Teacher Education

Robyn Brandenburg • Sharon McDonough
Jenene Burke • Simone White
Editors

Teacher Education

Innovation, Intervention and Impact

Editors
Robyn Brandenburg
Faculty of Education and Arts
Federation University Australia
Ballarat, Victoria, Australia

Jenene Burke
Faculty of Education and Arts
Federation University Australia
Ballarat, Victoria, Australia

Sharon McDonough
Faculty of Education and Arts
Federation University Australia
Ballarat, Victoria, Australia

Simone White
Faculty of Education
Monash University
Berwick, Victoria, Australia

ISBN 978-981-10-0784-2   ISBN 978-981-10-0785-9   (eBook)
DOI 10.1007/978-981-10-0785-9

Library of Congress Control Number: 2016943182

© Springer Science+Business Media Singapore 2016
This work is subject to copyright. All rights are reserved by the Publisher, whether the whole or part of the material is concerned, specifically the rights of translation, reprinting, reuse of illustrations, recitation, broadcasting, reproduction on microfilms or in any other physical way, and transmission or information storage and retrieval, electronic adaptation, computer software, or by similar or dissimilar methodology now known or hereafter developed.
The use of general descriptive names, registered names, trademarks, service marks, etc. in this publication does not imply, even in the absence of a specific statement, that such names are exempt from the relevant protective laws and regulations and therefore free for general use.
The publisher, the authors and the editors are safe to assume that the advice and information in this book are believed to be true and accurate at the date of publication. Neither the publisher nor the authors or the editors give a warranty, express or implied, with respect to the material contained herein or for any errors or omissions that may have been made.

Printed on acid-free paper

This Springer imprint is published by Springer Nature
The registered company is Springer Science+Business Media Singapore Pte Ltd.

Preface

> To identify what is important in our programs and to understand what our programs contribute to effective classroom instruction, we must operate from a *research rich foundation* that informs our efforts. (Wiseman, 2012, p. 90, emphasis added)

This inaugural publication from our scholarly community, *Teacher Education: Innovation, Intervention and Impact*, is both a product of, and seeks to contribute to, the changing global and political times in teacher education research. This volume also marks a significant shift in the collective work and outreach of the Australian Teacher Education Association (ATEA) as it endeavours to be an even more active contributor to what Donna Wiseman above describes as a *research rich foundation* for initial teacher education and more broadly to the teaching profession.

Increasingly, teacher educators and the research they produce are under *intense* scrutiny with an increased focus by politicians and the broader education community of their work. This attention, in turn, offers our ATEA membership both challenges and opportunities. Teacher education in Australia, like that of many other countries, such as England and the United States, has become a national priority with the increasing realisation that teacher education is central to preparing our future teacher workforce and thus ultimately a key in shaping all our childrens' futures. While many of us as teacher education researchers, would caution loudly against any reductionist and simplistic linear thinking that positions teacher educators and teachers as key alone in 'solving' all social inequalities, the prioritisation of teacher education research by governments and the broad benefits to a socially just society it offers is important.

As noted in the chapters within this volume, research *in*, *on* and *for* teacher education has now entered explicitly into the political landscape with the most recent review by the Teacher Education Ministerial Advisory Committee (TEMAG, 2014) into initial teacher education titled, *Action Now: Classroom Ready Teachers* acknowledging the vital importance of research to all areas of education reform. Importantly the review recommended "a national focus on research into teacher education" (TEMAG, 2014, p. 9). For those of us who have long been researching in the field of teacher education, this priority is most welcome and an opportune time to further explore multiple genres to disseminate, showcase and build from each other's work to productively engage with, and contribute to, shaping policy and practice.

Historically, ATEA has encouraged research dissemination through its annual conference and the publication of refereed conference papers: both traditional approaches for a scholarly community. While the ATEA membership base has increased and attendance at our conferences are at a record high, the past decade has witnessed a steady decline in researchers keen to take up the conference publishing opportunity. This phenomenon appears to be due to the growing accountability measures taking place within our universities where such publications do not 'count' so much against increasing impact and performance measures. Measures of impact lean towards such quality measures as citation counts and journal impact factors.

An authored chapter in a blind reviewed publication such as this volume, matters in the career opportunities of teacher educators and given the critique of teacher education research, it is vital that as a scholarly community we do more to support our colleagues and ensure that we do not further marginalise those in this field. Our desire through embarking on this new form of publication is that we raise both the status of teacher education research and those who research in the field. It is important to note that such internal 'impact' measures however are understood differently by practitioners and more recently by politicians who call for 'measures of impact' that make a difference to practice and as a community we also need to support both.

This volume has endeavoured to meet these dual expectations to both our teacher education research colleagues to promote and disseminate their important work and to provide research to be accessed by the wider education community. In regard to the latter, the volume has been produced by an Association *for* the profession, with a vision to contribute to a research-rich profession in the broadest sense. While some readers of this book might seek particular types of research or methodologies, the Association recognises the valuable contribution of diverse approaches. The recent BERA-RSA Inquiry into research into teacher education noted that research can make a contribution to teacher education in four different ways, namely:

- First, the content of teacher education programmes may be informed by research-based knowledge and scholarship, emanating from a range of academic disciplines and epistemological traditions.
- Second, research can be used to inform the design and structure of teacher education programmes.
- Third, teachers and teacher educators can be equipped to engage *with* and be discerning consumers *of* research.
- Fourth, teachers and teacher educators may be equipped to conduct their own research, individually and collectively, to investigate the impact of particular interventions or to explore the positive and negative effects of educational practice (BERA-RSA, 2014, p.11).

Throughout the chapters in this volume you will find evidence of all forms of contributions to research that can be utilised and considered in order to be taken up by a wide audience. Individually and collectively they have much to offer the broad education community. The next challenge for us as teacher education researchers and the ATEA community will be to seek out and to align strategically smaller-scale studies that when analysed and viewed together, will highlight common themes, as well as shine a light on diversity and context relevant matters.

As a first initiative, with the strong support of the Executive and outstanding dedication from the editorial team, I very much hope you enjoy reading and considering a 'snapshot' of the teacher education research conducted across Australia. I would like to take this opportunity to reiterate that the current political gaze into teacher education research offers us as teacher education researchers many opportunities and we need to seize these. More than ever, it is so important and valuable work to explain carefully why teacher education is not teacher training, to look for multiple ways to disseminate our research findings and to value highly the professionalization and preparation of our teachers and future leaders.

(ATEA President 2014–2016)   Simone White

References

British Educational Research Association (BERA). (2014). *Research and the teaching profession: Building the capacity for a self-improving education system.* Final Report of the BERA-RSA Inquiry into the Role of Research in Teacher Education. London: BERA.

Teacher Education Ministerial Advisory Group. (2014). *Action now: Classroom ready teachers.* http://www.studentsfirst.gov.au/teacher-education-ministerial-advisory-group.

Wiseman, D. L. (2012). The intersection of policy, reform, and teacher education. *Journal of Teacher Education, 63*(2), 87–91.

Acknowledgements

As editors we would like to thank most sincerely all who have contributed their research and scholarly endeavours to this volume, *Teacher Education: Innovation, Intervention and Impact*. The response to the call for chapters far exceeded our expectations and the collegial spirit to which everyone laboured within such a tight timeline, was most appreciated and quite a remarkable achievement.

We thank all those who reviewed chapters and who provided valuable feedback to authors. To the pre-service teachers, students, teachers and schools who participated in the various research projects, we extend our warm thanks for your on-going commitment to working together to contribute to building a research-rich teaching profession.

A special thank you to Springer and particularly to Nick Melchior who worked closely with us throughout the entire process, from conceptualisation to publication. Nick shared our vision for a new, productive and strategic partnership in teacher education research and we look forward to the continuation of this partnership in the future.

As always, many thanks are extended to our families for all their support and understanding, as without their support we would be unable to pursue these opportunities in our work.

Contents

Teacher Education Research and the Policy Reform Agenda 1
Robyn Brandenburg, Sharon McDonough, Jenene Burke,
and Simone White

**Reform and the Reconceptualisation of Teacher
Education in Australia** 15
Jennifer M. Gore

**Innovation and Transformation of Initial Teacher Education:
Employer and Graduate Perspectives**................................ 35
Sally Knipe, Rebecca Miles, and Stephanie Garoni

**Digital Credentialing: Does It Offer a Meaningful Response
to Initial Teacher Education Reform?**.............................. 49
Josephine R. Lang

**Innovating in First Year Pre-service Teacher Education:
"Buddy Up"**.. 63
Jennifer Elsden-Clifton, Kathy Jordan, and Nicky Carr

**Reconceptualising First Year Professional Experience:
Enacting a Repertoire of Learning Focused Talk
for Efficacy in Teaching Practice**................................. 79
Christine J. Edwards-Groves

**Rethinking the Observation Placement: A Community/Cohort
Approach to Early Professional Experiences** 99
Rachel Forgasz

**Images of Teaching: Discourses Within Which Pre-service
Teachers Construct Their Professional Identity as a Teacher
upon Entry to Teacher Education Courses**.......................... 117
Robyn Brandenburg and Ann Gervasoni

Exploring the Becoming of Pre-service Teachers in Paired Placement Models 139
Amanda Gutierrez

Internships in Initial Teacher Education in Australia: A Case Study of the Griffith Education Internship 157
Paula Jervis-Tracey and Glenn Finger

Advancing Partnership Research: A Spatial Analysis of a Jointly-Planned Teacher Education Partnership 175
Josephine Ryan, Helen Butler, Alex Kostogriz, and Sarah Nailer

Activating Teaching Dispositions in Carefully Constructed Contexts: Examining the Impact of Classroom Intensives 193
Amanda McGraw, Sharon McDonough, Chris Wines, and Courtney O'Loughlan

Classroom Ready? Building Resilience in Teacher Education 211
Caroline Mansfield, Susan Beltman, Noelene Weatherby-Fell, and Tania Broadley

Building Professional Learning Identities: Beginning Teachers' Perceptions of Causality for Professional Highs and Lows 231
Ellen Larsen and Jeanne M. Allen

Teaching and Teacher Education: The Need to Go Beyond Rhetoric 253
John Loughran

Index 265

Contributors

Jeanne M. Allen School of Education and Professional Studies, Griffith University, Nathan, Queensland, Australia

Susan Beltman School of Education, Curtin University, Perth, Australia

Robyn Brandenburg Faculty of Education and Arts, Federation University Australia, Ballarat, Victoria, Australia

Tania Broadley School of Education, Curtin University, Perth, Australia
Faculty of Education, Queensland University of Technology, Brisbane, Australia

Jenene Burke Faculty of Education and Arts, Federation University Australia, Ballarat, Victoria, Australia

Helen Butler Australian Catholic University, Melbourne, Australia

Nicky Carr RMIT University, Melbourne, Victoria, Australia

Christine J. Edwards-Groves School of Education, Charles Sturt University, Wagga Wagga, Australia

Jennifer Elsden-Clifton RMIT University, Melbourne, Victoria, Australia

Glenn Finger School of Education and Professional Studies, Griffith University, Gold Coast, Queensland, Australia

Rachel Forgasz Monash University, Melbourne, Australia

Stephanie Garoni School of Education, La Trobe University, Melbourne, Australia

Ann Gervasoni Monash University Australia, Melbourne, Australia

Jennifer M. Gore School of Education, University of Newcastle, Callaghan, Australia

Amanda Gutierrez Australian Catholic University, Melbourne, Australia

Paula Jervis-Tracey School of Education and Professional Studies, Griffith University, Mt Gravatt, Queensland, Australia

Kathy Jordan RMIT University, Melbourne, Victoria, Australia

Sally Knipe School of Education, La Trobe University, Melbourne, Australia

Alex Kostogriz Australian Catholic University, Melbourne, Australia

Josephine R. Lang School of Education, Deakin University, Melbourne, Australia

Ellen Larsen School of Education and Professional Studies, Griffith University, Nathan, Queensland, Australia

John Loughran Faculty of Education, Monash University, Melbourne, Australia

Caroline Mansfield School of Education, Murdoch University, Perth, Australia

Sharon McDonough Faculty of Education and Arts, Federation University Australia, Ballarat, Victoria, Australia

Amanda McGraw Faculty of Education and Arts, Federation University Australia, Ballarat, Victoria, Australia

Rebecca Miles School of Education, La Trobe University, Melbourne, Australia

Sarah Nailer Australian Catholic University, Melbourne, Australia

Courtney O'Loughlan Faculty of Education and Arts, Federation University Australia, Ballarat, Victoria, Australia

Josephine Ryan Australian Catholic University, Melbourne, Australia

Noelene Weatherby-Fell School of Education, University of Wollongong, Wollongong, Australia

Simone White Faculty of Education, Monash University, Melbourne, Australia

Chris Wines Faculty of Education and Arts, Federation University Australia, Ballarat, Victoria, Australia

About the Authors

Jeanne Allen is an Associate Professor of Teacher Education in the School of Education and Professional Studies at Griffith University. She has worked in Initial Teacher Education (ITE) since 2005 after spending an extensive career in secondary teaching and school leadership, both overseas and in Australia. Her work in ITE in four universities across three Australian States has provided her with first-hand experience in, and a sound understanding of, ITE stakeholder needs in the national arena. Jeanne is a Chief Investigator of a large Australia Research Council-funded project into student retention and a member of the Office for Learning and Teaching-funded "Project Evidence" extension team. Her publication output since 2005 includes an edited book, six book chapters and over 30 peer-reviewed journal articles. Jeanne is a Co-editor of the Asia-Pacific Journal of Teacher Education and she is on the Editorial Board of Linguistics, Culture and Education.

Susan Beltman is an Associate Professor who teaches and researches in the School of Education at Curtin University in Western Australia. Her current research interests involve using qualitative methods to examine mentoring, motivation, teacher resilience and identity. She was a team member for an Australian Learning and Teaching Council funded project *Keeping Cool*: *Embedding Resiliency in the Initial Teacher Education Curriculum* and is a project team member for two currently funded projects: a European Union Lifelong Learning Program project, ENTREE (*ENhancing Teacher REsilience in Europe*), and an Office for Learning and Teaching project BRiTE (*Building Resilience in Teacher Education*). Susan is a Fellow and current President of the Western Australian Institute for Educational Research.

Robyn Brandenburg is an Associate Professor in the Faculty of Education, Federation University Australia. For the past 15 years, she has taught mathematics education and professional experience courses in the Bachelor of Education, and student and teacher learning are at the core of her teaching and research. She has published widely and is nationally and internationally renowned for her work in reflective practice and student feedback and evaluation. Her books, *Powerful Pedagogy* (Springer, 2008) and *Pedagogies for the Future* (Co-edited, SENSE,

2013), are highly regarded by her peers. Robyn has led education research projects and has received awards for her research and teaching including The Vice-Chancellor's Award for Teaching Excellence (2010), an Australian Government Office for Learning and Teaching Citation for Outstanding Contributions to Student Learning (2011) and an Office for Learning and Teaching National Teaching Excellence Award (2013). Robyn is an executive member of the Australian Teacher Education Association.

Tania Broadley is an Associate Professor and Academic Lead at the Curtin Learning Institute. Tania provides leadership in professional learning and academic development at Curtin University. Her previous role in the Curtin Business School provided academic development and expertise in enhancing student learning through innovative teaching and technology strategies. Tania continues to conduct research into teacher education, which has developed from her background as Lecturer in Educational Technology for the School of Education at Curtin University. Tania has taught in undergraduate and postgraduate programs, both face-to-face and online including Open University Australia (OUA) and regional programmes. Tania is a project team member on the Office for Learning and Teaching projesct BRiTE (*Building Resilience in Teacher Education*).

Jenene Burke PhD, is a Senior Lecturer in the School of Education, and Associate Dean Learning and Teaching in the Faculty of Education and Arts at Federation University Australia. As a teacher educator, Jenene is the Program Leader of the Master of Special Education. She teaches and researches in the field of student diversity and inclusion in education settings and is also interested in school-university-community learning partnerships. As an executive member of the Australian Teacher Education Association (ATEA), Jenene coordinates the awards and grants. She has worked in initial teacher education for over 17 years after a career as secondary teacher and educational administrator. She is the recipient of the University of Ballarat Vice-Chancellors Award for Teaching Excellence (2012) and an Australian Government Office for Learning and Teaching Citation for Outstanding Contributions to Student Learning (2013).

Helen Butler is a Senior Lecturer, Education Victoria at the Australian Catholic University in Victoria. With a background in secondary teaching, she has led and participated in a range of teacher education research projects, particularly with a focus on family-school-community partnerships and student wellbeing.

Nicky Carr PhD, is a Lecturer and researcher in teacher education at RMIT. Nicky's teaching and research has a strong focus on the integration of digital technologies into teaching and learning in schools and within higher education. Of particular importance in this work is the need to ensure that the integration of digital technologies is connected to and supports sound pedagogy grounded in current educational theory. Nicky is also involved in the development and implementation of new approaches to initial teacher education, with a focus on strengthening the nexus between theory and practice through school partnerships and site-based delivery of programme elements in order to prepare classroom ready teachers.

Christine J. Edwards-Groves PhD, is a Senior Lecturer (Literacy) at Charles Sturt University (CSU), Wagga Wagga, NSW, Australia. Her current research focuses on classroom interaction and dialogic pedagogies, literacy, multimodal writing, professional learning and practice theory. She is co-leader of the "Speech, Language and Literacies" strand of CSU's Research Institute for Professional Practice, Learning and Education (*RIPPLE*) and is co-leader of international Pedagogy Education and Praxis (*PEP*) research network. Christine is co-recipient of the inaugural national *Primary English Teachers Association Australia* research grant studying dialogic pedagogies for literacy learning across the primary school. She was a 2013 Office for Learning and Teaching Citation recipient for her innovation project designed to develop dialogic pedagogies among pre-service teachers.

Jennifer Elsden-Clifton PhD, is an experienced school-teacher and university educator at RMIT University. Jen has a strong research interest in the areas of professional experience and professional issues in teaching and health education, and has received grants and published in these fields. She is currently involved in the field of placement or work-integrated learning and has developed a number of site-based and alternative pedagogical models for professional experience that blur theory/practice, schools/university, expert/novice and teachers/students in teacher education.

Glenn Finger is a Professor of Education in the School of Education and Professional Studies at Griffith University. He was the Dean (Learning and Teaching) of the Arts, Education and Law Group from 2011 to 2015, the Deputy Dean (Learning and Teaching) of the Faculty of Education from 2007 to 2010 and the Deputy Director, Centre for Learning Research, from 2005 to 2006. His academic appointment to Griffith University in 1999 enabled his research and teaching to focus on teaching the teachers. He has researched and published extensively with more than 150 publications on initial teacher education, teaching and digital technologies. Professor Finger has been acknowledged and recognised through prestigious teaching and outstanding conference paper awards. He commenced his teaching career in 1975 and served with Education Queensland for more than 24 years as a physical education specialist, primary school teacher, Deputy Principal and Acting Principal in a wide variety of educational settings.

Rachel Forgasz PhD, is a teacher educator in the Faculty of Education at Monash University, Australia. Her research centres on the pedagogy of teacher education, with a significant current focus on the professional experience dimension of initial teacher education. In particular, she researches and writes about mentor professional learning, innovations in professional experience curriculum design and the emotional dimension of mentor and pre-service teacher experiences during the professional experience. Rachel also publishes in the fields of embodied pedagogies, teacher emotion and self-study. She teaches across a range of programmes and specialises in drama education and reflective practice.

Stephanie Garoni is a Lecturer at LaTrobe University and has many years' experience as a classroom teacher, teacher librarian, learning support teacher, enrichment coordinator, literacy and numeracy advisor and deputy principal in both Australian and overseas schools. Since 2001, she has worked in the tertiary sector in Faculties of Education at Central Queensland, Charles Sturt and La Trobe Universities. She has extensive experience working with initial teacher education students and associate teachers, and her interest focuses on supporting graduate teachers as they move into new ways of learning and teaching in the twenty-first century. Her research at La Trobe University focuses on exploring how graduate teachers consider their readiness to teach and how this influences their transition from pre-service teacher to graduate teacher.

Ann Gervasoni is an Associate Professor, Numeracy, at Monash University. Ann has worked in teacher education, professional learning and primary teaching for 33 years. Ann was a member of the research team for the Early Numeracy Research Project (1999–2001) in Victoria and research director for the Bridging the Numeracy Gap project in Western Australia and Victoria (2009–2010). Ann's research interests include mathematics education in early childhood and primary education and the development of pre-service teachers' professional identities.

Jennifer M. Gore is a Professor in the School of Education at the University of Newcastle, Australia, where she was Dean of Education and Head of School for 6 years. Currently, Director of the Teachers and Teaching Research Centre and Co-editor of the prestigious international journal, *Teaching and Teacher Education*, Jennifer has managed several large-scale studies and has won more than AUD$4.9 million in research funding including nine grants awarded by the Australian Research Council. Of particular note is her decade-long programme of work on quality teaching (a framework she developed with James Ladwig in 2003), which has had significant impact in schools. The conceptualisation (with Julie Bowe) of an innovative approach to teacher development, *Quality Teaching Rounds*, takes this work further, as evidenced in a recent randomised controlled trial demonstrating impact on teaching quality.

Amanda Gutierrez is a Lecturer in Education and is the Professional Experience Coordinator in the secondary programme at the Australian Catholic University in Melbourne, Australia. She teaches and researches in the areas of English and literacy education, critical literacies and digital games, and professional practice and partnerships. Her research has a specific focus on teacher constructions and enactment of curriculum in these areas, and educators professional becoming. She has written about her work in *Digital Games: Literacy in Action* and journals such as *English in Australia*, *Critical Studies in Education* and the *Journal of Adult and Adolescent Literacy*.

About the Authors

Paula Jervis-Tracey PhD, is a Mid-Career Researcher in the School of Education and Professional Studies at Griffith University. Her work at the university has been characterised by strong links between teaching and research, with each informing the other. Her research and teaching has been primarily concerned with teacher professional issues, including ethics and professional standards, and beginning teachers, including rural education and preparation, induction and mentoring. She is Chief Editor (review) for the International and Australian Journal of Rural Education, which focuses on rural education and teacher professional issues. She has worked extensively with both final year pre-service teachers and industry partners in preparing and shaping new graduates as they enter the teaching profession. Prior to her appointment with Griffith University in 2005, Dr Jervis-Tracey served with Education Queensland for 12 years as a music education specialist, primary education teacher and Deputy Principal in both rural and urban educational contexts.

Kathy Jordan is an Associate Professor and researcher in the School of Education, RMIT University, and also Deputy Head of Higher Education. Kathy has strong research interests in changing notions of literacy, the use of ICT in school education and teacher decision-making particularly around ICT. She has also published widely in journals and conference papers. Kathy is also interested in initial teacher education, including the changing policy context that is shaping practice and the importance of work-integrated-learning to pre-service teacher development, with a focus on negotiating theory and practice and the development and implementation of innovative approaches using partnerships, shared responsibility and site-based learning.

Sally Knipe is an Associate Professor (Education) at the College of Arts, Social Science and Commerce at La Trobe University, in Wodonga, Victoria, Australia. Previously, she has been a Course Director at Charles Sturt University, where she was responsible for strategic leadership and academic management of a range of courses. She has been Chief Investigator for several research projects including the Australian Teacher Education Association and the Düsseldorf Skills Forum. Her publications include *Middle Years of Schooling*: *Reframing Adolescence* (Pearson Education Australia, 2007) and a chapter in *Big Fish Little Fish* (Mockler & Groundwater-Smith, 2015 (Eds.). Cambridge: Cambridge University Press). Sally is a national Standards Assessor – Teacher Education.

Alex Kostogriz is a Professor of Education and Head of Education Victoria at the Australian Catholic University. His research and publications focus on teacher education and professional ethics. Alex has been Chief Investigator on a number of projects funded by the Australian Research Council and other national and state-based funding schemes. These projects have explored the effectiveness of initial teacher education, mandated literacy assessment and reorganization of teachers' work, professional practice and ethics of language teachers, and literacy practices in diasporic communities

Josephine R. Lang PhD, is a Senior Lecturer and Associate Head of School, Teaching and Learning, at the School of Education, Deakin University, Australia. She has wide-ranging experience and leadership in the Higher Education sector. As a teacher educator, her teaching incorporates the area of professional studies in initial teacher education, which includes themes of curriculum, assessment, pedagogy and professional learning. Josephine's research interests include exploring the use of multimedia and information and communication technologies in education and particularly for pre-service teacher professional learning. In her research she investigates curriculum, pedagogical and assessment implications related to the affordances of information and communication technologies in their role for engaging professional learning, particularly of pre-service teachers.

Ellen Larsen is a doctoral student at Griffith University. She has over 25 years of teaching experience across both state and independent sectors in Queensland. Since 2011, Ellen has worked for Independent Schools Queensland, developing and implementing professional learning programs for classroom practitioners and school leaders, particularly in the areas of literacy, coaching, mentoring and teacher research in schools. Ellen has also served on an expert panel for the Queensland College of Teachers to provide feedback to Queensland universities regarding initial teacher education and post-graduate education courses. Ellen published and presented her research from her Master in Education thesis in 2014. Her primary areas of research interest include early career teachers, professional learning and development and ITE practices.

John Loughran is the Foundation Chair in Curriculum & Pedagogy and Dean of the Faculty of Education, Monash University. John was a science teacher for 10 years before moving into teacher education. He is well regarded in the fields of teacher education and science education and was the co-founding editor of *Studying Teacher Education* and an Executive Editor for *Teachers and Teaching: Theory and Practice*. He is the co-editor with Professor Mary Lynn Hamilton of the *International Handbook of Teacher Education* (Springer, 2016) and has written extensively about pedagogical content knowledge (*Understanding and Developing Science Teachers Pedagogical Content Knowledge*, Sense Publishers, 2012), expert teachers (*What Expert Teachers Do*, Allen & Unwin/Routledge, 2010) and a pedagogy of teacher education (*Developing a Pedagogy of Teacher Education*, Routledge, 2006).

Caroline Mansfield PhD, is a Senior Lecturer in the School of Education, Murdoch University, Western Australia. Her research broadly focuses on teachers and students in learning contexts, with emphasis on motivation, instruction and resilience. Caroline has led two successful funded projects on teacher resilience, *Keeping Cool: Embedding Resilience in Initial Teacher Education Curriculum*, and *BRiTE: Building Resilience in Teacher Education*. She is also a third country partner in *Keeping Cool Europe: ENhancing Teacher REsilience in Europe* and involved in an interdisciplinary resilience project *VetSet2Go: Building Veterinary Employability*.

She has received awards of excellence for research, teaching and professional service.

Sharon McDonough is an Early Career Researcher in the Faculty of Education and Arts at Federation University Australia where she is the Program Leader of the Master of Education Studies program. Sharon has a commitment to working closely with schools and researches learning and teaching in school and university contexts. Her research interests include pre-service teacher education, embodiment and emotion in education and professional learning. Sharon has been awarded an Australian Government Office for Learning and Teaching National Citation for Outstanding Contributions to Student Learning (2013). She is a member of the Australian Teacher Education Association (ATEA) executive where she is responsible for the Early Career Researcher/Higher Degree Research portfolio. She is interested in the use of social media in academic work, tweets at @Sharon_McD and is the Australian host of the online virtual writing group @SUWTues (https://suwtuesdays.wordpress.com/)

Amanda McGraw PhD, is a Senior Lecturer who coordinates the Master of Teaching (Secondary) program at Federation University Australia. The programme is known for its innovative practices in relation to preparing pre-service teachers. Central to the programme are school-based partnerships with regional and rural schools. Amanda's research interests focus on professional learning, teacher education and literacy. In 2010, Amanda was awarded the Vice Chancellor's Award for Teaching Excellence at Federation University, and in 2012, she was awarded an Australian Government Office for Learning and Teaching National Citation for Outstanding Contributions to Student Learning. Amanda taught for nearly 20 years in both state and independent schools and she has held a number of leadership positions in schools including Deputy Principal. She continues to work closely with practicing teachers in ongoing professional learning experiences and collaborative research projects.

Rebecca Miles is a researcher and teacher in pre-service teacher education at LaTrobe University, Victoria. Her research interests are centred on (1) knowledge, curriculum theory and inquiry; (2) teacher professional practice; (3) pedagogy in online teaching and learning; and (4) place-based education. Rebecca's teaching focuses on social and cultural contexts in education and teacher research. Rebecca's PhD research focused on place-based environmental education, drawing on practice theories to consider ways that place, knowledge and practice intersect in educating primary school students about being in the world. Her PhD dissertation was awarded the 2014 NSW Institute of Educational Research Beth Southwell Outstanding Thesis Award.

Sarah Nailer is a teacher educator and researcher at Australian Catholic University, Melbourne. Prior to this she taught for over a decade in secondary schools. For the past 3 years, she has been involved in longitudinal research investigating the role of school-university partnerships in teacher workforce development. Her main area of scholarship is teacher research engagement

Courtney O'Loughlan is a qualified secondary school teacher and a sessional academic in the Faculty of Education and Arts at Federation University Australia. She currently teaches in a community-based Bachelor of Arts programme that seeks to expand opportunities for students with non-traditional entrance pathways to attend university. Courtney is currently completing a Master of Education by research at Federation University Australia, with a focus on hearing the messages sent by disengaged secondary school students and on reconnecting those young people to meaningful educational contexts. Courtney's research interests include teacher education, inclusive education and student disengagement and the intersections between these areas.

Josephine Ryan PhD, is a Senior Lecturer in English/Literacy Education at Australian Catholic University, Melbourne campus. She teaches literacy education to students there and is engaged in researching successful approaches to teacher education, especially the value of school partnerships to creating strong teacher education, and how teacher education can be enhanced through technology.

Noelene Weatherby-Fell PhD, is a Senior Lecturer in School of Education at the University of Wollongong, New South Wales. Having taught for many years in both secondary and primary schools in city and regional contexts, Noelene's research interests include pre-service teacher preparation, epilepsy education (the focus of her PhD) and pastoral care of students and teachers. She has presented and written about her work with the *Response Ability Project* (*HIMH*), focusing on teacher education and social and emotional wellbeing /mental health, both nationally and internationally. Noelene is a project team member on the Office for Learning and Teaching project BRiTE (*Building Resilience in Teacher Education*).

Simone White is Chair of Teacher Education in the Faculty of Education at Monash University and currently the President of the Australian Teacher Education Association (July 2014–July 2016). Simone's publications, research and teaching are focused on the key question of how best to prepare teachers and leaders for diverse communities. Her current research areas focus on teacher education policy and research, professional experience and building and maintaining university-school/community partnerships. Through this work, she aims to connect research, policy and practice in ways that bring school and university teacher educators together and break down traditional borders between academics, policy makers, communities and practitioners. Simone currently leads a State-funded initiative *Teaching Academies for Professional Practice* (*TAPP*) to improve the professional learning of teachers across a broad geographic cluster. Some of the work, Simone has been involved in (with colleagues) can be accessed on the following websites: www.rrrtec.net.au; www.teacherevidence.net.au and www.teacherassessment.edu.au.

Chris Wines is a Lecturer and researcher in the Faculty of Education at Federation University Australia. He has been teaching for 24 years and also teaches at Ballarat High School as part of a formal collaborative relationship between the two institutions. This partnership allows him to conduct research in areas related to Science, Technology, Engineering and Mathematics (STEM) education, school/university partnerships and teaching and learning. Chris is currently the Institutional Team Leader for Federation University Australia for an Office for Learning and Teaching funded project titled, *It's part of my life: engaging university and community to enhance science and mathematics education.* This is a collaborative project with the Regional University Network (RUN) universities, Australia, that focuses on improving pre-service teacher confidence and competence in teaching mathematics and science and developing collaborations between university researchers, teacher educators and the community.

Teacher Education Research and the Policy Reform Agenda

Robyn Brandenburg, Sharon McDonough, Jenene Burke, and Simone White

> The Advisory Group believes that a national focus on research into the effectiveness of initial teacher education programs is needed. Research should focus on building an evidence base to inform the design of initial teacher education programs and teacher professional development (Teacher Education Ministerial Advisory Group 2014, p. 48).

1 Introduction

As reflected in the TEMAG (2014) report recommendation above, the demand for research as a means to improve teacher education in Australia is a political priority with numerous calls from politicians, policy makers, principals and the wider education community for an increased knowledge or 'evidence' base to inform schools, teachers and teaching practices. At the core of this demand is the key desire by those involved in teacher education to improve student learning, and to ultimately create increased opportunities for national, social and economic prosperity. While many policy makers are keen to utilise research to 'solve' teacher education policy problems (White, 2016), those who conduct teacher education research are cognisant of the view that the research, policy and practice connection is often non-linear, complex and cyclical. As Mertler (2016) suggests, "In most cases, educational research tends to be cyclical, or helical, as opposed to linear" (p. 7). Nevertheless, in the political context, research into teacher education is a high priority and teacher educators are increasingly called to demonstrate the effectiveness and the impact of

---

R. Brandenburg (✉) • S. McDonough • J. Burke
Faculty of Education and Arts, Federation University Australia, Ballarat, Victoria, Australia
e-mail: r.brandenburg@federation.edu.au; s.mcdonough@federation.edu.au; js.burke@federation.edu.au

S. White
Faculty of Education, Monash University, Melbourne, Australia
e-mail: Simone.white@monash.edu

© Springer Science+Business Media Singapore 2016
R. Brandenburg et al. (eds.), *Teacher Education*,
DOI 10.1007/978-981-10-0785-9_1

their programs. As Cochran-Smith (2005) argues, this pressure however requires the teacher education research community to carefully consider and communicate the connection between, and implications for research, policy and practice:

> The education research community needs to make it clearer to the public and to policymakers that there are significant complexities in what happens to policies on their way, as Susan Fuhrman (2001) puts it, from "capitols to classrooms." These complexities depend on the cultures and contexts of schools, the resources available, and the neighbourhoods, communities, and larger environments where schools are located. (p. 14)

It is within this context to not only increase research into teacher education, but to also consider more deeply what counts as evidence and the implications of research in specific contexts that this chapter, is focused. This chapter examines three areas: first; the focus on research in the Australian policy context, second; an examination of the current critique of teacher education research and third; a critical analysis and discussion of the various research conducted by the teacher educators within this volume. Findings highlight that within this volume, not only are teacher educators very keen to respond to policy reforms but they are also interested in providing research that provides a rich contextual discussion of their findings. Consistent with critique, the majority of the studies are small scale in nature but viewed collectively have much to offer the teacher education research community. More connected small scale studies that highlight both macro and micro levels of teacher education are recommended.

2 Teacher Education Research and Policy: An Analytical Discussion

The empirical studies and conceptual and theoretical frameworks explored in the chapters in this volume have much to offer the education community (including policy makers), both as individual chapters and collectively. As a snapshot, they highlight the tensions and complexity of connecting research to practice as identified by Cochran-Smith (2005). We, as editors of this volume and authors of this chapter, have examined the chapters as data to understand more deeply the current teacher education research landscape. We explore the broader policy context and demand for increased research into teacher education. Combined, an analysis of the chapters' key themes provide an insight into the contemporary practice of teacher educators in Australia and a mechanism to interrogate the ways in which policy, practice and research intersect. As such, we conducted a policy document analysis of the TEMAG (2014) report to begin to understand the ways in which 'research' is currently understood by politicians and policy makers. We also revisited the critique of teacher education research as a backdrop to do a comparative study across the chapters to consider the key themes.

2.1 Demands for Research into Teacher Education

Like other countries (for example, England and the United States), the demands for research into initial teacher education (ITE) have entered the Australian policy landscape, with the most recent review and report, titled, *Action Now: Classroom Ready Teachers*, identifying the vital importance of research to all areas of education reform. The Government report accepts the review's recommendation to establish a national focus on research into teacher education to address what is perceived as "not enough information to understand what the most effective teaching practices are and what teacher education approaches best prepare teachers for the classroom" (TEMAG, 2014 p. 9).

There are multiple conceptions of research within the policy documents (both the TEMAG review into teacher education and the Government's response) including to inform practice; to provide the rationale for key directions for reform in teacher education and to advise and shape teaching practice. For example, Recommendation 34 of the review calls for "The Australian Institute for Teaching and School Leadership's functions be reconstituted and expanded to provide a national focus on research into teacher education, including into the effectiveness of teacher preparation and the promotion of innovative practice" (p. xv). Research is specifically referred to as a crucial means to inform ITE curriculum and professional experience and "The design and delivery of initial teacher education programs must be based on solid research and best practice" (TEMAG, 2014, p. x). It is also implied as a skill and knowledge, that future teachers need to know how to research and that higher education providers need to "equip pre-service teachers with data collection and analysis skills to assess the learning needs of all students" (TEMAG, 2014, p. xiii).

Research is also referred to throughout the document as being largely synonymous with 'evidence,' highlighting a shift towards an approach that is focused on improving the effectiveness of graduates who will in turn improve student learning. The report specifically states that, "Better evidence of the effectiveness of initial teacher education in the Australian context is needed to inform innovative program design and delivery, and the continued growth of teaching as a profession" (TEMAG, 2014, p. xi).

Research defined as evidence is highly contentious "with heated debates about what counts as evidence and what the evidence indicates" (Sleeter, 2014, p. 146). As Whitty (2006, p.162) cautions:

> Research defined too narrowly would actually be very limited as an evidence base for a teaching profession that is facing the huge challenges of a rapidly changing world, where what works today may not work tomorrow. Some research therefore needs to ask different sorts of questions, including why something works and, equally important, why it works in some contexts and not in others. And anyway, the professional literacy of teachers surely involves more than purely instrumental knowledge. It is therefore appropriate that a research-based profession should be informed by research that questions prevailing assumptions – and considers such questions as whether an activity is a worthwhile endeavour in the first place and what constitutes socially-just schooling (Gale & Densmore, 2003).

Throughout the TEMAG document, and highlighted within the opening quote in this chapter, is the implication that research makes a difference to practice. By extension there exists a call by government for research to align more closely to policy, in order to impact teaching practice and learner outcomes. While this attention on teacher education research is acknowledged by teacher education researchers, the alignment of research to 'policy problems' requires further exploration. Concerns related to the disconnect between teacher education research and policy is not a new concept and as Sallee and Flood (2012) explain:

> In 1985, Keller argued that research in higher education was not useful to practitioners, suggesting that "if research in higher education ended, it would scarcely be missed" (p. 7). Similarly, Cochran-Smith and Lytle (1990) argued that teachers' voices are missing in research and, therefore, knowledge produced is neither useful nor applicable to teachers' daily experiences. In short, academics are frequently targeted for engaging in research that is out-of-touch and not relevant to those outside universities. (p. 137)

2.2 Considering the Critique of Teacher Education Research

In its entirety this volume affirms the role that teacher education researchers hold in 'speaking back' to the critiques of teacher education research. We begin by acknowledging some of the criticism and critique that has been levelled at teacher education research (and researchers) and then consider how the field might benefit from such critique.

Whitty (2006) summarised some of the principal criticisms of education researchers in the UK as "a failure to produce cumulative findings, ideological bias, irrelevance to schools, a lack of involvement of teachers and inaccessibility and poor dissemination" (p. 161). These criticisms seem to apply specifically to teacher education researchers as well. More recently both Cochran-Smith et al. (2015) and Zeichner, Payne, and Brayko (2015), in the US context, describe increasing criticism of teacher education research and researchers. Zeichner et al. (2015) note that researchers, who are usually located within the Universities, are perceived and defined as 'defenders' (p. 122) of the status quo of teacher education and associated with research, not focused on the interests of the public, and who are unable to translate and mobilise their research to speak to policy (White, 2016).

Teacher education research has also been criticised because "it is seen as narrow and operational in focus and more akin to course design and evaluation" (Ham & Kane, 2004, as cited in Murray, Nuttall, & Mitchell, 2008, p. 226). While not seeking to 'defend' this situation, these same authors provide explanations as to why teacher education research is largely small scale in nature, attributing factors such as:

> the relative newness of teacher education research as a legitimate field of empirical investigation, the relatively small-scale funding that teacher education research is able to attract, and a recognition within the field of the importance of investigating aspects of one's own practice in order to both understand and improve teacher education pedagogy. (Murray, Nuttall, & Mitchell, 2008, p. 235)

Having provided some of the context and policy environment within which this edited volume of chapters lie, we examine, discuss and explore the studies through the lens of teacher education research critique.

3 Learning from Teacher Education Research

A cross-section of universities is represented within this volume, ranging from regional, single-campus universities, to multi-campus regional universities and large metropolitan universities. While there are examples of research conducted in a single institution there are also examples of cross institutional collaborations. All of the research reported in this volume is collaborative, many in partnership with teachers and schools, supporting the contention that teaching, and learning about teaching, is underpinned by social interaction together with the establishment of communities of learning within which knowledge is created, shared and evaluated for impact. What is evident in the outcomes of the teacher education research is that regardless of geography, demographics and/or the relative size of the research projects and; whether they have been funded or not, there is a consistent focus which is to ultimately improve student learning and expand teacher educator pedagogical content knowledge. Chapters within this volume are clearly focused on schools, teachers and on improving initial teacher education. There are examples of projects explicitly focused on teachers and that highlight teachers' voices in their studies and showcase the complexity of the work of teachers and teaching. The teacher education research projects endeavour to heed the call made by John Loughran in this volume, which puts the onus on teacher educators to showcase the complexity of teaching. He explains:

> If teaching really is complex and sophisticated business, then teachers themselves need to be able to illustrate why that is so. The same applies in teacher education. There needs to be a concerted, coherent and thoughtful approach to illustrating what teacher education has to offer and how it makes a real difference in the development of the next generation of skilled professionals. If teacher education is to be a valued starting point for a career as a teaching professional, then teacher educators need to lead the way in responding to questions that have, for so long, been answered in less than convincing ways to the sceptical observer.

3.1 Teaching Is Research-Informed

What is highlighted throughout this entire volume is the diverse and contextually-driven ways in which teacher educators and teacher education more broadly have responded to the challenges and needs of the learners through the design and implementation of "needs-based research". This context is important as noted earlier to highlight the complexity that Cochran-Smith notes of policy to practice. The majority of the studies, within this volume are framed within a key aspect of the policy reform agenda and provide the in-depth examination in context of particular reform agendas. This goes against the critique of teacher education research being not focused on the needs of the education community but might explain the frustration of policy makers who are looking for scalable findings. For example McGraw, McDonough, Wines, and O'Loughlan examine the role of dispositions through the implementation of classroom intensives; Jervis-Tracey and Finger research the impact of internships in initial teacher education and Mansfield, Beltman, Weatherby-Fell, and Broadley report on a large-scale supported research project that examines the effectiveness of an online resource to build professional resilience. These examples demonstrate the diverse ways in which teacher educators are seeking to develop their own practices in order to support student learning, and contribute to the policy reforms and agendas that require graduate teachers to be 'classroom ready'. Jennifer Gore in her chapter, outlines two case studies of practice that specifically focus on improving classroom practice. As she notes, her own institution's endeavour is not alone here.

> Nonetheless, what should be striking to policy makers about our case studies is that teacher educators are clearly grappling with issues of the quality of classroom practice and quality of teacher education, regardless of the overall reform ideology. These and other case studies (Darling-Hammond, 2006), including others provided in this volume, provide a helpful basis for professional discussion between stakeholders about the best way of fostering excellent teaching in diverse settings across Australia and further afield.

Teacher educators are keen to work as problem-solvers and they are also keen to explain the complexity of their research and explore this from different perspectives. Perhaps one of the over-looked and under-addressed aspects of learning about teaching through research is the researcher's interpretation of complex variables and designing research questions and approaches that seek to reveal that which is not known, but clearly sought. Christine Edwards-Groves examines one of the most commonplace, features of classroom interaction – talk – and highlights the ways in which research about classroom interaction can lead to more dialogic, rather than 'monologic or teacher dominated talk'. She explains here the need to move away from a departmentalised narrow focus on a particular aspect of learning:

> It is argued that to know about the role of classroom talk in learning is simply not enough; what is required is an explicit practical focus on learning to listen, observe and interact with students in classrooms and be mentored in the process. Therefore, it will be proposed that developing a repertoire of learning focused, flexible and academically enriching interaction practices requires overt designed-in opportunities for pre-service teachers to both learn about and to practise.

3.2 Teacher Educators as Role Models for Research

> The recent review of Teacher Education in Australia (Teacher Education Ministerial Advisory Group, TEMAG, 2014) highlights the imperative that teaching graduates must be classroom ready. While the recommendations of the report focus predominantly on the need for Teacher Education programs to enable the acquisition and mastery of skills and pedagogical content knowledge, there is minimal recognition of the role of Teacher Education

in shaping PSTs' professional identities. Our contention is that graduates who are classroom ready must also have a deep understanding of the contextual factors, personal discourses and emotions that shape their professional self and appreciate that this identity is constantly changing. Often there is a disconnection between a graduate teacher's professional identity and the lived reality of that identity as they experience the (often) challenging school context in which they work. (Brandenburg & Gervsoni, this volume)

As noted above, Teacher educator researchers provide role models for PSTs, who participate in research and thereby come to understand more about the impact of research on learning. Numerous courses in teacher education programs now focus on 'student as researcher', whereby PSTs design, implement and assess the impact of small and large scale research projects on themselves, their students and their communities. This induction into a teaching/research culture is imperative if PSTs are to become lifelong learners and acquire the research and reflective skills needed for success as a teacher.

A key focus of the research presented in this volume relates to the 'sociality of teaching' and the ways in which interaction underpins learning, and learning about teaching. Both Gutierrez and Elsden-Clifton, Carr, and Jordan present research that examines the impact of paired placements as an innovative adaption of the one-to-one PST/Teacher mentor model. As Le Cornu (2015) reports, the conceptualisation and structure of professional experience placements remains a contested space whereby consensus, on the establishment of the most effective approach, remains elusive. What is revealed in the research related to paired placements however is the powerful learning that can be fostered and shared with peers, including increased confidence, development of problem-solving skills and belonging to a 'community of learners'.

Teacher research is literature and theory informed. As Elsden-Clifton et al., state:

the decision to buddy students was based on the literature around practicum to better facilitate professional conversations and learning that connect theory and practice. It was also informed by transition to university literature, with calls to foster learning communities and encourage social and professional networks.

Paired-placement research also highlights the ways in which teacher educators design research that can be responsive to contextually identified needs of both PSTs and teacher education programs. This flexibility and professional judgement is critical if teacher education programs are to meet the needs of all learners.

3.3 *Disruptive Innovations and Interventions*

Mansfield et al., in their chapter, highlight one of the key features of the work of teacher educators – that they seek to challenge and disrupt assumptions, knowledge and understandings as part of an ongoing process of learning and development. Disruptive innovations and interventions in teacher education challenge ideas: about the structure of programs and professional experience; about the way we design-in opportunities; and how we challenge our understandings of roles and identities.

This concept of disruption is embedded in work with PSTs and in teacher educators' own practice, with Loughran (2014) arguing that teacher educators' work is not only about responding to policy and curriculum change, but is "about an ongoing process of learning, development, and change driven by the players central to that work – teacher educators" (p. 3). Loughran also argues that teacher educators must transform teacher education and lead change. The development of innovations and interventions that seek to disrupt conventional understandings about the nature of teaching, learning and teacher education cause us to question our assumptions about education.

Some of these assumptions relate to the nature and structure of initial teacher education programs with Korthagen, Loughran, and Russell (2006) contending that changes to the program structures of teacher education necessitate "an attitudinal shift" (p. 1038) that progresses beyond matters of organisation and teaching. These attitudinal shifts can disrupt our traditional conceptions of what teacher education might look like, widely represented in the research presented in this volume.

4 Innovation, Intervention and Impact

The contribution that this volume makes to innovation, intervention and impact in teacher education is significant. The themes of innovation, intervention and impact are addressed throughout all of the chapters, and while each chapter can be read in isolation, combined they present a narrative. Jennifer Gore further discusses reform and the reconceptualisation of teacher education programs in Australia. She highlights the contested nature of what constitutes quality teaching and provides examples of successful teacher education programs that provides PSTs with a diverse range of learning and teaching experiences. Knipe, Miles and Garoni challenge us to consider new ways of structuring programs, including an F-12 teacher education qualification. They further argue, "It is time to challenge the age-based divisions in initial teacher education and develop different programs that are flexible and more responsive to the complexities of, and more appropriate to, the staffing needs of twenty-first century schools". In examining the feedback from graduates from an F-12 teacher education qualification and from their employers, they prompt others to consider what knowledge, content and pedagogy might prepare PSTs to teach across F-Year 12 contexts. Josephine Lang also disrupts our traditional understandings of the ways we have documented evidence of student learning in teacher education, and encourages us to consider how we might make use of digital credentialing to do this in the future. She argues that digital credentialing "offers promise and potential to address meaningfully the calls for initial teacher education reform". She argues digital credentialing enables PSTs to demonstrate their learning and receive digital badges to recognize their achievements. Elsden-Clifton et al., also argue that reform and "change in the regulatory environment has encouraged innovation" particularly in relation to the ways we conceptualise professional experience.

4.1 Professional Experience

Professional experience is regarded as a key element of teacher education programs, with the TEMAG report (2014) contending that professional experience provides a critical opportunity for PSTs to integrate theory and practice. Le Cornu (2015) argues that there are a "multiplicity of political, professional, economic and pragmatic issues that surround professional placements" (p. 5), with this multiplicity of challenges leading teacher educators to reconceptualise ways of structuring professional experience. The move towards collaborative sharing and knowledge generation in professional experience is present in the work of a number of authors in this volume with their research contributing to a broader understanding of the challenges and benefits of collaborative placement experiences for both PSTs and mentor teachers. For example, Elsden-Clifton et al., have responded to these challenges and the policy environment by developing a "Buddy Up" program that places cohorts of 12–16 PSTs in schools where they plan, teach and assess learning with partners. This concept of paired placements is also explored by Gutierrez with both identifying that these new models challenge PSTs to develop and understand more about the sophisticated nature of teaching.

Le Cornu (2015) argues that the mentor teacher is central in supporting PST learning during placement, but they can be challenged with the dual role of being both mentor and PST assessor. Rachel Forgasz contends that "interest in working as a community to collaboratively mentor pre-service teachers marks a significant shift in thinking about how to approach the mentoring task" however, she identifies a further challenge for mentors as working within these communities can disrupt traditional practices. This use of interventions designed to shift thinking and pedagogical practices can provide the impetus for interpreting experiences in new ways.

4.2 Transition to University

The transition to first year university study is a critical experience for students (Kift, Nelson, & Clarke, 2010; Krause, 2007; Masters & Donnison, 2010), and challenges academics to design programs that assist students in successfully navigating this transition. Christine Edwards-Groves and Robyn Brandenburg and Ann Gervasoni (consider how the first year program can be reconceptualised. Edwards-Groves argues that talk as a pedagogical tool is overlooked in teacher education, contending that what is needed is a "new default; one that shifts our thinking and practice towards a more dialogic and participatory approach." This disruption to our thinking and practice as teacher educators and PSTs occurs through "designed-in" processes that focus on classroom talk. This focus on designing in opportunities to challenge ways of thinking is also reflected in the research of Brandenburg and Gervasoni who also contend that teacher educators need to explicitly address professional identity formation and reformation with pre-service teachers. They argue that inviting PSTs to construct visual representations of teachers also provides opportunities for teacher educators to identify, and respond to, dominant and marginalized discourses of teachers and teaching. All of the innovations and interventions outlined offer insight into the ways in which teacher education curriculum can be reconceptualised and reformed to more adequately meet the needs of PSTs, teachers and other stakeholders.

4.3 Partnerships

Complex interrelationships exist within teacher education and universities seek to connect with a range of partners in order to establish programs that provide PSTs with opportunities to engage in a diverse range of learning and teaching experiences. Paula Jervis-Tracey and Glenn Finger describe the way that carefully constructed internships contribute to PST learning, while Ryan, Butler, Kostogriz, and Nailer explore the partnerships underpinned by "vision (conceived space), its particular program and approach (perceived space) and the experience of participants (lived space)". Research that examines the ways in which collaborative partnerships are established prompts us to consider partnerships that focus on transformational rather than transactional outcomes (Butcher, Bezzina, & Moran, 2011).

The teacher educator research presented in this volume demonstrates an awareness of the increased scrutiny of programs and of the policy agendas that demand that graduates are 'classroom ready'. In considering these agendas, teacher educators argue for a complex, holistic approach to PST learning, with McGraw et al., arguing that dispositions for teaching cannot be developed in isolation or measured in simplistic ways. Similarly, Mansfield, et al., contend that we require a more nuanced understanding of teacher resilience and programs that support PSTs to develop a range of strategies they can employ in their teaching. Larsen and Allen describe an approach whereby they consider what it is that beginning teachers attribute to their successes and failures, and offer us an opportunity to explore how we might effectively support graduate teachers as they enter the profession.

5 Research Methodologies in Teacher Education

In providing an overview of contemporary teacher education research in Australia, this volume represents research studies that utilize a broad array of research methodologies and approaches to examine a variety of issues and questions that emerge from teacher education practice. This diversity is not unexpected, and as Skukauskaiti and Grace (2006) highlight, it is "virtually impossible" for "any one approach to be used to address the complex issues being explored through research in education" (p. xi). Sallee and Flood (2012) note the benefits of qualitative research to the education community as: (a) its focus on context, (b) its use of an emergent design, and (c) its use of thick description.

On closer inspection, the range of methodological approaches adopted by the scholars who have contributed to this volume, encompass both qualitative method and mixed method research, and include: design-based research methodology; case study research: content and discourse analysis; spatial analysis and "bricolage". The various chapters feature data collected through such research methods including: surveys; interviews; focus group discussions; visual representations; document analysis, observations, filmed teacher-student interactions and field notes and frequently combinations of several methods.

The discipline of teacher education, interconnects with other disciplines such as Psychology, Information Technology, History, Sociology, Visual Arts and Spatial Geography. Shepard (2006) highlights that the inherent multidisciplinary nature of research in teacher education serves to broaden and shape the learning and perspectives of those who engage in the field, thus contributing to how various complexities are pondered, approached, challenged and understood. As Shepard states:

> Researchers in education work at the crossroads of multiple disciplines. Because of this interdisciplinarity, we are more aware than most social scientists of the ways in which narrow, disciplinary perspectives shape scholars' understanding of substantive problems... We appreciate the need to study significant issues at micro and macro levels of analysis and to synthesize research findings across methods and contexts'. (p. xi)

Through her consideration of the importance of both macro and micro levels of analysis, Shepard (2006) also highlights the role played by both large and small scale studies. Two of the studies described in this volume are longitudinal however the majority of the studies were small scale. As Loughran suggests, there is an inherent danger in dismissing small scale research as introspective and of minimal impact. Small scale studies however can assist researchers to interrogate their practice and to test new ideas. Through disseminating their research they assist others connect with, and understand what was learnt.

Teachers, students of teaching and teacher educators can adopt the roles of "public intellectuals and change agents" (Murray et al., 2008) and thus teacher education as a field of scholarship is reinforced, strengthened and extended. Furthermore, small scale teacher education research can speak back to policy and inform school reform. As Rust (2009) explains, "understanding what teachers do, how they do it, and why they do it is central to any effort at reshaping education policy around teacher education, teacher professional development, and school reform" (p. 1882).

As articulated in the National Research Agenda for initial teacher education (AITSL, 2015), one purpose of research is to "create a clear direction for initial teacher education" and stimulate "collaboration and research activity to meet the identified priorities articulated in *Action Now: Classroom Ready Teachers* (TEMAG, 2014, p. 1). It is essential that teacher education in Australia retains the broad interdisciplinary and multi-focused emphasis that is evident in this volume. Researchers should pursue research that both aligns with and critiques the National Research agenda. Research practice in the field of education involves "reflective and imaginative work, situational understanding, deliberation, sensibility and voice" (Punch & Oancea, 2014, p. xix), and has far more to offer the educational community than only supporting government initiatives and policy. Zeichner (2010) asserts that teacher education research should, importantly, assist those involved in the broad educational community to develop a critical consciousness, thus playing a pivotal transformational role within an education system in helping students to become critically aware and empathetic global citizens, knowing and understanding the sources and consequences of injustices.

6 Key Challenges for Teacher Education

Teacher education remains under scrutiny. What is clearly evident is that TEMAG (2014) has provided a further stimulus and guidelines for future teacher education research, and in this volume *Teacher Education; Innovation, intervention and impact*, teacher educators have presented examples of the ways in which research is indeed informing and impacting practice and pedagogical development in universities. Teacher education is research-informed and is generative, indicating that new knowledge about teacher education is ever expanding. There *is* evidence of impact, albeit is some cases localised, nuanced and contextually based.

However, a number of key challenges for teacher education, and teacher educators conducting research, have been identified. These challenges relate to the concepts of 'linking research' and focusing on the ways in which the impact of teacher education research can be measured. As Loughran (2013) suggests, "Approaches to sharing learning about pedagogical advances are important in pursuing scholarship of teaching and for inviting others to build on those advances in meaningful ways" (p. 8). Much of what is learnt through teacher education research remains as 'silo-research' and this remains an issue that teacher education researchers need to reconsider. Targeted, nuanced and context-driven research is critical as a means of responding to PST, teacher, course and student needs but more is required to provide both broad and deep responses. It is also imperative that teacher educators use their professional judgement, collaborative skills and pedagogical content knowledge to determine what these needs might be.

While the evidence based focus might arguably be broadened, the attention and spotlight on the important role of research *in* and *for* teacher education is timely. It suggests an opportunity for the teacher education research community to consider the "goals of their programs and invent new ways to trace their impact all the way to the ultimate destination – the nation's schoolchildren" (Cochran-Smith, 2005, p. 10). The focus on research in teacher education also raises further important questions, including: What counts as evidence of effectiveness and impact and for whom?; what are the appropriate research approaches and designs to be utilised?; who might be the researchers, co-researchers and participants? and what methods will best foster and enable the teacher education research community to communicate findings to a wide public and policy audience?

This volume, *Teacher Education: Innovation, intervention and impact* is a collective snapshot in time of teacher education research across Australia. It not only illustrates the nuances and complexities associated with researching teaching and teacher education, but it also highlights the powerful learning that is revealed when the research is designed to meet the needs of learners and teachers. The research outcomes and analysis presents for scrutiny the sophisticated ways in which students learn, and teachers teach and learn.

References

Australian Institute for Teaching and School Leadership (AITSL). (2015). Research agenda for initial teacher education. Retrieved from http://www.aitsl.edu.au/docs/default-source/aitsl-research/ITE-research-agenda.pdf?sfvrsn=4.

Butcher, J., Bezzina, M., & Moran, W. (2011). Transformational partnership: A new agenda for higher education. *Innovative Higher Education, 36*, 29–40.

Cochran-Smith, M. (2005). The new teacher education: For better or for worse? *Educational Researcher, 34*(7), 3–17.

Cochran-Smith, M., Villegas, A. M., Abrams, L., Chavez-Moreno, L., Mills, T., & Stern, R. (2015). Critiquing teacher preparation research: An overview of the field Part II. *Journal of Teacher Education, 66*(2), 109–121.

Kift, S., Nelson, K., & Clarke, J. (2010). Transition pedagogy: A third generation approach to FYE – A case study of policy and practice for the higher education sector. *The International Journal of the First Year in Higher Education, 15*(4), 370–386. doi:10.2167/irg201.0

Korthagen, F., Loughran, J. J., & Russell, T. (2006). Developing fundamental principles for teacher education programs and practices. *Teaching and Teacher Education, 22*, 1020–1041.

Krause, K. (2007). *New perspectives on engaging first year students in learning*. Brisbane, Australia: Griffith Institute for Higher Education.

Le Cornu, R. (2015). *Key components of effective professional experience in initial teacher education in Australia*. Melbourne, Australia: Australian Institute for Teaching and School Leadership.

Loughran, J. (2013). Stepping out in style. In Brandenburg & Wilson (Eds.), *Pedagogies for the future: Leading quality learning and teaching in higher education*. Rotterdam, The Netherlands: SENSE Publishers.

Loughran, J. J. (2014). Professionally developing as a teacher educator. *Journal of Teacher Education, 65*, 271–283.

Masters, J., & Donnison, S. (2010). First year transition in teacher education: The pod experience. *Australian Journal of Teacher Education, 35*(2), 87–98.

Mertler, C. (2016). *Introduction to educational research*. Thousand Oaks, CA: Sage.

Murray, J., Campbell, A., Hextall, I., Hulme, M., Jones, M., Mahony, P., et al. (2008). Mapping the field of teacher education research: Methodology and issues in a research capacity building initiative in teacher education in the United Kingdom. *European Education Research Journal, 7*(4), 459–474.

Murray, S., Nuttall, J., & Mitchell, J. (2008). Research into initial teacher education in Australia: A survey of the literature 1995–2004. *Teaching and Teacher Education, 24*(1), 225–239.

Punch, K., & Oancea, A. (2014). *Introduction to research methods in education*. Los Angeles: Sage.

Rust, F. O. (2009). Teacher's college record. Teacher research and the problem of practice. *Teacher's College Record, 111*(8), 1882–1893.

Sallee, M. W., & Flood, J. T. (2012). Using qualitative research to bridge research, policy and practice. *Theory Into Practice, 51*(2), 137–144.

Shepard, L. (2006). Handbook of complementary methods in education research. In J. L. Green, G. Camilli, & P. B. Elmore (Eds.), *American educational research association* (2nd ed., pp. xiv–xii). Washington, DC: Lawrence Erlbaum Associates.

Skukauskaiti, A., & Grace, E. (2006). On reading and using the volume. In J. L. Green, G. Camilli, & P. B. Elmore (Eds.), *Handbook of complementary methods in education research* (2nd ed., pp. xxi–xxiv). Washington, DC: Educational Research Association, Lawrence Erlbaum Associates.

Sleeter, C. (2014). Toward teacher education research that informs policy. *Educational Researcher, 43*(3), 146–153

Teacher Education Ministerial Advisory Group (TEMAG). (2014). *Action now: Classroom ready teachers*. Retrieved from: https://docs.education.gov.au/system/files/doc/other/action_now_classroom_ready_teachers_accessible.pdf.

White, S. (2016). Teacher education research and education policy makers: An Australian perspective. *Journal of Education for Teaching, 42*(2), 252–264.

Whitty, G. (2006, March). *Teacher professionalism in a new era*. General Teaching Council for Northern Ireland Annual Lecture, Belfast.

Zeichner, K. (2010). *Preparing globally competent teachers: A U.S. perspective*. Colloquium on the internationalisation of Teacher Education. Kansas City: NAFSA: Association of International Educators

Zeichner, K., Payne, K. A., & Brayko, K. (2015). Democratizing teacher education. *Journal of Teacher Education, 66*(2), 122–135.

Reform and the Reconceptualisation of Teacher Education in Australia

Jennifer M. Gore

1 The Australian Context

Reform of teacher education in Australia has been high on government, professional, and public agendas (Centre for Education Statistics and Evaluation, 2014; Louden, 2008; Mayer, 2014; Teacher Education Ministerial Advisory Group [TEMAG], 2014), intensifying during the past two decades. Underpinned by the view that improving the efficiency and equity of schooling depends on getting and keeping good teachers (Barber & Mourshed, 2007; Organisation for Economic Co-operation and Development [OECD], 2005), major recent reforms have included: extended programs of teacher education; the development of a national approach to accreditation of teacher education programs; and tighter regulation of who can teach and who can enter teaching programs. Unlike in other contexts, such as England where schools play a much more direct role, Australian reforms have all centred on universities as the key providers of teacher education.

1.1 Program Length and Professionalisation

From the late 1970s, the length of teacher education programs has been on the reform agenda, taking the majority of teacher education programs from 3-year diploma courses to 4-year baccalaureates (Aspland, 2006; Dyson, 2005). More recently, length of program concerns have targeted postgraduate teaching qualifications with most institutions moving from 1-year postgraduate diplomas to 2-year Master of Teaching awards, now a requirement for accreditation of postgraduate

---

J.M. Gore (✉)
School of Education, University of Newcastle, Callaghan, Australia
e-mail: jenny.gore@newcastle.edu.au

teacher education programs (Australian Institute of Teaching and School Leadership [AITSL], 2011).

Modifications to program length form part of a broader professionalisation agenda (Australian Council of Deans of Education [ACDE], 1998) to increase the status of teaching as an occupation by requiring preparation to be structured in similar ways to other professional occupations (Lovat & McLeod, 2006). This kind of move saw the amalgamation of teachers' colleges (at the time known as colleges of advanced education) with universities in 1988, to create a unified national system of higher education. In so doing, a range of new opportunities and challenges opened up (Aspland, 2006), including ongoing concerns about the status of teaching as a disciplinary field in higher education.

Since the vast majority of teacher education provision moved into universities during the late 1980s, public and political debate and academic commentary have focused more or less consistently on a range of desirable improvements to teacher education, mostly under the guise of partnerships with schools, time spent in schools, the discipline or content underpinnings of teacher preparation, and the adequacy of preparation particularly in relation to diverse student and community types. These kinds of issues have become constant challenges to teacher education in Australia – unresolved in part because each enhancement has significant consequences for government funding of teacher education, university student numbers, and the working conditions of teachers and teacher educators. For example, calls to increase time spent in schools as part of teacher education programs need to be balanced with the costs to universities of meeting demands of the industrial award which requires payment to teachers, as well as the perceived costs to schools of accommodating large numbers of student teachers. In Victoria alone, it is estimated that up to 25,000 placements are needed each year, highlighting the scale of the challenge (Victorian Department of Education and Early Childhood Development, 2013).

1.2 National Regulation

Regulation of teacher education has intensified throughout the period since amalgamation and especially with the establishment by the federal government of the Australian Institute for Teaching and School Leadership (AITSL) in 2010 as a public company funded by the Australian Government and the Minister for Education and Training as the sole member. While AITSL operates under its own constitution, with decisions made by an independent board of directors, and is intended to provide relatively independent national oversight of teacher education, its reliance on government funding and its need to be responsive to tasks and targets set by the Minister has significant consequences for the development of policy and processes. For example, a recent media release announced that "the Australian Government will provide an additional $16.9 million over 4 years to the Australian Institute for Teaching and School Leadership (AITSL) to improve initial teacher education and to ensure teacher graduates are 'classroom ready'" (Department of Education and

Training, 2015). The Minister said: "AITSL will also *be instructed* to monitor and revise accreditation arrangements on an ongoing basis to make sure the stronger quality assurance actually impacts on the classroom readiness of graduates" (emphasis added).

Furthermore, arguably, many of AITSL's policy outputs are underpinned by calls for submissions and opinion pieces rather than empirical evidence (not surprisingly given the timelines and budget restrictions on more rigorous forms of analysis to inform its policy statements), an irony not lost in the context of criticisms of teacher education for its inadequate evidence base (Riddle, 2015). At the time AITSL was established, several states in Australia had already set up their own regulatory authorities with responsibility for assuring the quality of teacher education (including Queensland, South Australia, New South Wales, and Victoria), but the national push through AITSL aimed to assure consistent high quality teacher education across the nation.

The development and implementation of teacher education program standards *Accreditation of Initial Teacher Education Programs in Australia: Standards and procedures* (AITSL, 2011) produced a tightening of program components and structures, with rigid requirements for program length, days of professional experience in schools (80 days in 4-year programs, 40 days in 2-year programs), specific amounts of discipline content, and attention to such matters as teaching Aboriginal and Torres Strait Islander students and students with special needs. In addition the program standards dictate who should be allowed entry into preservice teacher education programs, who should be employed as a teacher educator, and who can provide supervised teaching in schools (AITSL, 2011).

National policy has been notoriously difficult to implement in Australian education. Despite all State ministers of education agreeing to the establishment of AITSL and signing up to national standards, some states insist on stamping their own character (Tuinamuana, 2011). In NSW for example, so-called "elaborations" of the standards have been imposed, in the areas of classroom management, special needs, Aboriginal and Torres Strait Islander education, ICT, and literacy and numeracy, despite all of these matters being attended to in the articulation of the national standards. While perhaps trivial in the larger scheme of things, such additional requirements that impact directly and rather onerously on the already-cumbersome documentation required of teacher education providers, are illustrative of the over-regulation of teacher education not only through national requirements, but also state requirements, both of which also sit alongside already rigorous internal and external program development requirements within universities (Tertiary Education Quality and Standards Agency [TEQSA], 2014). The national effort by teacher educators to meet all of these requirements amounts to millions of dollars annually, in part because of the sheer scale of the teacher education enterprise in Australian universities with, for example, 8.7% of all commencing university enrolments in Education in 2014 (Australian Government Department of Education and Training, 2015b).[1]

---

[1] For all domestic students, total EFTSL in "Teacher Education" in 2014 was 52,536 (36,573 was at undergraduate level). Total EFTSL for all domestic students across all disciplines in 2014 was 719,363 – 7.3% (Australian Government Department of Education and Training, 2015a).

1.3 Current State of Teacher Education

Indeed, the scale of initial teacher education across Australia is significant. In 2013, there were more than 450 programs in 48 institutions (AITSL, 2014) (mostly universities, with a few colleges and TAFE providers also involved). While this number is sometimes derided as indicative of a foolhardy proliferation of programs, it is easily explained by the listing of discrete programs for each secondary specialisation – mathematics, science, physical education, English, social sciences, visual arts, languages, and so on – with considerable overlap in program requirements within each institution. Nonetheless, in 2013 there were 79,623 students enrolled as pre-service teachers (Australian Government Department of Education and Training, 2014a) in Australia. In the same year, higher education providers graduated 17,900 initial teacher education students, entering a workforce of 261,585 full time equivalent teachers (Australian Government Department of Education and Training, 2014b). This volume of activity poses significant challenges for accreditation and other regulatory processes which currently end up relying on "truckloads" of documentation (Mockler, 2015) comprised substantially of box-ticked matrices relating teacher education program assessments to the Professional Standards for Teachers.

With the increased regulation of both teacher education and teaching (through the Australian Professional Standards for Teachers (AITSL, 2011)), to qualify as a graduate teacher and be eligible for employment in Australian schools, participants must now hold a 4-year full-time equivalent higher education qualification, structured in one of the following ways:

- A 3-year undergraduate degree plus a 2-year graduate entry teaching qualification;
- An integrated qualification of at least 4 years combining discipline studies and professional studies;
- A combined degree of at least 4 years;
- Other combination approved by teacher regulatory authorities in consultation with AITSL deemed equivalent to the above.
- While the "other approved combination" leaves room for alternate modes of teacher education, there are currently very few such pathways into teaching in Australia, and even those existing, such as Teach for Australia, rely on strong university involvement.

Despite a strong system of initial teacher education in Australia, political and public dissatisfaction remains a prevalent feature of the discursive terrain. As put by the-then Minister for Education, the Honorable Christopher Pyne:

> There is evidence that our teacher education system is not up to scratch. We are not attracting the top students into teacher courses as we once did, courses are too theoretical, ideological and faddish, not based on the evidence of what works in teaching important subjects like literacy. Standards are too low at some education institutions – everyone passes. (Knott, 2014)

The adequacy of evidence for such statements aside, there are consistent calls for reform in teacher education, with the most recent federal government report *Action Now: Classroom Ready Teachers* (TEMAG, 2014) calling for an "overhaul" of teacher education in Australia:

> The evidence is clear: enhancing the capability of teachers is vital to raising the overall quality of Australia's school system and lifting student outcomes. Action to improve the quality of teachers in Australian schools must begin when they are first prepared for the profession. (p. viii)

The articulated goals of such reform, as with nearly all reform of teacher education, centre squarely on enhancing the quality of teaching in schools in order to improve outcomes for students (often meaning performance on standardised national and international tests), including more equitable outcomes.

Key strategies advocated in this context include restricting entry to teacher education to the best quality students (the top 30 % of the population) (Wilson, Dalton, & Baumann, 2015), improving the quality of teacher education programs, and enhancing partnerships with schools in order to ensure a better integration of theory and practice. The TEMAG (2014) report also concluded that many higher education providers and practitioners adopt strategies which reflect populist thinking (TEMAG, 2014), have not been linked with student learning, and are not well understood by those teaching them (Parliament of Victoria, 2005), rather than being informed by research (National Inquiry into the Teaching of Literacy, 2005). This view is echoed by Roberts-Hull, Jensen, and Cooper (2015) who declare that many programs are teaching obsolete or ineffective practices or strategies. Moreover, TEMAG reported that many teacher preparation programs are not modeling the practices they expect from students. Nor are they integrating theory and practice throughout program components. Note that the evidence for these claims comes primarily from submissions to reviews and the opinions of (often vocal) commentators or well-known critics of teacher education, including external companies with strong links to the federal government.

The *Action Now: Classroom Ready Teachers* (TEMAG, 2014) report named as key problems in Teacher Education (or more accurately, summarized as key concerns articulated by those who made submissions):

- *Australian Professional Standards for Teachers are weakly applied*;
- *Australians are not confident that initial teacher education entrants are the best fit for the job*;
- *not all programs are equipping graduates with evidence-based teaching strategies*;
- *teacher education providers are not assessing classroom readiness against the Professional Standards*;
- *insufficient support for beginning teachers*;
- *a lack of useful information on the effectiveness of the teaching program which hinders continuous improvement* (p. viii).

These concerns are poised to impact on the ongoing reform of teacher education in Australia. Accreditation of teacher education programs with a focus on outputs rather than inputs (AITSL/TEMAG), addressing the quality of entrants (e.g., Bowles, Hattie, Dinham, Scull, & Clinton, 2014), and gathering evidence of the impact of teacher education programs (AITSL, 2015a; see also Dinham, 2015; Gore, 2015a; Mayer, 2015) are at the forefront of the most recent pronouncements.

The impact of these latest government/public pushes for reform of teacher education in Australia remains to be seen. A focus on restricting entry to the 'best and brightest' (Smith, 2014) makes for persuasive government policy but its enactment alongside other (equally?) appealing calls to widen participation in higher education, including among historically under-represented groups (Bradley, Noonan, Nugent, & Scales, 2008), will test the resolve of reformers. This is especially so at a time when universities are under considerable financial strain and when attrition from teaching remains high (both among beginning teachers and with large numbers expected to retire in the near future) (McKinnon, 2016; Weldon, 2015). Focusing on outputs and the impact of teacher education programs also makes for compelling government rhetoric, but the enactment of such processes is enormously challenged by unresolved international efforts to measure the quality of teaching and the quality of teacher education (e.g., Darling-Hammond, 2015; Goldhaber, 2015; Goldring et al., 2015; Teachers College Columbia University, 2015).

It is against this backdrop that local teacher education programs in Australia are developed and refined. Within the tightly regulated program standards, and despite concerns about homogenising effects (Gannon, 2012) there is scope for innovation as illustrated in the following two case studies from the University of Newcastle – its implementation of the National Exceptional Teachers for Disadvantaged Schools (NETDS) Program and its development of a revised Master of Teaching (MTeach) Program. In the remainder of this chapter, I outline these 'new' teacher education programs in which I am involved and interrogate how far they go in providing 'solutions' to key 'problems' identified in and with teacher education. I consider the extent to which it is possible to create forms of teacher education that are professionally defensible from a higher education perspective while responding to public and political concerns.

2 Case Study 1. The Exceptional Teachers for Disadvantaged Schools Program

The Exceptional Teachers for Disadvantaged Schools (ETDS) program was pioneered by Jo Lampert and Bruce Burnett at Queensland University of Technology (Lampert & Burnett, 2011). It provides a pathway for high quality early career teachers to be professionally and personally prepared for roles within schools situated in low socio-economic areas, thus placing the "best" teachers into the most challenging schools (Rice, 2008). This program was developed in response to the finding that top-performing education graduates are far less likely to accept positions in disadvantaged schools (Cochran-Smith, Davis, & Fries, 2004), given that they are often snapped up quickly by independent schools or offered 'more attractive' positions at 'easier' schools within government school systems.

The ETDS program, funded by Social Ventures Australia (SVA),[2] identifies the highest-achieving education students at the end of their second year of study, combines this with data about student teachers' initial attitudes, dispositions, academic record, and social history, and then selects the top 5–10 % for invitation into the program (Lampert & Burnett, 2011). Mostly, GPA determines whether an invitation is issued.

Entry to the program provides participants with a specialised curriculum and practicum, partnering with low-SES schools, for part of their teacher education program, which otherwise is identical to that of their non-ETDS peers. Focus groups and interviews are conducted throughout the program to explore participants' perspectives and understandings of the impact on their teaching practice. As these 'exceptional' pre-service teachers finish their initial teacher education program, they are encouraged to pursue employment in low-SES schools. Designed to address both the distribution of 'effective' teachers in low-SES schools and the attrition of early career teachers/preservice teachers from those contexts through better preparation, ETDS offers extra support for working in disadvantaged contexts through focussed content in a cohort-based tutorial and extra academic visits and phone contact while on practicum.

According to SVA, three barriers to transformational social change on the scale required are addressed through the ETDS program: a lack of capital, experienced talent, and evidence to prove what works (Social Ventures Australia, 2015). Pitched as offering solutions to equity and workforce issues, ETDS is careful to avoid a 'missionary' or deficit model (Flessa, 2007; Labaree, 2010), instead emphasising academic excellence.

Tracking of the ETDS program, now with its fourth cohort of graduating students at QUT, is evaluating graduates' employment destinations, retention data, and performance. Preliminary data indicate a higher employment rate for ETDS graduates (from 85 % in 2011 to ~93 % in 2014) and a significantly increased proportion of EDTS graduates working in low-SES schools (from 35 % in 2011 to 88 % in 2014). Initial analysis by the program pioneers has suggested: student teachers in the program must have a passion for teaching in disadvantaged schools; they must have knowledge of low-SES contexts; and, although personal qualities such as resilience are desirable, a high grade point average is a strong measure of success (Lampert & Burnett, 2011). A question Lampert and Burnett (2011) seek to explore through ETDS is the capacity of the program to 'teach' social justice.

The early successes of the program, particularly in terms of employment destinations of graduates, has led to its expansion to other states and universities in the form of the 'National' Exceptional Teachers for Disadvantaged Schools (NETDS)

---

[2] SVA is a non-profit organisation that describes itself as "leading practitioners of venture philanthropy in Australia" (Social Ventures Australia, 2015).

program. Given its strong performance in equity with 27% of students from low-SES backgrounds (well above the sector average of 16%), the largest 'enabling' program in the country (University of Newcastle, 2016), and around 23% of the nation's Aboriginal teachers despite being one of 40 universities in Australia (Lester, Heitmeyer, Gore, & Ford, 2013), Newcastle was invited to be one of the first two universities to participate in this wider implementation of ETDS. The first cohort of 34 students was identified late in 2013 and commenced the program in 2014, the third year of their teacher education. Characteristics of the Newcastle cohort include 26% who attended low-SES high schools themselves (ICSEA[3] <1000), with 14 of the 31 for whom we have information the first in their family to attend university. The age of participants ranges from 19 to 47 years, with 65% of the cohort 'mature age' (over 25 years of age). The average GPA of the cohort is 5.88 (maximum possible is 7). As these students graduate, important comparisons with the Queensland and other cohorts will provide stronger evidence of the program's impact.

2.1 The Case for Reform

How far does NETDS take us in the reform or reconceptualisation of teacher education? To what extent does it address public and political calls for reform? In what ways does it move beyond traditional approaches to teacher preparation? What challenges does it face?

The program clearly responds to enduring concerns for the quality of teachers and quality of teaching, particularly for their role in improving outcomes for students from low-SES schools and communities. Unlike programs like Teach for Australia, which seek to attract graduates from any relevant degree program into teaching, NETDS builds on an existing vocational commitment to teaching as a career by targeting students in their second year of an undergraduate teacher education program. This is an important distinction with potential benefits in terms of satisfaction with, and retention in, teaching as a career.

By identifying and supporting high-achieving education students with additional academic content and additional contact with academic staff while on practicum in low-SES schools, the program also addresses concerns about the readiness of graduates, especially for more challenging teaching environments (TEMAG, 2014), thus setting them up for greater success. The numbers of ETDS graduates accepting employment in low-SES schools certainly suggests a level of confidence, potentially attributable to the program.

While providing extra support for the highest achieving teacher education students might be an effective strategy for delivering more equitable outcomes in

---

[3] ICSEA is the Index of Community Socio-Educational Advantage created by the Australian Curriculum, Assessment and Reporting Authority (ACARA), which enables meaningful comparisons of NAPLAN test achievement by students in schools across Australia. See http://www.myschool.edu.au/AboutUs/Glossary/glossaryLink for more details

schools, it raises questions about equity within the teacher education program itself. The extra support provided to a cohort of already high-achieving students is made possible through the special funding attached to the program. A more substantial reconceptualisation of teacher education, would require finding ways to make such support available for all teacher education students, not only for the chosen cohort.

Another limitation of NETDS might be the use of high academic achievement in the first two years of the teacher education program as a proxy for quality. Are these students 'exceptional teachers' or will they become 'exceptional' teachers? The international evidence of a relationship between academic achievement and success as a teacher is weak at present, although most studies have used academic achievement on entry to teacher education as the key measure. In the Republic of Ireland, admission to teacher education is highly selective (Department of Education and Skills, 2012) yet the country's performance on PISA in 2009 was indistinguishable from that of the United Kingdom, who maintain broader admission to teacher education. In Shanghai, teachers typically do not have high educational qualifications, but are given extremely high quality training both before and during their careers (Wiliam, 2014). In Sweden, higher university entry scores are not associated with higher performance by school students on standardised tests (Grönqvist & Vlachos, 2008). These findings, together with current debates about the adequacy of academic performance measures in the selection of teacher candidates (Bowles, Hattie, Dinham, Scull, & Clinton, 2014), raise questions about using academic performance as the key criterion for selection into the NETDS program.

There is also a risk that a program such as NETDS which encourages commitment to teaching in low-SES schools can err on the side of indoctrination, dogmatically exerting moral pressure on these high achieving students to make career choices with potentially negative consequences for some of its graduates. That is, if some of these exceptional teachers enter schools where they struggle to achieve their 'mission' of achieving good outcomes for students from low-SES backgrounds, attrition from teaching might even be greater. This 'social reconstruction' orientation of some teacher education programs (Zeichner, 1993) is particularly vulnerable to setting students up to fail unless they also have strong practical knowledge and support (Gore, 2001, 2015b). A 'reconceptualised' teacher education program would ensure the support provided includes practical know-how as well as deep theoretical underpinnings for understanding disadvantage, poverty, equity, and social justice.

Acknowledging these challenges is not to undermine the potential value of NETDS to those students who participate or the students they subsequently teach. They may well be better positioned to make a greater difference in low-SES schooling than graduates without this experience, delivering the high quality teaching and more equitable outcomes advocated across political, academic, and public discourses. As a model for the reconceptualisation of teacher education however, NETDS appears to face some substantial limitations.

Nonetheless in its reclamation of ideologically-driven government initiatives to ensure talented students are employed in the disadvantaged schools where ostensibly they are needed most by recruiting such students from within Education rather than without (as in the case of Teach for Australia) and to position NETDS within a teacher education program that conforms to all accreditation requirements, NETDS skilfully creates a more professionally defensible way of achieving the same kinds of goals. This defensibility of the NETDS program structure, at least from the perspective of the vast majority of teacher educators, sits in stark contrast to the abbreviated preparation of Teach for Australia candidates.

2.2 Summary

In short, NETDS represents a reconceptualisation of existing teacher education programs in a number of ways. It unapologetically identifies and supports the highest achieving students and encourages them away from the 'cushy' jobs they would easily win into more challenging and arguably more rewarding teaching careers in disadvantaged schools. This commitment interrupts traditional employment pathways whereby the 'best' students typically end up with the 'best' jobs and in so doing responds to national concerns about the quality of teaching in schools and equity of outcomes, particularly for groups that have traditionally not fared well in Australian schools (Indigenous and poor students). NETDS also reconceptualises the responsibility of the higher education provider to prepare graduates who will succeed and be sustained in some of the toughest schools. Addressing national levels of attrition by preparing graduates with the knowledge, skills, and experience to thrive in low-SES schools takes seriously this aspect of teacher education and begins to demonstrate what might be needed to prepare more teacher education candidates for success, wherever they may teach.

3 Case Study 2. The Master of Teaching Program at the University of Newcastle

The Master of Teaching program at the University of Newcastle was explicitly designed to address the quality of teaching.[4] It aims to develop beginning teachers who are not only well prepared when they arrive in schools, but are also adaptive and resilient learners and leaders. The MTeach ambitiously seeks to re-vision teacher education in ways that respond to enduring concerns about the quality and unique theory-practice nexus of teacher education. In so doing, it directly addresses the views encapsulated in various contemporary policy statements on teachers and teaching (such as the NSW Government's *Great Teaching, Inspired Learning* and AITSL's *Australian Teacher Performance and Development Framework*). It utilises knowledge derived from our own research into Quality Teaching and Quality

---

[4]The redesign of the existing Master of Teaching program at Newcastle took place in 2013 and 2014, with the first cohort enrolling in the revised program in 2015.

Teaching Rounds (see for example: Bowe & Gore, in press; Gore, 2014b; Gore & Bowe, 2015; Gore, Griffiths, & Ladwig, 2004; Gore, Ladwig, & King, 2004; Gore et al., 2015; Ladwig, 2007; Ladwig, Smith, Gore, Amosa, & Griffiths, 2007). It operationalises its aims through the following deliberate moves: the use of a specific pedagogical model to frame knowledge and analysis of practice; the explicit integration of course components; an emphasis on teaching as clinical practice; and specific engagement with local schools. Each of these innovations is outlined below.

3.1 The Knowledge Base for Teaching

A perennial problem of teacher education is the lack of an agreed knowledge base for understanding teaching practice (Shulman, 1986), which results in weak teacher education program effects (Zeichner & Tabachnick, 1981) and relatively poor student satisfaction (Gore, Griffiths, et al., 2004), with graduates lacking confidence in their abilities and unsure of how well prepared they are (McKenzie, Weldon, Rowley, Murphy, & McMillan, 2014). While some Australian universities have moved to initial teacher education programs that incorporate either an inquiry-based or clinical approach (most publicly The University of Melbourne) in order to strengthen the knowledge base for teaching, the MTeach at Newcastle draws on its 'signature' pedagogical framework, Quality Teaching, an empirically-tested model of good teaching developed by University of Newcastle academics (Ladwig and Gore).

This three-dimensional pedagogical framework,[5] Quality Teaching (NSW Department of Education and Training [NSW DET], 2003a, 2003b), has been the focus of more than a decade of research in schools with practising teachers. The studies have demonstrated positive impacts of the framework on teaching quality, teacher satisfaction, and student outcomes, whilst also narrowing achievement gaps for Aboriginal students and students from low-SES backgrounds (Gore, 2014a, 2014b; Gore & Bowe, 2015; Gore, Griffiths, et al., 2004, Gore, et al. 2015; Ladwig et al., 2007). All of these outcomes align precisely with the kinds of improvements sought by governments wanting to improve Australian schooling and so respond directly to the concerns of critics and reformers. Replicating these kinds of effects on the quality of teaching produced by preservice, rather than inservice, teachers is a major goal of the program. The framework itself, while seen as foundational in providing a firmer knowledge base for teaching, is only part of the MTeach program design. How the framework is used within the program is also critical, as elaborated below.

---

[5] The model focuses on intellectual quality, a quality learning environment, and significance.

3.2 Program Coherence

The MTeach program was designed to address longstanding criticisms of the fragmentation of knowledge in teacher education (Liston & Zeichner, 1991) which is seen to weaken the knowledge base and reduce students' confidence in their readiness to teach. The MTeach seeks to strengthen program coherence by using the Quality Teaching framework as a lens through which to analyse, interrogate, synthesise and evaluate other aspects of the teacher education program. Because the framework itself draws attention to what, how and who is being taught, it provides a lens with which to consider psychological, sociological, philosophical, historical, and policy perspectives on teaching and schooling. Moreover, it provides a framework for organising the discrete pieces of information that students typically encounter in teacher education.

In order to make this integration of knowledge explicit the program includes 'conferences' at the beginning of each semester and 'showcases' at the end, in which the various subjects studied during the semester are brought together. The conferences are intended to provide students with an overview of their studies for the semester and help them to see the relationship between discrete subjects. The showcases provide a forum for students to demonstrate their learning, with aspects of their assessment requiring integration of knowledge gained during the semester.

Essential to the success of this aspect of the program is a shared conceptual framework among the teacher educators involved and an agreed vision of what constitutes good quality teaching. In this respect, the Quality Teaching framework becomes a means of helping students to integrate the various components of their teacher education program, including its most theoretical and most practical components.

3.3 Clinical Practice

Another key component of the MTeach is its specific form of clinical work, designed to produce teachers who have superior diagnostic and strategic capacities for analysing and improving practice, reporting their impact on student learning, and leading their colleagues in continuous improvement. Other 'clinical' approaches to initial teacher education tend to focus either on diagnosing the needs of individual learners (e.g., Melbourne Graduate School of Education (MGSE) [MGSE], 2016) or on discrete teaching skills (as per approaches derived from 'clinical supervision' models (Glickman, 1981; Goldhammer, 1969)). The MTeach goes beyond such 'atomistic' approaches emphasising instead that professional practice requires neophyte teachers to draw on a full range of skills and insights to create meaningful learning experiences for whole classes of students within the complex multidimensional, unpredictable, simultaneous environments of classrooms (Jackson, 1968; Doyle, 1977).

Drawing on the University's research into teacher development and specifically its work on Quality Teaching Rounds as a way of effectively implementing the Quality Teaching model in schools (Bowe & Gore, in press; Gore, 2014a, 2014b; Gore & Bowe, 2015; Gore et al., 2015), the MTeach seeks to prepare knowledgeable and confident graduates with the clinical skills to help them deliver high quality teaching to students in all contexts and to continuously refine their practice in collaboration with colleagues. MTeach students thus work in 'professional learning communities' in which traditional conceptions of teachers working in relative isolation in their own classrooms are supplanted by extensive experience in approaching teaching problems in collaboration with colleagues.

3.4 School-University Alignment

Another feature of the MTeach lies in its alignment with goals of both the NSW Department of Education (NSW Government, 2013) and NSW Catholic school systems to identify clusters of schools as showcase environments for high quality professional experiences for pre-service teachers. Both organisations have articulated commitments to enhancing this core component of teacher education. Leveraging existing strong relationships with local schools built through the federal government's National Partnerships (Low SES, Teacher Quality, and Literacy and Numeracy) program, and other research relationships, the MTeach is partnering with a group of schools where there is a shared interest in Quality Teaching and willingness to work with student teachers in undertaking Quality Teaching Rounds. This university-school alignment in both substance (Quality Teaching) and process (Quality Teaching Rounds) lays the foundation for a smooth transition of graduates to employment and ongoing professional learning.

3.5 Possible Limitations

One challenge of the MTeach relates to the logistics for students, especially in finding times to meet with their PLCs outside of class. This is of particular concern when many of the students are mature aged with busy lives and families. Buy-in among teacher education colleagues could also impact on the program's delivery if, after agreeing to the program at the point of conceptualisation, some feel less supportive when the program requires changes to their own practice, integrating Quality Teaching or the new processes that characterise the program (professional learning communities, conferences and showcases). Such potential resistance would echo broader contestation throughout the field of teacher education over what constitutes and how to judge good teaching, and good teacher education. Arguably such contestation, manifest in longstanding paradigmatic differences (Gore, 2001; Zeichner, 1983), is a major impediment to the reform and success of teacher education and contributes to an ongoing mistrust of teacher education evident in the endless cycle of review, reform and government intervention – a topic for another paper.

3.6 Summary

The MTeach program seeks to overcome fragmentation of knowledge through its curriculum structure (conferences, showcases) and embedded use of the Quality Teaching framework. It seeks to prepare graduates for collaborative/inquiry-oriented/problem-solving professional practice through Quality Teaching Rounds and the experience of working in PLCs. It directly addresses the knowledge base for teaching through its theory/practice integration (Darling-Hammond, Hammerness, Grossman, Rust, & Shulman, 2005) and school/university continuity, and it develops productive relationships with partner schools through common understanding and shared practices (Quality Teaching Rounds/PLCs). Strongly aligned with pedagogical policy reform in schools (NSW Government, 2013), the program is well-positioned to support graduates in making a smooth transition between university teacher education and professional practice in schools.

While grounded more in our own research than in ideologically-driven government initiatives, the MTeach shares espoused government commitments to improving the quality of both teaching and teacher education, and addressing high levels of teacher attrition (Gore & Bowe, 2015; McKinnon, 2016). In this way, the MTeach offers a strong exemplar for the reform of teacher education; an exemplar that is professionally defensible through its basis in academic research on teaching and teacher education. The capacity of the newly-established program to deliver these outcomes remains to be seen.

In terms of reconceptualising teacher education, the MTeach confronts the knowledge base for teaching, the theory-practice nexus, and the preparation for ongoing learning about teaching through collaboration with colleagues. While none of these represent new concerns or practices among teacher educators, the MTeach brings them together in ways that offer new hope of genuine improvement. The recent success of the Quality Teaching Rounds approach for producing significant improvement in the quality of teaching among practising teachers (effect size 0.3–0.4) in the context of a randomised controlled trial (Gore et al., 2015) makes this hope seem tangible.

4 Discussion

Considerable commonality is evident, broadly speaking, in approaches to the reform of teacher education in Australia, both at the level of policy and at the level of teacher education program design and implementation. As the two case studies illustrate, efforts to improve teacher education remain centred on the quality of entrants, enhancement of teacher education programs, and a revised role of schools.

The NETDS program takes a new tack on the quality of teacher education students, not at the point of recruitment into teacher education, but by selecting the best performing students who are already enrolled and enhancing their preparation in a way that seeks to increase the likelihood that some of the best quality teachers will be successfully employed in low-SES schools. As a postgraduate program, the MTeach indirectly addresses the quality of entrants. Program enhancements for the NETDS focus on providing, for the selected cohort, a deeper understanding of the lives and learning needs of students from disadvantaged communities and additional support for students to practise teaching in schools in these areas. These enhancements respond directly to concerns about the adequacy of preparation and teacher attrition, particularly in these contexts. The MTeach takes a whole of program focus on coherence built through a shared vision and pedagogical knowledge base. The program enhancements are embedded in all aspects of the teacher education program. As a result, the potential benefits, for whole cohorts of graduates and their students, are far-reaching. Both the NETDS and the MTeach programs rely on the involvement of schools where there is a shared vision of and commitment to the specific program goals. Such continuity between schools and universities promises a substantial shift away from perceptions of teacher education programs as irrelevant to the realities of contemporary schools and classrooms.

The purported goals of nearly all reform in teacher education have consistently been to enhance the quality of teaching in order to improve outcomes, including (and sometimes especially) equity outcomes. These goals appear to encapsulate the discursive underpinnings of nearly all teacher education reform, despite varying political and professional agendas. The goals themselves are enduring and defensible. However, defining what counts as quality teaching and what counts as student outcomes remains contested and problematic. The strong evidence-based views of education academics are crucial to debates about such fundamental issues.

At this critical juncture, the future of teacher education appears poised to rely heavily on stronger evidence of program impact. New and more robust forms of research, including experimental studies, are being advocated from all quarters (AITSL, 2015b; Louden, 2015; Nuttall, Murray, Seddon, & Mitchell, 2006). Unless teacher educators can rise to this challenge, we may find ourselves stuck in a downward spiral of reform imposed externally, or left with the kind of serial fatigue that comes as (questionably) 'good' ideas are tried for a time and abandoned or replaced by the next good idea, following the next government review.

While high level policy rhetoric remains important in legitimating new policies in the political arena, the two case studies provided above demonstrate that teacher educators are able to occupy the space the reforms offer to reconceptualise our own practice in ways that go beyond (the sometimes simplistic) policy responses. Of course, robust evidence of the effects of these programs, as cohorts of students compete their studies, will strengthen the capacity of such innovations to play a role in pushing back against blunt reform initiatives. Nonetheless, what should be striking to policy makers about our case studies is that teacher educators are clearly grappling with issues of the quality of classroom practice and quality of teacher education, regardless of the overall reform ideology. These and other case studies (Darling-Hammond, 2006), including others provided in this volume, provide a helpful basis for professional discussion among stakeholders about the best way of fostering excellent teaching in diverse settings across Australia and further afield.

References

Aspland, T. (2006). Changing patterns of teacher education in Australia. *Education Research and Perspectives, 33*(2), 140–163.

Australian Council of Deans of Education. (ACDE). (1998). *Preparing a profession: Report of the national standards and guidelines for initial teacher education project*. Canberra, Australia: Australian Council of Deans of Education.

Australian Government Department of Education and Training. (2014a). *Higher education statistics: 2013 Special courses*. Retrieved from http://education.gov.au/higher-education-statistics

Australian Government Department of Education and Training. (2014b). *Selected higher education statistics: 2013 Student data*. Retrieved from http://education.gov.au/higher-education-statistics.

Australian Government Department of Education and Training. (2015a). *Selected higher education statistics: 2014 All student load*. Retrieved from http://docs.education.gov.au/system/files/doc/other/2014_all_student_load_0.xls.

Australian Government Department of Education and Training. (2015b). *Selected higher education statistics: 2014 Appendix 3 – Academic organisational units*. Retrieved from http://docs.education.gov.au/system/files/doc/other/2014_appendix_3.xls.

Australian Institute of Teaching and School Leadership. (AITSL). (2011). *Australian Professional Standards for Teachers*. Retrieved from http://www.aitsl.edu.au/docs/default-source/apst-resources/australian_professional_standard_for_teachers_final.pdf.

Australian Institute for Teaching and School Leadership. (AITSL). (2014). *Initial teacher education: Data report 2014*. Melbourne, Australia: Australian Institute for Teaching and School Leadership. (AITSL).

Australian Institute for Teaching and School Leadership. (AITSL). (2015a). *ITE reform: What is classroom ready?* Retrieved from http://www.aitsl.edu.au/initial-teacher-education/ite-reform-strengthened-accreditation/ite-reform-what-is-classroom-ready.

Australian Institute for Teaching and School Leadership. (AITSL). (2015b). *Research agenda for initial teacher education in Australia*. Retrieved from http://www.aitsl.edu.au/docs/default-source/aitsl-research/ITE-research-agenda.pdf?sfvrsn=4.

Barber, M., & Mourshed, M. (2007). *How the world's best-performing schools come out on top*. Retrieved from McKinsey & Company website: http://mckinseyonsociety.com/downloads/reports/Education/Worlds_School_Systems_Final.pdf.

Bowe, J. M., & Gore, J. M. (in press). Reassembling teacher professional development: The case for Quality Teaching Rounds. *Teachers and Teaching: Theory and Practice*.

Bowles, T., Hattie, J., Dinham, S., Scull, J., & Clinton, J. (2014). Proposing a comprehensive model for identifying teaching candidates. *The Australian Educational Researcher, 41*(4), 365–380.

Bradley, D., Noonan, P., Nugent, H., & Scales, B. (2008). *Review of Australian higher education: Final report*. Canberra, Australia: Department of Education, Employment and Workplace Relations. Retrieved from http://www.mq.edu.au/pubstatic/public/download.jsp?id=111997.

Centre for Education Statistics and Evaluation. (2014). *What works best: Evidence-based practices to help improve NSW student performance*. Sydney, Australia: NSW Department of Education and Communities.

Cochran-Smith, M., Davis, D., & Fries, K. (2004). Multicultural teacher education. In J. A. Banks & C. A. M. Banks (Eds.), *Handbook of research on multicultural education* (2nd ed., pp. 931–975). San Francisco: Jossey-Bass.

Darling-Hammond, L. (2006). *Powerful teacher education: Lessons from exemplary programs*. San Francisco: Jossey-Bass.

Darling-Hammond, L. (2015). Can value added add value to teacher evaluation? *Educational Researcher, 44*(2), 132–137. doi:10.3102/0013189x15575346

Darling-Hammond, L., Hammerness, K., Grossman, P. L., Rust, F., & Shulman, L. (2005). The design of teacher education programs. *Preparing teachers for a changing world: What teachers should learn and be able to do*. San Francisco: Jossey-Bass.

Department of Education and Skills. (2012). *Report of the international review panel on the structure of initial teacher education provision in Ireland*. Retrieved from https://www.education.ie/en/Press-Events/Press-Releases/2012-Press-Releases/Report-of-the-International-Review-Panel-on-the-Structure-of-Initial-Teacher-Education-Provision-in-Ireland.pdf.

Department of Education and Training. (2015). *$16.9 million to help lift teacher quality* (Media release). Retrieved from https://ministers.education.gov.au/pyne/169-million-help-lift-teacher-quality.

Dinham, S. (2015). *Issues and perspectives relevant to the development of an approach to the accreditation of initial teacher education in Australia based on evidence of impact. A paper prepared for the Australian Institute for Teaching and School Leadership*. Retrieved from http://www.aitsl.edu.au/docs/default-source/initial-teacher-education-resources/ite-reform-stimulus-paper-03-dinham.pdf.

Doyle, W. (1977). Learning the classroom environment: An ecological analysis. *Journal of Teacher Education, 28*(6), 51–55. doi:10.1177/002248717702800616

Dyson, M. (2005). Australian teacher education: Although reviewed to the eyeball is there evidence of significant change and where to now? *Australian Journal of Teacher Education, 30*(1), 37–54.

Flessa, J. (2007). *Poverty and education: Towards effective action. A review of the literature*. Toronto, Canada: Ontario Institute for Studies in Education.

Gannon, S. (2012). Changing lives and standardising teachers: The possibilities and limits of professional standards. *English Teaching: Practice and Critique, 11*(3), 59–77.

Glickman, C. D. (1981). *Developmental supervision: Alternative practices for helping teachers improve instruction*. Alexandria, VA: Association for Supervision and Curriculum Development.

Goldhaber, D. (2015). Exploring the potential of value-added performance measures to affect the quality of the teacher workforce. *Educational Researcher, 44*(2), 87–95. doi:10.3102/0013189x15574905

Goldhammer, R. (1969). *Clinical supervision: Special methods for the supervision of teachers*. New York: Holt, Rinehart and Winston.

Goldring, E., Grissom, J. A., Rubin, M., Neumerski, C. M., Cannata, M., & Drake, T. (2015). Make room value added: Principals' human capital decisions and the emergence of teacher observation data. *Educational Researcher, 44*(2), 96–104. doi:10.3102/0013189x15575031

Gore, J. M. (2001). Beyond our differences: A reassembling of what matters in teacher education. *Journal of Teacher Education, 52*(2), 124–135.

Gore, J. M. (2014a). Effective implementation of pedagogical reform through Quality Teaching Rounds. In *Proceedings of the annual national conference of the Australian College of Educators (ACE). What counts as quality in education?* (pp. 16–21). Melbourne, Australia: ACE.

Gore, J. M. (2014b). Towards quality and equity: The case for Quality Teaching Rounds. In *Proceedings of the Australian Council for Educational Research (ACER) research conference. Quality and equity: What does research tell us?* (pp. 86–91). Melbourne, Australia: ACER.

Gore, J. (2015a). My struggle for pedagogy. In D. Ford & B. Porfilio (Eds.), *Leaders in critical pedagogy: Narratives for understanding and solidarity* (pp. 81–92). Rotterdam, The Netherlands: Sense.

Gore, J. (2015a). *Evidence of impact of teacher education programs: A focus on classroom observations*. A paper prepared for the Australian Institute for Teaching and School Leadership. Retrieved from http://www.aitsl.edu.au/docs/default-source/initial-teacher-education-resources/ite-reform-stimulus-paper-2-gore.pdf.

Gore, J. M., & Bowe, J. M. (2015). Interrupting attrition? Re-shaping the transition from preservice to inservice teaching through Quality Teaching Rounds. *International Journal of Educational Research, 73*, 77–88. doi:10.1016/j.ijer.2015.05.006

Gore, J. M., Griffiths, T. G., & Ladwig, J. G. (2004). Towards better teaching: Productive pedagogy as a framework for teacher education. *Teaching and Teacher Education, 20*, 375–387. doi:10.1016/j.tate.2004.02.010

Gore, J. M., Ladwig, J. G., & King, B. (2004). *Professional learning, pedagogical improvement, and the circulation of power*. Paper presented at the annual conference for the Australian Association for Research in Education, Melbourne, Australia.

Gore, J., Smith, M., Bowe, J., Ellis, H., Lloyd, A., & Lubans, D. (2015). Quality Teaching Rounds as a professional development intervention for enhancing the quality of teaching: Rationale and study protocol for a cluster randomised controlled trial. *International Journal of Educational Research, 74*, 82–95. doi:10.1016/j.ijer.2015.08.002

Grönqvist, E., & Vlachos, J. (2008). *One size fits all? The effects of teacher cognitive and non-cognitive abilities on student achievement* (Working Paper 2008:25 for the Institute for Labour Market Policy Evaluation). Retrieved from http://www.ifau.se/upload/pdf/se/2008/wp08-25.pdf.

Jackson, P. W. (1968). *Life in classrooms*. New York: Holt, Rinehart and Winston.

Knott, M. (2014, February 19). Christopher Pyne turns spotlight on teacher training. *Sydney Morning Herald*. Retrieved from http://www.smh.com.au/federal-politics/political-news/christopher-pyne-turns-spotlight-on-teacher-training-20140218-32ykx.html.

Labaree, D. (2010). Teach for America and teacher ed: Heads they win, tails we lose. *Journal of Teacher Education, 61*(48), 48–55.

Ladwig, J. G. (2007). Modelling pedagogy in Australian school reform. *Pedagogies: An International Journal, 2*(2), 57–76.

Ladwig, J. G., Smith, M., Gore, J. M., Amosa, W., & Griffiths, T. (2007). *Quality of pedagogy and student achievement: Multi-level replication of authentic pedagogy*. Paper presented at the annual conference for the Australian Association for Educational Research, Fremantle, Australia. Retrieved from http://www.aare.edu.au/data/publications/2007/lad07283.pdf.

Lampert, J., & Burnett, B. M. (2011). Exceptional teachers for disadvantaged schools. *Curriculum Leadership, 9*(17). Retrieved from http://eprints.qut.edu.au/48419/2/48419.pdf.

Lester, J., Heitmeyer, D., Gore, J. M., & Ford, M. (2013). Creating and sustaining meaningful partnerships for supporting indigenous teacher education. *Journal of Australian Indigenous Issues, 16*(4), 3–18.

Liston, D. P., & Zeichner, K. M. (1991). *Teacher education and the social conditions of schooling*. New York: Routledge.

Louden, W. (2008). 101 Damnations: The persistence of criticism and the absence of evidence about teacher education in Australia. *Teachers and Teaching: Theory and Practice, 14*(4), 357–368.

Louden, W. (2015). *Standardised assessment of initial teacher education: Environmental scan and case studies*. A paper prepared for the Australian Institute for Teaching and School Leadership. Retrieved from http://www.aitsl.edu.au/docs/default-source/initial-teacher-education-resources/standardised-assessment-of-ite_environmental-scan-and-case-studies.pdf.

Lovat, T., & McLeod, J. (2006). Fully professionalised teacher education: An Australian study in persistence. *Asia-Pacific Journal of Teacher Education, 34*(3), 287–300. doi:10.1080/13598660600927174

Mayer, D. (2014). Forty years of teacher education in Australia: 1974–2014. *Journal of Education for Teaching: International Research and Pedagogy, 40*(5), 461–473.

Mayer, D. (2015). *An approach to the accreditation of initial teacher education programs based on evidence of the impact impact of learning teaching. A paper prepared for the Australian Institute for Teaching and School Leadership.* Retrieved from http://www.aitsl.edu.au/docs/default-source/initial-teacher-education-resources/ite-reform-stimulus-paper-1-mayer.pdf.

McKenzie, P., Weldon, P., Rowley, G., Murphy, M., & McMillan, J. (2014, April). *Staff in Australia's Schools 2013: Main report on the survey.* Retrieved from https://docs.education.gov.au/system/files/doc/other/sias_2013_main_report.pdf.

McKinnon, M. (2016, January 11). Teachers are leaving the profession – Here's how to make them stay. *The Conversation.* Retrieved from https://theconversation.com/teachers-are-leaving-the-profession-heres-how-to-make-them-stay-52697.

Melbourne Graduate School of Education. (MGSE). (2016). *Clinical teaching.* Retrieved from http://education.unimelb.edu.au/about_us/clinical_teaching.

Mockler, N. (2015, February 15). *EduResearch matters: More measuring, few solutions for teacher education under recommendations to Abbott Govt* [Blog post]. Retrieved from Australian Association for Research in Education website: http://www.aare.edu.au/blog/?p=903.

National Inquiry into the Teaching of Literacy. (2005). *Teaching reading: Report and recommendations.* Canberra, Australia: Australian Government Department of Education, Science and Training. Retrieved from http://research.acer.edu.au/tll_misc/5/

NSW Department of Education and Training. (NSW DET). (2003a). *Quality teaching in NSW public schools: An annotated bibliography.* Sydney, Australia: NSW Department of Education and Training/Professional Support and Curriculum Directorate.

NSW Department of Education and Training. (NSW DET). (2003b). *Quality teaching in NSW public schools: An annotated bibliography.* Sydney, Australia: NSW Department of Education and Training/Professional Support and Curriculum Directorate.

NSW Government. (2013, March). *Great teaching, inspired learning: A blueprint for action.* Retrieved from http://www.schools.nsw.edu.au/media/downloads/news/greatteaching/gtil_blueprint.pdf.

Nuttall, J., Murray, S., Seddon, T., & Mitchell, J. (2006). Changing research contexts in teacher education in Australia: Charting new directions. *Asia-Pacific Journal of Teacher Education, 34*(3), 321–332.

Organisation for Economic Co-operation and Development. (OECD). (2005). *Teachers matter: Attracting, developing and retaining effective teachers.* Paris, France: OECD.

Parliament of Victoria. (2005). *Step up, step in, step out: Final report on the inquiry into the suitability of pre-service teacher training in Victoria.* Melbourne, Australia: Education and Training Committee.

Rice, S. (2008). Getting good teachers into challenging schools. *Curriculum and Leadership Journal, 6*(14). Retrieved from http://www.curriculum.edu.au/leader/getting_good_teachers_into_challenging_schools,23264.html?issueID=11431.

Riddle, S. (2015, April 1). Teachers learn over many years in the job – Not just at university. *The Conversation.* Retrieved from https://theconversation.com/teachers-learn-over-many-years-in-the-job-not-just-at-university-39486.

Roberts-Hull, K., Jensen, B., & Cooper, S. (2015). *A new approach: Teacher education reform.* Melbourne, Australia: Learning First. Retrieved from http://static1.squarespace.com/static/531fd05ee4b00a4fbb7b1c67/t/55150cf0e4b0932ce9c67096/1427442928401/A+new+approach.pdf.

Shulman, L. S. (1986). Those who understand: Knowledge growth in teaching. *Educational Researcher, 15*(2), 4–14. Retrieved from http://www.jstor.org/stable/1175860.

Social Ventures Australia. (2015). *Social Ventures Australia.* Retrieved from http://socialventures.com.au/

Teacher Education Ministerial Advisory Group. (TEMAG). (2014). *Action now: Classroom ready teachers.* Retrieved from https://docs.education.gov.au/system/files/doc/other/action_now_classroom_ready_teachers_accessible.pdf.

Teachers College Columbia University. (2015, April 2). *Sachs lecture series. David Berliner: Evaluating teacher education and teachers using student assessments* [Video file]. Retrieved from https://youtu.be/lQkSnpFvbcs.

Tertiary Education Quality and Standards Agency. (TEQSA). (2014). *TEQSA snapshot May 2014*. Retrieved from http://www.teqsa.gov.au/sites/default/files/TEQSAsnapshotMay2014.pdf.

Tuinamuana, K. (2011). Teacher professional standards, accountability, and ideology: Alternative discourses. *Australian Journal of Teacher Education, 36*(12), 72–82. doi: 10.14221/ajte.2011v36n12.8

University of Newcastle. (2016). *Equity and excellence*. Retrieved from http://www.newcastle.edu.au/about-uon/our-university/equity-and-excellence.

Victorian Department of Education and Early Childhood Development. (2013). *From new directions to action: World-class teaching and school leadership*. Melbourne, Australia: Victorian Department of Education and Early Childhood Development. http://www.education.vic.gov.au/Documents/about/department/teachingprofession.pdf.

Weldon, P. R. (2015, March). *The teacher workforce in Australia: Supply, demand and data issues* (Policy Insights, Issue #2). Retrieved from Australian Council for Educational Research website: http://research.acer.edu.au/policyinsights/2/

Wiliam, D. (2014). *The formative evaluation of teaching performance* (Occasional Paper No. 137). Melbourne, Australia: Centre for Strategic Education. Retrieved from http://www.dylanwiliam.org/Dylan_Wiliams_website/Publications_files/The%20formative%20evaluation%20of%20teaching%20performance%20(CSE%202014)%20secure.pdf.

Wilson, R., Dalton, B., & Baumann, C. (2015, March 16). Six ways Australia's education system is failing our kids. *The Conversation*. Retrieved from https://theconversation.com/six-ways-australias-education-system-is-failing-our-kids-32958.

Zeichner, K. M. (1983). Alternative paradigms of teacher education. *Journal of Teacher Education, 34*(3), 3–9.

Zeichner, K. M. (1993). Traditions of practice in U.S. preservice teacher education programs. *Teaching and Teacher Education, 9*(1), 1–13.

Zeichner, K. M., & Tabachnick, B. R. (1981). Are the effects of university teacher education "washed out" by school experiences? *Journal of Teacher Education, 32*(2), 7–11.

Innovation and Transformation of Initial Teacher Education: Employer and Graduate Perspectives

Sally Knipe, Rebecca Miles, and Stephanie Garoni

1 Introduction

The dominant model of initial teacher education reflects the longstanding divisions in the organisation of schools based on the age and grade level of children. The structure of schools in the twenty-first century is changing and the way that teaching staff are allocated to teaching responsibilities is a model that does not always reflect the qualifications that teachers have acquired. It is time to challenge the age-based divisions in initial teacher education and develop different programs that are flexible and more responsive to the complexities of, and more appropriate to, the staffing needs of twenty-first century schools.

Historically, the formal years of school education began with primary schooling provided for children up to 12 years of age. Teacher preparation courses were established to provide training for teachers considered to be appropriate for this age group. As secondary school education developed, teacher preparation was expanded and designed to qualify teachers to teach adolescents. Primary school was separated into "infants" or preparation grade, the forerunner of early childhood education with training offered to prepare teachers to teach very young children. Teachers were organised in teaching positions based on their teacher preparation courses and restricted to employment in either a primary or secondary school, or a position in either an infants' school or the infants' section of a primary school (Hyams, 1979).

As school education expanded in the twentieth century, the majority of schools were organised as either primary or secondary schools, with primary schools having designated early childhood grades and in some cases separate schools. These longstanding models of schooling, however, are now being challenged by changes in school organisational structures and the need for greater flexibility in the way staff

S. Knipe (✉) • R. Miles • S. Garoni
School of Education, La Trobe University, Melbourne, Australia
e-mail: s.knipe@latrobe.edu.au; r.miles@latrobe.edu.au; s.garoni@latrobe.edu.au

© Springer Science+Business Media Singapore 2016
R. Brandenburg et al. (eds.), *Teacher Education*,
DOI 10.1007/978-981-10-0785-9_3

are allocated to teaching duties within a school. The growth of a range of different school structures, such as middle schools, F – Year 10 or F – Year 12, flexible learning schools, and senior colleges for Year 11 and Year 12 (and sometimes Year 10), has distorted the historic divisions of early childhood/primary/secondary (Knipe, 2012, 2015; Knipe & Johnston, 2007). Principals face on-going challenges deploying teachers to classes or particular programs within a school from a group of staff with restrictive age-based qualifications. This situation is further compounded when there is a shortage of qualified teachers, such as secondary mathematics, secondary/primary languages teachers or secondary science teachers (Australian Secondary Principals Association Incorporated, 2007; Productivity Commission, 2012).

In turn, universities experience pressure from teacher registration authorities regarding the specific content requirements expected of initial teacher education programs. These program standards predominantly reflect the age-based criteria of a primary or a secondary teacher (Reid, 2010). Given the evolving nature of school organisations, it may be time for universities to develop more flexible course structures in initial teacher education programs which remove the age-based divisions of early childhood, primary and secondary, and see schooling, and in turn a teaching qualification, as an educational continuum which spans a young person's schooling. This would produce teaching graduates with qualifications that better reflect the flexibility required for staffing schools and a teacher who has a good understanding of the school curriculum from Foundation to Year 12 (Knipe, 2012, 2015).

This chapter presents the perspectives of school supervisors who have recently employed graduates with qualifications to teach from the first year of school to Year 12. To enhance a discussion of current tensions affecting the design and models of initial teacher education courses, it is worthwhile to present a brief review of the historical evolution of teacher preparation courses in Australia to understand influences and changes on current course structure and content.

2 Teacher Preparation in Australia

The establishment of Colleges of Advanced Education (CAEs) in 1968 saw the subsequent transfer of teacher education to these institutions. Prior to this, teacher education had been undertaken in single purpose institutions (teachers' colleges or teacher institutes) typically dedicated to training teachers for a particular age group of schooling: primary, early childhood (infants/preparatory), secondary and technical (Mayer, 2014). The age group specialist nature of teacher training reflected the growth of education systems which had begun as education for children to acquire literacy and numeracy skills. Eventually, legislation was introduced to designate a school leaving age, so that all children received a basic education (Campbell & Proctor, 2014). As demand for educating older students rose, Years 7 and 8 were added to compulsory schooling. Eventually this led to the establishment of secondary schools, or high schools, with additional years up to Year 11 and ultimately Year 12 (Campbell & Proctor, 2014).

The documented history of teacher preparation in Australia from the early 1900s to the 1970s depicts a tightly controlled system with limited recruitment practices and training programs with varied quality (Hyams, 1979). In the early 1900s, teachers' colleges replaced the pupil teacher model that was established during the 1800s. The majority of graduates from teachers' colleges were employed in primary schools, with growing demands for teacher training through a 1-year Primary Teacher Certificate course. By the late 1930s, these teachers' colleges operated in most capital cities, with a few rural locations throughout Australia (Aspland, 2006). In 1930, a 2-year course was introduced; however, these did not become prevalent until the 1950s.

Teacher preparation for secondary teachers developed in a number of ways. Early secondary teacher preparation provided multiple pathways, including programs for primary teachers to acquire further training for a position as a secondary teacher, or employment for university graduates in combination with some on-the-job support. Post-graduate 1-year Diploma of Education courses for secondary teachers were not established until 1911 and were confined to the disciplines offered at universities, for example, English, mathematics, science, history and geography. For secondary teachers, the "apprentice" model remained the dominant pathway for some time, with a small percentage of secondary teachers with a university degree (Hyams, 1979). As the secondary school curriculum expanded, other disciplines such as music, physical education and visual arts were offered as electives not as compulsory subjects. In the 1940s, teachers' colleges introduced specialist qualifications for teachers of these subjects, effectively expanding the teacher training program of predominantly primary-focused teachers' colleges into the secondary arena.

The end of World War II saw a growth in population leading to increased school retention rates. This saw a demand for qualified primary school teachers as well as an increase in teachers qualified to teach in secondary schools (Reid, 2011). The number of places in Graduate Diploma of Education programs offered at universities increased and teachers' colleges, for the first time, began to offer Graduate Diploma of Education courses (Polesel & Teese, 1998). As a result, these teachers' colleges, that were already training secondary teachers in curriculum areas such as visual arts, music, and domestic science, expanded their secondary teacher training program into subject areas previously only offered at universities.

2.1 *A New Era in Teacher Preparation: 1965 to Present*

The Commonwealth Advisory Committee on Advanced Education was established in 1965 and this committee recommended the establishment of Colleges of Advanced Education (CAEs) to provide a non-university tertiary education system that would bring together a wide range of post-secondary courses that had developed as an outcome of the rapid expansion of the workforce after World War II. CAEs were to provide a "greater breadth of education" than technical colleges and would focus on "training in professional and technical skills" rather than postgraduate education and research which was the province of the university sector (Baker, 1975).

In 1972, teachers' colleges were absorbed into the CAE sector, which resulted in greater academic freedom and autonomy for these colleges, diminishing the influence and control of individual state departments of education (Knight, Lingard, & Bartlett, 1994). The setting up of the Commonwealth Schools' Commission, in 1994, arose from a policy on the part of the federal government to have greater involvement in school education, which was the responsibility of the states and territories. A major change for primary and early childhood teacher education courses was the increase in teacher training courses from 2 to 3 years, superseding the 2-year certificate courses that that had been a feature of the teachers' college programs since the 1950s. By the end of the 1970s, Tasmania CAE and Canberra CAE were offering a 4-year degree for both primary teaching and secondary teaching (Auchmuty, 1980).

Significant reform and restructuring of the tertiary education sector, consisting of universities, CAEs and Technical and Further Education (TAFE) Institutes, was undertaken by the federal government under the Commonwealth Minister for Education John Dawkins, with a view to develop CAEs into universities in 1987. During this time, the alignment of teacher preparation programs with universities was a contentious issue because CAEs were perceived as being sub-university in quality, and teacher education courses within CAEs were viewed with disdain due, in part, to the limited qualifications of some staff (Mayer, 2014).

With teachers' colleges amalgamated or absorbed into CAEs, a large number of staff were also absorbed, many of whom were now considered to be no longer appropriately qualified. This included those holding 2-year teaching certificates which had been superseded by 3-year primary Diploma of Education or a 4-year primary Bachelor of Education degree. These staff were mainly from the primary and early childhood sectors reflecting the longstanding differences between the divisions. Despite the development of university degree programs for teachers, the influence of the teachers' colleges remained, and it would be many years before teachers with 2-year teaching certificates were phased out of the school system. In the early 1990s, all teachers with a 2-year teaching certificate were required to 'upgrade' to a 3-year qualification, and from 2009 all teachers were required to be 4-year qualified; however, there was some variation in this timeline between states/territories and education systems.

2.2 Current Contexts for Teacher Preparation

Teacher preparation courses offered in Australian universities typically involve variations of two qualifications. Undergraduate Bachelor of Education degrees vary from a minimum of four years to four and half years. Postgraduate degrees, such as a Graduate Diploma in Education, a post-graduate Bachelor of Teaching or a Master of Teaching, involve 2-years of post-graduate coursework following completion of a 3-year, discipline-based undergraduate degree. There has been a trend to phase out 1-year post-graduate Diploma of Education programs in favour of 2-year Master of Teaching courses (Australian Institute of Teaching and School Leadership (AITSL) 2015; Hatton, 1996). Both the undergraduate Bachelor of Education degree programs and the post-graduate degree courses in education offer options for candidates to pursue a teaching qualification for the various stages of schooling such as early childhood, primary and/or secondary courses.

Further to this, universities have developed courses that are designed as "double degrees" as an alternative to a 4-year Bachelor of Education, enabling a secondary teacher to qualify concurrently with a Bachelor of Education degree and a Bachelor Degree in a discipline area (such as science). The alternative post-graduate degree pathway for later entry to the profession offers access to teaching after completion of a university degree. However, with the phasing out of 1-year post graduate courses in education the post-graduate pathway will now constitute 5 years of study (AITSL, 2015).

The early childhood sector remains the most complex. With recent national policies regarding early childhood education, and the expansion of the child-care and before-school age sector, the development of specialist early childhood courses has been growing. With changed qualifications required for staff employed in the before-school-age sector, courses are being developed for teaching the age-groups of birth to aged 8 years or birth to aged 12 years. Restrictions remain, however, regarding teacher placement, with graduates of early childhood courses acceptable for employment in teaching across early childhood and primary school settings from birth to Year 6. Primary trained teachers, however, are not accepted as teachers of children younger than the Foundation year.

2.3 *Recent Developments Impacting on Teacher Preparation*

Teaching degrees in Australia have undergone a wave of change especially in regard to structure, content and duration, compared to the early models of teacher preparation that were largely practitioner based, particularly for early childhood and primary teachers (Campbell & Proctor, 2014; Mayer, 2014; Williams, Deer, Meyenn, & Taylor, 1995). The debate concerning course design and course content has been significantly influenced by teacher registration institutes and the development of national guidelines and state requirements for teacher certification and registration, which is also supported by education departments as employing authorities. Guidelines for the accreditation of courses have placed demands upon course designers required to structure programs that satisfy initial teacher education accreditation requirements (Parkes, 2013).

Initial teacher education programs are now required to contain specific skills and understandings including: content knowledge and how to teach that knowledge; theories underpinning how students learn; planning for and implementing effective teaching and learning; classroom management including challenging behaviours;

assessing and reporting student learning; engaging in professional learning; engaging with colleagues, parents and the community as well as mandatory studies in areas such as literacy and numeracy, teaching English language learners, teaching Indigenous students, inclusive education; and technology education together with a specific number of teacher practicum days (AITSL, 2015).

Despite the expansion in post-graduate pathways for teacher preparation, enrolments in initial teacher education programs tend to reflect the longstanding differences between teacher preparation pathways for secondary and primary/early childhood. Data from the Department of Education, Employment and Workplace Relations (2012) indicates that there are greater numbers of Year 12 leavers enrolled in early childhood/primary undergraduate degrees than in undergraduate secondary programs. In addition, there are a greater number of students enrolled in post-graduate teaching qualifications for secondary teaching than for early childhood/primary teaching (as cited in Initial Teacher Education: Data Report, AITSL, 2014).

The growth in initial teacher education courses that have deviated from the more traditional teacher education structure of "primary teacher education" or "secondary teacher education" and, qualify a candidate to teach across the primary and secondary school sectors has been gradually increasing. This trend has challenged models of what constitutes an initial teacher education program. There are currently 30 undergraduate courses that qualify teachers across the primary/secondary school divide, a rise over the past several years. As indicated on the Australian Institute of Teaching and School Leadership website, at the post-graduate level there are seven programs that qualify a candidate to teach primary and secondary education, which is significantly fewer than at the undergraduate level (http://www.aitsl.edu.au/initial-teacher-education/accredited-programs-list). The number of undergraduate and post-graduate courses that qualify a graduate to teach from Foundation to Year 12 are significantly less than the number of initial teacher education programs that qualify a teacher to teach in the age-based divisions of "primary only" and "secondary only".

This plotted history of initial teacher education in Australia provides an understanding of how the current proliferation of age-based teacher education courses has evolved. We argue, however, that there is a need for conceptualizing, and delivering, teacher education which prepares teachers to have discipline content knowledge and pedagogy across the breadth of F – Year 12. Presenting evidence to support this argument, the remainder of this chapter reports on findings from a project tracking graduates from initial teacher education programs that qualify teachers to teach from the first year of school through to Year 12 from one Australian university. The results reported here provide the perceptions of these graduates and supervisors regarding the benefits of graduate teachers qualified to teach across the primary and secondary sectors.

3 Method and Participants

The participants involved in this project were drawn from a purposive and convenient sample of graduate teachers and their school supervisors. All graduates discussed in this paper came from an initial teacher education program that graduated Foundation to Year 12 qualified teachers and were selected from government and Catholic schools located across Victoria. The school supervisors were mostly principals but in some secondary settings the supervisor was a head teacher. Approval to conduct this research was gained from the presiding university, the Department of Education in Victoria, and the four Victorian Catholic Education Office dioceses. In total there were 14 graduates and 8 supervisors involved in these interviews.

Some of the authors had been involved in teaching the graduates therefore a project officer was employed to interview the graduates and their school supervisors. Following transcription, initial data was coded by a research assistant using NVivo to identify themes and patterns in the data. Due to the author's involvement in the teaching of the graduates, this was considered an important element in establishing credibility in data analysis. Using multiple analysts, as well as multiple sources allowed for the data to be triangulated providing the results of the study with credibility.

4 Analysis and Discussion

A number of themes have emerged from the data relevant to teachers with a F – Year 12 teaching qualification. Specifically, much of the focus of the discussion centred on: graduate employment opportunities and the flexibility of staffing; a breadth of understanding of the teaching and learning continuum, including curriculum and pedagogy; and the benefits of knowing the developmental needs of young people in regard to their work as a teacher. These themes are discussed in the following sections.

4.1 Employment Opportunities and Flexibility of Staffing

Several of the supervisors highlighted the benefits of employing a graduate teacher with a qualification to teach primary and secondary students, particularly in terms of the flexibility for staffing and the opportunities for greater employability. It was acknowledged that "a F – Year 12 qualification produced a graduate that is more employable and can apply for more jobs" (Supervisor I-1). There was recognition that F – Year 12 qualified teachers can draw from a range of curriculum knowledge and pedagogical experiences to enhance their work as a teacher, something that was seen as a major benefit to employment, as indicated by the following quote: "He's teaching from Foundation through to Year 6 this year so his teaching qualification (it's) has enabled him to pick that up and roll with that. I can see that [he's] brought a lot to the table" (Supervisor E-1).

There was also recognition amongst supervisors that graduates with a F – Year 12 teaching qualification and with diverse personal experiences and skills were able to make a positive contribution to the school and to teaching teams. In particular, Supervisor J-1 highlighted that in the school teaching team, several staff held a F – Year 12 teaching qualification. This, along with having an initial undergraduate degree, was seen as an advantage to school staffing, as indicated by the following quote:

> [I] think that it's a real positive. Those F – Year 12 graduates bring a lot more skill into the school system. So here we've got staff including myself, Cherie and April, so 4 out of 6, went through that (F – Year 12) course. And as a group we've got backgrounds in health science, April was an accountant and so was Cherie. So that expertise makes a difference. The wealth of knowledge that comes into our team is fantastic (Supervisor J-1).

The opportunity for employment was consistent with the graduates' perspectives, where most of the participants discussed the increased options for employment that were available to them with a F – Year 12 qualification, as indicated by the following quotes:

> I thought if I ever change my mind and move into another sector I have the option available (Graduate F-1).
>
> A F – Year 12 qualification (it's) given me more opportunities I guess to get extra work. And also what it's like to work in a high school. It gives you that insight, so that's good. So if I don't get a job in primary schools, it's given me more options. I can go to high school. That's good (Graduate G-1).
>
> I think it's really about the options. When coming into the course, I didn't really know where to go. So having that F – 12 is a really good option and gave me a little bit of experience in all year levels and helped me to figure out exactly what I wanted to do (Graduate J-1).
>
> The thing that attracted me to the F – 12 to begin with was that I wasn't quite sure whether I wanted to do primary or secondary teaching. And so the F – Year 12 was going to give me exposure to both (Graduate K-1).

There was recognition from several graduates that although they had initial "set ideas" regarding the school sector they wished to teach in when they commenced the course, experiences and opportunities during their studies and exposure to different stages of schooling served to show the strengths and benefits of teaching across the different year levels, as indicated by the following quotes:

> By being forced to do something else, I really found what I'm supposed to do. So that was good. Like, I never planned to go to primary (Graduate D-1).
>
> I was [only interested in] teaching secondary, I wouldn't have known if my skills were adaptable to primary school. Now I know I'd be great and it opens up opportunities for me because I can apply anywhere (Graduate E-1).

Given the changing nature of schools in the twenty-first century, the complexity of employment and the need for a more diverse and flexible workforce, it is time that initial teacher education programs better reflect the staffing needs of schools.

As indicated by Knipe (2012, 2015), the development of teacher education programs have been significantly influenced by divisions that reflect the evolution of education rather than the developmental pedagogical and organisational needs of schools. Therefore, it was not surprising that that some supervisors expressed concern about the breadth of content that is needed to be covered in a F – Year 12 degree. Some secondary school supervisors expressed a perceived concern about the difficulty in covering course content in sufficient depth to be a F – Year 12 qualified teacher, as indicated by the following comments:

> I think that we often teach different skills in the secondary and perhaps graduate teachers may not be getting that exposure on their teaching rounds to lots of secondary students. If they've done primary experiences, then they won't be doing the secondary school ones. That's a huge expectation, a huge ask on the students because of the broad spectrum Prep through to 12. I like more the idea that you specialise in secondary and that's where you do your teaching rounds and that's where you have your experience (Supervisor B-1).
>
> I think you could spread yourself a little bit thin in terms of what you're really developing and what you think is the most valuable kind of information for students that teachers need to have when they're in schools. And when you go on professional experience, you're essentially over such a broad range it becomes a little bit difficult to really develop those specialised skills you need (Supervisor A-1).

Universities that have developed F to Year 12 degree programs are appealing to graduate teachers who may not wish to be "locked in" to a particular age group. The flexibility of the school's teaching staff can be critical for principals managing workloads, school programs and subject availability. These findings support the need for more initial teacher education programs to graduate teachers who are flexible in the sectors in which they can be employed. However, there are still some in the profession who endorse the more traditional view of what constitutes initial teacher education. This is not surprising given the long-standing and entrenched model of how to qualify a teacher, a model that is currently reflected in most university programs.

4.2 The Teaching/Learning and Curriculum Continuum

A teacher who can teach across the foundation grades, primary and secondary is a great benefit to schools in adapting to the teaching and learning needs of young people. Teachers with generic pedagogical skill, discipline knowledge in one or two secondary teaching areas were acknowledged by supervisors as having a deeper understanding of the teaching and learning continuum and the benefits that understanding offers both sectors. It was clear that for many of the supervising teachers, the distinction that exists between primary and secondary schooling is ingrained, which is not surprising given that the majority of initial teacher education programs continue to be age-based. The distinctions between primary and secondary school teaching have been highlighted with primary teaching considered to be more pedagogical, whereas secondary teaching is more content focused (Williams et al., 1995). This was also evident in the interviews with the supervisors, as indicated by the following quotes:

> The opportunity to be qualified F – Year 12 and seeing more classroom settings would give you a greater appreciation of different styles of teaching. Primary teaching is very different to senior secondary but we can certainly learn from primary teachers and use that as an asset (Supervisor F-1).

> I work closely with my local primary school and the one thing I notice is that primary school teachers know so much about learning as an art but my degree in secondary education was primarily content focused. Historically in secondary schools, it's probably covered a great deal of content and I feel, if I could change anything over the last couple of years, it would be about focusing on the learning (Supervisor D-1).

Overall, the graduate teachers felt that one of the key benefits of a F – Year 12 qualification was their understanding of the F – Year 12 learning continuum. This understanding enabled them to develop their approach to student engagement, as well as a strong curriculum knowledge across the primary and secondary continuum, which was a great advantage when teaching students with diverse cognitive development and abilities, as indicated by the following quotes:

> The continuity of learning; how learning can be scaffolded to meet different students' needs. That's really helped with that … scaffolding it for all learners, so everyone can access the curriculum in the best possible way (Graduate C-1).
>
> Knowing where each year level could lead to. Having experience in all the year levels. When I was with Year ones on placement, I could see where this was going to lead to, the concepts. We did a narrative section and knowing where that was going to lead to. Having that continuity of learning is a great benefit (Graduate J-1).

Understanding and knowing the primary curricula and approaches to different teaching styles, as well as understanding and knowing specialist discipline/s for secondary teaching was acknowledged by graduates especially by those who had gained teaching positions in secondary schools. Graduates indicated that their awareness and understanding of the general "prior" learning and curriculum experience of their students was an asset and assisted them with their approach to secondary teaching, as indicated by the following quotes:

> [It's] given me an understanding of how that learning journey starts. From the younger years and all the way through. So it's been very much more holistic view of teaching and in that way it's been quite beneficial (Graduate F-1).
>
> I definitely can see the benefit of having a P to 12 degree as opposed to pure secondary or primary. It's given me a better understanding to some degree of what's been built up prior to when they get to me. This I wouldn't know if I hadn't have done the primary curriculum stuff (Graduate I-1).

Given the evolving nature of school organisations especially in terms of curriculum implementation it is time for universities to develop more flexible and innovative course structures for initial teacher education programs that removes the age-based divisions. This would enable universities to produce teaching graduates with qualifications that better reflects the school curriculum from Foundation to Year 12 (Knipe, 2012, 2015).

4.3 Child Development

Biological, psychological and environmental factors impacting on the transition from childhood to adulthood require understanding by those involved in teaching young people. There are a range of individual differences in the emotional, cognitive and behavioural development of young people that manifest in numerous ways, including interpersonal and intra-personal conflict, risk-taking behaviour and biological changes (Hollenstein & Logheed, 2013). Teachers qualified to teach from F – Year 12 are well placed to understand the various stages of development of young people no matter what age group or developmental differences that may be present in a group of young children and adolescents (Knipe, 2015). Principals and school supervisors and graduate teachers discussed the benefits that F – Year 12 qualified teachers have in regard to "having an awareness of the whole development of a child" (Graduate A-1), as indicated by the following quotes:

> Learning all about the cognitive and physical development; that really made sense to me and helped me understand how students learn. So how I learn now as an adult is really different to the way I learnt [as a child] (Graduate C-1).
>
> Even though he's teaching younger children now that always won't be the case and the work he's done on adolescents will come in handy (Supervisor A-2).
>
> As a teacher (you) have a better understanding of those students in higher grade levels and in-classroom stuff (Supervisor G-1).

As children grow throughout the compulsory years of schooling, changes in their emotional, social and intellectual development become an ever increasing challenge for teachers. The traditional separation of school years into primary and secondary, with a break between the two that occurs in the middle of the adolescent years, creates a disruption for many students coping with these changes (Haynie, 2003). Concerns about the need for different school structures and programs to improve the educational and overall school experience for young people, especially those in the 10–15 year age group, was the focus of several research and government reports during the 1990s and 2000s (Barratt, 1998; Carrington, 2004; Chadbourne, 2001; Cumming & Cormack, 1996; Schools Council, 1992). Over time, many schools have introduced programs to address the issues associated with the primary/secondary school separation with many new schools now being purpose built such as F -9/10/12.

5 Conclusion

A teacher education degree that qualifies a candidate to teach from the first year of school through to Year 12 challenges the restrictions of the traditional early childhood/primary/secondary school model and facilitates greater flexibility with teacher employment. The advantage of F – Year 12 teacher preparation programs to a range of stakeholders, such as potential candidates, graduates and employers, lies in the flexibility of employment pathways for those interested in teaching as a profession, and the options for a graduate to expand their teaching experience within a school. This perspective has been endorsed by many of the principals and supervising managers interviewed as part of this study. Reservations by some of the school supervisors regarding the pressure that F – Year 12 qualification places on teacher education candidates, was negated by the overwhelming support for such teachers.

The longstanding age-based/grade-based divisions in teacher education have been challenged for some considerable time whereby teacher shortages in particular in secondary school disciplines, have resulted in employing teachers from primary schools or other secondary disciplines to fill staffing gaps. More recently the introduction of middle schools or middle school programs and the rise of F-9/10/12 school structures requires teaching staff with broad generic teaching skills. A F – 12 teaching qualification provides opportunities for teachers to move through the school system and increase their employment opportunities, as well as meeting the diverse staffing needs of learners and schools. A teacher qualified to teach across the foundation grades/primary and secondary sectors, is of great benefit to schools providing flexibility in terms of staffing. In many high schools in Australia, where fluctuating student enrolments place pressure on staffing for different subject areas, flexibility of staffing can be critical. The findings from this study indicate that schools are keen to employ graduate teachers who have the flexibility to teach across primary and secondary schools, endorsing the F to Year 12 qualification model.

Some universities have responded to changes with the development of degree programs that equip graduates to teach across different age sectors and to expand options for teachers to develop different career paths in education. Universities that have developed F to Year 12 degree programs are appealing to graduate teachers who may not wish to be "locked in" to a particular age group. This study has presented the perspectives of employers and graduate teachers regarding the benefits of employing a teaching graduate who can teach across the primary and secondary school sector. These findings support the need for more initial teacher education programs to graduate teachers who are flexible in the sectors in which they can be employed and have developed a sound understanding of the continuum of F-12 schooling from pedagogical, developmental and curriculum perspectives.

Acknowledgements The authors wish to acknowledge that the collection of data for this research project was supported by Strategic Initiates Funding, La Trobe University.

References

Aspland, T. (2006). Changing patterns of teacher education in Australia. *Education Research and Perspectives, 33*(2), 140–162.

Auchmuty, J. (Chair) (1980). *Report of the national inquiry into teacher education.* Canberra AGPS.

Australian Institute for Teaching and School Leadership. (2015). *National professional standards for teachers.* http://www.aitsl.edu.au/initial-teacher-education-program-accreditation.html. Melbourne: AITSL.

Australian Institute for Teaching and School Leadership. (2014). *Initial teacher education: Data report 2014.*http://www.aitsl.edu.au/docs/default-source/initial-teacher-education-resources/ite-data-report-2014.pdf. Accessed 30 Apr 2015.

Australian Secondary Principals Association Incorporated. (2007). Survey – Beginning teachers. http://www.aspa.asn.au/images/surveys/2007beginningteachersreport.pdf. Accessed 24 Sept 2009.

Baker, L. J. (1975). *Governance of the Australian colleges of advanced education.* Queensland, Australia: Darling Downes Institute of Advanced Education.

Barratt, R. (1998). *Shaping middle schooling in Australia: A report of the national middle schooling project.* Canberra, Australia: Australian Curriculum Studies Association.

Campbell, C., & Proctor, H. (2014). *A history of Australian schooling.* Crows Nest, Australia: Allen & Unwin.

Carrington, V. (2004). Mid-term review; the middle years of schooling. *Curriculum Perspectives, 24*(1), 30–41.

Chadbourne, R. (2001). *Middle schooling for the middle years; what might the jury be considering?* Victoria, Australia: Australian Education Union.

Cumming, J., & Cormack, P. (1996). *From alienation to engagement; opportunities for reform in the middle years of schooling.* Canberra, Australia: Australian Curriculum Studies Association.

Department of Education, Employment and Workplace Relations. (2012). *Summary of the 2012 full year higher education student statistics.* Canberra, Australia: Department of Education.

Hatton, N. (1996). Changing initial teacher education: Limitations to innovation in the United States, Australia and the United Kingdom. *Australian Journal of Teacher Education, 21*(2), 50–61.

Haynie, D. (2003). Contexts of risk? Explaining the link between girls' pubertal development and their delinquency involvement [electronic version]. *Social Forces, 82*(1), 355–397.

Hollenstein, T., & Logheed, J. (2013). Beyond storm and stress: Typicality, transitions, timing and temperament to account for adolescent change [electronic version]. *American Psychologist, 68*(6), 444–454.

Hyams, B. K. (1979). *Teacher preparation in Australia: A history of its development from 1850 to 1950.* Hawthorn, Australia: Australian Council for Educational Research.

Knight, J., Lingard, B., & Bartlett, L. (1994). Reforming teacher education policy under labour governments in Australia 1989–03. *British Journal of Sociology of Education, 15*(4), 451–466.

Knipe, S. (2012). Crossing the primary and secondary school divide in teacher preparation. *Australian Journal of Teacher Education, 37*(5). Accessed http://dx.doi.org/10.14221/ajte.2012v37n5.6.

Knipe, S. (2015). A generic teacher education program that meets contemporary schools' needs. In S. Groundwater-Smith & N. Mockler (Eds.), *Big fish, little fish; teaching and learning in the middle years* (pp. 223–235). Melbourne, Australia: Cambridge University Press.

Knipe, S., & Johnston, K. (2007). Problematising middle schooling for middle schools and middle years education. In S. Knipe (Ed.), *Middle years of schooling; reframing adolescence* (pp. 3–20). Frenchs Forest, Australia: Pearson Education Australia.

Mayer, D. (2014). Forty years of teacher education in Australia: 1974–2014. *Journal of Education for Teaching: International Research and Pedagogy, 40*(5), 461–473.

Parkes, R.J. (2013). Challenges for curriculum leadership in contemporary teacher education. *Australian Journal of Teacher Education, 38(7).* Accessed http://dx.doi.org/10.14221/atje.2013v38n7.8.

Polesel, J., & Teese, R. (1998). *The 'Colleges' growth & diversity in the non-university tertiary studies sector (1965–74).* Canberra, Australia: Department of Education, Training & Youth Affairs, Commonwealth of Australia.

Productivity Commission. (2012). *Schools workforce.* Research report. Canberra, Australia.

Reid, J. (2010, November 8). [AARE Presidential Address 2010]. *Doing it by numbers? Educational research and teacher education.* Speech presented at the Australian Association for Research in Education Conference. Melbourne, Australia.

Reid, J. (2011). A practice turn for teacher education? *Asia-Pacific Journal of Teacher Education, 39*(4), 293–310.

Schools Council. (1992). *In the middle schooling for young adolescents.* Project Paper no. 7 Compulsory Years of School Project. Canberra, Australia: NBEET, AGPS.

Williams, D., Deer, C., Meyenn, B., & Taylor, A. (1995). Reform, restructuring & innovation in teacher education down under. Paper presented at the a*nnual meeting of the American Association of Colleges for Teacher Education* (47th Washington, DC, February 12–15 1995).

Digital Credentialing: Does It Offer a Meaningful Response to Initial Teacher Education Reform?

Josephine R. Lang

1 Introduction

The purpose of this chapter is to highlight key features of the disruptive technological innovation identified as digital credentialing and also known as digital badging or Open Badges. The chapter discusses the current policy reform landscape in Australia for the initial teacher education (ITE) context and then offers the possibility of how digital credentialing may create opportunities to meaningfully address policy recommendations, particularly in relation to the concepts of graduates being 'classroom ready'. While not an extensive review of the literature about digital credentialing, the chapter discusses the disruptive innovation and emerging understandings and design frameworks that can support new ways of approaching initial teacher education.

2 What Is Initial Teacher Education (ITE) Reform?

There are national and international calls for improving the quality of initial teacher education, which is creating a policy landscape seeking innovative frameworks and processes to rethink how to represent teacher professional learning and demonstrate impact on school student learning that have been embodied, for example, in national teaching standards.[1] In the current Australian regulatory policy context, initial teacher education is required to meet the academic standards outlined in the

---

[1] http://www.aitsl.edu.au/australian-professional-standards-for-teachers/standards/list

J.R. Lang (✉)
School of Education, Deakin University, Melbourne, Australia
e-mail: j.lang@deakin.edu.au

Australian Qualifications Framework (AQF)[2] and the teaching profession as defined by the national accreditation program standards including the graduate teaching standards. The most recent call for improving initial teacher education in Australia is the Australian government's advisory committee's report released in early 2015 entitled *Action Now: Classroom Ready Teachers* (Teacher Education Ministerial Advisory Group (TEMAG), 2014). A key pillar informing 'initial teacher education reform'[3] is the attempt to make direct links between pre-service teachers' learning and their practice through an evidence-based approach that also incorporates the impact of that teaching on student learning. While this policy (linear) direction may superficially appear as issues of accreditation and accountability, there is scope to re-think how this can trace back to the more 'enduring questions' in initial teacher education (Cochran-Smith, Feiman-Nemsar, & McIntyre, 2008) such as teacher professional learning (Feiman-Nemser, 2008). In particular, how do the interrelationships between learning, theory and practice manifest as professional knowledge and practice for our initial teacher education graduates i.e., that enduring quest in teacher education to bridge the theory-practice gap so often associated with the messiness (or swampy lowlands) of learning within the professions (Schön, 1983, 1987). With innovation in teacher education pedagogy (Loughran, 2006), can we re-frame how initial teacher education conceptualises evidence of pre-service teacher professional learning by exploiting the affordances of disruptive technologies such as digital credentialing?

3 What Is Digital Credentialing?

Digital credentialing is based on the metaphor of earning and issuing (physical) badges, which is embedded in the traditions and culture of youth organisations such as Scouts and Guides (e.g. see the 'proficiency badges' for South Australian Scouts: http://scouts.sa.scouts.com.au/proficiencybadges). Alternatively, the video-based game industry has also enculturated the badge metaphor to provide a meta-level architecture outside the game itself to allow players to showcase their achievements via "merit badges". This contributes to the player's online profile of "achievements" in gaming that can be seen by others via the internet Achievements (video gaming), 2015). Similarly, innovative businesses in health-oriented personalised gadgets also issue badges to wearers to recognise daily or weekly health goals (e.g., see Fitbit wristband that monitors health indicators such as number of steps taken daily: http://help.fitbit.com/articles/en_US/Help_article/How-do-I-manage-my-Fitbit-badges). As has been seen in these examples of gaming and health, the concept of digital badges is re-imaging what and how achievements might be recognised. The process of earning and issuing digital badges can be known as digital or open badging or, increasingly in the education sector, as digital credentialing.

---

[2] AQF: http://www.aqf.edu.au/
[3] Refer to AITSL's webpage: http://www.aitsl.edu.au/initial-teacher-education/ite-reform

In recent years, digital credentialing has gained momentum and has entered the field of education, often as a tool to motivate or reward learning and recognise achievement of knowledge or skills; and, in other contexts, evoking a game based approach (Abramovich, Schunn, & Higashi, 2013; Gibson, Ostashewski, Flintoff, Grant, & Knight, 2015; Randall, Harrison, & West, 2013). Digital credentialing often uses Open Badges[4] platforms (such as Mozilla or Credly) to recognise learning, which may be formal or informal, and validated by the issuer of the digital credential (badge) through rigorous assessment process. The (l)earner of the digital credential is required to curate artefacts of her/his evidence of the learning, knowledge and/or skill to gain the credential. A series of digital credentials may be interlinked or necessary to demonstrate achievement of significant learning. In the field of education, digital credentialing is an emergent and disruptive innovation that may signify opportunities to respond meaningfully to the recent calls for demonstrating and re-imagining what and how evidence of impact may be exhibited by pre-service teachers, graduates and initial teacher education providers. This may move initial teacher education reform from one of a "problem of policy" to re-focus to the challenges of working towards "teacher education as a learning problem" (Cochran-Smith, 2012, pp. 30–31). How might the affordances of digital credentialing go beyond compliance and focus on learning-to-teach within a purposeful, evidence-based framework? This use and approach to digital credentialing is just beginning to emerge as a research issue in the literature (e.g., Abramovich et al., 2013; Devedzic & Jovanovic, 2015; Gamrat, Zimmerman, Dudek, & Peck, 2014).

3.1 What Are the Characteristics of a Digital Credential?

Similar to the badge metaphor, the digital credential is a symbol of the recipient's achievements. These achievements are not like a scrapbook of experiences pasted together; rather the series of digital credentials should reflect a narrative of the pre-service teacher's learning to teach journey, representing her complexity of her professional knowledge, practices, beliefs and dispositions to illustrate her passion for teaching and her students' learning (Gamrat et al., 2014). The affordances of the online environment that a digital credential operates within, creates the opportunity for the [l]earner to use the online environment to manage, curate and display the evidence of that achievement for others to observe, such as educators, prospective employers or peers. This strong link to demonstrating evidence of the (learning) achievement is significant within the education context and goes beyond the limitations of past symbolic representations of achievements such as a degree testamur, certificate or a letter grade in a transcript. In this way, the digital credential provides a space to represent within an online environment a claim of the learning achieved as well as its particular details of the evidence (O'Byrne, Schenke, Willis, & Hickey, 2015).

---

[4] Open Badges (Mozilla): http://openbadges.org/ or Credly: https://credly.com/

Table 4.1 Characteristics of the digital credential

Characteristic	Function
Recipient/earner of digital credential	Identification of who earned the achievement
Issuer	Individual, consortium or organisation taking the responsibility for issuing the badge into the OBI (Open Badge Infrastructure) to the required specifications; usually an entity that has firsthand knowledge or evidence of the earner's achievement
Criteria and description	Criteria to be demonstrated by the recipient to achieve the recognition associated with the digital credential
Evidence	Authentic representation, or connection (often in the form of a url to a website/digital portfolio) to the work performed or contribution made by the recipient to earn the badge
Date	Precisely when the badge was awarded
Expiration	When, if ever, the credential issued is no longer valid; e.g., if the knowledge/skills have to be refreshed such as First Aid certificate is valid for 3 years
Certificate or assertion	A connection to an official form of verification vouching for the validity of the award
Endorser/signer	An organisation, consortium or individual who validates the badge/digital credential by signing it with their private encryption key. Trusted third party signers may emerge in the design or implementation process

Adapted from Finkelstein, Knight and Manning (2013), p. 7; and Mozilla Open Badge Infrastructure (OBI) Wiki 2011, viewed 17 Nov 2015, https://wiki.mozilla.org/Badges/infrastructure-tech-docs

Like the physical badge, the digital credential (or badge) develops an interrelationship between a tripartite partnership between the earner (or recipient), issuer (of the credential), and observer (who is reviewing the recipient's representation of an achievement) and where trust, validity and value of the achievement, represented by the digital credential, must underpin the partnership. If the digital credential is not valued by all in the partnership, the digital 'currency' within the digital credentialing ecosystem is lost or becomes invalid. The trust and validity are created through careful design of how the evidence is embodied within the digital credential. Therefore, digital credentialing offers "a socially constructed and valued encapsulation of [learning] experiences through metadata" embodied in the credentialing framework and processes such as criteria, assessment processes and issuer (Gamrat et al., 2014, p. 1136). Table 4.1 outlines the characteristics of a digital credential that assists in developing high value or currency (Finkelstein, Knight, & Manning, 2013).

3.1.1 Is There a Connection Between Portfolios and Digital Credentialing?

In the TEMAG (2014) report, three of the 38 recommendations pertain to or imply the use of a portfolio within initial teacher education as a key strategy to "assure classroom readiness" (refer to Section four of the TEMAG report). The

Table 4.2 Recommendations to embed a portfolio of evidence in ITE within the TEMAG (2014) report

TEMAG recommendation no.	Description
Recommendation 26	The Australian Institute for Teaching and School Leadership develop a national assessment framework, including requirements for a Portfolio of Evidence, to support higher education providers and schools to consistently assess the classroom readiness of pre-service teachers throughout the duration of their program
Recommendation 27	Pre-service teachers develop a Portfolio of Evidence to demonstrate their achievement of the Graduate of the Professional Standards
Recommendation 28	Higher education providers and schools work together to assist pre-service teachers to develop and collect sophisticated evidence of their teaching ability and their impact on student learning for their Portfolio of Evidence

recommendations suggest that the portfolio will illustrate how pre-service teachers provide evidence of meeting the graduate level of the Australian Professional Standards for Teachers, and thus be ready to enter the teaching profession. Table 4.2 outlines these three recommendations to assure classroom readiness through the portfolio.

Portfolios have formed a basis in teacher education pedagogies since at least the 1980s (Loughran & Corrigan, 1995) and particularly in the US where it became associated with teacher licensure (Zeichner & Wray, 2001). While acknowledging that the portfolio is appropriated from other disciplines such as artists and architects, teacher educators continue to see its potential to support reflection in order to improve teaching and help pre-service teachers bridge the theory-practice gap. With the TEMAG (2014) recommendations as highlighted in Table 4.2, it is apparent that policy makers also share this aspiration for the value of portfolios within initial teacher education.

An in-depth critical appraisal of portfolios presents the arguments as to why portfolio use in initial teacher education has been inefficient as a tool for learning or assessment, and highlights that there is little research to understand the impact of portfolios used for employment purposes (Delandshere & Petrosky, 2010). Reviewing and building on the work of other researchers in initial teacher education, Delandshere and Petrosky review the research literature to unpack the inconsistencies between the hopes for portfolios in initial teacher education and the pedagogical practices that seem to consistently fall short of meeting the goals. A number of factors are attributed to the contested space of portfolio claims and what portfolios may achieve in the reality of practice. Three potential purposes are identified for the portfolio in initial teacher education: learning, assessment and employment. A fundamental factor contributing to tensions and poor curriculum constructive alignment between purpose, curriculum and outcomes are exposed particularly when the one portfolio is used for more than one purpose within a program. Moreover, the portfolio is frequently attributed to enabling pre-service teachers to reflect deeply on their practice and learning. In their review of the portfolio research

Delandshere and Petrosky (2010) argue that the creation of portfolios by pre-service teachers doesn't guarantee deep reflections and connections with the teaching being represented and there are further limitations if the portfolio is viewed as a repository for 'pasting' in teaching events or artefacts. "A scrapbook of uninterrupted teaching artifacts, even if varied and sampled over time, is not very useful for the assessment or understanding of someone's teaching" (Delandshere & Petrosky, 2010, p. 21).

Like others before (Zeichner & Wray, 2001) and since their literature review (Boulton, 2014; Chung & van Es, 2014; Moran, Vozzo, Reid, Pietsch, & Hatton, 2013), Delandshere and Petrosky (2010) argue for the need to develop teacher education pedagogies (Loughran, 2006) associated with the use of portfolios in initial teacher education. Such pedagogies need to develop the knowledge and skills (e.g., understanding the role of evidence to support professional learning and how to use evidence to reflect on practice and inform future teaching and student learning) to engage deeply with the act of creating meaningful portfolios that articulate the pre-service teachers' professional identities and practices as teachers. Consequently, identifying a 'portfolio of evidence' in the TEMAG (2014) report is not necessarily a new insight into the potential of portfolios to demonstrate "classroom readiness". Yet, despite more than two decades of portfolio use in initial teacher education, there is still the need for research to better understand how 'evidence' is identified, analysed and curated to represent a pre-service or graduate teacher's professional understanding and practice of their teaching and students' learning in its multifaceted complexity.

Ultimately, the use of digital credentialing is underpinned and strengthened by the appropriate use of digital portfolios in initial teacher education. For this reason, the lessons learned from the use of portfolios are important to the work of digital credentialing within initial teacher education. In contrast to the practice of using portfolios, from the outset, digital credentialing needs to focus on the roles that evidence, assessment, moderation and judgements are made to validate the curated work that the pre-service or graduate teacher represents in order to create value and trust of the digital credentials being earned, issued and endorsed. To successfully generate a 'currency' of value within the teacher education sector, the digital credentialing ecosystem necessitates consideration of how to engage all stakeholders in the system design. Such a multidimensional approach to digital credentialing ensures that issues of "evidence of impact" and "classroom readiness" are examined and challenged within and beyond the sector to develop common understandings and shared practices.

3.2 Why Might Digital Credentialing Be a Disruptive Innovation?

> Disruptive innovation adopts cutting edge technology and ideas that enable new and novel applications to sustain exponential growth. A disruptive innovation increases long term productivity and changes the way people experience and live daily life (Baughman, Pan, Gao, & Petrushin, 2015 p. 5).

According to Baughman and his colleagues (2015), disruptive innovations are characterised by three dimensions that lead to change for creating highly functioning and productive societies:

- *imagine* – (re)imagine the future
- *innovate* – innovate to achieve the imagined future through, for example (innovative), technologies and processes
- *impact* – understand the (positive) impact of the disruptive innovation on society and the need for it to create a better or desirable environment.

Digital credentialing meets all three dimensions of disruptive innovations. It is a new technological innovation recently adopted within education and consequently it is re-imagining the future of the educational landscape (Randall et al., 2013). The new affordances of the digital credentialing technologies presents new possibilities of representing evidence in multimodal and expansive ways. The positive impact of establishing digital credentialing within ITE will, for example, enhance the graduates' capabilities to provide evidence of their classroom readiness on entering the teaching profession. More significantly is the potential for digital credentialing to disrupt what and how evidence is represented and incorporate new positive ways of learning and assessment within schools. The disruptive innovation is readily manifested once design of digital credentialing frameworks enable, for example: learners to create their own learning pathways; nurture life-long learning habits; encourage transdisciplinary learning; and re-think the way learning achievements may be assessed and recognised including incorporating knowledge and skills achieved through formal and informal learning contexts (e.g., Ahn, Pellicone, & Butler, 2014; Bowen & Thomas, 2014; Finkelstein et al., 2013).

3.3 How Is Digital Credentialing Being Used in Education?

Digital credentialing is a new innovation in education, and particularly in teacher education as is readily confirmed by a systematic review of research literature using ERIC EBSCO*Host* database and key words of *badges* OR *digital credential* AND *pre-service teacher education*. The initial search result yielded 181 articles and yet a quick scan suggested that many items were not directly related to the above keyword fields. Since Mozilla announced the Open Badge Infrastructure Project https://blog.mozilla.org/blog/2011/09/15/openbadges/ in 2011, which signified the badging technology becoming available in a form that was open and transparent, further filtering the literature review data by years (2009–2016) resulted in 50 literature items. Of these 50 item results, 25 related directly to Open Badges (or digital credentialing) within a broad, education context. This means that the Open Badges was referred to across diverse education sectors: formal schooling such as higher education; primary and secondary school curriculum; and also in informal or non-formal learning contexts. Of these 25 items, six items were linked to Open Badges but were not peer reviewed items; the remaining 19 items were peer reviewed articles. Out of the 25 items with Open Badges in an education context two articles were related to teacher education. One article was based within the in-service teacher education context and discussed using digital credentialing to foster personalised, professional development for teachers within their work environments (Gamrat et al., 2014). The other article included a discussion of initial teacher education at Purdue University working with secondary pre-service teachers to develop their ICT literacies (Randall et al., 2013). This literature review illustrates the concept and practice of digital credentialing within teacher education is in its very early stages and other education sectors may provide insights of what may be possible within initial teacher education. A further analysis of the literature suggests that there is a higher proportion of theoretical articles often discussing the conceptualisations and debating the benefits or otherwise of digital credentialing; and case studies, representing empirical data of implementation, are only beginning to surface in the research literature.

3.3.1 Recognition of Complexity of Learning

Central to the emergence of digital credentialing technologies is the necessity to acknowledge the complexity of learning within the twenty-first century and that these technologies offer a granular system for recognising the achievements of that learning. The complexity of learning involves active learning, often based on social, collaborative and inclusive principles and incorporates progressive acquisition of knowledge and skills that can be applicable and transferable into new contexts; as well as growth and development of attitudes and dispositions, (professional) beliefs and values that can be adapted in real world scenarios (Knight & Cassilli, 2012). Such learning is often 'inter' or 'trans' disciplinary in nature and, in formal education such as initial teacher education, disrupts the conventional ways pre-service teachers can demonstrate and represent their learning and for teacher educators to have alternative ways for assessing the pre-service teachers' learning achievements. In particular, digital credentialing offers the prospect of assessing and evidencing learning across the initial teacher education course, for example between university course work and professional experience. Digital credentialing has the potential to create a system for this kind of assessment, recognition and representation of learning achievements. In particular, the potential for a digital credentialing ecosystem to offer new opportunities for working with employers, the profession and evidencing learning in authentic ways via the online platform calls for new ways to assess and validate learning achievements and recognition of mastery (e.g., Gibson et al., 2015).

3.3.2 Fostering Deep Engagement for (Professional) Learning

A constant theme within the literature is the role that digital credentialing plays in motivation and engagement for learning; a link often associated with its roots in gamification (e.g., Codish & Ravid, 2014; Jovanovic & Devedzic, 2015; O'Byrne et al., 2015; Tunon, Ramirez, Ryckman, Campbell, & Mlinar, 2015). Advocates for digital credentialing argue that it can support students to develop aspects of deep engagement for learning through the development of metacognitive skills such as self-regulation (e.g., Devedzic & Jovanovic, 2015; Randall et al., 2013) and cross curricular deep learning skills such as critical thinking, cross disciplinary learning and team work (e.g., Bowen & Thomas, 2014; Davies, Randall, & West, 2015).

Abramovich and his colleagues' (2013) seminal work in this area analysed and identified two types of models for badges reflective of the sources that inspired the creation of digital credentials. One model is based on merit associated with the Scouts' conceptualisation of badges that represent achievement of specific knowledge and skills, which acts as a type of certification. Within this merit-based model there is a theoretical assumption that the motivation and curiosity for earning a badge will transfer to intrinsic motivation for setting goals for future learning of knowledge and skills. The second model is based on playfulness and the "metagaming features common to videogames…[that allow] players to earn recognition of their in-game achievements outside of the game itself" (Abramovich et al., 2013, p. 219). In this model, there is a theoretical assumption that the extrinsic motivation of publicly displaying your virtual profile of your mastery for others to see will support the player to continue his/her quest to earn further badges. Abramovich and his colleagues (2013) argue that educational digital badges blend the features of these two models.

In their empirical study, Abramovich and his colleagues examine students' motivation for learning from the perspectives of goal theory and mastery in conjunction with the impacts of students' prior knowledge and how these factors interact with the overlay of earning digital badges. The context for the empirical study is based in measuring the motivation of junior secondary students in a low socioeconomic, urban school while earning digital badges during a computer-based mathematics program. Using Elliot's (Elliot, 1999, cited in Abramovich et al., 2013) goal theory as a key theoretical framework to analyse their data, Abramovich and his colleagues' empirical study found that various badge types (participatory or mastery of knowledge/skills) affected the motivations of learners differently. A key conclusion these authors presented is that low performing students tended to gravitate towards earning participatory badges and provided motivation for learning that was often extrinsic or reward based. In contrast, the high performing students tended to choose to earn the mastery badges that highlighted an intrinsic motivation to learn content and often interacted negatively with the participatory badges that represented low level engagement with mathematical content learning. Hence, Abramovich and his colleagues argued that this finding has implications for instructional and curriculum designers in their development of the types of badges that are integrated into the curriculum. They suggest that participatory badges should be limited, or even removed, from the curriculum because of the negative patterns associated with them for low performing students (fostering extrinsic motivation learning behaviours) and high performing students (often led to a negative correlation with motivation). This finding provides the basis of one of their key recommendations to designers of digital credentialing ecosystems within curricula: that they "must consider the ability and motivations of learners when choosing what badges to include in their curricula"

(Abramovich et al., 2013, p. 230). A similar conclusion has been reached by another research team, Codish and Ravid (2014), who studied personality differences and interactions with playfulness in a program that had an overlay of digital badges using a gamification approach and its effects on undergraduate engineering students. They concluded that to successfully increase playfulness in the learning environment, digital credentialing and curriculum designers need to consider the right mix of "game mechanics" and these might need to be changed through the program to accommodate the needs of learners such as introverts and extroverts as each group responded differently to the gamification use of badges (Codish & Ravid, 2014, p. 144). They also recommended further research is needed to better understand the learners and their learning processes when using digital credentialing embedded in formal learning contexts. These studies begin to advance the conception that learning within digital credentialing ecosystems is complex with many interacting factors.

3.3.3 Personalising the (Professional) Learning Journey

Digital credentialing can also act positively as a significant disruptive innovative technology in its capacity to create opportunities for personalising the learning journey. This design principle gives agency to learners to make choices about how they gain their learning experiences and provide evidence to demonstrate and be recognised for their learning achievements. This is particularly useful to support lifelong learning and there are instances where digital credentialing is being used for professional learning and development of staff, such as librarians attending conferences and earning digital badges to consolidate and demonstrate their professional learning (Fontichiaro, Ginsberg, Lungu, Masura, & Roslund, 2013); and library staff undertaking a non-award training program related to customer service (Ippoliti, 2014). Another example is the proposal to design an Open Badge system and framework to certify a professional association's (i.e., American Evaluators Association [AEA]) members who are evaluators (Davies et al., 2015). The proposed digital certification system would focus on recognising the fine-grained skills, knowledge and experience of an AEA evaluator using valid and reliable assessment processes and provide the evaluator a platform to showcase the quality of their expertise to potential clients using an evidence based approach.

Being able to draw on lifelong and life-wide learning experiences to curate into evidence of mastery of knowledge, skills and dispositions that are needed for working in particular careers, provides a powerful platform for the learner to make strong connections between formal, informal and non-formal learning. Such potential affordances of the digital credentialing ecosystem and its associated processes builds on authentic or real world learning and developing valuable employability skills enabling demonstration of career readiness (Bowen & Thomas, 2014; Knight & Cassilli, 2012; O'Byrne et al., 2015; Thigpen, 2014). This type of learning achievement and ability to represent digitally through a rigorous, valid and trusted assessment process illustrates the divergence of the digital credentialing framework and processes from conventional course transcripts and testamurs. The evidence curated and represented via a digital credentialing system has the potential for transparency of assessment process and far more fine-grained detail, or evidence base of learning achievement and experience that is not often associated with modularised learning, but rather reflective of connected learning, building bridges between learning experiences (Bowen & Thomas, 2014).

4 Can Digital Credentialing Be a Disruptive Innovation in ITE Reform? The Challenges and Future Research Possibilities

At the heart of the most recent call for initial teacher education reform in Australia through the TEMAG (2014) report is the requirement to seek graduates who are able to provide evidence of their professional learning and practice and demonstrate how student learning is enhanced in order to illustrate their classroom readiness. This policy requirement is no small endeavor. In identifying this goal, the Advisory Group has recommended the use of the digital portfolio as cornerstone (e.g., formative assessment) and capstone (e.g., summative assessment) strategies that will significantly work towards addressing the challenge of preparing graduates that are 'classroom ready' as they enter the teaching profession. As previously discussed, the portfolio approach has an extensive history within initial teacher education since at least the 1980s and while 'going digital' has significantly increased the potential affordances of the portfolio, the pedagogical approaches have been shown to have critical limitations of success; particularly in relation to its use to demonstrate classroom readiness.

The intention of the TEMAG (2014) reform is to seek new ways of learning and working to build enriched and stronger bridges between diverse, high quality learning experiences for pre-service teachers in their coursework and professional experience contexts. To take up such a reform intention is to call for a disruptive innovation that re-imagines future teacher education pedagogies rather than return to past practices such as the digital portfolio that has constraints to deliver on the policy intention. This chapter has outlined some of the potential for digital credentialing to offer a disruptive innovation. This includes the potential of the digital credential ecosystem and its associated processes to strengthen metacognitive capabilities to nurture reflexivity within the 'learning to teach' for our pre-service teachers. Such pedagogical use of the digital credentialing ecosystem can also facilitate greater experiential learning opportunities leading pre-service teachers to connect their learning across and between their diverse formal, informal and non-formal learning experiences.

However, as with any new digital technology and innovation, there are challenges for the teaching profession should they engage with the digital credentialing approach to respond meaningfully to the call for using evidence to demonstrate classroom readiness. A number of these challenges and tensions are already surfacing in the research literature (e.g., Devedzic & Jovanovic, 2015; Finkelstein et al., 2013) and as these are yet to be explored in the teaching profession, there will be nuances and, no doubt, new challenges that will emerge to reflect the profession's particularities. Issues of designing the digital ecosystems are paramount to embedding the technology within teacher education sector and many of the lessons already learned can be used to guide attempts within the sector. For example, through their comprehensive Open Badges development framework, Devedzic and Jovanovic (2015) provide multiple lenses to consider during the design process within a systemic approach. Others provide further insights into the design such as identifying successful and challenging design principles associated with recognition, assessment and motivation (O'Byrne et al., 2015); and discuss the value and potential of disruptive innovation and design frameworks within specific contexts such as adult literacy in the USA (Finkelstein et al., 2013). The issue of status of the recognition (i.e., what value are afforded by the digital credentials and by whom) and subthemes of equity and privacy are also raised by these research teams and others in their frameworks (e.g., Gibson et al., 2015; Thigpen, 2014). A particular useful discussion of challenges and tensions that further these debates of what should be considered in design of digital credentialing frameworks is offered by Ahn and her colleagues (2014). They add further complexity through the lenses of motivation, pedagogy and credentials; and then overlay it with a discussion about the nature of openness in the digital credential, which has implications for how far the digital disruptive technology may extend.

Digital credentialing offers promise and potential to address meaningfully the calls for initial teacher education reform; particularly in areas of evidence and classroom readiness. Yet as a disruptive technological innovation it also presents its own sets of challenges and tensions. In addition to the technical and pedagogical issues that have been discussed here, the overarching issue is one of learning for all stakeholders within the sector and building a culture of shared understanding of digital credentialing frameworks that respects the value of what this new digital innovation may bring to enhancing initial teacher education. Such change requires a multifaceted approach. It requires re-imagining our cultures and the ways we work as well as examining how we can make digital credentialing work purposefully for our sector's (learning) needs in order to enhance the learning of students in our schools. As an emerging field, this chapter indicates there are many possibilities for research to underpin and support implementation of digital credentialing frameworks in ITE, for example: examining and developing pedagogies; gaining a better understanding of the complexities of learning processes; exploring effective design frameworks, principles and processes; investigating the cultures of learning; the role of formative feedback and assessment; and exploring the potential for collaborative learning.

References

Abramovich, S., Schunn, C., & Higashi, R. M. (2013). Are badges useful in education?: It depends upon the type of badge and expertise of learner. *Educational Technology Research and Development, 61*(2), 217–232.

Achievements (video gaming). (2015). *Wikipedia*, viewed 17 Nov 2015, https://en.wikipedia.org/wiki/Achievement_(video_gaming).

Ahn, J., Pellicone, A., & Butler, B. S. (2014). Open badges for education: What are the implications at the intersection of open systems and badging? *Research in Learning Technology, 22*, 1–13.

Baughman, A. K., Pan, J., Gao, J.-Y., & Petrushin, V. A. (2015). Disruptive innovation: Large scale multimedia data mining. In A. K. Baughman, J. Gao, J.-Y. Pan, & A. P. Valery (Eds.), *Multimedia data mining and analytics: Disruptive innovation*. Cham, Switzerland: Springer.

Boulton, H. (2014). EPortfolios beyond pre-service teacher education: A new dawn? *European Journal of Teacher Education, 37*(3), 374–389.

Bowen, K., & Thomas, A. (2014). Badges: A common currency for learning. *Change: The Magazine of Higher Learning, 46*(1), 21–25.

Chung, H. Q., & van Es, E. A. (2014). Pre-service teachers' use of tools to systematically analyze teaching and learning. *Teachers and Teaching: Theory and Practice, 20*(2), 113–135.

Cochran-Smith, M. (2012). Trends and challenges in teacher education: National and international perspectives. In F. Waldron, J. Smith, M. Fitzpatrick, & T. Dooley (Eds.), *Re-imagining initial teacher education: Perspectives on transformation*. Dublin, Ireland: The Liffey Press.

Cochran-Smith, M., Feiman-Nemser, S., & McIntyre, D. J. (Eds.). (2008). *Handbook of research on teacher education: Enduring questions in changing contexts* (3rd ed.). New York: Routledge, Taylor & Francis Group and the Association of Teacher Education.

Codish, D., & Ravid, G. (2014). Academic course gamification: The art of perceived playfulness. *Interdisciplinary Journal of E-Learning and Learning Objects, 10*, 131–151.

Davies, R., Randall, D., & West, R. E. (2015). Using open badges to certify practicing evaluators. *American Journal of Evaluation, 36*(2), 151–163.

Delandshere, G., & Petrosky, A. R. (2010). The use of portfolios in pre-service teacher education: A critical appraisal. In M. Kennedy (Ed.), *Teacher assessment and the quest for teacher quality: A handbook*. San Francisco: Jossey-Bass.

Devedzic, V., & Jovanovic, J. (2015). Developing open badges: A comprehensive approach. *Educational Technology Research and Development, 63*(4), 603–620.

Elliot, A. J. (1999). Approach and avoidance motivation and achievement goals. *Educational Psychologist, 34*(3), 169–189.

Feiman-Nemser, S. (2008). Teacher learning: How do teachers learn to teach? In M. Cochran-Smith, S. Feiman-Nemser, D. J. McIntyre, & K. E. Demers (Eds.), *Handbook of research on teacher education: Enduring questions in changing contexts*. New York: Routledge and Association of Teacher Educators.

Finkelstein, J., Knight, E., & Manning, S. (2013). *The potential and value of using digital badges for adult learners: Draft for public comment*. Washington, DC: American Institutes for Research.

Fontichiaro, K., Ginsberg, S., Lungu, V., Masura, S., & Roslund, S. (2013). Badging a conference. *School Library Monthly, 29*(7), 5–7.

Gamrat, C., Zimmerman, H. T., Dudek, J., & Peck, K. (2014). Personalized workplace learning: An exploratory study on digital badging within a teacher professional development program. *British Journal of Educational Technology, 45*(6), 1136–1148.

Gibson, D., Ostashewski, N., Flintoff, K., Grant, S., & Knight, E. (2015). Digital badges in education. *Education and Information Technologies, 20*(2), 403–410.

Ippoliti, C. (2014). Are you being served? Designing the customer service curriculum. *Public Services Quarterly, 10*(3), 177–192.

Jovanovic, J., & Devedzic, V. (2015). Open badges: Novel means to motivate, scaffold and recognize learning. *Technology, Knowledge and Learning, 20*(1), 115–122.

Knight, E., & Cassilli, C. (2012). Mozilla open badges. In D. G. Oblinger (Ed.), *Game changers: Education and information technologies*. Washington, DC: EDUCAUSE.

Loughran, J. (2006). *Developing a pedagogy of teacher education: Understanding teaching and learning about teaching*. London: Routledge.

Loughran, J., & Corrigan, D. (1995). Teaching portfolios: A strategy for developing learning and teaching in pre-service education. *Teaching and Teacher Education, 11*(6), 565–577.

Moran, W., Vozzo, L., Reid, J., Pietsch, M., & Hatton, C. (2013). How can technology make this work? Pre-service teachers, off-campus learning and digital portfolios. *Australian Journal of Teacher Education, 38*(5), 116–130, Article 8.

O'Byrne, W. I., Schenke, K., Willis, J. E., III, & Hickey, D. T. (2015). Digital badges: Recognizing, assessing, and motivating learners in and out of school contexts. *Journal of Adolescent & Adult Literacy, 58*(6), 451–454.

Randall, D. L., Harrison, J. B., & West, R. E. (2013). Giving credit where credit is due: Designing open badges for a technology integration course. *TechTrends, 57*(6), 88–95.

Schön, D. A. (1983). *The reflective practitioner: How professionals think in action* (First edition, reprinted in 1995 ed.). Hants, England: Arena.

Schön, D. A. (1987). *Educating the reflective practitioner*. San Francisco: Jossey-Bass Publishers.

Teacher Education Ministerial Advisory Group (TEMAG). (2014). *Action now: Classroom ready teachers*. Canberra, Australia: Department of Education and Training, Australian Government.

Thigpen, K. (2014). *Digital badge systems: The promise and potential*. Washington, DC: Alliance for Excellent Education.

Tunon, J., Ramirez, L. L., Ryckman, B., Campbell, L., & Mlinar, C. (2015). Creating an information literacy badges program in blackboard: A formative program evaluation. *Journal of Library & Information Services in Distance Learning, 9*(1–2), 157–169.

Zeichner, K., & Wray, S. (2001). The teaching portfolio in US teacher education programs: What we know and what we need to know. *Teaching and Teacher Education, 17*(5), 613–621.

Innovating in First Year Pre-service Teacher Education: "Buddy Up"

Jennifer Elsden-Clifton, Kathy Jordan, and Nicky Carr

1 Introduction

Professional experience (placement/practicum) describes the aspect of Teacher Education whereby PSTs spend time in schools to observe practice, gain authentic experience and develop their professional identity. Professional experience is recognised as an essential part of initial teacher education programs (Le Cornu, 2015; Ure, Gough, & Newton, 2009) yet it is also the site of contestation around how it is conceptualised, structured and supervised (Le Cornu, 2015). Professional experience takes multiple forms across universities from block placements (PSTs are sent to schools for a set number of weeks at a time) to models such as one day a week over a period of time, internships and more extended placements. There are also examples of different placement location settings such as virtual placements, overseas placements and placements in alternative educational settings.

Despite the diverse constructions of practicum across universities, national reports into initial teacher education continue to question the quality of professional experience programs. In 2007, the Australian House of Representatives Standing Committee on Education and Vocational Training tabled the *Top of the Class* (Commonwealth of Australia) report into teacher education. In this report, it iterated that "high quality placements for school-based professional experience are a critical component of teacher education courses" but that there was little consensus around "how much practicum there should be, when practicum should begin and the best structure for practicum" (p. 67).

Despite calls for reform, any innovation in professional experience is influenced by regulatory, political and historical contexts. In 2011, the Australian Government introduced a national approach to accreditation for initial teacher education

J. Elsden-Clifton (✉) • K. Jordan • N. Carr
RMIT University, Melbourne, Victoria, Australia
e-mail: jennifer.elsden-clifton@rmit.edu.au; kathy.jordan@rmit.edu.au; nicky.carr@rmit.edu.au

regulated by the Australian Institute for Teaching and School Leadership (AITSL). Teacher education providers are now required to meet a set of national program standards that relate to the development, structure and delivery, as well as student selection of their courses. Currently, professional experience needs to consist of at least 80 days for undergraduate programs and 60 days for graduate entry and must involve "well-structured, supervised and assessed teaching practice in schools" (AITSL, 2011, p. 15). Providers need to document the practicum component of their programs including partnership relationships with schools. For some universities, change in the regulatory environment has encouraged innovation. It has meant a rethink in the way professional experience is conceptualised, a reconsideration of the curriculum and pedagogy of placement-based courses and the development of different practicum models.

Innovation in the area of professional experience is also bound by historic notions of what practicum is. Stakeholders such as school leadership, teacher mentors and the teacher education students themselves have formed, and hold, values and expectations based on their own experiences and "by history and tradition and by the universal qualities that are embedded in the tradition of the profession" (Mattsson, Eilertsen, & Rorrison, 2011, p. 3). This history can "facilitate as well as hamper certain practices" (Mattsson et al., 2011, p. 3) and innovation.

It is within these histories, regulatory environment and political times that innovation around placement in first year courses discussed in this chapter was introduced. The site-based professional experience model reported in this chapter has been developed by the School of Education at RMIT University and 13 partner primary schools in Melbourne, Victoria, Australia. Drawing on a view that learning is fundamentally a social process (Brown, Collins, & Duguid, 1989; Vygotsky, 1978), where context or situatedness is key in knowledge construction (Lave & Wenger, 1991), this model involved placing 209 first year PSTs in small groups (12–16 students) in partner schools, then pairing the students, their buddy, for their professional experience placement. Whilst in schools, the small groups were taught course content by a school-based tutor.

Two sets of literature informed the development of this model including: literature related to professional experience, the importance of partnerships between university and schools, and the value of paired placements; and literature related to transition into higher education and best practice strategies for supporting first year students. This chapter begins by examining these two sets of literature then describes the elements of the innovation, its method of delivery and examines, through focus group data, PSTs' perceptions of being paired/buddied. A number of key implications in relation to buddies are then discussed.

2 Literature

2.1 Professional Experience Partnerships

Numerous reports into initial teacher education in Australia refer to the need to improve the quality, with consistent concerns about the lack of connection between theory and practice (Ure et al., 2009). This rhetoric drives political commentary and has been the premise for a number of reports and initiatives. For instance, the *Top of the Class* report (Australian Parliament House of Representatives Standing Committee on Education and Vocational Training, 2007), argued that at the centre of the issue around interconnection was the "current distribution of responsibilities in Teacher Education" (p. 2); whereby theoretical components are typically taught on campus by faculty and the teaching practicum undertaken on-site in schools by practising teachers. The more recent Teacher Education Ministerial Advisory Group (TEMAG) report (2014) shared similar sentiments; schools and universities need to form closer partnerships and practising teachers should be more involved in preparing PSTs.

Practicum is generally acknowledged as one site where universities and schools can connect, as well as being vital for the development of practical skills for future teachers (Ure et al., 2009). Yet, how the practicum should be designed and implemented, and its relationship to university coursework is heavily contested by policy makers, practising teachers, university educators as well as students. Zeichner (2010) is critical of the way universities approach the practicum, arguing that they typically have very little involvement in its details, leaving these to be worked out between PSTs and their teacher mentors. Drawing on his own extensive experience, Zeichner suggests that practicum is often perceived by universities as an administrative task. Another problem with the practicum he suggests is that schools and teacher mentors know very little about the university coursework, and university educators have little knowledge of what happens in schools. Darling-Hammond (2010) similarly suggests that:

> ... [*the practicum*] *side of teacher education has been fairly haphazard, depending on the idiosyncrasies of loosely selected placements with little guidance about what happens in them and little connection to university work.* (p. 40)

While there is acknowledgment by policy makers, academics, researchers and practitioners alike, that university-based coursework and practicum should be more connected, achieving this connection is complex. As noted by Grossman, Hammerness, and McDonald (2009):

> ... *though scholars of teacher education periodically revise the relationship between theory and practice, teacher education programs struggle to redesign programmatic structures and pedagogy to acknowledge and build on the integrated nature of theory and practice as well as the potentially deep interplay between coursework and field placements.* (p. 276)

In response, initial teacher education providers have attempted to improve professional experience through various innovations involving partnerships with schools, including versions of a teaching schools, site-based curriculum (Lang, Neal, Karvouni, & Chandler, 2015) and teacher residencies between universities, schools and school districts (Klein, Taylor, Onore, Strom, & Abrams, 2013). This chapter adds to research around innovations that connect schools and universities and focuses on how this partnership has been structured to support the transition of first year students to university and the profession.

2.2 Transition to Higher Education

Many of the pedagogical and organisational decisions around this innovation were influenced by the literature in relation to transitioning to university that is understood as challenging. This is particularly challenging within initial teacher education, as PSTs often feel vulnerable in their placements (Le Cornu, 2009). Given this course was located in first semester of first year, it was designed to acknowledge both the transition to university and the profession.

Studies have repeatedly shown that transition to university, whether entering university directly from school or from other starting points, is characterised by stress, challenges and a sense of being overwhelmed (Harvey, Drew, & Smith, 2006; Kift, Nelson, & Clarke, 2010; Tinto, 1993). Indeed, the highest academic failure and attrition occurs in the first year of tertiary education (McInnis, James, & Hartley, 2000) and brings with it substantial social and economic costs (Kuh, Cruce, Shoup, Kinzie, & Gonyea, 2008).

Institutional changes to higher education have also influenced transition to university. The shift to blended and online models of learning and teaching within the university sector also means fewer days on campus (James, Krause, & Jennings, 2010). The massification of higher education, that is the move to larger and larger class sizes, is placing small group teaching practices under threat (Black & MacKenzie, 2008). Students also face external pressure from the need to take employment alongside their study, which may reduce attendance on campus for both formal classes and networking with fellow students (Bowles, Dobson, Fisher, & McPhail, 2011; Hillman, 2005; James et al., 2010). The combined effects of these recent trends means that students spend less time on campus compared to 10 years ago, and less time interacting with one another. There has also been a significant decline in the proportion of first year students who feel confident that they are known by name by at least one teacher, and only 26 % of students believe that staff take an interest in their progress (James et al., 2010). The potential for social isolation that results from these trends is concerning since social connectedness is increasingly recognised as key to successful transition (James et al., 2010; Kift et al., 2010; Masters & Donnison, 2010).

To counter these effects, the literature suggests that there needs to be an effective transition strategy for both student well-being and academic success (Bovill, Bulley, & Morss, 2011). Some specific strategies include creating a curriculum where students have a sense of belonging and address the personal, social and academic literacies of first year students (Krause, 2007; Reason, Terenzini, & Domingo, 2007). Other strategies include: orientation activities; academic support programs such as study skills (Harvey et al., 2006); formal and informal social events (Kift et al., 2010); and explicit forms of peer support through year levels, with more experienced students mentoring first year students (Bowles et al., 2011; James et al., 2010). More recent initiatives designed to support the first year experience involve creating learning communities, where students are allocated to a specific learning community for tutorials and seminars and remain in that learning community, sharing common classes for a semester or longer (Black & MacKenzie, 2008; Bowles et al., 2011; Masters & Donnison, 2010).

3 The Innovation

In 2014, the School of Education at RMIT University reconceptualised professional experience for its 4 year Bachelor of Education program. Drawing on the literature outlined above, the new program centres on forming partnerships with schools to bring about better connections between theory and practice including a co-constructed curriculum. Each year of the program has a different model/approach to professional experience.

The first year model focuses on providing effective transition to university and to the profession in the course *Orientation to Teaching*. The course content and assessment has been designed collaboratively by practising teachers and teacher educators. The course begins at university, with PSTs undertaking eight two hour workshops involving tasks recommended in the transition literature including academic skills development, getting to know you activities, and scaffolded tasks which progressively introduce students to key teaching skills, such as questioning and feedback.

Based on the transitional literature, we encouraged peer engagement and social support through a number of social activities, including establishing a shared Facebook page between university staff and students. In keeping with research that supports fostering belonging and improving engagement through creating communities of learners (Black & MacKenzie, 2008; Harvey et al., 2006), we placed the PSTs into small groups of 12–16. We "buddied" them with a peer for support, both socially and academically.

The course then continued at 13 partner primary schools in Melbourne. Two hundred and nine PSTs observed and experienced teaching first-hand for two weeks, supported by five two hour tutorials taught by a school-based tutor (a practicing teacher employed by the university) who customised the core curriculum to the individual school context. As they undertook the course they applied their knowledge and skills in a teacher mentor's classroom through activities such as audits and observations. The PSTs were required to complete a number of tasks that were assessed by the school-based tutor.

While there were many aspects of this innovation, such as co-constructed curriculum with schools, site-based learning, peer learning communities in schools, audits that critically question observation, this chapter examines the key element of pairing up PSTs; which was referred to as "buddies". This pairing was random and no effort was made to match partners although PSTs were given some direction as to how to work together as "buddies".

Previous approaches to buddied practicum experiences suggest that the benefits include overcoming the sense of isolation that many first time PSTs report (Lang et al., 2015) by providing a source of personal and professional support in a situation where PSTs often feel vulnerable and intimidated (Lang et al., 2015; Le Cornu, 2009). Being paired fosters opportunities for critical reflection on practice (Manouchehri, 2002) in the belief that reflecting with a peer is not as intimidating as reflecting with a mentor teacher (Smith, 2004; Walsh & Elmslie, 2005). PSTs were also exposed to other approaches and perspectives about the same observed experiences, helping to broaden their teaching repertoires (Smith, 2004). Sharing the classroom with a buddy also enculturates PSTs into a profession increasingly characterised by team teaching, reflective practice, collegiality, collaborative relationships and socialised knowledge (Le Cornu, 2009; Manoucherhi, 2002).

4 Method

The course, *Orientation to Teaching* was delivered in Semester 1, 2014 to 209 PSTs who were predominantly preparing to be generalist primary school teachers. The majority of the PSTs were female (86%), aged between 18 and 39 years (mean age of 21), and Australian-born (89.3%) with English as their language spoken at home (81.3%). Following the completion of the course, we invited the PSTs to participate in a variety of focus group discussions led by an independent facilitator. Some 42 PSTs participated across the four focus groups that were held on separate days over a two week period. The focus group discussions used a number of open questions to prompt discussion around their experiences in the course and its design. The four focus groups included:

1. a random sample of PSTs who were buddied from a cross section of schools (only one of the buddies was invited to participate);
2. a selected group of PSTs who had not been buddied (due to student withdrawal or uneven numbers);
3. a selected group of international PSTs; and
4. an open forum where everyone was invited to attend.

Discussions were audiotaped and transcribed. The research team then identified in the transcript when being buddied was discussed. Findings from each focus group are presented in Sect. 5. The main issues identified are then discussed thematically to examine the buddy role in placements in first year courses.

Innovating in First Year Pre-service Teacher Education: "Buddy Up" 69

5 Findings

5.1 Focus Group: Buddied Group

This focus group included 12 PSTs participated in this focus group. When asked specifically about having a buddy, several of the PSTs commented favourably. "Loved it" was one response, and "I had a really good buddy experience," was another. Often, as each PST gave their response they offered a justification for their response, and these differed from supporting learning to personal reasons. For example, in terms of learning, one PST commented that having a buddy enabled her "just to clarify my views and things that were happening in the classroom." Another PST commented that having a buddy exposed her to other ways of handling situations:

> I thought it interesting, like I'd see some of the ways my buddy would approach the kids about certain things, topics. I was like, I hadn't thought about it like that before but it's really interesting to see.

This PST also added:

> At the end of the day we would always like debrief, how we felt about the day and ... upcoming tasks and stuff, what we're going to do to prepare, do we need help with this.

Another PST perceived that having a buddy enabled her:

> ... to find out as well how you work best. Like sometimes there are certain activities where we do decide we're going to do this because that's what works for us. So, I think just as a learner as well, it's good to work out how you like to do this.

However, other PSTs provided less favourable responses to being paired with a buddy. One PST commented that having a buddy "took away from the work". Another PST elaborated on this theme and added:

> I was really having to help her get through the task and just constantly supporting her. All my focus was on her most of the time and not actually what I'm supposed to be doing.

Not all the PSTs had a definitive view; one PST highlighted this tension. Initially, when he had not been assigned a buddy he was pleased. "I was really lucky because I didn't have a buddy" adding that as a result, "It was about me all day long. Whatever I needed I got. I had all the attention on me and I loved that. I didn't need to compete with anybody else".

When he realised that a buddy was being assigned he commented, "it was the first day panic set in." As he elaborated, he became very suspicious and quite nervous about the motives underpinning the buddy design, commenting "I thought that they designed this buddy system for a reason. Maybe PSTs in the past weren't very confident?" and this possible motivation seemed to make him anxious. Later in this same conversation he turns full circle commenting that when his buddy was assigned, he realised there were benefits:

> ... because I got to not keep so many things to myself. Like if I thought about what was happening with the kid or interaction between the student and the teacher I could go to my buddy and ask him what did you think of this? What did you think of that?

Many of the negative comments about having a buddy were mostly personality based, including "I was with a lovely girl but I found her very hard to work with and although I was patient and professional at all times, I know there was a lot of extra stress".

Others felt that even if the pairing was not ideal, it was a reality of what they may experience in schools. One PST commented, "if you're put with someone who doesn't work well with you, you'd have to take that on board as an experience in itself." Another commented, that experiencing such a pairing could prepare for the workplace "because there is always going to be people in your profession that you might not be best friends with, you might not get along with, so experiencing that now, you're sort of more prepared for it".

Another PST, who acknowledged that while she didn't "have the best experience" added that "you've got to think of everybody else in the course and how it can benefit them."

The issue of whether PSTs should have been able to choose their own buddy was one that generated considerable discussion in this focus group. This is typified in the following comment:

> the buddy system was a huge hit and miss ... it was pretty much pot luck for all of us because we didn't know who we were going to be partnered with and I don't think that, you know, the coordinators of this course researched all of us and our personalities and said let's mash these two up together and create this awesome union. So, it was really just random.

The issue of choosing your own buddy didn't come up in the non-buddy group or the international group, but was raised in the open forum discussed in Sect. 5.4 (below).

When asked about how they specifically related with their buddy, again mixed views were expressed. One PST responded that she thought this relationship was one-sided and felt under pressure and assumed more of a parental relationship with her buddy:

> I was always having to touch base with her and make sure that she understood what was required of her to do. And yeah, I emailed her like every night just to remind her about little things because I was a buddy. I felt like that if she didn't do something it would let us both down, so I always feeling that pressure that I had to keep on, that things were getting done. It's a joint effort and at times I felt like I was doing more work.

Another commented that her relationship with her buddy was very different:

> I think it helped that I already knew my buddy, so like I would pick her up from the bus every morning and we would go together, everything together. As far as our assignment went, we would send emails back and forth, 'oh I've added this, what do you think of what I've added in that'.

And yet another PST commented that she and her buddy worked rather independently from one another; "we had a lot of discussion and that but when it came to actually teaching and doing class stuff we were very independent."

In summary, members of this focus group found benefits in using their buddies as a sounding board, to explore ideas and different perspectives about the same experiences. Being with a buddy exposed them to different approaches to situations and helped to develop their own practice. Many buddies worked in highly collaborative and supportive ways, whereas other buddies supported each other, but operated at more independent levels. For some, however, particularly where PSTs perceived themselves to be more experienced or capable, buddies were seen as a burden.

5.2   Focus Group: Non-buddied Group

This group of eight PSTs was not assigned a buddy. We were interested to research their views to see how not having a buddy may have influenced their experience. For this group being placed in the one school with a peer group rather than having a buddy seemed to matter more, "I think that having a buddy isn't necessary but having a group of teachers like learning teachers is a really good thing."

This group of PSTs commented that they liked not having a buddy. As one of them said, "I preferred being alone" as she thought that having a buddy would restrict what she was able to do. As she elaborated, "I was by myself in the classroom, I really felt like I can just do everything as my teacher mentor wanted me to do by myself and just like, be more me than both of us". As another PST similarly commented, "I got to do so much more than they got to do because it was simply that there was one of me". Not surprisingly, this focus group paid minimal attention to the issue of buddies, preferring to discuss other core aspects of the course.

5.3   Focus Group: International Pre-service Teachers Group

To this group of four PSTs having a buddy was one of the best features of the course. For the most part, PSTs in this group commented that they felt anxious about placement, and that having a buddy provided them with support:

> ...for me, stepping into a new environment like a primary school in Melbourne, I was really daunted by the prospect. I was really worried about what I was going to do in that environment. But having a buddy was really helpful in the sense that she motivated me and encouraged me to do well.

Also commenting that, "I know nothing about Australia's schools. When I first met her, she just tell me, no worries, I'll help you. That actually comforted me a lot." The buddy feature was seen as important: "Especially for the first placement for first year. Because we're so confused. We worry about what we are going to do, just in class by ourselves, but with two persons, we can talk to each other, discuss".

This assistance and support was a common theme throughout the comments:

> *My buddy just assists me and helps me a lot. So she [my buddy] tells me if there's something I don't know, just ask her. Sometimes in some classes I have to ask her to explain what the teacher is talking about, or the process. I am really glad and thankful for the buddies.*

Having a buddy to some also meant that they could work as a team:

> *He [my buddy] doesn't have experience with the children like I had experience with children, so I could help him with the children, but he could help me with how to organise my work, put my lesson plan together.*

However as one of the PSTs commented, not all pairs worked in teams.

> *...there was no team work. They were just doing it for themselves, working in competition with each other. This moved on to the others in the school. Everyone started to become more competitive. Even my buddy started to become more competitive. There was a lot of change over the weeks. She started to become a bit rude to me in front of the teachers: "It's your turn now, come on!"*

Buddies, for the international students, were a conduit to understanding the unfamiliar culture of Australian classrooms. However, varying perceptions of ability by some of the Australian PSTs over the period of the practicum lead to a sense of competitiveness.

5.4 Focus Group: Open Group

This group was the largest focus group with 42 PSTs in attendance. Many of their opinions echoed that of the buddied focus group (Sect. 5.1) and tended to support the notion of being paired, especially as this was their first placement: "For first year students and first placement in primary school, it was just a huge support for my buddy and we helped each other a lot". It was also seen as providing support from a peer: "It was really good to have someone at the same level as you so it's not quite as scary because you are not there by yourself being shoved into that situation".

Similar to the buddied focus group (Sect. 5.1), the reasons for liking the buddy ranged from personal, learning and professional understanding, and for some PSTs multiple reasons, for example:

> *Initially when I found out we were going to have buddies in the classroom with us I was a little bit disappointed... in the end I ended up loving it because I actually felt more confident more than I probably would have done on my own in the classroom. I would have really ... I could stand up there and I could do the questioning and I really felt a lot more confident. We did things that I probably wouldn't have done otherwise. I found it really good.*
>
> *I spent the first week with a buddy, I spent the second week alone and I did not like that at all. It was, I just, it was all right, it was good because I got more opportunities to learn but I didn't have that person to lean on and sort of help me through it all as well.*

An issue that didn't arise in any of the other focus groups was around self-imposed comparisons when buddied. For example, one PST commented:

> During class time I found that I would watch my buddy and how he interacted with the kids and I would kind of reflect on myself. So I was constantly comparing myself ... I thought he was a little bit more ahead. So, I was like all right, how can I, you know, change my teaching so I'm on par with him.

In a similar vein, another noted:

> I found at certain times I would again watch my buddy and how she was reacting and I'd kind of sometimes I'd feel, I think the kids like her a little bit better or they are just becoming a little bit more attached or she's acting more natural and fluent with them than I am.

As with the other groups, there were a number of PSTs who weren't supportive of the buddy model:

> I think in our classroom especially it was very crowded and like its exactly like you have different views and you just go about things totally differently ... I would much prefer to just like for the first day sit back and be able to watch the teacher interacting with the student.

Again, however, the issue of uneven relationships with a buddy arose:

> My buddy was lovely. It's nothing against her but having years of experience in early childhood and teaching we weren't on the same level. And although she was here to support me and that was great and if I had a question that was fine, but working together we had very different views and I get that that's a great introduction into teaching because there will always be somebody in your teaching staff that is different, but different levels of professionalism, different levels of what I would expect from a buddy and what I expect to be as a buddy.

The findings demonstrate that the relationships between buddies are complex and variable. Focus group data suggests that a number felt that buddying had advantages such as overcoming the sense of isolation, providing support and being able to share ideas and debrief on lessons with peers rather than teacher mentors. Others were less favourable. The issue of whether PSTs should be able to choose their buddy generated considerable discussion. Focus group data also suggested that working in a pair, or even in a group, requires more support and planning than was originally assumed. However, a number of themes arose that need further discussion (see Sect. 6) to better understand this innovation being utilised in a first year placement.

6 Discussion

6.1 Buddy Up: Learning Potential

This study reinforces much of the research around the benefits of pairing PSTs for placement as identified in the literature.

Many of the PSTs in this study felt that the paired placement allowed them to share problems, concerns and worries with a person in the same situation who was not assessing them (Smith, 2004) and they valued the support of a peer (Gardiner & Robinson, 2010). This support came in multiple forms: practical support, "picking me up from the bus"; personal support, "I felt more confident"; supporting reflective practice, "just to clarify my views"; and support with learning. This was similar to King's (2006) research that found that pairing students increased confidence, provided a peer to share problems, the highs and lows of the classroom, and to share resources.

Some PSTs reported that they learned vicariously from watching each other teach (Smith, 2004) and provided different perspectives about the teaching process, "I hadn't thought about it like that before" and helped each other take pedagogical risks, "we did things that I probably wouldn't have done otherwise" (Gardiner & Robinson, 2010). It seemed that working in pairs provided PSTs with an additional layer of support that enabled them to make meaning from their early teaching experiences; "it's not quite as scary." Working in pairs also helped them gain confidence in their ability as teachers and they began to see themselves as teachers as they engaged in learning conversations with their partners (Harlow & Cobb, 2014). This may not have been the case if they had been placed alone with their mentor as research has found that often the dialogue between PSTs and their mentors tends to be "directive and focused on pragmatic tasks, such as which lessons to teach, what to do to differently next time" (Gardiner & Robinson, 2010, p. 204). There was evidence that some PSTs engaged in more open-ended brainstorming and problem solving as well as feedback on each other's teaching. This may be because the peer relationship is more equal than the mentor/student relationship and the peers were more comfortable questioning and analysing each other's teaching than they would be engaging in similar talk with their mentor teacher (Gardiner & Robinson, 2010). This was evident in comments where PSTs felt they might "annoy" their mentor with questions and concerns but felt more "on the same level" as a peer.

6.2 Buddy Up: Transition Potential

The buddy approach, set within learning communities of students placed in schools and taught by a school-based tutor, supports elements of a transition pedagogy. The innovation supported social networks amongst first-year PSTs and many of the students spoke about how the intimacy of buddying up acted to promote close bonds and a sense of belonging to a community of learners in ways that larger, university tutorial classes may not have supported.

The focus group with the most positive views about the buddy system was the international focus group. International students, particularly those from non-Western backgrounds, face significant challenges that can impede their successful transition to their new university environment (Goldingay et al., 2014). Teacher education students can struggle with communication issues, cultural differences, financial burdens, heavy workloads and difficulty in developing relationships with local students. This can lead to high levels of anxiety. One of the benefits of the new first year program is that, whilst on placement, international students are with students who are familiar with the culture of Australian classrooms and, through peer and group discussions both formally and informally, support is there for the international students to understand and interpret what they were seeing and experiencing.

6.3 Buddy Up: Potential for Competition

Pairing worked well when both PSTs had a positive attitude to learning, were respectful and helpful towards each other and the teaching staff (Walsh & Elmslie, 2005) and perceived each other as being on relatively equal footing (Gardiner & Robinson, 2010). However, competitive individualism (Schniewind & Davidson, 1998) emerged in some instances. Being buddied made it difficult for some PSTs to avoid comparison, either overtly or covertly, "I was constantly comparing myself". They buddying system was less successful where there were perceived differences in ability, either academic or practical; "we weren't on the same level" which created a sense of competition (King, 2006). Perceptions of disparity emerged from a PSTs' comparison of their own performance and ability with their buddy's, or if one PST perceived that the teacher mentor favoured their partner over them, or had not created a balance of individual and shared learning experiences within the classroom. Feelings of competition and comparison (Walsh & Elmslie, 2005) also emerged in relation to assessments. Tensions sometimes arose where PSTs were encouraged to work as a team but were assessed individually.

Universities often pre-suppose that students arrive with the maturity and skills necessary to work in a professional setting with peers, but such skills are rarely explicitly taught. Many first year PSTs generally come from backgrounds where individualism and winning is valued, rather than from a more collectivist or collegial stance.

6.4 Buddy Up: Potential for Teacher Education

While some of the literature tends to report pairing of PSTs for organisational or pragmatic reasons, for example, the relative scarcity of school placements and teacher mentors (King, 2006), in this study they were purposefully paired to support transition and the belief that working together may build "collegiality, peer feedback and socialised knowledge" (Manouchehri, 2002, p. 735). The idea that from first year, we are embedding professional dialogue, peer feedback, working in teams, collaboration and reflective practice in initial teaching education may make it more likely to become a foundation of their practice (King, 2006). However, the focus group data revealed that paired placements present complexities such as unprofessional behaviour, individualised competition and at times seeing peers as a burden. PSTs questioned the random buddying of students and recommended that we spend more time researching personalities and capabilities to engineer more productive buddying. However, setting aside the practical and resource implications from this suggestion, one of the foundations of teaching is working with others, therefore it is imperative that we provide opportunities, especially for first year PSTs, to collaborate and develop these skills. We acknowledge that we have our role to play in preparing them for this challenge. We may have to focus time and energy in teaching collaboration skills, problem solving, active listening, and overcoming personality challenges as this will be a feature when they enter the teaching profession.

7 Conclusion

> So, I guess the constructive criticism would be then for the coordinators to emphasis so no matter who you've been paired with there are positives… because if [they] don't get along with their buddy and they are not working together they could be really … let down, and saying "this sucks I don't get along with this person"… There are always positives… (PST, buddied group)

This chapter provided comment and research around PSTs' perceptions of the buddy model for professional experience using data from four focus groups. The decision to buddy students was based upon the literature around practicum to better facilitate professional conversations and learning that connect theory and practice. It was also informed by the transition to university literature, with calls to foster learning communities and encourage social and professional networks.

The findings from the focus groups offer insights into the complexities involved in buddying PSTs on practicum. Some PSTs felt there were positives including: learning possibilities, professional engagement through dialogue and personal benefits such as increased confidence. Others were less favourable, often citing personality clashes or differences in workplace experience, commitment or knowledge of course requirements as well as competitive individualism. Focus group data suggested that working with a buddy does require a certain skill-set. There is much we can do in an initial teacher education program to support the development of teaching professionals that goes beyond classroom instruction, behaviour management and content. Given the current demands of the teaching profession, we will need to create innovative professional experience models such as buddying to prepare them for the challenges of collaboration. Further, it is necessary that we provide development opportunities for PSTs to learn about themselves and strategies for working with others and the skills to become reflective practitioners.

References

Australian Institute for Teaching and School Leadership (AITSL). (2011). *Accreditation of initial teacher education programs in Australia*. Carlton South. http://www.aitsl.edu.au/docs/default-source/default-document-library/accreditation_of_initial_teacher_education_file. Accessed Oct 2015.

Black, F. M., & MacKenzie, J. (2008). *Quality enhancement themes: The first year experience – Peer support in the first year*. Glasgow, Scotland: The Quality Assurance Agency for Higher Education.

Bovill, C., Bulley, C. J., & Morss, K. (2011). Engaging and empowering first-year students through curriculum design: Perspectives from the literature. *Teaching in Higher Education, 16*(2), 197–209.

Bowles, A., Dobson, A., Fisher, R., & McPhail, R. (2011). An exploratory investigation into first year pre-service teacher transition to university. In K. Krause, M. Buckridge, C. Grimmer, & S. Purbrick-Illek (Eds.), *Research and development in higher education: Reshaping higher education* (Vol. 34, pp. 61–71). Gold Coast, Australia, 4–7 July 2011.

Brown, J. S., Collins, A., & Duguid, P. (1989). Situated cognition and the culture of learning. *Educational Researcher, 18*(1), 32–42.

Commonwealth of Australia. (2007). *Top of the class. Report on the inquiry into teacher education*. http://www.aph.gov.au/parliamentary_business/committees/house_of_representatives_committees?url=evt/teachereduc/report.htm. Accessed May 2015

Darling-Hammond, L. (2010). Teacher education and the American future. *Journal of Teacher Education, 61*(1–2), 35–47. doi:10.1177/0022487109348024

Gardiner, W., & Robinson, K. S. (2010). Partnered field placements: Collaboration in the "real world,". *The Teacher Educator, 45*(3), 202–215. doi:10.1080/08878730.2010.487928

Goldingay, S., Hitch, D., Ryan, J., Farrugia, D., Hosken, N., Lamaro, G., et al. (2014). "The university didn't actually tell us this is what you have to do": Social inclusion through embedding of academic skills in first year professional courses. *The International Journal of the First Year in Higher Education, 5*(1), 43–53. doi:10.5204/intjfyhe.v5i1.194

Grossman, P., Hammerness, K., & McDonald, M. (2009). Redefining teaching, re. *Teachers and Teaching: Theory and Practice, 15*(2), 273–289. doi:10.1080/13540600902875340

Harlow, A., & Cobb, D. J. (2014). Planting the seed of teacher identity: Nurturing early growth through a collaborative learning community. *Australian Journal of Teacher Education, 39*(7), 70–88. doi:10.14221/ajte.2014v39n7.8

Harvey, L., Drew, S., & Smith, M. (2006). *The first-year experience: A review of literature for the Higher Education Academy*. York, UK: Higher Education Academy.

Hillman, K. (2005). *The first year experience: The transition from secondary school to university and TAFE in Australia* (Longitudinal Studies in Australian Youth Research Report No 40). Camberwell, Australia: Australian Council for Educational Research.

James, R., Krause, K., & Jennings, C. (2010). *The first year experience in Australian universities: Findings from 1994 to 2009*. Melbourne, Australia: Centre for the Study of Higher Education, The University of Melbourne. Accessed Sept 2015.

Kift, S., Nelson, K., & Clarke, J. (2010). Transition pedagogy: A third generation approach to FYE – A case study of policy and practice for the higher education sector. *The International Journal of the First Year in Higher Education, 1*(1), 1–20.

King, S. (2006). Promoting paired placements in initial teacher education. *International Research in Geographical and Environmental Education, 15*(4), 370–386. doi:10.2167/irg201.0

Klein, E. J., Taylor, M., Onore, C., Strom, K., & Abrams, L. (2013). Finding a third space in teacher education: Creating an urban teacher residency with Montclair State University and the Newark Public Schools. *Teaching Education, 24*(1), 27–57. doi:10.1080/10476210.2012.711305

Krause, K. (2007). *New perspectives on engaging first year students in learning*. Brisbane, Australia: Griffith Institute for Higher Education.

Kuh, G. D., Cruce, T. M., Shoup, R., Kinzie, J., & Gonyea, R. M. (2008). Unmasking the effects of student engagement on first-year college grades and persistence. *The Journal of Higher Education, 79*(5), 540–643.

Lang, C., Neal, D., Karvouni, M., & Chandler, D. (2015). An embedded professional paired placement model: "I know I am not an expert, but I am at a point now where I could step into the classroom and be responsible for the learning". *Asia-Pacific Journal of Teacher Education, 43*(4), 338–354. doi:10.1080/1359866X.2015.1060296

Lave, J., & Wenger, E. (1991). *Situated learning: Legitimate peripheral participation*. Cambridge, UK: Cambridge University Press.

Le Cornu, R. (2009). *Crossing boundaries: Challenges of academics working in professional experiences*. Refereed paper presented at 'Teacher education crossing borders: Cultures, contexts, communities and curriculum' The Annual Conference of the Australian Teacher Education Association (ATEA), Albury, 28 June–1 July.

Le Cornu, R. (2015). *Key components of effective professional experience in initial teacher education in Australia*. A paper prepared for the Australian Institute for Teaching and School Leadership, http://www.aitsl.edu.au/docs/default-source/initial-teacher-education-resources/aitsl_key-components-of-effective-professional-experience.pdf. Accessed Sept 2015.

Manouchehri, A. (2002). Developing teaching knowledge through peer discourse. *Teaching and Teacher Education, 18*(6), 715–737.

Masters, J., & Donnison, S. (2010). First-year transition in teacher education: The pod experience. *Australian Journal of Teacher Education, 35*(2), 87–98.

Mattson, M., Eilertsen, T. V., & Rossison, D. (2011). *A practicum turn in teacher education*. Rotterdam: SENSE.

McInnis, C., James, R., & Hartley, R. (2000). *Trends in the first year experience in Australian universities*. Canberra: Department of Education, Training & Youth Affairs. Retrieved from http://www.cshe.unimelb.edu.au/downloads/FYEReport05KLK.pdf.

Reason, R. D., Terenzini, P. T., & Domingo, R. J. (2007). Developing social and personal competence in the first year of college. *The Review of Higher Education, 30*(3), 271–299.

Schniewind, N., & Davidson, E. (1998). *Open minds to equality: A sourcebook of learning activities to affirm diversity and promote equality*. Needham Heights, MA: Allyn & Bacon.

Smith, J. D. N. (2004). Developing paired teaching placements. *Educational Action Research, 12*(1), 99–125.

Teacher Education Ministerial Advisory Group (TEMAG). (2014). *Action now: Classroom ready teachers*. https://docs.education.gov.au/system/files/doc/other/action_now_classroom_ready_teachers_accessible.pdf. Accessed Sept 2015.

Tinto, V. (1993). *Leaving college: Rethinking the causes and cures of student attrition* (2nd ed.). Chicago: The University of Chicago Press.

Ure, C., Gough, A., & Newton, R. (2009, October). *Practicum partnerships: Exploring models of practicum organisation in teacher education for a standards-based profession final report*. Strawberry Hills, NSW: Australian Learning and Teaching Council. http://www.altc.edu.au/project-practicum-partnerships-exploring-melbourne-2009.

Vygotsky, L. S. (1978). *Mind in society: The development of higher sociological processes*. Cambridge, MA: Harvard University Press.

Walsh, K., & Elmslie, L. (2005). Practicum pairs: An alternative for first filed experience in early childhood teacher education. *Asia-Pacific Journal of Teacher Education, 3*(1), 5–21.

Zeichner, K. (2010). Rethinking the connections between campus courses and field experiences in college- and university-based teacher education. *Journal of Teacher Education, 61*(1–2), 89–99. doi:10.1177/0022487109347671

Reconceptualising First Year Professional Experience: Enacting a Repertoire of Learning Focused Talk for Efficacy in Teaching Practice

Christine J. Edwards-Groves

1 Introduction

> I didn't realise that listening, really listening to the children, was pretty hard. I really had to focus and practise it. So having the chance to interact with the children in small groups gave me the opportunity to interact with a focus and apply theory we have learnt in lectures and workshops. (Melanie, First Year Pre-service Teacher, 2013).

This chapter calls for teacher education programs to reconceptualise approaches for developing and enacting quality pedagogical interactions among pre-service teachers (PSTs). This focus emerged from a concern that research examining what PSTs learn through authentic experiences in classrooms is overwhelmingly dominated by reports on what they learn from supervising teachers. Coupled with this there is a dearth of research specifically investigating what PSTs learn through classrooms interactions with students; an issue of practical concern for education globally (Grossman, Hammerness, & McDonald, 2009; Woodruff & Brett, 1999; Zeichner, 2010). To counter this tendency, the specific innovation reported in this chapter was premised on a need for PSTs to overtly focus on [re]conceptualising the efficacy of pedagogical interactions with students in professional experience classrooms.

A central argument of this chapter is that a focus on classroom talk must be 'designed-in' to teacher education. This attention would provide a strategic pathway for PSTs to understand classroom interaction practices in a strongly reasoned and grounded way. Such a policy direction would ultimately launch practical foundations for developing and implementing quality lessons initially across their teaching degree, but in the longer term form a strong platform for PST's teaching efficacy in their future profession. To make the argument, the chapter draws on findings from a

---

C.J. Edwards-Groves (✉)
School of Education, Charles Sturt University, Wagga Wagga, Australia
e-mail: cgroves@csu.edu.au

© Springer Science+Business Media Singapore 2016
R. Brandenburg et al. (eds.), *Teacher Education*,
DOI 10.1007/978-981-10-0785-9_6

3 year empirical study conducted at a regional Australian university that called for an explicit focus on developing quality classroom interactions and dialogic pedagogies. The overarching emphasis was for PSTs to examine the particular interactive practices or strategic *talk moves* required to achieve the outcomes of the curriculum at the same time create a more dialogic and participatory classroom culture.

This chapter re-theorises the development of quality teaching practices in teacher education by illustrating how a focus on practising interacting with students in classrooms influences what PSTs learn about teaching from listening to and interacting with students in first year school placements. Taking a 360° view, accounts from classroom teacher mentors, teacher educators and PSTs, such as Melanie in the opening quote, will be presented as illustrative empirical material that suggests that learning teaching practices is not only informed but formed through interrogating the theory-practice nexus *in enactment* (Edwards-Groves, 2014a).

2 Research Context

The research is set against both a political context and a social context. Politically, teacher education is increasingly subject to and challenged by standardised neoliberal approaches characterised by a globally-influenced, accountability-driven, performative culture. Socially, teacher education is entrenched within a media climate that pushes education towards a 'back to basics' line in the quest to raise the quality of teaching, sometimes at the expense of creativity and innovation. However, to understand teaching as it is developed there is a pressing need to understand that it is fundamentally anchored in sociality.

The sociality of teaching is well documented. In fact, the essence of teaching has long been associated with language and interaction (Bakhtin, 1981; Mehan, 1979). The role of teacher-student talk in classrooms has been the topic of educational research for many decades, and connections between teacher talk and student's learning have been well researched (Alexander, 2008; Barnes, 1976; Cazden, 2001; Edwards & Westgate, 1987; Freiberg & Freebody, 1995). Despite the attention pedagogical talk receives in academic and professional literature, there have been relatively modest impacts on the interactive practices of teachers (Fisher, 2010). This may well be because explicit instruction about the role of talk as a pedagogical tool receives little prioritised space in teacher education. Consequently, this lack of attention often leaves PSTs to interact with students in classroom lessons in a default mode of practice based on replicating known or 'remembered' patterns of interaction from their own schooling (Love, 2009). Such default practices (seemingly more traditional, didactic, prescribed, teacher dominated talk) limit the scope for student participation in their lessons and so, in their learning. What is needed is a new default; one that shifts thinking and practice-in-action towards a more dialogic and participatory approach.

3 An Overview of the "Talking to Learn" Research and Innovation

The *Talking to Learn* was an intervention designed to raise the profile of classroom interaction as critical for producing lesson talk with highly focused intellectual rigor. In the project, first year Bachelor of Education PSTs were guided by teacher educators and classroom teacher mentors to pay explicit attention to the details and patterns of discourse in teacher-student exchanges. The focus on interaction practices-in-interaction is critical since it is at this level of granularity that the ways that classroom talk works pedagogically is made visible.

The project involved five layers of *talking to learn*: first, PSTs learned about classroom talk and interaction; second, they observed and listened to talk between teachers and students in classrooms; third, PSTs observed talk between students; fourth, they practised, initially in pairs, interacting with small groups of four to five students in classrooms; and, fifth, they participated in mentoring conversations. Each layer was interconnected in its underlying focus to provide PSTs with opportunities to:

1. participate in overt instruction about classroom interaction and the role of talk for learning;
2. focus their observations on the teacher's repertoire of interaction practices in classrooms;
3. listen to students;
4. develop their own quality dialogic practices through authentic, situated interaction experiences with small groups of students;
5. talk with peers and classroom teacher mentors in mentoring conversations involving focused reflection, feedback and debriefing (adapted from Timperley, 2001); and to
6. systematically monitor and record evidence of individual learning (Edwards-Groves & Hoare, 2012).

Specifically, PSTs focused on how lessons unfolded interactionally to pay attention to particular pedagogical "talk moves" (Edwards-Groves, 2014b) that influenced classroom learning experiences.[1] This formed the basis for feedback offered in mentoring conversations centred on how teachers *and* PSTs:

- Engaged in whole class, small group and individual interactions
- Focused on building dialogue
- Invited students to sustain and extend responses
- Encouraged other children to expand on the responses of others
- Demonstrated active listening by reframing, repeating or revoicing
- Allowed appropriate wait time for thinking and rehearsing

---

[1] This focus was initially based on the collective work of Alexander (2008), Churchill et al. (2010) and Anderson, Chapin, and O'Connor (2011).

- Gave timely and learning focused feedback
- Provided specific [and stage appropriate] curriculum information
- 'Vacated the floor' so students had opportunities to direct their talk, and
- Enabled reflection

Prior to the in-school experience, volunteer classroom teacher mentors participated in three 2 h workshops conducted by participating university academics (including the author). These sessions focused on classroom interaction, enacting dialogic approaches for classroom participation and facilitating mentoring conversations.

4 Aims/Objectives

This chapter aims to illustrate the nature and extent of PSTs learning about dialogic teaching from observing, listening to and interacting with students in classrooms. Research examining the development of a repertoire of classroom interaction practices among PSTs is limited. Indeed, research reporting on PSTs observations of teaching interactions appears to be mainly located in analysing videoed lessons (Xio, 2013), or in lessons focused on mathematics (Harkness & Wachenheim, 2008) or music (Haston & Russell, 2012). This chapter argues that unless teacher educators directly lead PSTs to look deeply beyond the surface level 'activity' of classroom teaching and view interactive practices as the object of overt instructional focus, understandings about effective pedagogy will simply remain superficial (Edwards-Groves, 1999).

5 Background Literature

Classroom talk, in practice, remains a taken-for-granted routinised dimension of the everyday activity of the classroom.

> But herein lies the key point, it is so commonplace, so regular, so ordinary and mundane that as teachers we often take-for-granted its purposes, its power and its position in pedagogy. We often neglect to consider it as our practice – and as a core practice – so it slides into the background as a focus of our deliberate reflection, critique and development. (Edwards-Groves, Anstey & Bull, 2014, p. v)

In one way, its everyday*ness* has rendered classroom talk to be rarely the subject of overt, continuing and in-depth focus in teacher education courses. Indeed, 'if students [PSTs] are striving after a form of knowledge, which they believe to be 'out there', rather than mutually constructed [through talk], and subject to change, they may well undervalue dialogue as a cognitive stepping-stone and fail to use it in practice' (Fisher, 2010, p. 38). So, to claim a focus on purposeful classroom talk within the realm of teacher education, this section will foreground its purposes, its power and its position as an important pedagogical resource for enacting quality teaching. As this chapter argues, if as suggested by decades of research it is important for teaching and learning, then purposeful classroom talk must hold a central place in teacher education programs. This section will describe:

- the sociality of teaching and learning,
- the nature of classroom talk,
- talk as a pedagogical resource; and
- mentoring conversations for learning teaching practice.

5.1 The Sociality of Teaching and Learning: Intersubjectivity, Interaction and Interrelationships

Participating in interaction is a locally produced social accomplishment among speakers and hearers (like teachers and students). In these interactions teachers and students encounter one another in intersubjective spaces as interlocutors (or co-participants in dialogues), in interactions and in interrelationships (Kemmis et al., 2014). These intersubjective spaces form particular communicative avenues for participating in lessons that unfold in moment-by-moment teacher-student interactions (Barnes, 1976). From this, lessons are evolving interactive events (Edwards-Groves, 1999) comprised of simultaneously constituted language, activities and relationships that, as a social enterprise, take place in:

- *semantic space* whereby through 'sayings' a shared language, in which meanings are shared and mutually understood in talk exchanges, is possible;
- *physical space-time* whereby through 'doings' in shared locations and activities in space and time are possible; and,
- *social space* whereby through 'relatings' shared encounters with others afford different kinds of interrelationships, roles, agency and power are possible. (Kemmis et al., 2014)

These spaces are always and ever interconnected, intertwined and mutually constitutive; each forming, reforming and transforming the space of the other. As lessons unfold in these three spatial-temporal dimensions teachers and students encounter one another in an interlocutory activity of meaning making that simultaneously creates the social-political context in which they rely (Edwards & Furlong, 1979). As meaning makers, participants in interactions orient towards one another and the world through language as a mechanism to come to shared understandings about, or make sense of, what one another is saying, doing or how they are relating to each other and the world. To accomplish lessons, teachers and students use language to make sense of and to comprehend what is necessary and relevant to the particular classroom context, community and discipline at the moment of enactment; thus forming a discourse that is shared, mutually produced and understood.

5.2 The Nature of Classroom Talk: Language Games, Learning and Lessons

Participating in classroom talk is distinctive from participating in everyday conversations. Decades of research into the nature of classroom talk have identified a number of patterned ways language is used to orient teachers and students towards one another and the world (in their lessons). Lesson talk is easily recognisable by its dominant three-part turn-taking exchange system described as the Initiation-Response-Feedback (IRF) structure (Mehan, 1978; Sinclair & Coulthard, 1975). Typically teachers orchestrate the IRF by taking the first turn formulated as an initiating question (I); the second turn is generally allocated to students to respond (R); the third turn generally returns to the teacher who provides feedback or an evaluation (F). As a result the IRF creates an exchange structure that provides two turns for teachers and one for students; and it is the teacher who generally controls who gets a turn to talk, the development of a topic and what counts as relevant to it (Cazden, 2001). Consequently, lesson-talk "involves a largely subordinate communicative role in which turns are allocated by the teacher" (Edwards & Westgate, 1987, p. 175).

Classroom talk is characterised by other distinctively patterned and routinised social exchange systems, for example 'asking pseudo questions and right-answer seeking' (Edwards & Westgate, 1987) or 'trial and collect' (Freiberg & Freebody, 1995).[2] These patterns, forming recognisable classroom "language games" (Wittgenstein, 1958)[3], often limit scope for extending thinking, displaying reasoning and exercising initiative through discussion or dialogue (Alexander, 2008). Noting, that the IRF structure remains the default pattern of classroom talk; its place in organising students behaviourally and socially is undisputed.[4] In fact, it is considered important for managing instructional interactions. Nonetheless, it remains a covert taken-for-granted pattern in classroom talk. In its most basic form, it can lead to a very teacher-centric pattern of interaction unless deliberate *and* conscious moves are made by the teacher to achieve more dialogic practices rather than monologic or teacher dominated talk.

---

[2] Note: for a fuller description see Edwards-Groves, Anstey, & Bull, 2014.

[3] According to Wittgenstein (1958) a language game is a shared, collective, intersubjective achievement involving one or more interlocutors who share broad 'forms of life' (like particular teachers and students participating in a particular lesson in a particular classroom).

[4] Note: It is not the intention of the author to criticise the IRF (it forms an important, and possibly necessary, organisational mechanism for teaching); the intention is to raise consciousness of its *taken-for-grantedness* and the constraints it can put on creating dialogic and participatory classroom interactions.

5.3 Dialogic Talk as a Pedagogical Resource

Dialogic talk is considered a pedagogical resource that promotes thinking and learning (Mercer & Littleton, 2007) with exchange structures that lead classroom interaction to be collective, reciprocal, supportive and inclusive, purposeful and explicit, cumulative and reflective (Alexander, 2008, p. 37–43). At its most influential, it opens up the communicative space to build currency that supports students to use language more flexibly, productively and purposefully (Edwards-Groves, 2014b). More dialogic approaches give students opportunities to vocalise, organise their thoughts into coherent utterances, hear how their thinking sounds out loud, listen to how others respond, and hear others add to or expand on their thinking (Anderson et al., 2011); making thinking and learning empirically visible.

To develop participatory lessons, Edwards-Groves et al. (2014) outlined particular dialogic *talk moves* that build in interactive mechanisms that enable students to learn through both vocalising and listening (see pp. 88–105). Teacher practices such as pressing for reasoning, repeating and revoicing (O'Connor & Michaels, 1996), allowing wait time, using open ended questioning and vacating the floor to allow student-student interactions, "reduces unsubstantiated illogical reasoning and opens up the possibility for multiple interpretations to be explored and challenged, minimises risk and error, and expedites the 'handover' of concepts and principles" (Alexander, 2008, p. 103). Such practices form new language games that produce more rigorous, academically enriched, purposeful lesson talk that can accomplish high intellectual engagement. It is argued that PSTs need to be explicitly taught and then practice enacting these.

5.4 Mentoring Conversations for Learning Teaching

Edwards (1995) suggested that mentoring is "the constant zigzag of action and discussion with someone more expert in the practice" providing a platform for PSTs to

> translate their experiences into frames provided by public knowledge and to acquire the more powerful language frameworks so that they become insiders in the professional discourse and able to articulate it and keep it public and open to scrutiny rather than tacit or private (p. 598)

From this, mentoring conversations have been defined as both

> dialogic and pedagogical. It is a communicative and transformative practice whereby two or more people engage in learning conversations facilitated by an experienced other. These conversations are focused on learning, are critical in nature, based on evidence from experiences and actions, are accountable for making connections between theory and practice and involve timely responsive feedback and collaborative goal setting. The intersubjective dimensions of mentoring practice – their sayings, doings and relatings – are coherent and comprehensible to each interactive participant. (Edwards-Groves, 2014a, p. 163)

Therefore, facilitating mentoring conversations 'specifically focused' (Hudson, 2004) on classroom dialogue requires conversations that are:

(i) *critical* – whereby PSTs are challenged to be analytic, to justify or interpret, extend and critique their own and others' actions and responses;
(ii) *focused on learning* – whereby PSTs are led beyond arbitrary descriptions of practice to examine their actions and interactions about:

   (a) the learning of students in classrooms, and
   (b) their learning as novice teachers.

(iii) *based on evidence* – whereby dialogues are substantive and utilise evidentiary talk (connected to authentic actions and interactions as experiences) to exemplify learning and extrapolate meanings;
(iv) *connected to theory* – whereby conversations are framed as being accountable to the professional discourse supporting PSTs to become insiders to the profession as they translate practices into language, activities and concepts informed by theory; and
(v) *responsive* – whereby timely feedback is provided and space is created for collaborative goal setting. (Edwards-Groves, 2014a, p. 163)

This chapter maintains that to be instructive, mentoring conversations conducted with classroom teacher mentors need to accompany the learning encountered in teacher education courses in the university setting. As interdependent learning contexts, both are pivotal in leading PSTs (through collaboration, support and guidance) towards the development of knowledge and skills in interpreting, critiquing and adapting interactive practices for themselves (Edwards-Groves & Hoare, 2012).

6 Theoretical Framework

Participating in classroom practices requires coherence and comprehensibility among the interactive participants about *what counts* as relevant at the time; that is, at the moment of saying particular things, doing particular things and relating to others in particular ways *in practice*. From this, the chapter is positioned within the realm of practice theory and draws on the theory of practices architectures (Kemmis et al., 2014) which seeks to describe, in fine-grained ways, the practices, arrangements and spaces that influence and shape teaching and learning as it happens in particular sites in particular ways.

6.1 The Theory of Practice Architectures

The theory of practices architectures (Kemmis et al., 2014)[5] pays close attention to the details of practices formed by interconnected sayings, doings and relatings. It attends to the interconnectedness between the dimensions of language, work and interrelational power found in particular intersubjective spaces where people meet one another. Kemmis and colleagues 2014 propose that broader education practice fields – like teacher education, teaching and student learning – are comprised of other constitutive practices that are always organised, informed and shaped by three kinds of mutually influential and interconnected practice architectures:

1. *cultural-discursive* arrangements formed in semantic space and relate to *sayings*, thinkings, language and discourse,
2. *material-economic* arrangements formed in physical space-time and relate to *doings*, activities, material resources and the organisation of physical set-ups, and
3. *social-political* arrangements formed in social space, and relates to *relatings*, interrelationships, power, solidarity and agency. (Kemmis et al., 2014)

These arrangements are always interconnected and overlapping (also described by Kemmis et al. as *enmeshed*).

The theory of practice architectures is fundamentally an ontological approach (after Schatzki, 2002) that emphasises that practices, like teaching and learning, need to be understood in relation to the place where they happen. These places (like classrooms) are distinctive, particular, unique and peculiar and because of this, the practices that take place there are also distinctive, particular, unique and peculiar.

7 Methodology

The study was a three-year qualitative research conducted by a regional university in New South Wales, Australia, in partnership with a local school system. The study (reported in Edwards-Groves & Hoare, 2012) investigated the implementation of the *Talking to Learn* project, outlined in Section 3 above.

Data collection periods were mainly in the first semester in each year of the study. Semi-structured focus group interviews (Mertens, 1998) were conducted with volunteer PSTs, classroom teachers and academics at the end of the semester. Interviews were audio-recorded and transcribed to build participant accounts and

---

[5] The description of theory of practice architectures presented in this chapter is a necessarily brief and somewhat malnourished account of the theory; a fully articulated description can be found in Springer text:

Kemmis, S., Wilkinson, J., Edwards-Groves, C., Hardy, I., Grootenboer, P. & Bristol, L. (2014). *Changing Practices, Changing Education*. Singapore: Springer

associated attributions of participant experiences and explanations of the interactive practices in focus (Freebody, 2003). Over the three-year period, total participants included 346 PSTs (participating in the in-class program) of which 24 PSTs (arranged in pairs) volunteered to video-record their small group interactions with students in classrooms. Other participants included 16 classroom teachers, six teacher educators and all PSTs who participated in the final survey.

Classroom teachers and volunteer PSTs were issued with a small recorder (Flip Camera) for the duration of the study to record classroom observations, mentoring conversations and small-group interactions. Additionally, all PSTs recorded their ongoing experiences, insights and learning in a reflection journal. Informed consent was given by participating PSTs, teachers, principals, students, care-givers and teacher educators.

8 Analysis and Discussion

This section draws on selected excerpts from the corpus including semi-structured focus groups with PSTs, and interviews with classroom teachers and teacher educators. These excerpts are typical of the accounts offered by others in each group. Thematic analysis of participant accounts reveals four central points: observing and learning to listen, practising and learning to interact, the role of mentoring conversations and what this means for reconceptualising teaching as interactive practice. All names are pseudonyms.

8.1 Observing and Learning to Listen

Focused observations of classroom lessons, with the specific intention of listening to teacher-student interactions emerged as pivotal for PSTs conceptualising and framing views about what teaching entails. PST comments such as "I didn't realise that really listening to the children was so hard. I really had to focus and practice it" (Bethany) directly connected to the value placed on intentional listening within the realm of developing listening pedagogies (Egan, 2009). For PSTs, it emerged as a dynamic aspect of learning about teaching. Like Bethany, Harrison (next) identified that listening was harder than he had expected:

> By listening to their responses [to teacher's questions], straight away I realised I would need to work on my vocabulary and not to talk down to these students. I didn't realise they knew so much; their knowledge was very impressive. (Harrison)

Their realisations oriented to the importance of listening for learning (Zyngier, 2007); and that they had to practise it. For them, listening emerged as a personal resource for developing a strong foundation for understanding student knowledge. This insight is mirrored by Charlise and Ryan who acknowledged the need to treat students' knowledge and contributions to classroom discussions as genuine resources for advancing learning and thinking.

> For me active listening was a key to how much I learnt. I actually had to learn to listen to them with more careful precision ... I completely underestimated how much they already knew and could do ... I[need to] listen with intent. (Charlise)
>
> Through listening I learnt I really need to build on what they know; they know so much already. It completely changed my view that I just give them the content. (Ryan)

For these PSTs, learning about teaching, learning to teach and enacting teaching required listening to be developed as a pedagogical practice. Listening to student's responses oriented PST's thinking towards clarifying the pedagogical meanings attributed to classroom practices. As Ryan's comment illustrates, listening reconceptualised his view about the nature of pedagogy "that [he] really needs to build on what they know", and of teaching in that he "completely changed [his] view that [he] gives them the content". Their comments show genuine engagement with listening as a pedagogical practice that develops responsivity.

8.2 *Practising and Learning to Interact*

In this study, practising and learning to interact was enabled by changing the broader intersubjective spaces in which PSTs encountered students and mentor teachers. PSTs had early experiences to observe classroom interactions and practice interacting with group groups of students in classrooms with the focus on interacting rather than waiting for a later formal placement then being assessed on their teaching. Accounts below offer personal insights into their understandings and experiences "practising" pedagogical talk.

> Authentic interactions in classrooms are the only way to truly gain an understanding of the role of teacher talk in children's learning; it allows you to experience it. For me I didn't really get that the interactions were so important; I had to work at it. (Joel)
>
> Engaging in classroom interaction ... helped me understand and relate to the theory we do... You can put things like open questions and wait time into practice and observe the real impact it has as you are doing it... you don't realise until you are actually in the classroom interacting with children that you get a real sense of what that means for their learning. (Elana)

Empirically, their comments highlight shifting understandings among first year PSTs about the value they placed on firstly, 'actually' practising interacting with students in classrooms; and secondly, how they attributed much of what they had learned about teaching to learning to listen and interact with students. For example, Elana and Joel clearly recognised that through their practice-in-action they came to know that different types of classroom talk practices do different kinds of pedagogical work. In general it was found that the many underlying beliefs held by PSTs about what teaching actually entailed were re-conceptualised, summed up by Oliver, who stated "It wasn't as easy as I thought; I had to really practise and work on it, how hard would it be to talk to kids. I was surprised by that."

8.3 Understanding the Repertoire of Dialogic Practices Through Mentoring Conversations

Mentoring conversations provided the collaborative and communicative space for PSTs to deepen understandings about the repertoire of dialogic practices. Through their interactions with peers and their mentor teacher, PSTs were guided to interpret, critically reflect on and evaluate their practice development within this interdependent relationship (Darwin, 2000). This arrangement formed a distinctive relational space between PSTs and mentors that over time enabled their 'practice' to be refined and developed in connection to theory. Importantly, PSTs recognised the democratic and collaborative nature of the mentoring practices being likened to "being in a team" as Tom pointed to below:

Tom: Working with Andrea was like being in a team, with no judgement… through the mentoring I learnt I need to ask more open questions … allow the students to take the floor … get them to talk amongst themselves… they learn and grow in knowledge with each other, the student who understands can solidify their own knowledge and for the student who does not, they may learn from their friend.

Characterising Tom's mentoring experiences were collaborative social-political arrangements that enabled him to "practise without judgement". For him, this enabled the development of specific ideas about questioning and the reciprocity between students' learning as they interacted with one another. These practice architectures were instrumental for forming practical knowledge about the repertoire of classroom talk practices; there was a direct interconnection between practising, mentoring and learning.

Learning about the range of interactive mechanisms for developing engaging teaching and learning practices were interconnected with mentoring feedback; a point reinforced in the next extract.

Ruby: … focusing on the different ways the teacher gets the kids involved was so important. Like how my mentor got the kids to explain more about the topic; just saying things like "tell me more about that" was so easy; it really got the kids talking. Then discussing it with him [teacher mentor] after made it make so much sense because he could explain the difference it made to the kids learning; I could see it actually.

Mary: The whole feedback thing was … the most important part … it helped me to know where to improve in things like "wait time"… it was based on what I was doing…and we didn't have the pressure of being formally assessed.

Hamish: The mentoring helped encourage and support us in how they [mentors] observed how we worked with students … I could really understand why thinking and talking about talk was so important for student's learning.

Encouragement and support were recognised by Hamish to be an important characteristic of the kind of mentor feedback "which assisted them to really understand" (Hamish) "the difference it made to the kid's learning" (Ruby). Such responses illustrated PST's acknowledgement that focused and timely feedback offered in the mentoring conversations enabled consideration be given "why thinking and talking about talk was so important for student's learning". PSTs attended to the distinctive ways their mentor used talk for different pedagogical outcomes, for instance, using wait time for thinking or having students explain or extend their point further.

Classroom teacher mentors also valued the focus on interaction in mentoring conversations as a space for learning about teaching. As suggested by Edwards-Groves (2014), practising and critically reflecting on their experiences is a central goal for mentoring conversations; a point highlighted by teacher mentor Andrea in this interview extract:

> ... their questioning had developed by the end of the eight weeks,... they were able to draw the information out of the kids without telling them what to put on the page... At the start you could see them thinking about how they were going to say things ... when they were questioning it was a lot of leading questions, they were giving the children answers ... and a lot of them picked up on that after the first day, like they were saying "oh my gosh I can't believe I even asked that question"...
> One thing about the process was that we had time, time to learn, time to practise, and time to adjust their practices...

Andrea suggested that time and regularity were influential factors for enabling the development of particular kinds of dialogic practices (described earlier by PSTs). PSTs needed time to translate their practical interaction experiences into the professional discourse (Edwards, 1995) and so enter the shared discourse or 'sayings' of dialogic teaching. Andrea continued:

> It was really interesting watching their teaching growth ... at the same time it was about them talking directly about what they experienced and trying to use professional ways to describe it...
> By the end ... [mentoring conversations] were becoming a lot more open, everyone was contributing and it was a real conversation... which after time...they were able to take the theory and then try it ... put it into practice ... apply it ... it was a real cycle of action, reflection and change...They could begin to understand what teaching is really about.

Andrea oriented to the reciprocity between her actions as a mentor and those of the PSTs. She acknowledged their shared roles and suggested the close interconnectivity between her expert support and their openness to learn. Her comments also point to both the pedagogical nature of the conversations and the complexity of "learning to interact with children in classrooms" at the same time to "learning to participate in the conversations" whilst taking on the professional discourse to describe their experiences. Andrea also recognised that participating in "real conversations" that were both dialogic and analytic, grounded in the evidence of their practical experiences and involved an increasingly reflexive relationship between university and classroom contexts.

8.4 Reconceptualising Teaching as Interactive Practice

To conceptualise their understandings of the sociality of pedagogy, PSTs observed, practised, reflected on and analysed classroom practice in and through site-based interactions; that is, at the "primordial" level of teaching (Freiberg & Freebody,

1995). As PSTs observed teaching practices in action and then practised listening to and interacting with students, they reconceptualised what constituted teaching and learning. This is highlighted in Dylan's comment:

> Being in the classroom and really focusing on how the teacher organises the talk is so important, it really gave me confidence to have a go myself without being in the formal practicum situation. Now I really have a feel for teaching and what difference talk makes to kid's learning. (Dylan)

Here Dylan explicitly articulated his shift in perspective about the role of teacher talk and its direct connection to learning. Responses from PSTs in a focus group interview (below) illustrated the development of understandings about the intricate and consequential patterns of classroom interactions.

Belle: I couldn't believe how the different prompts the teacher used changed what kids said, I never thought about that part of it before. Simple things like how she asked them to explain more about their ideas

Harry: It's about getting kids to talk more

Terry: I noticed when the students work in groups or pairs they all work together, bouncing ideas off each other... it really encourages them to talk and to listen to each other.

Claudia: I think that might have something to do with Andrea's teaching style ... like she vacates the floor... And like she'll say like 'what are the biggest challenges facing Antarctica?' and these kids are just bam, bam, bam, and they're all just building on each other's points.

Terry: And there's no hands, there's no waiting, there's just give us all your knowledge, share it.

Claudia: ... you know when you've asked a good question you just don't get a word in because they just keep building on each other's knowledge and I'm thinking, my teacher is going to think the kids do all the talking and I'm doing nothing ((all laughing))...

Dane: I think the knee-to-knee is actually a good way the teacher 'vacates the floor' and gives all the kids the chance to talk, give their opinion, say what they have learned. I was honestly amazed about how different it was.

Matt: At the start I did all the talking, I thought that was my job. But the thing I learnt from Andrea was with the 'no hands up' ... ' I was amazed it worked at all.' was like the children were actually learning a lot of things that a lot of people our age don't even know how to do, and that's just wait for somebody else to finish speaking before they come in and speak... and they were very good at it, and they sat there silently and let this person speak ... They're getting it, to know when they can go and speak without cutting the other person off, and so you could tell they were really listening to each other; that's part of language for the rest of your life...

Across this excerpt, PSTs oriented to different ways classroom talk worked. For them, teaching was bound up with practice architectures; that is, PSTs identified the interconnectedness between the 'sayings' or discourse (the language structures or what was spoken e.g. Antarctica), the 'doings' or physical set-ups (group work or sitting knee-to-knee partner work), and the 'relatings' or the social-political arrangements (by talking in pairs or small groups, taking turns, sharing knowledge).

PSTs oriented to the construction of purpose-built teaching-learning exchanges (Freebody, 2003, p. 127). For instance they could distinguish between the different ways turn-taking was managed; for example, some students were organised to turn 'knee-to-knee'; others experienced the 'no hands up' approach; others applied wait time or open-ended questions. Others identified that *because* the teacher 'vacated the floor' students were mobilised to build on each other's points and share knowledge. These comments form reconceptualisations about teaching and learning interactive practices with important implications for their formation as teachers.

9 Reconceptualising First Year Professional Experience

The innovation reported in this chapter overtly centred on changing the practice architectures in teacher education by re-designing opportunities for PSTs to examine the development of the "language games" associated with teaching (Edwards & Westgate, 1987). Through a focus on classroom interaction and dialogic pedagogies (Churchill et al., 2011; Eilam & Poyas, 2009), engaging in classroom observations, practising or rehearsing (Ball & Forzani, 2010), and participating in mentoring conversations (Timperley, 2001), PSTs formed particular intersubjective mechanisms for understanding the role of talk for learning in teaching. Re-designed practices provided an authentic context for 'informed participation' in learning about teaching (Edwards, Gilroy, & Hartley, 2004) that provoked reconceptualised notions of what constitutes teaching.

Results revealed that PSTs experiences overtly shifted towards understanding the sociality of classroom practice by (i) treating classroom talk (theoretically) as a pedagogical resource that leads learning in lessons to be active and participatory, and (ii) enacting pedagogies (practically) that facilitate deeper engagement with curriculum. Through their experiences, PSTs were guided to interpret not just their observations (as in Hennissen, Crasborn, Brouwer, Korthagen, & Bergen, 2011) but connect their practical in-practice experiences to particular theoretical frameworks for teaching, acknowledged in Sarah's comment:

> When I am doing my reading I think, 'I saw that happening'. I could see how the teacher tried to bring them in through her talk, and I could see how group work really helped the children talk and learn from each other. Now that I have seen it, practised it and can understand it, and it has helped me write more critically about it.

By drawing on demonstrations, the enactment of practices and guided by the expertise of experienced classroom teachers PSTs were explicitly able to connect classroom experiences directly with their university learning and the realities of their future profession. As Patrick, the teacher mentor, indicated, "practising interacting prepared PSTs with the basics … to develop their understanding of how to respond differently to each child, and how to talk and act *for* student learning". The program recognizably contributed to the PSTs ability to communicate professionally; expressed here by teacher mentor, Peta, "they have noticeably improved their ability to talk in a focused manner with students; we now have a shared language to talk about teaching." This shift was also identified by Fran the teacher mentor,

We really notice the change when they come in later in the year for their official ...placement; there is a higher level of ease as they talk with other teachers and with children in classes. From the beginning they act like professionals ... are able to interact with the kids, it is a definite and noticeable change to the university students we have had previously.

Another teacher Robyn stated:

The power and value of Talking to Learn has been phenomenal... We found that these preservice teachers have learnt to value the power of spoken word and the impact it has on the lives of students. I've found this program directly allowed these young teachers to develop their ability to reflect on their understandings and their practice, gaining a deeper understanding of the processes, skills and strategies being used and how to develop talking and learning within the classroom.

Threaded through the above excerpts, classroom teacher mentors provide dynamic descriptions of the particular conditions and practice arrangements that stimulated and supported the practice development of PSTs. Comments revealed their perceptions about how PSTs formed, reformed and transformed notions of teaching and their reconceptualised views about the social intricacies and substantive nature of the dialogues encountered in classroom interactions.

Academic staff similarly endorsed the influential nature of this approach for connecting theory with the practical realities of teaching well. The program influenced student engagement in university courses as highlighted in this remark by teacher educator Tonia (English), "It has changed how PSTs talk in class and the professional and technical language they use, they make real connections between the theory we cover and what they experience by engaging with children in classrooms". This view resonated with observations made by Graham (Mathematics) who stated:

It is this program that can be attributed to way our university students interacted and engaged with the children who come in for the yearly Maths Day. I was amazed how different this year's group were compared to previous years; they seemed so natural with the children ... the program had a real influence on learning to be with children and how to interact with them in learning situations... this is a real flow on from what participating in the Talking to Learn program teaches them.

These data illustrate the importance of connecting theoretical propositions made within teacher education programs with authentic interactions between PSTs and students in classrooms, signifying the nexus between theory and practice.

In conclusion, it was found that framing the in-class experience around dialogic teaching practices and situating these in the classroom made the focus authentic and timely for first year PSTs. Specifically, PSTs identified that:

1. they had to learn to listen, it didn't come naturally;
2. they had to learn to interact, for many it was taken to granted and time for practising was needed;
3. listening was a foundation for understanding student knowledge; many didn't realise, and were surprised by, what students knew;

4. responsivity was important in teaching; that is, by listening closely to what students said provides valuable information to which teachers should respond;
5. that classroom interactions form an intersubjective mechanism for teaching and learning;
6. classroom interaction was a pedagogical tool; and
7. their role was both as a teacher and as a learner.

Overall, outcomes have the potential to directly inform the wider global debate questioning the efficacy of teaching and teacher education. To meet ongoing political and social expectations, pressures and challenges concerned with teacher quality and pedagogy, the focus on classroom interaction needs to move swiftly and more directly into teacher education programs. Results presented in this chapter suggest the need for teacher education to take a "practice turn" (Reid, 2011) and reconceptualise its own practices by explicitly orienting PSTs towards the complexity of teaching-learning processes by developing talk and interaction as dynamic pedagogical resources. To do this teacher education policy needs to prioritise the practical and theoretical implications of classroom interaction as pillars for developing teaching efficacy.

10 On Becoming a Teacher: Conclusion

Becoming a teacher involves entering and participating in the practices and practice architectures of teaching and teacher education. Undeniably, a key goal of teacher education is to create spaces for PSTs, in their processes towards becoming a teacher, to make sense of what constitutes quality teaching, both theoretically and practically. And so to conclude, I return to some words from Melanie (First Year PST, 2013), who remarked:

> This approach is so fantastic for scaffolding your learning in all subjects at university. Becoming a teacher is a process, I never thought about it like that. But by going into the classroom and working with the children every week from the beginning, and being supported by my peers and the classroom teacher in our mentoring conversations I have learnt about the way talk works, how to bring kids along in their learning. You know the finer ways to get them engaged and extend them, things I never considered at all. I can now see and feel the stuff we are learning at uni and it somehow makes so much more sense.

Acknowledgements First, I wish to acknowledge Professor JoAnne Reid, Charles Sturt University, for her vision in setting this research in motion. Second, I acknowledge collaborator Mrs Rhonda Hoare for her influence in directing the research. And third, I thank the PSTs, classroom teacher mentors and members of the first year academic team for participating in the study over the three years. Without your energy in engaging in change focused on "talking to learn" the study would not have been possible.

References

Alexander, R. (2008). *Towards dialogic teaching: Rethinking classroom talk*. Cambridge, UK: Dialogos.
Anderson, N., Chapin, S., & O'Connor, C. (2011). *Classroom discussions in math: A Facilitator's guide to support professional learning of discussion and the common core*. Sausalito, CA: Maths Solutions, Scholastic.
Bakhtin, M. (1981). *The dialogic imagination*. Austin, TX: University of Texas.
Ball, D., & Forzani, F. (2010). Teaching skilful teaching. *The Effective Educator, 69*(4), 40–45.
Barnes, D. (1976). *From communication to curriculum*. Harmondsworth, UK: Penguin Books.
Cazden, C. (2001). *Classroom discourse: The language of teaching and learning* (2nd ed.). Portsmouth, UK: Heinemann.
Churchill, R., Ferguson, P., Godinho, S., Johnson, N. F., Keddie, A., Letts, W., et al. (2011). *Teaching: Making a difference*. Queensland, Australia: Wiley.
Darwin, A. (2000). Critical reflections on mentoring in work settings. *Adult Education Quarterly Journal, 50*(3), 197–212.
Edwards, A. (1995). Teacher education: Partnerships in pedagogy? *Teaching and Teacher Education, 11*(6), 595–610.
Edwards, A., & Furlong, V. (1979). *The language of teaching*. London: Heinemann.
Edwards, A., Gilroy, P., & Hartley, D. (2004). *Rethinking teacher education: Collaborative responses to uncertainty*. London: Routledge.
Edwards, A., & Westgate, D. (1987). *Investigating classroom talk*. London: Falmer Press.
Edwards-Groves, C. (1999). *Explicit teaching: Focusing teacher talk on literacy* (Primary English Notes, PEN, Vol. 118). Newtown, Australia: Primary English Teachers Association.
Edwards-Groves, C. (2014a). Learning teaching practices: The role of critical mentoring conversations in teacher education. *Journal of Education and Training Studies, 2*(2), 151–166.
Edwards-Groves, C. (2014b). *Talk moves: A repertoire of practices for productive classroom dialogue* (PETAA PAPER, Vol. 195). Newtown, Australia: Primary English Teaching Association Australia.
Edwards-Groves, C., Anstey, M., & Bull, G. (2014). *Classroom talk: Understanding dialogue, pedagogy and practice*. Newtown, Australia: Primary English Teaching Association Australia.
Edwards-Groves, C., & Hoare, R. (2012). Talking to learn: Focusing teacher education on dialogue as a core practice for teaching and learning. *Australian Journal Teacher Education, 37*(8), 82–100.
Egan, B. A. (2009). Learning conversations and listening pedagogy: The relationship in student teachers, and developing professional identities. *European Early Childhood Education Research, 17*(1), 43–56.
Eilam, B., & Poyas, Y. (2009). Learning to teach: Enhancing pre-service teachers' awareness of the complexity of teaching–learning processes. *Teachers and Teaching, 15*(1), 87–107.
Fisher, A. T. (2010). Creating an articulate classroom: Examining pre-service teachers' experiences of talk. *Language and Education, 25*(1), 33–47.
Freebody, P. (2003). *Qualitative research in education: Interaction and practice*. London: Sage.
Freiberg, J., & Freebody, P. (1995). Analysing literacy events in classrooms and homes: Conversation-analytic approaches. In P. Freebody, C. Ludwig, & S. Gunn (Eds.), *The everyday literacy practices in and out of schools in low socio-economic urban communities* (pp. 185–369). Canberra, Australia: Commonwealth DEET.
Grossman, P., Hammerness, K., & McDonald, M. (2009). Redefining teaching, re-imagining teacher education. *Teachers and Teaching, 15*(2), 273–289.
Harkness, S., & Wachenheim, K. (2008). Using listening journal in math method. *The Teacher Educator, 43*(1), 50–71.
Haston, W., & Russell, J. (2012). Turning into teachers: Influences of authentic context learning experiences on occupational identity development of pre-service music teachers. *Research in Music Education, 59*(4), 369–392.

Hennissen, P., Crasborn, F., Brouwer, N., Korthagen, F., & Bergen, T. (2011). Clarifying preservice teacher perceptions of mentor teachers' developing use of mentoring skills. *Teaching and Teacher Education: International Journal Research Studies, 27*(6), 1049–1058.

Hudson, P. (2004). Specific mentoring: A theory and model for developing primary science teaching practices. *European Journal Teacher Education, 27*(2), 139–146.

Kemmis, S., Wilkinson, J., Edwards-Groves, C., Hardy, I., Grootenboer, P., & Bristol, L. (2014). *Changing practice: Changing education*. Singapore, Singapore: Springer.

Love, K. (2009). Literacy pedagogical content knowledge in secondary teacher education: Reflecting on oral language and learning across the disciplines. *Language and Education, 23*(6), 41–60.

Mehan, H. (1979). *Learning lessons: Social organization in the classroom*. Cambridge, MA: Harvard University Press.

Mercer, N., & Littleton, K. (2007). *Dialogue and the development of children's thinking: A sociocultural approach*. Oxon, UK: Routledge.

Mertens, D. (1998). *Research methods in education and psychology: Integrating diversity with quantitative and qualitative approaches*. Thousand Oaks, CA: Sage.

O'Connor, M. C., & Michaels, S. (1996). Shifting participant frameworks: Orchestrating thinking practices in group discussion. In D. Hicks (Ed.), *Discourse, learning and schooling* (pp. 63–103). Cambridge, MA: Cambridge University Press.

Reid, J. (2011). A practice turn for teacher education? *Asia-Pacific Journal Teacher Education, 39*(40), 293–310.

Schatzki, T. (2002). *The site of the social: A philosophical account of the constitution of social life and change*. University Park, TX: University of Pennsylvania Press.

Sinclair, J., & Coulthard, R. (1975). *Toward an analysis of discourse*. Oxford, UK: Oxford University Press.

Timperley, H. (2001). Mentoring conversations designed to promote student teacher learning. *Asia-Pacific Journal Teacher Education, 29*(2), 111–123.

Wittgenstein, L. (1958). *Philosophical investigations* (G. E. M. Anscombe, Trans., 2nd ed.). Oxford, UK: Basil Blackwell.

Woodruff, E., & Brett, C. (1999). Collaborative knowledge building: Preservice teachers and elementary students talking to learn. *Language and Education, 13*(4), 280–302.

Xio, Z. (2013). *"You Are Too Out!": A mixed methods approach to the study of "Digital Divides" in three Chinese senior secondary schools*. Retrieved December 14, 2013, from http://etheses.dur.ac.uk/8456/1/thesis.pdf.

Zeichner, K. (2010). Rethinking the connections between campus courses and field experiences in college and university-based teacher education. *Teacher Education, 89*(11), 89–99.

Zyngier, D. (2007). Listening to teachers-listening to students: Substantive conversations about resistance, empowerment and engagement. *Teachers and Teaching: Theory and Practice, 13*(4), 327–347.

Rethinking the Observation Placement: A Community/Cohort Approach to Early Professional Experiences

Rachel Forgasz

1 Introduction

In 2014, the report of the Australian Federal Government's Teacher Education Ministerial Advisory Group (TEMAG, 2014) found that during the Professional Experience (PE) component of initial teacher education, "quality is limited by a lack of integration of theory and practice, and by a lack of integration of the work of providers and schools" (p. 31). It subsequently identified the establishment of formal PE partnerships with stronger links between theory and practice as a strategic area for the improvement of initial teacher education.

This chapter reports on one university's response to the TEMAG (2014) challenge to bridge the theory-practice gap in initial teacher education through better integrated PE partnerships. It focuses on an innovative school-university partnership model designed to improve the quality of early "observation-focused" PE. Specifically, the partnership aimed to develop shared understanding between school and university partners about how to teach pre-service teachers about teaching in this context. With this shared understanding, school-based and university-based teacher educators collaborated to develop and implement a structured PE curriculum for two 5-day observation-focused PE blocks for pre-service teachers in their second year of a Bachelor of Education program. The chapter reports on the effectiveness of that program from the perspectives of the mentors who delivered it.

R. Forgasz (✉)
Monash University, Melbourne, Australia
e-mail: Rachel.forgasz@monash.edu

2 Aims

Recognising the crucial role that mentors play in assisting pre-service teachers to connect theoretical concepts to their daily practices in schools (Goodnough, Osmond, Dibbon, Glassman, & Stevens, 2009), the study sought to develop a model for early PE. The aim of the model was to encourage theory-practice integration amongst pre-service teachers by cultivating quality mentoring practices grounded in mutual understanding of how best to create educative PEs at the early stages of initial teacher education. Specifically, the purpose of the study was to:

- counter the traditional allocation of one mentor to one pre-service teacher, instead exploring the educative possibilities of a community of mentors working with a cohort of pre-service teachers;
- develop, implement and evaluate a structured PE curriculum for two 5-day observation-focused PE blocks in the second year of a Bachelor of Education program; and
- understand the influence of university-led mentor professional learning on mentors' approaches to working with pre-service teachers during the PE.

3 Background

The following section elucidates the background to the study. It includes both the research background (key literature and conceptual frames) and the contextual background to the partnership at the centre of the study.

3.1 Literature

According to Clarke, Triggs and Neilson (2014): "although [mentors] have a considerable influence on the ways in which [pre-service teachers] come to know and participate in the profession, they are not always fully aware of the extent and strength of this influence" (p. 31). The TEMAG (2014) report similarly recognised the fundamental role of quality mentoring in ensuring educative school-based PEs for pre-service teachers. At the same time, it emphasized both the uneven quality of individual mentoring and the systemic "lack of structured training to ensure that [mentors] have the necessary skills to supervise, provide support and feedback, and assess [PE] placements" (p. 32). Lack of preparation for mentors is identified as a key problem across a range of international teacher education contexts (Clarke et al. 2014), leading to calls by researchers for more and better preparation for their roles (see, for example, Graham, 2006; Leshem, 2012; Maynard, 2000).

Professional learning has been shown to improve mentors' understanding about how to teach pre-service teachers about the more complex aspects of quality teaching. Collaborative, university-led professional learning is especially productive as an approach to changing and improving practices (Graham, 2006; Maynard, 2000). Ongoing mentor professional learning situated during the PE itself is particularly powerful since it provides an immediate context to explore and apply new ideas, thus offering immediate benefits to pre-service teachers as well (Forgasz, White, & Forsyth, 2015).

The Community/Cohort partnership model at the heart of the current study is premised on engaging the significant involvement of tenured university-based teacher educators in the PE as a fundamental strategy to bridge the divide between school and university based learning (Allen, Ambrosetti, & Turner, 2013; Beck & Kosnik, 2002). The partnership arrangement reflects the kind of work undertaken in some Professional Development school contexts, such as Graham's (2006) work in which mentors and university based teacher educators collaborated to develop a "formal experiential curriculum" (p. 1122) for the PE.

3.2 Conceptual Frames

This study is significantly influenced by Zeichner's (1990) categorisation of six obstacles that hinder pre-service teachers' PE learning. Despite speaking from the US context some 15 years ago, many of these obstacles persist and continue to apply across a range of international contexts (including in Australia):

1. The tendency to understand the PE as an "unmediated and unstructured apprenticeship."
2. The absence of a structured PE curriculum and the attendant lack of connection between school-based and university-based learning about teaching.
3. Lack of professional learning for mentors about how to enact their roles.
4. Poor resourcing of the PE by universities, including low status within the university of PE related work.
5. Similarly poor resourcing and low status of the PE in schools.
6. The confusing and discrepant framing of teachers as reflective practitioners on one hand and as technicians on the other (Zeichner, 1990).

In order to respond meaningfully to these challenges, Zeichner (1990) called for PE reform on three levels: organizational, curricular, and structural. More recently, Zeichner (2010) outlined a range of models and approaches as examples of powerful innovation and reform. A unifying feature of what are otherwise quite disparate approaches is the focus on creating hybrid, third-spaces that offer theory-practice integration by reimagining the relationships between universities and schools.

Third space theory (Bhabha, 1994) has been enthusiastically taken up in teacher education research (see, for example Martin, Snow, & Franklin Torrez, 2011; McDonough, 2014; Williams, 2013; Zeichner, 2010). As its metaphorical associations imply, it offers a powerful alternative to the problematic binaries that plague teacher education discourse: in particular, theory/practice and university/school.

Instead, third space theory offers the alternative view of teacher education transpiring in hybrid, third spaces that "bring practitioner and academic knowledge together in less hierarchical ways to create new learning opportunities" (Zeichner, 2010, p. 92). The PE model that is the focus of the current study was designed to respond to Zeichner's obstacles and offers one example of this new kind of third space PE partnership in action.

Another key concept is Graham's (2006) categorisation of mentors' understandings of their roles in one of two ways. She captured the essential difference as that of maestro versus mentor. According to Graham:

> *Maestros are excellent teachers who provide models of practice, [whereas] mentors incorporate the role of teacher educator into their vision of cooperating teacher. Mentors consciously and carefully structure the clinical experience to nurture the professional growth and development of the intern.* (p. 1122)

Graham's distinction between maestro and mentor is helpful because it articulates the influence of the mentor's role perception on how the PE will ultimately be enacted, as either Dewey's (1904) apprentice (maestro) or laboratory (mentor) model. A key aim of the Community/Cohort PE model designed for the current study was to engage mentors in professional learning about their roles in order to consciously engender a "mentor" mindset.

4 Context

The partnership pilot study involved pre-service teachers enrolled in their second year of a secondary Bachelor of Education double degree program at a research-intensive university in Melbourne, Australia. The nature of the double degree program means that pre-service teachers undertake five days of PE per semester in each of their first three years of study, finishing off with 25 days of PE in each of their final two semesters in their fourth year of study. Pre-service teachers are traditionally placed in schools that are geographically close to their homes, and allocated to mentors on a one-to-one basis. In their first year, pre-service teachers are placed in primary school settings. In their second year, they are placed in secondary schools but they are not necessarily placed with a mentor who teaches in their method area. The curriculum and focus for the second year PE is, therefore, somewhat unclear.

The school partner, Keymore Secondary College,[1] is situated across two campuses (A and B) in Melbourne's southeast. It is a government school with a high proportion of students from non-English-speaking and refugee backgrounds. The school is strongly committed to pre-service teacher education and provides PEs to large numbers of pre-service teachers from multiple Victorian universities each year.

---

[1] Pseudonyms are used throughout the chapter to maintain the confidentiality of school and individual participants.

The Community/Cohort model that is the focus of this study was the second PE pilot undertaken between the school and university partners. The first pilot project was conducted in 2014 and involved mentor participants in a structured and ongoing mentor professional learning program and has been reported elsewhere (see, for example, Forgasz et al., 2015).

The mentors who participated in the Community/Cohort pilot study were also involved in the mentor professional learning pilot program. As such, they had already undertaken some professional learning about their roles as mentors. There were eight mentor participants in total, four from each Keymore College campus. Six of these eight participated in the research interviews that form the basis of the current study. There were three males and three females. Two research participants were from the Campus A community of mentors. They were Jona (Sciences, Maths, and Investigate[2]) and Peter (Maths). Four Campus B mentors participated in the research interviews. They were Linda (Sciences), Stuart (Maths, Game Design, and Daily Organiser), Greta (Visual Arts and Year 10 Coordinator), and Emma (Drama, English, Investigate and Year 8 Coordinator).

5 The Community/Cohort Model

The Community/Cohort model piloted an approach to early observation-focused PE which would break with the traditional allocation of one mentor to one pre-service teacher. Instead, a *community of mentors* would collectively mentor a *cohort of pre-service teachers* within a single school site. Although each mentor was allocated a pair of pre-service teachers for whom they would be primarily responsible, the model was premised on the notion of a mentor community working collaboratively to support the entire cohort of pre-service teachers allocated to their campus (and occasionally, across campuses).

The Community/Cohort model began with two days of professional learning and curriculum design during which mentors and university-based teacher educators collaborated to develop a PE curriculum framework and the content for a pre-service teacher handbook. It included induction information, mentor timetables, co-curricular event calendars, observation protocols, and a daily diary with data entry fields structured according to the Australian Professional Standards for Teachers (APSTs).

With the handbook as a curriculum resource, pre-service teacher pairs were able to autonomously plan a 5-day timetable for their own PE learning, with pairs working at different times with different mentors. Pre-service teachers also assigned themselves to participate in co-curricular activities, and occasionally to observe teachers and classes outside the mentor community. Participation in classes often involved combinations of structured observation (using observation protocols from

---

[2] 'Investigate' is a compulsory, integrated humanities subject that is taught at Keymore College to students from Year 7 to Year 9 in large open learning spaces.

the handbook) and one-on-one and small group student interactions. Every day, pre-service teacher pairs met with their assigned mentor to debrief their experiences, reviewing their observations in an extended reflective dialogue.

The PE curriculum also included several whole-group information sessions which were overseen by mentor community members according to their expertise. These covered topics such as student welfare, innovations in Science, Technology, Engineering and Maths (STEM), teaching in open learning spaces, and opportunities to complete coursework tasks such as mentor interviews.

6 Research Approach

With its interest in developing a deep understanding of participants' experiences and evaluations of the Community/Cohort PE pilot, a qualitative research design was deemed most appropriate for the current study.

6.1 Data Generation

Qualitative data for the study were collected from mentor and pre-service teacher participants in a range of forms.[3] Three data sets related to the mentor experience were generated. Open-ended questionnaires were completed at the end of the 2-day professional learning program to capture participants' evaluations of the purpose and quality of the professional learning program. One-hour focus groups were conducted on each campus during each semester's 5-day PE and captured the collective experiences of each mentor community. Extensive semi-structured interviews of 30–45 min were conducted with six out of eight participants 2–3 weeks after the conclusion of the PE pilot in order to generate an in-depth understanding of each mentor's individual experiences, including their evaluations of the Community/Cohort model.

Individual interviews were deemed important on top of focus groups in order to provide time and space for each participant to share more fully their individual experiences. Given its constraints, this chapter draws exclusively on data from those interviews in which participants responded to the following questions:

1. What is your understanding of the purpose of this second year Community/Cohort pilot?
2. What is your sense of what and how PSTs can learn about teaching/learning through their PE in schools? And has it changed in any way?

---

[3]The project and all data collection processes were approved by the Monash University Human Ethics Research Committee and by the Department of Education & Training.

3. What were the implications of working in this model for your role and approach as a mentor?
4. What were the challenges/benefits/surprises of working as a community of mentors with a cohort of PSTs?
5. What were some of the key learning experiences that impacted the PSTs? What was it about those experiences that affected them?
6. What advice can you offer us about improving this model and/or implementing it in another setting?

6.2 Data Analysis

Full transcripts of the interviews were inductively coded and categorised according to the substantive content of each participant's individual interview responses (Gillham, 2000). Themes were then sought across categories from the six participants' responses. Three key themes emerged in relation to participants' perceptions and experiences of the Community/Cohort model: structure, curriculum and pedagogy, and emotional experiences. Data were then further categorised into subsections under each broad theme.

7 Outcomes

There can be a tendency when reporting this kind of research to summarise the essence of multiple participant perspectives in order to leave more space for presenting and theorising the findings. But this study is philosophically premised on Zeichner's (2010) third-space notion of flattening the traditional hierarchy of academic over practitioner knowledge, of university over mentor authority. I aim to support this philosophical end in the reporting of the findings by foregrounding participants' voices through the inclusion of extensive direct quotations. In doing so, it is my intention to visually represent the philosophical rebalancing of participant and researcher voices.

This commitment to highlighting participant voice limited the space available to report the findings. As such, findings are presented below in relation to the first two of three broad themes, the first being participants' views of the model's structure, and, the second, its curriculum and pedagogy. Key findings related to participants' emotional experiences with the Community/Cohort model are presented within the discussion of each of the other two themes as appropriate.

7.1 Structural Features of the Community/Cohort Model

Participants reflected on two key structural features of the Community/Cohort pilot: the community of mentors and the cohort of pre-service teachers. In the following section, each of these is explored in turn.

7.1.1 A Community of Mentors Sharing the Work of Mentoring

The first key structural feature of the Community/Cohort model was the notion of a community of mentors working collaboratively to engage pre-service teachers in PE learning. Given that mentors nominate lack of time as the "biggest impediment to an effective practicum" (Hastings, 2004, p. 144), a significant aim of the Community/Cohort pilot was to investigate whether this approach could reduce the workload associated with one-to-one mentoring, without compromising the quality of experience mentors were able to offer. This aim was certainly achieved for Elana who described being alleviated of the mental exhaustion she would typically feel when she had a pre-service teacher following her around "like a shadow" all day long. While working in the Community/Cohort model meant that any number of the cohort of pre-service teachers might attend a mentor's classes at any time, Elana explained that the fact that they would soon move on to another experience was liberating.

Individual mentors' daily time commitments were further reduced by sharing responsibility for debriefing pre-service teachers' observations. Elana explained:

> *Other teachers were doing that as well, so it didn't seem so intense ... I felt that I didn't have to share so much because everybody was sharing things, so I could just pick a few things that I thought were important.*

In this sense, the value of the community of mentors was not only pragmatic, but also pedagogical. Sharing the work of reflective debriefing meant that mentors felt less concerned about the quantity of ideas they should discuss, instead focusing on the quality of each conversation. For Elana, this meant engaging in less transmissive and more dialogical exchanges about teaching. She explained:

> *Normally, I'm like "ok, I've got 40 minutes" [to spend with the pre-service teacher] and so I end up talking at them because I'm in a hurry, whereas I felt like my chats to them, it was much more two-way and we could have a proper discussion, which was a lot more helpful.*

While responsibility for these kinds of conversations fell to the four teachers who comprised each campus' mentor community, the model also opened up the PE beyond the immediate community of mentors, encouraging pre-service teachers to observe teachers across the whole school over the course of any given day. Paul described this approach as "really critical" because it meant that pre-service teachers could "learn so much more rather than just working with one person, which has always been the historical way of doing it."

This aspect of the Community/Cohort model was beneficial not only for pre-service teacher professional learning, but also for the mentors themselves. Linda explained:

I also love when my student teachers go out to other teachers' classes and come back and say "this teacher is doing this awesome stuff, they're doing this and this and this"... I love the insight into other people's practice and also their ideas about teaching too.

But not all participants were initially so positive about sharing the work of mentoring. Jona was very clear about the fact that "I wouldn't feel comfortable [about pre-service teachers] seeing particular teaching styles that I would deem, say, ineffective." Furthermore, the idea of sharing responsibility for mentoring amongst the community of mentors created a confusing shift in role perception for him. Jona explained:

I'm used having someone follow me... I'm quite stubborn. I'm a stubborn person in general. So, when I, because I've had so many pre-service teachers before, and I've selected a particular way or method, and I've seen that it's, so to speak, worked for me, to see this [Community/Cohort model] and see, like, a completely different approach, initially for me it was quite "Whaaat?"

Jona and the other mentors in the Campus A community had, in fact, more or less ignored the Community/Cohort model during the first 5-day PE and approached it as a traditional placement. But when the mentor communities from the two campuses met to reflect and refine the model at the end of the first week, Jona heard about the positive experiences of the Campus B mentors and reconsidered his position:

So the second time round – because I've heard that the other group went quite well – this time I just thought, "You know what? What the hell!" I'm always open to new ideas. I am stubborn, but I am open to listening and at least giving it a go, and this time it was just like, it's more freedom for [the pre-service teachers], so they can actually observe different aspects. So just changing my frame of mind, which is tough to do, I'm not going to lie, it ended up working for the best, not just for me, but for them, because they were able to get a much better experience. And I found the second round was a lot smoother for them, they enjoyed the second round a lot more and I myself enjoyed it a lot more because I was able just to say "You know what? Go for it."

This evolving understanding about how to teach pre-service teachers about teaching represents precisely the shift from a maestro to mentor mindset that the project set out to explore and develop. And with a mentor mindset, Jona began to recognise the value of offering his pre-service teachers a range of learning experiences beyond simply observing him at work in the classroom.

No less significant than the shift in mindset is the sense of how challenging it is for mentors to make this leap. As evident in Jona's early reaction to the model, it might be understood as a reconsideration of questions of power and authority in the PE relational dynamic of "powerlessness and surveillance" (Bloomfield, 2010, pp. 229–30) between pre-service teachers and their mentors. In this regard, having the community of mentors share responsibility for the cohort of pre-service teachers created what Linda described as something "more flattened, more egalitarian, more democratic" than Bloomfield's "conditions of hierarchy [in which] power is commonly conceptualised in terms of contested possession" (2010, p. 228).

7.1.2 A Community of Mentors: Feeling Like Part of a Community

For Linda, being part of the Campus B community of mentors engendered a strong sense of belonging and connectedness and these feelings extended beyond the life of the pilot. She attributed this shift to the sense of professional trust that developed within the mentor community:

> We don't see each other that much. We're like ships passing in the night but I knew that I could trust them. And that's the thing: I could trust them to do what they said they were going to do and there was (sic) no issues. And I think that's part of it too is that it just builds trust between people and from that also comes respect and it's just a really good, a positive thing.

Greta too described her participation in the community of mentors as positively influencing her sense of connectedness to her colleagues. The collaborative process of designing the curriculum for the Community/Cohort model was particularly significant in this regard:

> Sometimes I used to think, "oh my goodness, I feel so different from the way this teacher teaches" and then I'm thinking, "hang on a second, now I've got to know you and now we've really got to unpack what we think teaching is all about, and now I'm really listening to your value system, perspective, philosophy – whatever – of teaching"... I think I'm discovering other teachers and I'm realising that our differences are reasonably superficial compared to the things that we share in common at the core... I feel more "belonged" and confident in being different in the way that I'm different, which is really a nice feeling.

As Greta's comments suggest, collaborating as a community of mentors provided a platform for the mentor community to share deeply their values and philosophies of teaching and in that process, significant shifts in professional relationships were evident.

But while two of three female mentor teacher participants who were interviewed, Linda and Greta, experienced a strong and enduring sense of belonging, all three male participants, Stuart, Paul and Jona, expressed something of the opposite sentiment. Stuart reflected:

> When you say "community of mentors" it brings up this image of we're sort of really working together, but we're not... really we're all different people working at different year levels in different subjects and because of our timetabling situations, we don't get a chance to get together.

Paul had a similarly functional understanding of what it meant to be part of a community of mentors and, like Stuart, associated the sense of community with the idea of time spent working together. For Paul, to feel more of a sense of community, "we needed to have a bit more opportunity for us as a team to get together and work out how we were doing things."

But even if they did not all feel themselves to be part of a tight-knit community in practice, even their interest in working as a community to collaboratively mentor pre-service teachers marks a significant shift in thinking about how to approach the mentoring task. It certainly challenges the traditional one-to-one model of the PE as an unmediated and unstructured apprenticeship (Zeichner, 1990) and not all participants were initially open to it. As discussed, for Jona, for example, there was something ideological at stake in sharing responsibility for the pre-service teachers in his charge and he acknowledged that he was initially resistant to the Community/Cohort model because of what he described as the challenge of "letting go of that control."

7.1.3 A Cohort of Pre-service Teachers

The second key structural feature of the Community/Cohort PE model was the deliberate placement of a cohort of pre-service teachers at a single school site. Within each Keymore College campus cohort, pre-service teachers were paired up and each pair was allocated to a "home" mentor within the community. Mentor participants shared their experiences of both pair and cohort groupings.

The pairing of pre-service teachers was, at least in part, a pragmatic design feature of the Community/Cohort model which, if successful, would effectively halve the number of mentors required to work with pre-service teachers during these early PEs. But pairing also offered the additional efficiency of relieving mentor workload. Elana explained, "When I do get busy, they're not just waiting for me to give them some guidance, they've got each other to sort of talk to and to have those discussions." In this sense, from the mentor perspective, the benefit of pairing pre-service teachers was as much pedagogical as it was pragmatic because pairs of pre-service teachers were able to engage with each other in reflective sense-making of their observations.

These conversations offered an alternative when mentors were too busy to talk but they also had the effect of lifting the level of reflective dialogue with mentors since, as Greta explained, "the conversations are being discussed [in pairs] and maybe even unpacked and refined a little bit before the question is posed [to the mentor]." Jona likewise found that conversations with his pre-service teacher pair were more focused because, "They knew what they wanted to discuss with me" and that having "two different [pre-service teacher] perspectives" further enhanced the quality of their reflective dialogue.

If pairing pre-service teachers was effective, so too was placing multiple pairs together as a cohort. Indeed, the degree to which the cohort placement encouraged pre-service teachers' sense of belonging at each campus was an unanticipated outcome of the model. PE can often be a daunting experience for pre-service teachers who must quickly acclimate to an unfamiliar environment. The challenge is often exacerbated in one-to-one placements which do not encourage pre-service teachers to form broad relationships or to get a sense of the workplace except from the perspective of their mentor. In contrast, Linda explained that the Community/Cohort model offered pre-service teachers an opportunity to "experience the complexity of school life without it being confrontational. They get to experience it in a very gentle way in some ways because they're together."

Linda explained further the way in which the cohort approach encouraged pre-service teachers to experience a sense of belonging:

> [Y]ou're already orientating the right way into a school, you're not the outsider, the outsider coming to be a voyeur or an intruder. You're part of the school… And I think that the group dynamic was just lovely to see. I never saw a long face or a stressed out person or someone who looked embarrassed, it was just a lot more gentle.

These feelings of belonging to a cohort were made tangible for the pre-service teachers who were physically housed together in the main staffroom. Elana noted that while, "in the past, I always thought it was so important that a PST have their own desk," the cohort had shared with her that, "it was really good having the staff room because if they went there, there were always other people there from their community."

These benefits of being part of a pre-service teacher cohort may be understood in terms of Zeichner's (2010) notion of the PE transpiring in a third space between the school and the university. In this case, the in-between-ness of that third space enabled the pre-service teachers to inhabit simultaneously their student and teacher identities. They were gently being eased into a sense of belonging to the broader teacher and school communities, at least partly because of the confidence and comfort of concurrently feeling a part of the cohort as its own independent community of practice. Paul described powerfully the sense in which those feelings of belonging influenced the pre-service teacher cohort's engagement with whole school community:

> They were really seeing themselves as part of the staff of the school first of all, they weren't just visitors they were here, and belonged, and were welcome… They just seemed a lot more confident about even themselves just going up to someone else on the staff, not part of the [mentor] team, saying, "I believe you teach this class this subject and this is who I am - would you mind if I observed." And that seemed to be again a reflection that they felt really comfortable and welcome in the place.

In all, the reorganisation of relationships in the Community/Cohort model, including its mentor community and pre-service teacher pair and cohort dimensions, reflects Le Cornu's (2010) learning communities approach to PE in which PSTs are expected to work together with their peers and to actively contribute to all of the learning relationships in which they are engaged.

7.2 Curriculum and Pedagogy

Participants identified three significant curriculum features of the Community/Cohort model: the whole-school focus for the PE, the use of structured observation, and engagement in reflective dialogue. The research findings in relation to each of these is now discussed in turn.

7.2.1 Broadening to a Whole School Focus

The 2-day professional learning program that preceded the implementation of the Community/Cohort pilot was very much focused on engaging the community of mentors in an exploration of questions around what, and how, pre-service teachers can learn about teaching during early PEs which are not necessarily teaching-focused. This professional learning focus broadened participants' understandings of the purpose and learning potential of the PE. Stuart reflected:

> *Often there's a lot of emphasis on content and less about the pedagogy. Here, the emphasis has been about "What does a teacher do?" not "What does a teacher teach?" and I probably hadn't really thought of that so much before this.*

This comment by Stuart marked a significant change in his thinking, one that was critical in contributing to participants' shifts in mindset from maestro to mentor. Mentors who had previously been unable to imagine how pre-service teachers could learn anything except by practising teaching now began to reconceptualise both what they might learn and how that learning might be achieved. Even the most fundamentally taken for granted assumptions about PE learning were open for rethinking, as seen in Paul's comments about placing the pre-service teachers outside of their method areas of specialisation:

> *[Y]ou learn so much more when you're actually observing someone where, frankly, you're not that interested in the subject but you're really learning about the teacher's method. And that's I think one of the big benefits of the way we've done it this time.*

Having established a shared vision to focus PE learning on the question, "What does a teacher do?" mentors and university based teacher educators set about developing a curriculum by collaboratively answering it. In this way, the community of mentors developed ownership over the PE curriculum design to which they were actively and collaboratively contributing. Linda explained:

> *We were having quite interesting debates about what was important, what wasn't important, what should be valued, what shouldn't be valued and so on… So there was a bit of debate, a bit of soul searching… and hearing other people's opinions and ideas … moves the conversation along to a different point.*

Having invested themselves in determining what was important for the pre-service teacher cohort to learn and to consider about teaching and the fullness of teachers' work, mentors were sensitised to drawing out these ideas during the PE. In doing so, they understood through their own experience the degree to which their knowledge of practice is tacit (Polyani, 1958) and needs to be explicitly unpacked in order to be seen and appreciated by pre-service teachers. Jona reflected:

> I think many of them are quite amazed, so to speak, of (sic) what is actually involved in the teaching profession. It's not just standing up in front of a class for 40 minutes and just imparting information. There's lots of other things you do… So it's just trying to give them the whole aspect of teaching as much as I possibly can.

7.2.2 Focused Dialogue About Practice

Having pre-service teachers observe their mentors teaching is a common pedagogical strategy for PE learning, especially during early PEs. Despite this, Loughran (2006) observes:

> There is little to suggest that students of teaching are encouraged to unpack the professional knowledge or beliefs of their teaching mentors…or that their teacher mentors themselves see that unpacking their professional knowledge and beliefs comprises part of their role in teaching about teaching (p. 45).

As part of the mentor professional learning that preceded the Community/Cohort pilot, mentors explored these ideas around unpacking teacher professional knowledge and pedagogical reasoning as a dimension of initial teacher education. With a newfound appreciation of the problematic absence of this kind of conversation, mentors agreed to engage their pre-service teacher pairs each day in what Graham (2006) describes as "focused dialogue about practice" (p. 1126). This daily reflective dialogue would aim to surface both pre-service teachers' and mentors' understandings of the knowledge underlying the various teacher actions that the pre-service teachers had observed throughout the day.

The idea of unpacking practice as part of mentoring work was new for the mentor participants. Linda observed, "I was more self-conscious as far as the tacit, being able to explain what I was doing and why. That's what was really the big difference for myself as a mentor, I think, through this whole process." Having come to understand that the pedagogical reasoning underlying their decisions and actions was not apparent unless it was deliberately surfaced, they developed various strategies for engaging in this daily dialogue. Stuart explained:

> People aren't going to necessarily see [the pedagogical reasoning that underlies decisions and practices] unless both people, the PST and the mentor, are aware that that's what we're looking for so that afterwards you have your conversations and say, "Well I did this because – " or the PST says, "Why did you do that?" or "I like the way you did this," and then the mentor, such as myself, says, "Oh yeah, I didn't even realise that. I'm glad you told me that. I've got to actually think about that in future."

Stuart's openness to his pre-service teacher pair being able to offer him new insights about his teaching is noteworthy. It suggests a repositioning of roles and a redistribution of authority that enabled genuinely two-way professional learning between mentor and pre-service teacher.

Jona reflected similarly that focused dialogue about practice surfaced aspects of his professional knowledge in ways that contributed to his own reflection and professional learning: "It's been really, really good for me to see specifically things that I naturally do, without trying to sound cocky, things that I naturally do without noticing it and then seeing, hey, that really works." Like the mentors in Nguyen's (2013) study, mentor participants in the current study took seriously their pre-service teachers' observations and drew on them as opportunities for ongoing professional learning and reflection. In this sense, making explicit their tacit knowledge of practice was useful to both mentor and pre-service teachers alike.

7.2.3 Structured Observation

If unmediated observation is a problem for PE in general then it is particularly problematic in the case of early PEs in which pre-service teachers spend much of their time "observing" classes in action. In the absence of reflective dialogue, much of this experience is uneducative since pre-service teachers don't know what they are looking at or what to look for. Worse still, PE observation may also prove miseducative since, according to Loughran (2006), when pre-service teachers observe, they tend to see what they expect to see and "interpret classroom events in light of their own experiences as learners" (p. 45).

As discussed, to counter this problem, the Community/Cohort PE curriculum required that pre-service teachers reflected with their mentors on their observations during daily focused dialogue about practice. But this approach assumes that mentors themselves know what pre-service teachers should be looking at and what to look for, an assumption proven grossly unfounded in light of these candid comments by Paul:

> For a lot of years, really until now I think, even though I've had lots of PSTs I really haven't been able to guide them as to "this is what you need to look at"... I think we were just saying "right, you follow the teacher around and you observe some classes and you try and observe as many different people as you can." But we weren't really guiding them as to what they should be looking for.

To scaffold both pre-service teachers' classroom observations and mentors' daily focused dialogue about them, the Community/Cohort handbook included a series of observation protocols which had been collaboratively adapted/designed by mentors and university-based teacher educators during the initial 2-day professional learning program. Even when pre-service teachers chose not to use the protocols themselves, Elana observed that simply including them as a resource "gave them some ideas of what things they could notice" which in turn "opened up what they could write about, whereas I think in the past they weren't really sure what to write."

Greta also noted that the observation protocols lifted the quality of pre-service teacher reflections. She explained:

> I've really been impressed with the quality of conversations that we've been having... A deeper level of conversation. And I think it's because of the structure that's been put in

place encouraging the pre-service teachers to look at "this" and then to ask questions about "this" and then it gives you the opportunity to have [these conversations] with everyone rather than just with the ones that it seems to naturally evolve with.

In this regard, structured observation was a valued pedagogical strategy used to create distinct learning opportunities as opposed to relying on the "natural" reflective capabilities of individual pre-service teachers.

Structured observation and focused dialogue about practice in the context of a broad focus on the fullness of teachers' work offered the community of mentors a distinct pedagogical approach, curriculum, and set of practices which they were able to enact in order to offer a powerfully educative PE for the pre-service teacher cohort.

8 Implications and Conclusion

It is, perhaps, unusual for a study of a PE partnership model to focus exclusively on the mentor experience with no reference at all to the pre-service teachers themselves. And indeed, pre-service teacher experiences and evaluations will be the focus of future reporting on this Community/Cohort partnership pilot. But aside from the limitations of space for this chapter, the stated aims of the study also make sense of this exclusive focus on mentor perspectives.

Accusations of a theory-practice gap in initial teacher education abound (Loughran, 2006; Zeichner, 1990) and they are, arguably, felt most strongly during the PE (Darling-Hammond & Bransford, 2005) when pre-service teachers frequently report being encouraged by their mentors to let go the apparent abstractions of theory in order to handle the "realities" of practice. This goes some way towards explaining Zeichner's sixth obstacle to PE learning in that teachers are framed as reflective practitioners by teacher educators in the university space while being discrepantly framed as technicians by their mentors during the PE. The current study sought to dissolve this problematic theory-practice divide by creating a third space of shared vision and purpose. Aligning teacher educators' and mentors' understandings about the aims for PE learning and how best to achieve them was a foundation upon which this third space was built.

Shared understanding was largely achieved through professional learning about the purposes and pedagogies of teacher education (Loughran, 2006) and how these can find expression in the PE. With a sense of the educative value of PE beyond merely providing opportunities to practise teaching (Graham, 2006), mentor participants collaborated with university-based teacher educators to determine how best to teach about teaching during the PE. Structurally, a learning communities approach (Le Cornu, 2010) in which a community of mentors shared responsibility for a cohort of pairs of pre-service teachers was essential to shifting away from the traditional master-apprentice model for PE learning towards the laboratory approach of exploration and experimentation encouraged by Dewey (1904). With a laboratory approach in mind, mentors aimed to make explicit some of the tacit dimensions of teaching practice (Polyani, 1958). They achieved this largely by focusing pre-service teacher observations and then modeling and encouraging reflection as a strategy for understanding and improving practice (Graham, 2006; Loughran, 2006; Nguyen, 2013).

Shifting mentor mindset from a maestro to mentor approach (Graham, 2006) is difficult but without this shift, a Community/Cohort approach to PE cannot succeed. Such shifts require university-led professional learning for mentors. The current study makes a strong case that embedding mentor professional learning as a feature of quality PE partnerships goes a long way towards addressing all six of Zeichner's (1990) obstacles to PE learning by:

7. Explicitly challenging common mentor conceptions of the PE as an unmediated and unstructured apprenticeship;
8. Jointly constructing a structured PE curriculum that draws deliberate connections between school-based and university-based learning about teaching;
9. Offering university-led professional learning for mentors about how to enact their roles;
10. Better resourcing the PE with academic support which also serves to raise the status of PE related work;
11. Similarly raising the quality of resourcing and the status of PE work in schools; and
12. Redressing the discrepant framing of teachers as reflective practitioners on one hand and as technicians on the other.

Policy reforms such as those flagged by TEMAG (2014) can be understood as bureaucratic impositions that reduce the autonomy of teacher education providers and can be responded to in panicked reactions to sign up schools as "partners." Theoretical constructs such as the third space might then be cynically invoked to smokescreen these "partnerships," effectively disguising the failure to respond meaningfully to calls for reform. Alternately, such calls for reform can be viewed as opportunities for teacher education providers to review, reflect on, and genuinely renegotiate the terms of their PE partnerships with schools in order to develop stronger connections and coherence in purpose. As the current study evinces, authentic third space partnerships have the potential to do far more than simply *reform* PE. Much more compellingly, they have the potential to *transform* PE learning (Martin et al., 2011) by creating and enacting a shared vision for engaging pre-service teachers in learning about teaching.

Acknowledgments This project was funded by a 2014 Education Portfolio grant from the Faculty of Education, Monash University.

References

Allen, J. M., Ambrosetti, A., & Turner, D. (2013). How school and university supervising staff perceive the pre-service teacher education practicum: A comparative study. *Australian Journal of Teacher Education, 38*(4), 108–128.

Beck, C., & Kosnik, C. (2002). Professors and the practicum involvement of university faculty in preservice practicum supervision. *Journal of Teacher Education, 53*(1), 6–19.

Bhabha, H. K. (1994). *The location of culture*. London: Routledge.

Bloomfield, D. (2010). Emotions and "getting by": A pre-service teacher navigating professional experience. *Asia-Pacific Journal of Teacher Education, 38*(3), 221–234.

Clarke, A., Triggs, V., & Nielsen, W. (2014). Cooperating teacher participation in Teacher Education. *Review of Educational Research, 84*(2), 163–202.

Darling-Hammond, L., & Bransford, J. (2005). *Preparing teachers for a changing world: What teachers should learn and be able to do* (1st ed.). San Francisco: Jossey-Bass.

Dewey, J. (1904). The relation of theory to practice in education. *The third yearbook of the national society for the scientific study of education*. Chicago: The University of Chicago Press.

Forgasz, R., White, S., & Forsyth, A. (2015). *Building mentoring capacity*. Paper presented at the ATEA 2015 Conference: Strengthening partnerships in teacher education, Charles Darwin University, Australia.

Gillham, B. (2000). *The research interview*. London: Continuum.

Goodnough, K., Osmond, P., Dibbon, D., Glassman, M., & Stevens, K. (2009). Exploring a triad model of student teaching. *Teaching and Teacher Education, 25*(2), 285–296.

Graham, B. (2006). Conditions for successful field experiences. *Teaching and Teacher Education, 22*(8), 1118–1129.

Hastings, W. (2004). Emotions and the practicum: The cooperating teachers' perspective. *Teachers and Teaching: Theory and Practice, 10*(2), 135–148.

Le Cornu, R. (2010). Changing roles, relationships and responsibilities in changing times. *Asia-Pacific Journal of Teacher Education, 38*(3), 195–206.

Leshem, S. (2012). The many faces of mentor-mentee relationships in a pre-service teacher education programme. *Creative Education, 3*(4), 413.

Loughran, J. J. (2006). *Developing a pedagogy of teacher education: Understanding teaching and learning about teaching*. Oxon, UK: Routledge.

Martin, S., Snow, J. L., & Franklin Torrez, C. A. (2011). Navigating the terrain of third space: Tensions with/in relationships in school-university partnerships. *Journal of Teacher Education, 62*(3), 299–311.

Maynard, T. (2000). Learning to teach or learning to manage mentors? *Mentoring and Tutoring, 8*(1), 17–30.

McDonough, S. (2014). Rewriting the script of mentoring pre-service teachers in third space: Exploring tensions of loyalty, obligation and advocacy. *Studying Teacher Education: A Journal of Self-Study of Teacher Education Practices, 10*(3), 210–221.

Nguyen, H. T. M. (2013). Peer mentoring: A way forward for supporting preservice EFL teachers psychosocially during the practicum. *Australian Journal of Teacher Education, 38*(7), 31–44.

Polyani, M. (1958). *Personal knowledge. Towards a post critical philosophy*. London: Routledge.

Teacher Education Ministerial Advisory Group (TEMAG). (2014). *Action now: Classroom ready teachers*. Canberra, Australia: Department of Education and Training.

Williams, J. (2013). Boundary crossing and working in the third space: Implications for a teacher educator's identity and practice. *Studying Teacher Education: A Journal of Self-Study of Teacher Education Practices, 9*(2), 118–129.

Zeichner, K. (1990). Changing directions in the practicum: Looking ahead to the 1990s. *British Journal of Teacher Education, 16*(2), 105–132.

Zeichner, K. (2010). Rethinking the connections between campus courses and field experiences in college-and university-based teacher education. *Journal of Teacher Education, 61*(1–2), 89–99.

Images of Teaching: Discourses Within Which Pre-service Teachers Construct Their Professional Identity as a Teacher upon Entry to Teacher Education Courses

Robyn Brandenburg and Ann Gervasoni

1 Introduction

> Teacher professional identity then stands at the core of the teaching profession. It provides a framework for teachers to construct their own ideas of 'how to be', 'how to act' and 'how to understand' their work and their place in society. Importantly, teacher identity is not something that is fixed nor is it imposed; rather it is negotiated through experience and the sense that is made of that experience. (Sachs, 2005, p. 15)

The recent review of Teacher Education in Australia (Teacher Education Ministerial Advisory Group (TEMAG), 2014) highlights the imperative that teaching graduates must be *classroom ready*. While the recommendations of the report focus predominantly on the need for Teacher Education programs to enable the acquisition and mastery of skills and pedagogical content knowledge, there is minimal recognition of the role of Teacher Education in shaping PSTs' professional identities. Our contention is that graduates who are *classroom ready* must also have a deep understanding of the contextual factors, personal discourses and emotions that shape their professional self and appreciate that this identity is constantly changing. Often there is a disconnection between a graduate teacher's professional identity and the lived reality of that identity as they experience the (often) challenging school context in which they work. Beauchamp and Thomas (2009) suggest that pre-service teachers "undergo a shift in identity as they move through programs of teacher education and assume positions as teachers in today's challenging school contexts" (p. 175). Anticipating that a professional identity is constantly evolving empowers new teachers to adapt and respond to the challenges and demands of their

---

R. Brandenburg (✉)
Faculty of Education and Arts, Federation University Australia, Ballarat, Victoria, Australia
e-mail: r.brandenburg@federation.edu.au

A. Gervasoni
Monash University Australia, Melbourne, Australia
e-mail: ann.gervasoni@monash.edu

© Springer Science+Business Media Singapore 2016
R. Brandenburg et al. (eds.), *Teacher Education*,
DOI 10.1007/978-981-10-0785-9_8

new profession, rather than reverting to survival mode strategies or choosing to leave the profession altogether. After researching the shifting identity of first year graduate teachers, Beauchamp and Thomas recommended that teacher education must explicitly address *identity* as a critical program component. The implication is that PSTs need to be aware of their professional identity and the factors that influence its evolution so that they can remain the key agents in constructing and reconstructing their professional identities.

This chapter examines the discourses of teaching and professionalism that PSTs appropriate when they first begin a four-year degree course in Education. The research was conducted at the Ballarat campuses of Federation University Australia (FUA, formerly, the University of Ballarat) and Australian Catholic University (ACU). The research presented and discussed in this chapter constitutes Phase One of a longitudinal study that explored how PSTs' conceptions of a teacher and teaching change over the course of a four-year teacher education program. Our examination includes an overview of the content and discourse analyses of 181 representations. The themes that were identified provide insight about PSTs' conceptions of teachers and teaching in their first month of a Bachelor of Education degree and we discuss these findings in relation to how these PST images produce and/or reproduce particular understandings of teachers (Moore, 2004). The analyses reveal a range of predominantly stereotypical images of teaching and teachers. These images and discourses provide teacher educators with insights that enable them to design experiences and course content (interventions) that may assist PSTs to construct professional identities as teachers who are change agents, advocates and pedagogical leaders who are *classroom ready*.

2 The Literature

2.1 *The Construction of Identity*

This research draws primarily on the Foucauldian poststructuralist constructs of discourse, subjectivity, power-knowledge and agency to inform the analysis of the multiple sources of data and interpret the findings. Whilst the central concern of this study is the development of an identity as a teacher, the notion of identity draws on identity as subjectivity/subjectivities that are constructed in and through discourse. By discourse we mean systems of meaning, often institutionally based, that act as the truth according to which individuals understand the world and their life in that world (MacNaughton, 2000). Discourses provide norms, values, principles, rules and standards, for example, about how to be a 'good' teacher and what constitutes a teacher in Australia in the twenty-first century. They make it possible to think, speak and act in some ways and not others (Ball, 1990). Subjectivity refers to "the conscious and unconscious thoughts and emotions of the individual, her sense of herself and her ways of understanding her relation to the world" (Weedon, 1987, p. 32). Subjectivities are shaped as the individual participates in the discourses to which s/he has access. Agency is the ability to form one's own subjectivity, rather than simply being a pawn of discourse(s). It is not just a matter of being constituted in and through discourses as a result of particular institutional practices. There is always a choice, as the individual resists particular subject positions and actively takes up others, reflects on "the discursive relations which constitute her" and chooses "from the options available" (Weedon, 1987, p. 121). The choices available, however, may be very limited, depending on the discourses (and subsequently the subject positions) accessible to particular individuals. The concept of power-knowledge as an analytical construct within this study draws on Weedon who claims that, "power is exercised within discourses in the ways in which they constitute and govern individual subjects" (p. 110). The constitution of subjectivity is therefore an exercise of power. Subjectivity is about knowledge – using knowledge about how to be a particular (normal) human being, or, in this study a (good) teacher, and knowledge of the self.

2.2 Professional Identity

There is significant and ongoing interest in the development of teachers' professional identity (Beauchamp & Thomas, 2009, 2011; Beijaard, Meijer, & Verloop, 2004; Coldron & Smith, 1999; Lasky, 2005; Sachs, 2001; Walkington, 2005) including the development of PSTs' professional identity (Thomas & Beauchamp, 2011). It is likely that the experience of Pre-Service Teacher Education over four years at university has a significant impact on the development of PSTs' professional identities. Moore (2004) has argued that too little attention has been paid to the impact that personal biography and the constructions of teaching and teachers that PSTs *bring* to teacher education on the teachers they become. Critical commentators (see for example Ball, 2003; Sachs, 2001, 2003; Stronach, Corbin, McNamara, Stark, & Warne, 2002) foreground the role of discourses in making possible certain constructions of teacher professionalism and excluding others, and in doing so, shaping teacher identities. In this chapter, we examine the teacher identity constructions that PSTs portrayed when first beginning a teacher education course. We contend that research on teachers' professional identity formation is relevant for teacher educators in order to gain insight about how they might support student teachers to understand themselves as teachers (Korthagen, 2004).

3 Method

Phase One of our research explored the initial discourses of teaching and professionalism within which PSTs understand what it means to be a teacher and the discourses they appropriate as they initially construct themselves as teachers (Ball, 2003; Sachs, 2001, 2003; Stronach et al., 2002). The data for Phase One were collected in 2010 from 181 pre-service teachers (PSTs) from the Ballarat campuses of two Australian universities; Federation University Australia (FUA, formerly, the University of Ballarat) and Australian Catholic University (ACU). The PSTs were enrolled in the first year of a Bachelor of Education Degree with specializations in Early Childhood and Primary, Preparatory-Year 6 or Preparatory-Year 10. The research project was approved by the FUA and ACU Human Research Ethics Committees. According to the ethical guidelines for the research, the purpose and processes of the *Visual Representations* research were explained to each cohort at both universities by the researchers, and all participating PSTs provided written informed consent to participate in Phase One of the research project. Neither of the researchers was involved in teaching the cohorts. Tutors who were teaching each of the cohorts presented the *visual representation* task and collected the artifacts produced. The PSTs enrolled in the courses at FUA completed the visual representation as an off campus learning task, during week three of Semester One, 2010 and PSTs enrolled at ACU completed the task during class time during week four, Semester One, 2010. All PSTs were asked to produce a visual representation of a teacher, which could include, but was not limited to, drawing, collage, photography, construction and/or sculpture. Collecting visual representations as data enabled us to gain deeper insights into the identity constructs PSTs depict in the first month of a teaching degree.

Visual methodologies and methods have become more widely used in educational and social research and as such, provide opportunities for producing and reproducing knowledge and understandings of the world in a different way than that offered by speech or writing (Guillemin, 2004). We collected the data, conducted an initial sorting, and then conducted an analysis of the visual representations that involved two levels of analysis: (1) content analysis and (2) discourse analysis. Once completed, the 181 PST visual representations were collated, scanned and digitized, all being labeled with a sequential number together with an identifying reference code (for example, 2AFP6 refers to A = Australian Catholic University; F = female; P6 = Preparatory-6 Degree).

3.1 Level One: Initial Sorting of Representations and Content Analysis

Once these representations were collected, they were next grouped according to university, program and the general content of each representation. During the initial sorting we noted that some PSTs used pictorial images of teachers, some used symbols, some used words, and others used combinations of these. Figure 1 shows the percentage of each representation category for each PST specialization.

At least 10 % of each group produced representations that included an image of a teacher accompanied with words, artifacts and symbols. We undertook the initial tabling and sorting of the visual representations as a way of immersing ourselves in

Images of Teaching: Discourses Within Which Pre-service Teachers Construct Their... 121

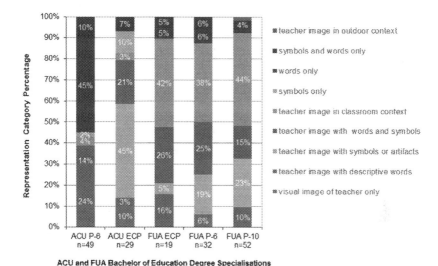

Fig. 1 Percentage of each visual representation of a teacher category for each PST, university and course specialization

the data and identified recurring visual images, key words and outlying images, a process that is quite different from formal analysis and classifying frequencies. Our first level of content analysis (Rose, 2007) focused on identifying key themes and patterns across the different cohorts and universities and within cohorts and universities. The images were initially sorted into broad categories: (1) visual image of teacher only; (2) teacher image accompanied by descriptive words; (3) teacher image accompanied by symbols or artifacts (e.g., chalkboard, books, clock, heart, apple); (4) teacher image accompanied by words and symbols; (5) teacher image in classroom context; (6) symbols only; (7) words only; (8) symbols and words only and (9) teacher image in outdoor context.

Figures 2, 3, and 4 depict examples of the visual representations produced by the PSTs from both universities. These are examples of Category 4: Teacher image in a classroom context.

Figure 2 is an example of one PST's visual representation of a teacher in a classroom context. The teacher is a white Caucasian male who is standing back-centre with three students standing in the foreground. He is dressed casually in a red t-shirt and is waving with his left hand open. There are two male students and one female who portray the range of school uniforms. The background of the classroom reproduces images of a whiteboard with numbers that include addition to ten. The pin-up board includes the upper and lower case alphabet along with drawings of animals that begin with the letters. There are also readers on a lower shelf, a birthday chart and a clock (1:00 pm). The teacher and all students have smiling facial expressions.

Fig. 2 Representation of a teacher in the classroom context

Fig. 3 Representation of a teacher in the classroom context

Fig. 4 Representation of a teacher in the classroom context

In contrast, Fig. 3 depicts a smiling teacher in a dinner suit behind a desk and a male and female student, one of who is writing on the board, and the other smiling broadly. The desk displays a globe of the world, a document and pencils. Student work is displayed on the wall.

Figure 4 depicts a female teacher reading to a large group of attentive students. The room is well resourced, and many images are displayed on the walls. A duties list is shown and letters of the alphabet are shown on the whiteboard.

Content analysis was employed as a means of 'understanding the symbolic qualities' of the representations, that is "the way that elements of a text [the visual representations] refer to the wider cultural context of which they are a part" (Krippendorf, 1980, in Rose, 2007, p. 60). The content analysis involved devising categories for coding the representations (in our case the categories were developed in relation to the research questions, the literature and our knowledge of the field), coding the representations, counting the frequency of certain visual elements and words, and identifying categories and themes. This process involved individually viewing each representation and coding each time key words or images occurred. The content analysis was completed with the knowledge that our analysis of the results would focus on identifying the discourses that PSTs drew on to produce their representations. Following this initial coding, seven themes were identified: (1) Teacher appearance; (2) Teacher activity; (3) Teacher location (Teacher standing at front of classroom – 51; Teacher sitting at front of classroom – 12; Teacher sitting at desk – 5; Amongst children and at their level-20; Standing over children – 7; Working one-to-one – 11; Teacher standing in front of a board – 25); (4) Symbols (alphabet 50, Numeracy 62, glasses, 37, Hearts 17, apples 13, clocks); (5) Tools/artifacts;

(6) Personal qualities, characteristics and attributes; (7) Gender (125 female; 33 male). A key difference between the representations produced by PSTs from the two universities was that approximately 40% of the FUA PSTs produced representations of a teacher in a classroom setting. However, in comparison this representation was much less evident amongst the ACU PSTs. Reasons for this could be explained by differences in the way the task was presented to PSTs, or by differences in the course content and professional placements at the two universities during the first month of Semester One. For example, at the time of producing the visual representations, the FUA PSTs had completed three days, one day each week, of a professional experience observation placement as part of the Successful Learners Bachelor of Education Course. The ACU cohort had not yet undertaken any formal professional experience placements. This may highlight the influence of course content on PST construction of their professional identity even in the initial weeks of a course.

3.2 Level Two: Discourse Analysis

The second level of analysis for Phase One of the study focused on identifying the discourses of teaching produced and reproduced in and through key elements of the images identified in the content analysis. We were interested in how these PSTs had come to understand and represent a teacher and teaching in the way/s that they had. Analysis at this level attended specifically to how the PSTs' images produced and reproduced particular understandings of teachers (Moore, 2004). The analysis at this level identified both the dominant and marginalized discourses and we also addressed the missing and/or silenced discourses. The dominant discourses were: (1) Teaching as transmission; (2) Teacher as the charismatic and caring subject; (Moore, 2004); (3) Teacher as professional; (4) Teacher as knowledgeable and (5) Teaching as complex. The silent or marginalized discourses were: (1) Teaching as collaborative; (2) Partnerships with parents, colleagues and others; (3) Discourses of diversity and difference; (4) Use of contemporary technology and (5) Reflective practice.

4 Findings and Discussion

A surprising feature of this research was the number of PSTs who chose words alone to create their visual representation of a teacher. Many of these words related to the theme, *Personal qualities and attributes of a teacher and* an integral aspect of the content analysis was the tally of the frequency of the occurrences of each word. The highest frequency of words used to describe the teacher were: fun (25); caring (24); knowledgeable (24); friendly (19); happy (16) and helpful (16). This analysis indicates that a teacher having the attributes of fun, happy and friendly was very frequent which is apparent in the compilation of images from PSTs (Fig. 5). The number of smiling happy faces is striking representing, perhaps, an idealistic image

Fig. 5 Key symbolic representation of personal qualities/attributes: fun, happy, friendly

in that teachers are always smiling. Only one PST from the 181 representations noted that teachers sometimes get stressed and frustrated.

The Content analysis of all the representations led to the identification of seven key themes:

1. Personal appearance
2. Teacher location/positioning
3. Teacher activity
4. Symbols
5. Tools/artifacts related to teaching/curriculum
6. Personal qualities/attributes
7. Gender

Teachers and teaching were represented in stereotypical and traditional ways, using traditional tools, in the context of the classroom and positioned at the front of the room. Teachers were predominantly pointing to the board, or at students who had raised hands, talking to students and physically positioned above students, on a teacher sized chair or leaning over students seated at tables. If positioned at the child's level, most teachers assumed a physical position of authority that is evident by teachers pointing to something in child's work, demonstrating or observing rather than being actively engaged.

4.1 Discourses

Identifying the discourses within which the PSTs constructed their image of a teacher involved examining the representations with care for detail through immersion in the data and the identification of key themes. As expected in research involving data comprising visual representations, we accept that our interpretations are subjective and that just like written texts, visual representations research invokes varied interpretations (Weber & Mitchell, 1995). This requires researchers, when reporting findings, to be clear about the lens through which they interpreted the data that ultimately enables the reader to ascertain the trustworthiness of the interpretations. Our focus was primarily on identifying PSTs' underpinning assumptions about what it means to be a teacher and the representations included teacher in control, teacher as the authorized source of knowledge, dressed in a professional manner, and possessing an extensive and impressive range of personal qualities. We examined these seemingly natural and uncontested ways of being recognized as a teacher through the analysis of the data. As such, we do not claim that our analyses are the only interpretation of the data. A study by Weber and Mitchell, while it did not use discourse analysis or a poststructuralist framework for analysis, found that the images of teachers produced by PSTs and children revealed "the persistent and pervasive presence of traditional images of teaching as transmission of knowledge from all-knowing teacher into empty vessel student … a white woman pointing or expounding, standing in front of a blackboard or desk" (p. 28). Weber and Mitchell also concluded that the traditional stereotypes "remain firmly entrenched in today's children (some of who will be tomorrow's teachers) and in today's teachers (all of who were among yesterday's children) despite the common perception that teaching methods nowadays are radically different" (p. 28).

In the following section, we present data and evidence for the five main discourses we identified:

1. A teacher and teaching is focused on the *transmission of knowledge*, evident in representations of the teacher positioned at the front of class, in front of a board, directing, pointing and talking;
2. A teacher is *charismatic and caring* which is most evident in the words used to describe a teacher. For example, 'care' was one of the most mentioned three words used to describe a teacher and other words included 'patient', 'loving', 'helpful' and 'supportive'. There was a sense of idealism in the positive descriptions and images including smiling faces, words (smiling, fun, inspirational, passionate) and images, including candles, hearts, stars, apples, and flowers;
3. A teacher is and looks *professional and is knowledgeable*, which is evident in the personal appearance and descriptions of a teacher's attributes as they were often described as knowledgeable (n=24), and often depicted as wearing glasses (n=30) to represent this knowledge;
4. A *teacher is connected to learning and ideas* as demonstrated by the words used to describe the teacher, symbols (images of Einstein, books, brains, light bulbs), and depiction of specialized professional knowledge (literacy, numeracy, range of curriculum areas) and,
5. *Teachers and teaching are complex* which was indicated through annotations such as: multiple roles (wears lots of hats); variety of practices/approaches (one to one, groups, reading, transmission); variety in terms of content to be taught and the range of skills needed. Inherent in complexity are tensions and contradictions, representing multiple subjectivities. Several PSTs described teachers as needing to be 'strict yet friendly'.

Images of Teaching: Discourses Within Which Pre-service Teachers Construct Their... 127

Fig. 6 (**a, b**) Dual discourse: teacher as the charismatic and caring subject and teaching as complex

4.1.1 Teacher as Charismatic and Caring Subject

Moore (2004) argues that constructing a teacher as a charismatic and caring subject is the discourse that student teachers most often bring with them to their Education courses. It is a discourse circulated in films and in conversations with family and friends. Moore's point is that this is not necessarily a deficit discourse but that it can lead to PSTs feeling discomfort or self-imposed failure when they discover that they cannot achieve this subjectivity consistently. In other words, they cannot be the charismatic and caring teacher all the time. Figures 6a, b are examples of representations that display two discourses to biographize teaching: the discourse of the teacher as the charismatic and caring subject and the Teaching as complex discourse.

4.1.2 Teaching as Transmission

A dominant discourse used to represent teaching was one of the portrayal of the teacher as the transmitter of knowledge. Figure 7 (below) depicts a stick figure teacher with stars floating from the mouth, drifting above the heads of the students and falling into funnels above the students' heads. The image of the *empty vessels to be filled* is one that was prevalent and "reveals the persistent and pervasive presence of traditional images of teaching as transmission of knowledge from

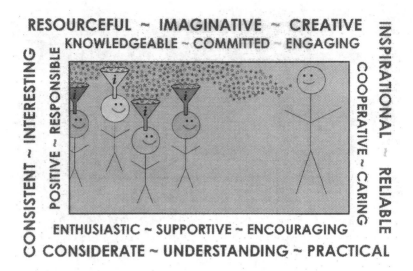

Fig. 7 Teacher as the transmitter of knowledge

all-knowing teacher into empty vessel student" (Weber & Mitchell, 1995, p. 28). Many representations also included the word *knowledgeable* as part of their description of a teacher.

4.1.3 Conventional Images of the Teacher

Multiple images portrayed teachers in conservative dress from a bygone era with twentieth century artifacts. For example, the most common downloaded image from the Web presented by PSTs was an image of Doris Day[1] pointing to a blackboard and using a pointer while dressed in a suit and stiletto shoes. This image represents firmly entrenched stereotypes. As Vick (2008) suggests,

> conservative representations of teachers and teachers' work have a tenacious hold on both established educational professional and pre-service teachers. It argues that such representations are highly problematic for the sort of progressive transformation of professional practice ... Our own complicity in such conservative representations is even more acutely problematic, and opens up questions about our own self-representational practices. It suggests that a transformation of our own self-representations might be a critical condition of transformations of other aspects of our practices ... (p. 2)

What, then, is the link between stereotypes and teacher identity? The research findings concur with Britzman (1991) who suggests that such [stereotypical] images tend to subvert a critical discourse about the lived contradictions of teaching and the

---

[1] For an example of the image of Doris Day as a teacher used by a number of PSTs in their representations see http://www.dorisdaytribute.com/wp-content/uploads/2005/04/Doris-Day-Teachers-Pet.jpg

actual struggles of teachers and students. Stereotypes engender a static and hence repressed notion of identity as something already out there, a stability that can be assumed ... trapped with these images, teachers come to resemble things or conditions " (p. 5). In many ways then, it is the responsibility of teacher educators to address and disturb stereotyped images and explicitly challenge the conventional view.

4.1.4 Teaching as Complex

The PST who produced the image depicted in Fig. 8 included an explanatory text. He explained that the "image shows two personalities of the one person. I believe that a teacher should be strict and formal with how they run their class yet at the same time, seem relaxed and fun to help make the class more enjoyable for the students ... By having these separate personalities in the one class the students need to learn to listen to the teacher and do their work but also find class enjoyable at the

Fig. 8 Teacher with dual roles

same time." This representation highlights the complexity of teaching and the challenges for teachers to be both strict and formal but also relaxed and fun. Teacher education needs to enable PSTs to explore these complexities and resolve any tensions that may emerge.

4.1.5 Teacher as Professional

Teachers in the majority of images were portrayed as professional in appearance. Clothing constituted a key factor in the images of teachers. For example, in the following representation we noted that the dominant feature was the professional dress, including necklace, bracelets, red shoes and a professional bag. Both researchers interpreted the illustration of the bag as a briefcase. It was only during a subsequent interview with the PST that we discovered that the bag was a computer-bag. A notebook computer is viewed here as an essential tool for a teacher (Fig. 9).

Fig. 9 Teacher as a professional

Fig. 10 Teacher and teaching as complex

4.1.6 Teaching and Teacher as Complex: Multiple Roles and Activities

Many images, such as the example in Fig. 10, used words and images to represent the teacher and teaching as complex. The representations depicted multiple roles, varying contexts, a variety of teaching approaches and the demand of curriculum content. The 'Teacher and teaching as complex' discourse suggests multiple subjectivities, tensions and contradictions.

5 Silences and Marginalized Discourses

5.1 *Silent Discourses*

An important aspect of discourse analysis is reading for what is not seen or said (Rose, 2007). The researcher needs to identify what is absent or seldom present. Our discourse analysis highlighted that there were few images that depicted parents. Only one downloaded image showed a teacher talking together with parent and student. There were three instances of written text that mentioned teachers' relationships with parents. There were no images where teachers had body adornment such as piercings or tattoos. Some downloaded images portrayed African American teachers and children but no hand drawn images portrayed ethnic diversity, and only

Fig. 11 The teacher working outdoors was a marginalized discourse

two of the written images mentioned diversity in terms of multiculturalism, but not necessarily in relation to the teacher. In a multi-cultural country such as Australia, this is a 'loud' silence. Also absent in most images were references to forms of technology with only three of the 181 representations including any technological reference. Figure 11 is one of three representations of teachers working outside of a traditional classroom environment. The remaining two were part of collages constructed from images downloaded from the internet.

Moore (2004) cites research suggesting that PSTs often learn very little in their pre-service courses that may actually challenge or change pre-existing views of teaching and learning. Fundamentally, they are more likely to remain influenced by previous experiences of school, by memorable teachers of their own, by media representations of teachers and teaching and by the opinions of family and friends (Moore, 2004). Our aim was to discover what our PSTs *bring with them* to the initial stage of their teacher education in terms of the discourses within which they understand what it means to be a teacher and to teach so that we could invite them to reflect on what their conceptualizations might mean for how they will teach or react to the challenges of professional experience. Our analysis suggests that many PSTs construct teaching and what it means to be a teacher within different, overlapping and often contradictory discourses. Walkerdine (1990) argues that because discourses overlap it is possible to challenge them "to struggle against and to contest the ways in which we are encouraged to identify ourselves and others and to make sense of the social world" (p. 199). As teacher educators, we can facilitate this goal by being explicit, addressing silences, and through using these data with PSTs and teacher educator colleagues in order to disrupt stereotypes and taken-for-granted assumptions about what it means to be a teacher. Weber and Mitchell achieved this by asking PSTs to reflect on and comment on the pictures they drew. They found that they "became aware of the power that past experience and stereotypes seem to have on them. They expressed, often with consternation, their ambivalence in relation to the dominant transmission images of teaching culturally [and historically] embedded in the teaching profession" (p. 29).

Moore (2004) also argues that discourses are 'neither immutable or impenetrable' and he suggests that their evolving nature and our ability to be aware of (and wary of) them means that they are contestable and challengeable. Moore suggests that an essential aspect of developing and improving one's teaching lies in the capacity and willingness to learn and that this learning relates not just to teaching skills, strategies and knowledge but also to understanding and critiquing the discourses within which our formal and informal learning about teaching is framed. Weber and Mitchell (1995) also suggest that we

> need to face more explicitly the probability that ambiguity, and multiple, even if seemingly contradictory images that are integral to the form and substance of our self-identities as teachers. By studying images and probing their influence, teachers can play a more conscious and effective role in shaping their own and society's perceptions of teachers and their work. They could ponder ways of using and even celebrating heterogeneity, viewing it not only as a problematic source of caution and critique, but also as a potential source of renewal and affirmation. (p. 32)

These perspectives are reminiscent of Foucault (1983) who argued "my point is not that everything is bad, but that everything is dangerous, which is not exactly the same as bad. If everything is dangerous then we always have something to do" (pp. 231–232). This is something for us as educators to ponder, something to contest and work on. One specific way of coming to this recognition is to access poststructuralist frameworks for understanding the world. Teacher educators can do this by referring to the representations with PSTs to facilitate reflection and identification of the discourses within which they have produced their images of a teacher. Making poststructuralist perspectives accessible to PSTs will therefore provide the opportunity to gain a deeper understanding of the discourses within which they are producing their understandings of what it means to be a teacher and how these discourses subject and constitute them, and the effects of this in terms of their identities as teachers and how they teach.

6 Enacting Shifts in Practice as Teacher Educators

The key research focus for Phase One was the identification of the ways in which PSTs visually represented teachers and teaching. In response to this data, we undertook to examine the impact of this new knowledge on our practice and we implemented altered approaches to teaching and curriculum development, and thereby challenged not only the PSTs' assumptions about teachers and teaching, but also our own. In the following section of this chapter, we individually describe and reflect on one example of how this Visual Representation research has impacted our practice as teacher educators in our respective Bachelor of Education Courses.

6.1 Responding to Silent and Dominant Discourses

Analysing the rich data collected during this research led to the identification of opportunities for enacting changes in curriculum and practice that would improve the effectiveness of teaching and student learning in the fourth year elective course, (Bachelor of Education program at ACU: EDMA201 *Numeracy in the Early Years*.). In particular, the aim was to focus on three discourses that were critical in mathematics education and could be important for these students' learning: silent discourses related to diverse learners and child-centred classrooms; the dominance of stereotypical images of teachers (for example, the teacher being situated by a chalkboard); and the teacher represented as 'all-knowledgeable' and one who transmits knowledge to students, all of which are important discourses for transforming mathematics learning and teaching. Learning experiences were developed for the PSTs to challenge key assumptions about teachers and teaching mathematics that would enable deeper learning. In contrast to the traditional unit structure of a one hour lecture followed by a two hour workshop, a two hour workshop in partnership with The Smith Family was conducted in two economically disadvantaged communities for 10 weeks to enable PSTs to conduct two weekly after-school *Maths Clubs* for Grade 3 and Grade 4 children. Following a curriculum framework explored in the one hour lectures, the PSTs experienced teaching small groups of children from diverse backgrounds in a non-traditional setting – school multi-purpose rooms. This challenged the dominant discourse that mathematics learning only takes place in formal classroom settings. The Maths Club curriculum for each group was personalised and based on the assessed needs for the individual children. Further, the PSTs identified games and activities that enabled the students to construct mathematical concepts in practical contexts as opposed to memorising and practising mathematical concepts and procedures. PSTs developed and conducted a workshop for the children's parents about ways they could support their children's mathematics learning in everyday contexts. This experience and relationship building with parents was quite transformational for many PSTs. The Maths Club experience with the addition of the assessment tasks for the unit challenged the silences in discourses related to diverse learners and child-centred classrooms, and the dominance of stereotypical images of mathematics teachers being situated by a chalkboard and represented as the all-knowledgeable one who transmits knowledge to students. The PSTs reported in their Action Research Reports at the conclusion of the unit that this was one of the most powerful learning experiences they had undertaken at university as it enabled them to reconstruct their understanding of mathematics learning and teaching and the role of parents and community in children's mathematics learning, and to appreciate their role in transforming mathematics teaching and learning when they graduated at the end of the year. Teaching this unit was transformative, and this was achieved through the explicit addressing of the silent, marginalised and dominant discourses identified in the research. This approach is now an embedded practice within the EDMA201 *Numeracy in the Early Years*.

6.2 Enacting Research-Informed Change in Teacher Education Curriculum

As a response to the visual representation data, the Course, *Professional Policy, Practice and Responsibility* (EDBED4004), a compulsory Fourth Year Bachelor of Education Course, was modified to include the specific challenging of PST assumptions through the completion and shared analysis of the visual representation task during class. The PSTs completed the visual representation of 'self as teacher' and shared their representations with peers in groups and noted the key features evident in each response. These were examined and the ensuing discussions highlighted the dominant and the marginalized discourses that were represented by the tutorial groups and then contrasted with the examples from the Visual Representation research. The silences and marginalised discourses noted during Phase One – for example, catering for the needs of diverse students, technology and community connections – was less marginalized. PSTs explicitly represented their understandings and student needs. Technology was more evident and iPads, computers, iPhones and interactive smart-boards were prevalent in their representations. The following representation includes one PST's image reflecting group work and peer-to-peer learning, small guided-group learning and the teacher, using an ipad and a smart-board to teach the guided group. Key classroom attributes are identified – trust, honesty, respect and responsibility – together with references to a 'school-community' relationship. The PST has identified the dominant discourses represented in this image as 'multi-tasking, technology and group work' (Fig. 12).

Another example reflected a student in a wheelchair with extra wide classroom doors to enable access, leading to a discussion that revealed the PSTs' passion to teach students with specialist needs. Class discussions provided a focused opportunity to address stereotypical and traditional representations of teachers and teaching and provided opportunities to challenge PST assumptions.

The identification of the themes from the analysis of the images – silences related to diverse learners; technology and child-centred classrooms; dominance of stereotypical and conservative images of teachers and teacher as knowledgeable – led to modifications in teacher education courses, and both researchers have, and continue to address dominant and marginalized discourses related to PST's initial, developing and graduating conceptions of teachers and teaching.

Fig. 12 Multi-tasking, technology and group work

7 Conclusion

Teaching is complex, personalized and influenced by context. As Weber and Mitchell (1995) have suggested, even when PST professional identity is acknowledged and explicitly addressed as part of the teaching curriculum, "teacher identity is too often treated as unproblematic and singular in nature" (p. 25). Much to our surprise, however, many of the images presented by the first year PSTs were very alike those produced decades earlier by children and student teachers whose images were presented in Weber and Mitchell's research. Asking PSTs to produce a visual representation of themselves *as a teacher* may seem a simplistic task. In this chapter we have explored the complexity of what underpins a developing professional identity and exposed more about what this means for students of teaching. Professional identity is not fixed or stable but is ever-evolving. To be *classroom ready*, graduate teachers must have a deep understanding of their teaching role and the ways in which their professional identity will impact this role as teacher; the two are not synonymous. Dilemmas and tensions can occur when graduate teachers experience a disconnection between these two spaces.

We acknowledge that our interpretation of the visual images produced by the PSTs is but one interpretation and as such, it *is* a subjective analysis. However, visual methodology research has provided profound insights for us and for the students we teach. Visual methodology research encourages an alternative means of expression, a form of data gathering that is less traditional and allows for creative freedom of expression. The images themselves revealed two critical insights: the first being the predominance of stereotypical and traditional images of teachers and teaching, and the second being the important silent or marginalized discourses that were not or seldom evident in the images. These findings point to ways in which teacher educators can provide learning opportunities through specifically incorporating visual image research within the curriculum as a means to develop and refine PST professional identities as beginning teachers.

The response to the outcomes of visual methodologies research has meant that our assumptions as teacher educators have also been challenged and we have enacted changes in our own practices so that now we address professional identity formation and reformation with PSTs. Through focusing explicitly on marginalized and silent discourses and directly examining these discourses in conjunction with the dominant discourses, opportunities and experiences are provided within the curricula to enable PSTs to identify and begin to articulate their own identity. Education courses that take account of PSTs' professional identities upon entry to university are well placed to assist them to construct professional identities as teachers who are change agents, advocates and pedagogical leaders.

Acknowledgements This research was supported through a Collaborative Research Grant from both Federation University Australia and the Australian Catholic University. We would like to thank the PSTs and colleagues who participated in this research and who have contributed to a deeper understanding of understanding teachers and teaching through visual image representation and analysis.

References

Ball, S. (Ed.). (1990). *Foucault and education: Disciplines and knowledge*. London: Routledge.
Ball, S. J. (2003). The teacher's soul and the terrors of performativity. *Journal of Education Policy, 18*(2), 215–228.
Beauchamp, C., & Thomas, L. (2009). Preparing prospective teachers for a context of change: Reconsidering the role of teacher education in the development of identity. *Cambridge Journal of Education, 39*(2), 175–189.
Beauchamp, C., & Thomas, L. (2011). New teachers' identity shifts at the boundary of teacher education and initial practice. *International Journal of Educational Research, 50.1*, 6–13.
Beijaard, D., Meijer, P. C., & Verloop, N. (2004). Reconsidering research on teachers' professional identity. *Teaching and Teacher Education, 20*, 107–128.
Britzman, D. (1991). *Practice makes practice: A critical study of learning to teach*. Albany, NY: State University of New York Press.
Coldron, J., & Smith, R. (1999). Active location in teachers' construction of their professional identities. *Journal of Curriculum Studies, 31*(6), 711–726.
Foucault, M. (1983). On the genealogy of ethics: An overview of work in progress. Afterword. In H. L. Dreyfus & P. Rabinow (Eds.), *Michel Foucault: Beyond structuralism and hermeneutics* (2nd ed.). Chicago: University of Massachusetts Press.
Guillemin, M. (2004). Understanding illness: Using drawings as a research method. *Qualitative Health Research, 14*(2), 272–289.

Korthagen, F. (2004). In search of the essence of a good teacher: Towards a more holistic approach in teacher education. *Teaching and Teacher Education, 20*, 77–97.

Lasky, S. (2005). A sociocultural approach to understanding teacher identity, agency and professional vulnerability in a context of secondary school reform. *Teaching and Teacher Education, 21*, 899–916.

MacNaughton, G. (2000). *Rethinking gender in early childhood education.* St Leonards, Australia: Allen & Unwin.

Moore, A. (2004). *The good teacher: Dominant discourses in teaching and teacher education.* London: RoutledgeFalmer.

Rose, G. (2007). *Visual methodologies: An introduction to researching with visual materials.* London: Sage.

Sachs, J. (2001). Teacher professional identity: Competing discourses, competing outcomes. *Journal of Education Policy, 16*(2), 149–161.

Sachs, J. (2003). *The activist teaching profession.* Buckingham, UK: Open University Press.

Sachs, J. (2005). Teacher education and the development of professional identity: Learning to be a teacher. In P. Denicolo & M. Kompf (Eds.), *Connecting policy and practice: Challenges for teaching and learning in schools and universities* (pp. 5–21). Oxford, UK: Routledge.

Stronach, I., Corbin, B., McNamara, O., Stark, S., & Warne, T. (2002). Towards an uncertain politics of professionalism: Teacher and nurse identities in flux. *Journal of Education Policy, 17*(1), 109–138.

Teacher Education Ministerial Advisory Group (TEMAG). (2014). *Action now: Classroom ready teachers.* Retrieved from: https://docs.education.gov.au/system/files/doc/other/action_now_classroom_ready_teachers_accessible.pdf.

Thomas, L., & Beauchamp, C. (2011). Understanding new teachers' professional identities through metaphor. *Teaching and Teacher Education, 27*(4), 762–769. doi:10.1016/j.tate.2010.12.007

Vick, M. (2008). *Imagine (like) this: The work the representation of teachers' work does.* Proceedings of the 2008 Australian teacher Education Association National Conference in: Teacher Educators at Work: What works and where is the evidence? July, Queensland, Australia.

Walkerdine, V. (1990). *The mastery of reason: Cognitive development and the production of rationality* (Critical Psychology Series). London: Routledge.

Walkington, J. (2005). Becoming a teacher: Encouraging development of teacher identity through reflective practice. *Asia-Pacific Journal of Teacher Education, 33*(1), 53–64.

Weber, S., & Mitchell, C. (1995). *That's funny you don't look like a teacher: Interrogating images.* London: RoutledgeFalmer.

Weedon, C. (1987). *Feminist practice and poststructuralist theory.* Oxford, UK: Blackwell.

Exploring the Becoming of Pre-service Teachers in Paired Placement Models

Amanda Gutierrez

1 Introduction and Background

In light of a recent review into teacher education (Teacher Education Ministerial Advisory Group (TEMAG), 2014) emphasising quality placement experiences and stronger partnerships with schools, along with literature on paired placements, the Australian Catholic University (ACU) Melbourne trialled paired placements in 2015. The ACU trial was developed during a time of change at the university: enrolments were increasing making finding placements more complex; various alternative placement and partnership options were trialled; and changes in course design included the merging of placements with specific academic coursework units (known as embedded placement units). The paired placement pilot was based on an arrangement whereby two pre-service teachers (PSTs) were assigned to the same supervising teacher's classroom for the duration of their placement. Typically this model revolves around the idea of collaborative team teaching, with two PSTs planning, teaching and reflecting together with the support of their supervising teacher. It is an approach that has been used both internationally and in Australia (for example see Gardiner & Robinson, 2009; Lang, Neal, Karvouni, & Chandler, 2015) and has been found to have many positive outcomes.

This chapter discusses survey and interview data collected from PSTs and their supervising teachers involved in the paired placement pilots to focus on the professional becoming of those involved in the model. It explores the ways PSTs negotiated the triadic arrangement and the ways it influenced the development of their voice on teaching. It also discusses the research aim to explore the supervising teachers' contribution to the paired relationship, and their own development of

A. Gutierrez (✉)
Australian Catholic University, Melbourne, Australia
e-mail: amanda.gutierrez@acu.edu.au

professional identities in this space. Finally, this chapter draws on the analysis to consider the future of alternative models of placement such as paired and group placements in cluster style partnerships and embedded placement units.

2 Literature Review

2.1 The Changing Political Space: Reviewing Teacher Education and Standards

The policy landscape of teacher education, both nationally and internationally is shifting. Australia, like many other nations, is in a political context in which accountability and a focus on 'evidence' is at the forefront of policy changes. Significant recent changes in this area are the introduction of the Australian Institute for Teaching and School Leadership (AITSL) in 2010, which was established to develop national standards for teaching. These national standards came into use in 2013 and have become the criteria used for assessment of PSTs on their placements. In early 2014 a review into teacher education was conducted by the Teacher Education Ministerial Advisory Group (TEMAG) and in late 2014 'Action Now: Classroom Ready Teachers' (referred to as the TEMAG report henceforth) containing 38 recommendations was released. The impact of this changing political environment has manifested at ACU through: an increased focus on accreditation of university courses; exploration of ways to merge course work with placements; and an increased impetus to develop effective and sustainable partnerships between universities, schools and educational organisations.

In relation to PST placements in schools, the TEMAG report highlights variability in the type and quality of experience. The report also identifies the challenges universities are facing in terms of costs of placement and in locating placements in Victoria, stating that "up to 25,000 professional experience placements are needed in that state alone" (TEMAG, 2014, p. 23). Another area affecting the quality experience of PSTs and supervising teachers in school placements is the variability in contact from the provider (TEMAG, 2014). While at the researcher's university we are exploring a new model for partnerships, our previous approach to placements in the Victorian secondary context included: a one supervisor and one PST model; one visit to the PST and supervising teacher for our third year undergraduate Bachelor of Teaching/Bachelor of Arts degree; and a contact call to the PST's supervising teachers for the remaining placements in both the undergraduate and postgraduate Graduate Diploma of Education and Master of Teaching courses. Any PSTs identified by a school to be at risk of failing their placement would receive two visits from one of our sessional tertiary supervisor staff members. The TEMAG report also raises concerns that supervising teachers have not been provided with formal training in the mentoring of PSTs. The variability and quality of school placements are important considerations when trialling non-traditional approaches such as paired placements.

2.2 Exploring the Literature on Paired Placements

There is a growing body of research evidence that highlights benefits for participating schools and PSTs within a collaborative or paired model of placement (Ammentorp & Madden, 2014; Baker & Milner, 2006; Bullough et al., 2003; Gardiner & Robinson, 2009; Harlow & Cobb, 2014). While this evidence cites many benefits that contribute to PSTs' experiences on placement and the supervising teachers' experiences, many also examine the challenges this kind of model can pose.

Bullough et al. (2002) define paired placements as challenging the typical pattern of PST placements, being one PST to one supervising teacher/mentor. Instead, a paired placement has two PSTs placed with one supervising teacher. The paired placement model has evolved internationally and nationally due to: increasing pressure to secure places for PSTs (King, 2006; Smith, 2002); the need for PSTs to develop collaboration skills (Bullough et al., 2003; Smith, 2002; Walsh & Elmslie, 2005); and to provide more scaffolding support (Smith, 2002; Walsh & Elmslie, 2005). The theoretical underpinnings of paired placement are framed in Vygotskian theory, in particular around the zone of proximal development, scaffolding and the benefits of cooperative practices (King, 2006; Smith, 2002; Walsh & Elmslie, 2005). As indicated in the literature, there are multiple ways to set up paired relationships with a variety of guidance mechanisms. Some models provide limited guidance (Bullough et al., 2002; Nokes, Bullough, Egan, Birrell, & Hansen, 2008), while others provide set roles and responsibilities for each member of the pair to assist with team teaching in the classroom (Parsons & Stephenson, 2005; Smith, 2002).

2.3 Benefits and Challenges of Paired Placements

Multiple benefits for both the PSTs and their supervising teachers are identified in the literature. Authors such as Gardiner (2010) and Nokes et al. (2008) suggest this model increases opportunities to meet the needs of classroom students through three way professional dialogue between the school supervising teacher and PSTs. Gardiner (2010) also argues the targeted exploration of different pedagogical models including team teaching and tandem teaching is an additional benefit. Smith (2002) listed positive outcomes of paired placements such as: emotional support for the PSTs (also identified by King, 2006); the potential of learning more from their pair due to a smaller gap in experience compared to their supervising teacher; and more support in the classroom for school students. Bullough et al. (2002, 2003) also identified this learning potential, as well as the opportunity for PSTs and school supervisors to engage in rich and authentic scaffolded feedback. They suggest "fresh" ideas and the process of rethinking their roles as mentors can reinvigorate supervisors. Other benefits discussed included developing stronger confidence in PSTs to trial approaches and problem solve (Harlow & Cobb, 2014; King, 2006) and the strengthening of collaborative skills and approaches to working in teams (Manouchehri, 2002).

The literature also traces the challenges that exist in paired placements with Lang et.al. (2015), for example, suggesting some principals do not believe a paired placement arrangement prepares PSTs for the real world of teaching. This view was also evident in PSTs' responses in Gardiner and Robinson's (2009) research where some PSTs suggested they developed an overreliance on their pair in their weaker areas and, therefore, did not push themselves to improve in these areas, describing using their pair as a "crutch". In addition, Bullough et al.'s (2003) research identified PST concerns that schools would not view their paired placement experiences as worthwhile when looking for employment. Some literature identifies issues regarding personality conflicts (Smith, 2002; Wynn & Kromrey 2000) that impact on PSTs' ability to plan together and concerns about relationships in which one PST was more dominant than the other (Smith, 2002). Related to this concern is the reality that PSTs are individually assessed on their placement rounds which can raise issues relating to equitable and objective assessment and feedback, and being compared by the supervising teacher (Smith, 2002; Walsh & Elmslie, 2005).

Other challenges associated with these models relate to a supervisor's workload. Some supervisors identified a perceived increased workload as they came to terms with the different style of placement (Baker & Milner, 2006; Bullough et al., 2002; Walsh & Elmslie, 2005). It was also identified that some supervisors provided less individualized attention and feedback (Baker & Milner, 2006), and others viewed a paired placement as an opportunity to decrease their supervisor workload providing less attention for PSTs, instead expecting the pairs to support each other (Smith, 2002). A final difficulty identified by Smith is limited understanding in the triad team about how to team-teach, which can create classroom management issues.

2.4 Tensions, Identity and Learning in the Paired Placement

Nokes et al. (2008) examine the role of tension, dialogue and reflection in the paired relationship and of particular interest to this chapter is their identification of the way the resolution of tension varied when the PSTs were in dialogue with each other rather than with their supervising teacher. The actions of the supervising teachers when tension and conflict was evident between the PSTs were also interesting with some supervisors seeing this as an opportunity for professional growth, whereas others avoided the conflict and split the pair into two solo placements. What is missing, however, is a discussion of how the power of the voices within the triad relationship influenced the actions the PSTs and supervising teachers took and this is something addressed within this chapter.

Harlow and Cobb (2014) draw on the notion of community of practices and Wenger's (1998) discussion of PSTs' negotiation of learning and identity development within these social spaces to explore developing teacher identity and the contribution of the placement to PSTs' 'becoming' as a teacher. They argue that multiple levels of community can contribute to teachers' experiences and deeper and reflective understanding of teaching. They also identified confidence as playing "a critical role in either constraining or enabling the development of teacher identity" (Harlow & Cobb, 2014, p. 84). Harlow and Cobb's work is one of the few that theorise the multilayered relationships that exist in 'communities of practice' and most closely aligns with the analysis focus of this research. For the purpose of my research, I focus on the Bakhtinian concept of dialogism rather than the notion of community of practice.

While the literature on paired placements has identified the positive aspects and challenges of this kind of arrangement, the discussion does not venture into how the combination of these experiences, and conflicts with certain voices contribute to the PST and supervising teachers' overall ideological understanding of what the teaching profession is. There is little exploration of how the overlapping of social worlds, such as school discourses, university discourses, and pre-existing discourses within each individual interweave in triadic relationships to add to, disrupt or normalise notions of professional becoming as a teacher.

3 Theoretical Framework

3.1 *Professional Becoming*

The notion of 'professional becoming' is central to the findings and analysis in this chapter. To develop a theoretical understanding of the concept professional becoming one can draw on recent discussions in this area, and for the purpose of my research, I have drawn on Bakhtinian views of knowledge creation. Publications by Kostogriz (2007), Kostogriz and Peeler (2007), and Mulcahy (2011) explore the connection between 'professional' and 'becoming' in educational settings. Drawing on Lefebvre (1991), Kostogriz explores the spatial dynamics and socially constructed nature of professionalism and professional knowledge. He argues, "the focus on the interplay between official and unofficial knowledge in learning uncovers teachers' professional becoming as multidimensional and related to their daily lives" (Kostogriz, 2007, p. 34). Mulcahy develops an understanding of professional becoming through actor-network theory, emphasizing professional becoming as not only a process, but also a material practice incorporating multiple heterogeneous networks.

These views compliment a Bakhtinian conceptualization of *professional becoming* using a concept from Bakhtin called 'ideological becoming' (Bakhtin, 1978). Bakhtin's use of ideology relates to the ways social groups view the world. Ideological becoming describes the complex process humans move through when engaging with social groups and the influence this has on one's views about the world. Kostogriz and Peeler's (2007) renegotiation of traditional uses of context to the concept of space when discussing professional learning is useful in describing the process of ideological becoming. The notion of space enables an appreciation of the multiplicity of voices and ideological environments (Bakhtin, 1978) that contribute to one's ideological becoming. In this chapter ideological becoming has been appropriated and relabeled 'professional becoming' to acknowledge the particular social group in this research, teachers, who exist in discursive spaces in which 'professional' processes and material practices exist on levels from school expectations through to legislative requirements.

Bakhtin argued that the voices we come into contact with can become assimilated without challenge, dismissed or modified. The outcome of this mixing of voices and discourses with our own is that we create a hybridized (Bakhtin, 1981, 1986) version that meets our own needs and contexts. Freedman and Ball (2004) explore the concept of hybridization in their research on teacher professional learning arguing:

> the role of the other is critical to our development; in essence, the more choice we have of words to assimilate, the more opportunity we have to learn. In a Bakhtinian sense, with whom, in what ways, and in what contexts we interact will determine what we stand to learn. (p. 6)

The kinds and variety of voices available in a teacher's environment will influence their learning and, hence, constructions and understandings of what it means to be a teacher.

3.2 Authoritative Discourses

Another important consideration for this particular research is the influence of what Bakhtin (1986) labelled "authoritative discourses". His conceptualization of language and meaning represents the multifaceted relationships that exist between voices as individuals and authorities as they attempt to create stability for themselves and others within discourse. Various forces form a complex matrix through space and time, which results in discourses not only reaffirming social systems but also contributing to the renegotiation and change of systems (Lemke, 1995). The paired placement challenges a traditionally accepted social system in which one supervisor has one PST and this concept is also a consideration in the triadic relationship. While Bakhtin's use of authoritative discourse tends to be in the context of dictatorships or religious scriptures, in this context the supervising teachers' voice represents a powerful force that PSTs sometimes struggle to challenge as this voice can be represented by the educational social system, and at times by the supervising teachers themselves, as the authority on how to be a teacher. It is important to consider the possibility of the supervisors' voice acting as an authoritative discourse, and the influence this has on the professional becoming of both the PSTs and the supervising teachers.

4 Participants and Context

A paired placement research study was conducted in Semester One and Semester Two of 2015. In this pilot PSTs were allocated to a school based on their geographical location and method area. The Semester One study comprised of a group of Postgraduate Diploma of Education PSTs (n = 12), with data collected essentially for evaluative purposes. During Semester Two, two cohorts were placed in paired arrangements and this research draws on data from seven Postgraduate Diploma of Education PSTs (five female/two male) and two supervising teachers (one male/one female) from this placement. Participants completed an online survey and were invited to participate in a follow up interview, with two PSTs participating in an interview. All data presented in this chapter uses pseudonyms.

Like Bullough Jr. et al. (2002), I chose to encourage the supervising teachers to negotiate the implementation and structure of the paired placement to suit their context and their perceived needs of the PSTs. Participants were provided with information outlining the concept of paired placements and recent research in this area. It was expected that PSTs planned and taught as pairs, as well as each PST having an opportunity to teach solo and provide peer feedback for each other. During pre-placement workshops PSTs were provided with material about conducting professional conversations with peers and their supervising teacher.

5 Aims and Method

The research discussed in this chapter was based on four key aims which were to:

1. examine the contributions paired placements can make to the professional becoming of PSTs;
2. examine the contributions paired placements can make to the professional becoming of supervising teachers;
3. examine the ways PSTs and their supervising teachers in paired placements negotiate unfamiliar situations and conflicts; and,
4. develop an understanding of the kinds of spaces that enable alternative placement models such as paired placements to succeed.

5.1 Data Collection Methods

The study drew on a mixed methods approach, using survey and interview data. The survey included ranking scales and open ended questions and was designed in SurveyMonkey, a familiar survey tool for teachers and PSTs. As identified above, survey data was drawn from seven PSTs and two teachers, and interview data from two PSTs. The analysis in this chapter draws primarily from the open ended question responses and transcribed interview responses as they provided the most valuable data about the participants' professional becoming and their negotiation of tensions. The data was analysed using a combination of thematic grouping and item analysis, with the Bakhtinian theoretical framework applied to develop a more detailed understanding of the participants' comments in relation to the research aims.

5.2 Limitations

This is a small scale research project that does not enable generalisations about the effectiveness of the paired placement to be drawn, however the surveys and interviews point to interesting findings about the effect a paired placement can have on teachers' development of professional understandings about themselves and the teaching profession. Rather than making generalisations about a larger population, this research was interested in the particularity of the ways PSTs and supervising teachers negotiate the voices within the paired placement space.

6 Analysis and Discussion

As identified in the review of the literature there are positive and negative outcomes associated with paired placements and while this analysis illustrates the benefits and challenges, I focus particularly on the contribution of tensions and conflicts to the professional becoming of the participants, and to the renegotiation or perpetuation of particular discourses in teaching. More specifically, I explore the ways these dialogues exist in ideological environments and the internal struggles participants had as they developed their own hybridized voice in the process of their professional becoming. The analysis begins by examining the PST data and then moves on to examine the survey data from the supervising teachers.

6.1 Pre-service Teacher Surveys and Interviews

This section reports on key themes emerging from the survey and interview data of the PSTs. The pseudonyms used for the participants whose responses were selected for the analysis are Ellie, Rebecca and Ashley. Rebecca and Ashley volunteered to be interviewed and the interview data has been used in combination with their survey responses to explore their professional becoming in more depth.

6.1.1 The Influence of Conflicts and Constraints on Professional Becoming

The tensions identified by PSTs in the survey with the voices around them in the triadic relationship, and their actions, illustrated the struggles PSTs often have when they have to negotiate difficult professional conversations and conflicts. Two PSTs suggested no conflicts arose, however all seven who completed the survey identified some form of constraint and/or challenge. Some of the comments were troubling, suggesting a great deal of preparation would be required to enable PSTs to learn from multiple voices they encounter in paired placements, rather than perceiving their partner as competition, inferior, or of no benefit to their own professional becoming.

Ellie stated that her pair "was not really interested in my reflections on her lessons so I stopped doing them for her. She never typed up any reflections on my lessons. We sometimes shared verbally about lessons". The potential to learn as one negotiates heterogeneous voices in a triadic space was limited by the reluctance from Ellie's partner to engage in dialogic interactions. It appeared Ellie initiated a process in which peer to peer voices could form an additional contribution to their professional becoming, rather than just the traditional more authoritative supervising teacher to the often-compliant PST (Nokes et al., 2008). It was unfortunate that this experience became such a challenge for Ellie that she chose to cease her involvement in this process rather than develop a dialogue in the triad, or even with her partner, about the tension she felt in this space. Ellie also raised the issue of a conflict with her supervisor's approach to assessment stating,

> I felt conflicted internally since I witnessed testing that resulted in a 40% average for the Year 7 class and was not able to go back over the test or have a discussion with the class. I was told to move on to the next topic. This had nothing to do with the paired placement but with the strategy for assessment being used by my supervising teacher.

To state that this had "nothing to do with the paired placement" demonstrates the multiplicity of dialogic struggles that existed within this relationship. Not only did she cease sharing reflective feedback with her partner, but Ellie felt an internal conflict about her supervising teachers' approaches. Her comments disassociating this conflict with the relationship she had with her partner suggests she did not view the paired placement as an opportunity to explore with her partner areas of conflict with their supervising teacher. One of the benefits discussed in much of the literature relating to paired placements refers to the emotional and pedagogical support that comes from working with a peer. A combination of unreconciled conflict with her partner and an unchallenged authoritative discourse through her supervising teacher meant Ellie was unable to engage in this space in a productive way on ideological discourses around professional understandings of teaching.

Ashley's responses in the survey suggested a complete break down in the relationship. He stated "my partner didn't want me in their class after two weeks. This caused a little awkwardness. This was her decision not mine," and he attributed this break down to "different styles of teaching, different levels of expectation about what was expected, different ideas about what would work, different levels of experience". Ashley's interview provided further information on how he negotiated the tension leading up to and as a result of splitting the pair, and the influence this had on his professional becoming.

Ashley had been a teacher's aide in a school for a number of years, and expressed excitement about team teaching in a situation where he was one of the lead teachers rather than an aide. He said it is "often frustrating being in the teaching aide role because you can't control the classroom". His interactions in the space of teaching aide had provided him access to multiple voices on teaching, however his frustrations reflect the desire to be the dominant voice in the classroom. He reported no conflicts with his supervising teacher on placement, saying that she "was fantastic, very considerate, looked for both myself and my pair's voice in the process and gave us control over the process". The placement experience provided the potential for Ashley to have the control he felt was lacking in his teaching aide role. He also said she:

> made us aware very early that she was going to listen to us, take into account what we thought, plan with us and it was going to be a very collaborative approach, as opposed to her just being the figure that told us what we were going to do and when we were going to do it.

Ashley's description suggests the supervising teacher in the early stages of the paired placement enabled a dialogic approach to planning and teaching supporting the collaborative nature of the paired placement arrangement. Ashley's statements also suggest he did not believe his supervisor was going to make attempts to represent herself as an authoritative discourse on teaching, which, for someone with established internal discourses on teaching, created less tension and more willingness to engage with the voice of this person.

Ashley's perception, however, of the collaborative process and dialogic possibilities in the triad seemed to be contradicted by his description of the events leading up to the separation of the pair. He stated at the commencement of the round that he and his pair "both went into it with very positive intentions, we tried to make it work, definitely at the start" and that he was "willing to make it work". The decision to split the pair, however, was not collaborative as he stated,

> after a week and a half my supervising teacher and pair had a discussion in private and my supervising teacher said that it would be better if I didn't go to anymore of the classes that my pair was teaching. Obviously my pair felt it was not going to work.

Neither Ashley's pair nor their supervisor spoke with Ashley about their concerns prior to the decision to split the pair. While "at the time I wasn't too perturbed about it", Ashley "felt perhaps my pair could have come to me and spoken to me about it". By removing a key voice in the triadic relationship the potential for a dialogic approach to working through and learning from the ideological tension and the potential for this process to contribute to both Ashley, his partner and supervising teacher's professional becoming was stifled.

Ashley's actions in this situation were to accept rather than challenge the decision delivered by his supervising teacher stating "as the placement went on me and my pair were at different stages of teaching perhaps and that became very apparent to my mentor teacher". He rationalised the decision by commenting that his supervisor "saw that I wanted to control the class but that I kept stopping because my pair was there" and that "in my pair's case, she saw that I was a more dominant figure so she felt like my presence in the room, like she would give me more control instead of having to do it herself". His concerns reflect the issue raised by Gardiner and Robinson (2009) that sometimes a pair may use their partner as a "crutch" and not challenge themselves to develop to their full potential. It appeared the potential for the triadic interaction of voices assisting in the professional becoming of those in the relationship was severely limited after this point as the pair "did not work on planning together after this point either". While Ashley told his pair he was more than happy to share what he was preparing, his comment that "if I went off what she was preparing I would have felt underprepared" illustrated a lack of confidence with his partner's professional decisions about teaching, and an apparent acceptance by the supervising teacher that collaboration between the three was not able to provide further opportunities to assist both PSTs to 'become' more effective teachers.

6.1.2 The Role of Confidence in PST Professional Becoming

The importance of feeling confident was touched on by some PSTs, but was particularly evident in Rebecca's survey and interview. Harlow and Cobb (2014) state "lack of confidence seemed to inhibit the ability for pre-service teachers to actively involve themselves in teaching experiences, which impacted on their perceptions of their identities as teachers" (p. 84). This inhibition was evident in Rebecca's responses, which acted as a barrier to her professional becoming.

In her survey Rebecca stated "I didn't like having my pair in my classroom, in the end my supervisor and I decided it was best we both taught alone". Rebecca felt intimidated by her partner as he was "slightly older and had worked in a school before [which] made him much more confident and made me look terrible in the classroom". Rebecca highlighted one of the issues raised by Smith (2002) and Walsh and Elmslie (2005) in that she viewed the relationship as competitive. She felt her partner had a closer relationship with the supervisor and he tended to arrive earlier and leave later, which she perceived as an effort to "make me look bad". She also identified a concern that the university supervisor (not the researcher) who made a phone call to the school to check on their progress did not speak to her individually and that she was "basically grilled about my teaching style and how I was going to improve" in front of both her supervising teacher and her partner.

Rebecca's diminished confidence influenced her ability to negotiate the internal dialogic struggle that was a result of differing ideologies on teaching with her partner, and the authoritative voice of her supervisor. Her lack of confidence at times impacted the ways she constructed her identity creating conflict in her understanding of who she was as a professional. In her interview she stated that she was perceived as very quiet, which she reasoned as only because she was being compared to her "outgoing and loud" partner. Part of the tension for Rebecca was her perception that the relationship with her partner was competitive, and this conflict inhibited her confidence in speaking to her partner about the situation. In addition, her feelings of inferiority due to her partner's experiences in schools made her perceive her power status within the triadic space as the lowest, number three. Nokes et al. (2008) suggested "having one's ideas questioned by a peer is fundamentally different than having ideas questioned by an experienced mentor teacher" (p. 2173), however when two people in the triad are perceived as more experienced a situation may arise where "it is much safer for a student teacher to disengage from the dialogue" (Nokes et al., 2008, p. 2173). In particular, if the peer is perceived as more experienced, as Smith (2002) found, this may create more tension as it challenges the expectations of this relationship.

This is evident in Rebecca's situation as she said the decision to split was "the supervising teacher's from the beginning. In the end she came up to us quietly and said you're both on your way now, I think you should take one class each". The supervisor in this situation chose to protect both PSTs from what she perceived as an unproductive relationship. However, these vast differences in ideologies which created tension, if managed carefully, may have allowed critical engagement with the 'other' to develop a stronger sense of where predispositions about how and what to teach come from, and how to combine one's understandings with those of experienced supervising teachers to contribute to one's professional becoming. As Nokes et al. (2008) argue, "when two student teachers disagree there is an enhanced potential for rich interaction and reflection" (p. 2173), however to be successful this requires dialogue between the partners. When one peer removes their voice and limits the other's voice, and the supervising teacher encourages the shift to solo teaching, dialogue and the learning experience opportunities decreases. It is cases such as these in which additional professional voices with expertise in negotiation in adult interactions could enable positive dialogic outcomes leading to professional growth.

6.1.3 PST Voices: A Summary

For many of the PSTs in this study their hybridized versions of being a teacher professional in a secondary context does not include positive ideological positioning towards the ability to work collegially within the classroom space. Many identified tensions with the voices within their placement arrangement, and that they struggled to find ways to learn from these tensions. There were suggestions that a paired approach was useful for planning, but very few saw the approach as useful for their professional becoming in the implementation of teaching in the classroom.

6.2 Supervising Teacher Feedback

One of the limitations of the research was the lack of data generated from supervising teachers, with only two teachers completing the survey, with this limitation pointing the way for future research. Both supervisors were experienced, having supervised several PSTs previously in solo arrangements. This was their first experience working with a pair of PSTs. The experience of supervision of a pair was perceived as positive and they identified benefits that focused on the social, emotional and pedagogical support of the paired model, as reflected in the literature on paired placements.

The supervising teachers identified that the paired arrangement may not have worked as effectively if there were "really clashing personalities" or if "they don't get along so well", with this data echoing the comments from PST's in the literature review who had tensions of this nature. The perception of success in a paired placement appears to be associated with the PST's ability to "get along" or develop rapport. The supervising teachers did not identify what the PSTs could learn from contrasting or conflicting voices, or their role in providing alternative voices to encourage critical reflection on ingrained ideologies about education.

Each of the supervisors identified the positives of having the pair with Anne stating it meant "as a part timer, didn't feel so guilty on my day off" as she knew the PSTs could support each other, reflecting Smith's (2002) discussions on the expectation by supervising teachers that the pairs *will* support each other in their absence. Tim stated having a PST meant he had to "take the time to again note the professional standards and consider how closely one is actually doing what is expected of a teacher. This is because of the need to model behaviour and also offer feedback", however, this could be interpreted more as a general statement about supervising PSTs, rather than something specific to the paired placement itself. The survey responses from the supervisors did not provide insights into the intricacies of being traditionally the more authoritative voice in the relationship and how they managed triadic collaboration. These gaps are ones that can be addressed in future research.

7 Outcomes of the Paired Research

While the PSTs and supervising teachers in this research identified multiple complexities of paired placements that challenged their own persuasive discourse on what teaching should be, with some saying it created barriers to their professional becoming, this does not mean paired approaches are not of value. While some literature suggests a better outcome may be reached by asking PSTs to volunteer to be a part of a pair (Smith, 2002), this results in only a select few developing the negotiation skills required in collaborative teaching arrangements. Rather than adopt this approach there are ways to improve paired placement experiences for large cohorts and through reflecting on this research, and considering ways to address the issues and recommendations raised by TEMAG (2014), a more effective paired placement model can be conceptualised.

7.1 Conditions for Paired Placements to Contribute to Professional Becoming

An effective way to utilise paired placements is in coursework units that embed the placement experience into course work. In 2016 we will be implementing a second year embedded placement that requires pairs to focus specifically on a smaller group, rather than the task of teaching the whole class. The course work component of the academic study will incorporate workshops and role-plays on professional conversations with the pairs before they commence their placement, along with the inclusion of a small paired or a group research project on differentiation with specific groups of students, or the implementation of particular pedagogies or theories. This enables all parties to negotiate theoretical voices with their own, each other's and supervisors' voices, as well as the classroom student voices, contributing to the PST's professional becoming in relation to their understanding of the nexus between theory and practice, and collaborative approaches.

In relation to the professional becoming of the supervising teachers, the provision of mentoring training would be highly beneficial. The mentoring of supervising teachers would benefit from an 'outside' voice that may be able to disrupt established and ingrained ideologies. Professional learning focused on professional conversations and conflict negotiation also needs to occur with both supervising teachers and PSTs. The PST group who completed the survey appeared to need more workshops than were provided in this area with data indicating that some PSTs have strong internal persuasive discourses around what becoming a secondary teacher means, including the idea that close collaboration, particularly in classroom teaching, is not a requirement. Collaborative approaches to teaching and open classrooms where teaching is critiqued by peers, leaders and 'outside' critical friends are becoming more common place and these are essential skills for teachers to develop.

7.2 Importance of Strong Partnerships

To improve trials of alternative placement models, it is important that stronger intersections between universities and schools are developed to provide supportive dialogic spaces. Along with leadership team members and staff in the secondary component of the placement program, I am introducing a cluster partnership system in which academics are connected geographically to a number of schools. These academic staff will become integral parts of the school community. In this model they will provide support to the PSTs and their supervising teachers in the schools while they are on placement. This model also incorporates mentoring training, collaborative options for school-university partnership work on school improvement plans and support for staff around action research. The clusters also provide the opportunity for more integrated teaching of academic content in schools, and trials of alternative placement models that develop a better understanding of the theory and practice nexus. These partnership spaces can become Communities of Practice where multiple voices negotiate the improvement of school student outcomes through research and practice. The TEMAG (2014) report states "close working relationships through effective partnerships between providers and schools can produce mutually beneficial outcomes and facilitate a close connection between teaching practice and initial teacher education" (p. 25). Effective partnerships in this space will assist the implementation of collaborative models of placement such as paired placements and strengthen the professional becoming of not only pre-service, early career, experienced and leadership educators in schools but also tertiary educators and researchers involved in the clusters.

8 Conclusion and Future Directions

This research has highlighted the ways in which PSTs negotiate the triadic relationship that comes with paired placement in schools. While these models of placement have the potential to provide multifarious forms of support and contributions to PST and supervising teachers' professional becoming, this research has revealed that there needs to be careful construction of links between university and schools to assist both supervisors and PSTs in negotiating these complex spaces. The future directions for this researcher in relation to paired placement research is to explore how a more targeted use of paired placements in the new cluster partnership model, combined with a paired assessment task in an embedded placement unit contributes to the professional becoming of PSTs, supervisors and tertiary staff. It is anticipated that establishing clusters with academics linked to each cluster will enable the development of a stronger relationship between the university and schools, provide better conditions for dialogue and positive outcomes for the professional becoming of those involved in alternative professional placement models.

References

Ammentorp, L., & Madden, L. (2014). Partnered placements: Creating and supporting successful collaboration among preservice teachers. *Journal of Early Childhood Teacher Education, 35*(2), 135–149. doi:10.1080/10901027.2014.905805

Baker, S., & Milner, J. (2006). Complexities of collaboration: Intensity of mentors' responses to paired and single student teachers. *Action in Teacher Education, 28*(3), 61–72.

Bakhtin, M. (1978). *The formal method in literary scholarship: A critical introduction to sociological poetics* (A. Wehrle, Trans.). London: John Hopkins University Press.

Bakhtin, M. (1981). *The dialogic imagination* (C. Emerson & M. Holquist, Trans.). Austin: The University of Texas Press.

Bakhtin, M. (1986). *Speech genres and other late essays* (V. McGee, Trans.). Austin: University of Texas Press.

Bullough, R., Jr., Young, J., Birrell, J. R., Cecil Clark, D., Winston Egan, M., Erickson, L., et al. (2003). Teaching with a peer: A comparison of two models of student teaching. *Teaching and Teacher Education, 19*(1), 57–73. doi:10.1016/S0742-051X(02)00094-X

Bullough, R., Jr., Young, J., Erickson, L., Birrell, J., Clark, D., Egan, M., et al. (2002). Rethinking field experiences: Partnership teaching vs single-placement teaching. *The Journal of Teacher Education, 53*(1), 68–80. doi:10.1177/0022487102053001007

Freedman, S., & Ball, A. (2004). Ideological becoming: Bakhtinian concepts to guide the study of language, literacy and learning. In A. Ball & S. Freedman (Eds.), *Bakhtinian perspectives on language, literacy and learning* (pp. 3–33). Cambridge, UK: Cambridge University Press.

Gardiner, W. (2010). Mentoring two student teachers: Mentors' perceptions of peer placements. *Teaching Education, 21*(3), 233–246. doi:10.1080/10476210903342102

Gardiner, W., & Robinson, K. S. (2009). Paired field placements: A means for collaboration. *The New Educator, 5*(1), 81–94. doi:10.1080/1547688X.2009.10399565

Harlow, A., & Cobb, D. J. (2014). Planting the seed of teacher identity: Nurturing early growth through a collaborative learning community. *Australian Journal of Teacher Education, 39*(7), 70–88. doi:10.14221/ajte.2014v39n7.8

King, S. (2006). Promoting paired placements in initial teacher education. *International Research in Geographical and Environmental Education, 15*(4), 370–386. doi:10.2167/irg201.0

Kostogriz, A. (2007). Spaces of professional learning: Remapping teacher professionalism. In A. Berry, A. Clemens, & A. Kostogriz (Eds.), *Dimensions of professional learning: Professionalism, practice and identity* (pp. 23–36). Rotterdam, The Netherlands: Sense Publishers.

Kostogriz, A., & Peeler, E. (2007). Professional identity and pedagogical space: Negotiating difference in teacher workplaces. *Teaching Education, 18*(2), 107–122. doi:10.1080/10476210701325135

Lang, C., Neal, D., Karvouni, M., & Chandler, D. (2015). An embedded professional paired placement model: "I know I am not an expert, but I am at a point now where I could step into the classroom and be responsible for the learning". *Asia-Pacific Journal of Teacher Education, 43*(4), 338–354. doi:10.1080/1359866X.2015.1060296

Lefebvre, H. (1991). *The production of space*. Oxford, UK: Blackwell.

Lemke, J. (1995). *Textual politics: Discourse and social dynamics*. London: Taylor and Francis.

Manouchehri, A. (2002). Developing teaching knowledge through peer discourse. *Teaching and Teacher Education, 18*, 715–737. doi:10.1016/S0742-051X(02)00030-6

Mulcahy, D. (2011). Teacher professional becoming: A practice-based, actor-network theory perspective. In L. Scanlon (Ed.), *"Becoming" a professional: An interdisciplinary analysis of professional learning* (pp. 219–244). Houten, The Netherlands: Springer.

Nokes, J., Bullough, R., Jr., Egan, W., Birrell, J., & Hansen, J. (2008). The paired-placement of student teachers: An alternative to traditional placements in secondary schools. *Teaching and Teacher Education, 24*, 2168–2177. doi:10.1016/j.tate.2008.05.001

Parsons, M., & Stephenson, M. (2005). Developing reflective practice in student teachers: Collaboration and critical partnerships. *Teachers and Teaching: Theory and Practice, 11*(1), 95–116. doi:10.1080/1354060042000337110

Smith, J. D. N. (2002). The development of tandem teaching placements. *Mentoring & Tutoring: Partnership in Learning, 10*(3), 253–274. doi:10.1080/1361126022000022507

Teacher Education Ministerial Advisory Group (TEMAG). (2014). *Action now: Classroom ready teachers – Australian Government response*. Canberra: Australian Government. Retrieved from: https://docs.education.gov.au/system/files/doc/other/action_now_classroom_ready_teachers_accessible.pdf.

Walsh, K., & Elmslie, L. (2005). Practicum pairs: An alternative for first field experience in early childhood teacher education. *Asia-Pacific Journal of Teacher Education, 33*(1), 5–21. doi:10.1080/1359866052000341098

Wenger, E. (1998). *Communities of practice: Learning, meaning and identity*. Cambridge, UK: Cambridge University Press.

Wynn, M., & Kromrey, J. (2000). Paired peer placement with peer coaching to enhance prospective teachers' professional growth in early field experiences. *Action in Teacher Education, 22*(2A), 73–83. doi:10.1080/01626620.10463041

Internships in Initial Teacher Education in Australia: A Case Study of the Griffith Education Internship

Paula Jervis-Tracey and Glenn Finger

1 Introduction: The Aim of the Chapter

This chapter focuses on the importance of Internships in initial teacher education (ITE) in Australia. Internships are situated within the wider attention being afforded to improving ITE programs, evident through the reviews and their terms of reference in recent years. To illustrate, the TEMAG report *Action Now: Classroom Ready Teachers* (TEMAG, 2014a) stated that it "…grew out of two clear propositions: that improving the capability of teachers is crucial to lifting student outcomes; and that the Australian community does not have the confidence in the quality and effectiveness of new teachers" (p. 1). The scale of this initial teacher education agenda in Australia was highlighted in the preceding *Teacher Education Ministerial Advisory Group Issues Paper* (TEMAG, 2014b, p. 5) which stated that, "In 2012, there were around 76,000 domestic pre-service teachers enrolled in these programmes – 62,000 in undergraduate programmes and 14,000 in postgraduate programmes". That issues paper acknowledged other reviews conducted in most Australian jurisdictions in the previous two years, including:

- New South Wales – *Great Teaching, Inspired learning: Blueprint for Action* (New South Wales Government Education and Communities, 2014)

P. Jervis-Tracey
School of Education and Professional Studies, Griffith University,
Mt Gravatt Campus, 176 Messines Ridge Road, Mt Gravatt, Queensland 4122, Australia
e-mail: p.jervis-tracey@griffith.edu.au

G. Finger (✉)
School of Education and Professional Studies, Griffith University,
Gold Coast Campus, Gold Coast, Queensland 4222, Australia
e-mail: g.finger@griffith.edu.au

- Victoria – *From New Directions to Action: World class teaching and school leadership* (State of Victoria Department of Education and Early Childhood Development, 2013)
- Queensland – *A Fresh Start: Improving the preparation and quality of teachers for Queensland schools* (Department of Education & Training and Employment, 2013)
- South Australia – *Building a Stronger South Australia: High Quality Education* (Government of South Australia, 2013)

Disturbingly, these reviews highlighted important areas for strengthening both accountability processes and improvement agendas in the quality of ITE programs (Finger, 2013). For example, the six key findings of the most recent review by TEMAG (2014a) included the following three findings: evidence of poor practice in a number of programs; insufficient integration of teacher education providers with schools and systems, and, inadequate application of standards.

Consequently, the design and implementation of quality ITE programs should address those concerns through producing quality graduates and ensure public confidence. Importantly, Internships are located in the final semester of an ITE program during which ITE students are expected to demonstrate the expectations of the *Australian Professional Standards for Teachers – Graduate Teachers* (AITSL, 2014).

The authors outline the context of this research by summarising the emergence of Internships in ITE programs in Australia. More specifically, we note the historical development of *The Griffith Education Internship* which had its genesis more than 21 years ago in 1994. That Internship model has been scaled up as a mandatory course for all students undertaking the Bachelor of Education (Primary) at Griffith University, which is located in Queensland, Australia. That context, and a review of relevant literature, informs the development of the conceptual framework, shown in Fig. 1 later in this chapter, and used to guide the qualitative case study research design and methodology.

Subsequently, the methodological approach outlined is designed to enable a particularistic, descriptive, heuristic, and inductive description and analysis of *The Griffith Education Internship*. In that case study, the current Internship design is discussed in terms of its structure, the University-School partnership, and the importance of the Internship Action Plan (IAP). The case study concludes with a succinct identification of the outstanding features of *The Griffith Education Internship* model, including the shift in the relationships between the ITE student as a student teacher supervised by a teacher in the "Final Professional Experience/Practicum", and the ITE Intern transitioning to a Co-teacher working with a Mentor Teacher in the Internship as an advanced capstone professional experience. This account provides insights and implications for others who might be designing ITE capstone professional experiences, such as Internships.

Internships in Initial Teacher Education in Australia: A Case Study...

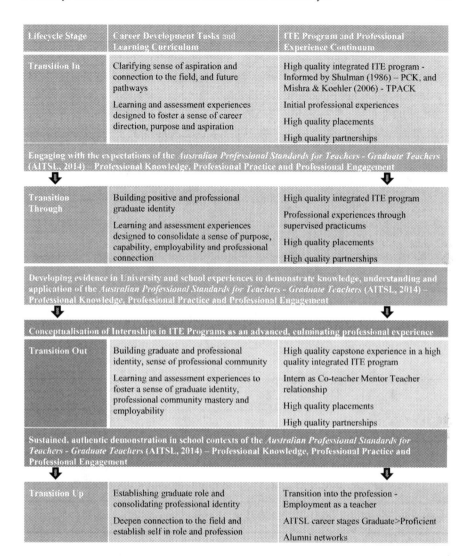

Fig. 1 Conceptual framework – internship as an advanced ITE professional experience

2 The Context of the Research: Internships in Initial Teacher Education in Australia

The context of this research which provides a case study of *The Griffith Education Internship* needs to be understood within the wider developments of Internships in ITE in Australia.

As outlined in *The Multiple Faces of Internships*, a report of the Working Party on Internships in Teacher Education (Queensland Board of Teacher Registration,

2004), it appears that "Active trialling on internship models in teacher education programs took place around Australia in the mid-1990s. For example, Jones, Ball and Smart (1995) described a pilot internship program conducted during 1994 at Griffith University Gold Coast in the Bachelor of Education (extension) program" (Queensland Board of Teacher Registration, 2004, p. 3). The case study presented in this chapter can be traced back to these beginnings in 1994, which reflects that it has been sustained, reviewed, and improved over the subsequent 21 years.

Moreover, that report outlined that "A School Based Semester (SBS) was offered to students in the final year of the Bachelor of Education (Primary) program at Edith Cowan University from 1994 (Campbell-Evans, 1995; Chadbourne, 1995)." In addition, similar trials of variable 'Internship' designs were being conducted at Southern Cross University (Young, 1995), the 'Practernship' at the Queensland University of Technology (Millwater & Yarrow, 1997), and at the University of Sydney (Hatton, 1996). A review of relevant literature on Internships in ITE in Australia presented later in this chapter elaborates on the emergence and approaches to Internships. Thus, 21 years after the trial of the Internship at Griffith University in 1994, this chapter will provide a case study of *The Griffith Education Internship* in 2015, situated within that context.

3   Review of the Literature and the Conceptual Framework Guiding the Case Study

In this section, a review of relevant literature on Internships in initial teacher education is provided. This informs the development of a conceptual framework which draws upon the *Australian Professional Standards for Teachers – Graduate Teachers* (AITSL, 2014), and the TEMAG's key findings and recommendations. It will draw upon the theoretical frameworks of the knowledge base for teaching of Shulman's (1987) pedagogical content knowledge (PCK) and Mishra and Koehler's more recent work (2006) on technological pedagogical and content knowledge (TPACK).

The accreditation of ITE programs in Australia is governed by the Australian Institute of Teaching and School Leadership (AITSL), and, in particular, the *Accreditation of ITE Programs in Australia: Standards and Procedures* (AITSL, 2012). Inherent in these standards and all ITE programs is the development of pedagogical content knowledge (PCK) which draws upon Shulman's seminal work (1987) in which he proposed the knowledge base for teaching, including a model of pedagogical reasoning and action. PCK informs strategic decisions about how best to represent content for effective learning in a given context. Subsequent to dynamic technological changes, Mishra and Koehler (2006) argued that these changes should be recognised by expanding Shulman's concept of PCK to include technological knowledge (TK), and that teachers now require technological pedagogical and content knowledge, commonly referred to in the literature as TPACK. While not extensively elaborated upon in this chapter, PCK and TPACK provide a theoretical framing of the knowledge base for teaching and are inherent in the *Australian Professional Standards for Teachers – Graduate Teachers* (AITSL, 2014).

As outlined earlier, *The Multiple Faces of Internships, a report of the Working Party on Internships in Teacher Education* (Queensland Board of Teacher Registration, 2004) provided a useful review of Internship models and approaches. That report noted that most early Internships "were designed on a selective or elective basis" (p. 4) and, as these were positively regarded by ITE students and the school communities, "most universities in Queensland have begun to include an internship as part of their professional experience program" (pp. 4–5). They also noted that the duration varied from four weeks to an entire school term, and that, in some models, ITE students progress from a supervised practical experience to the Internship whereby the supervising teacher becomes the Intern's mentor teacher.

In an Appendix to that report, examples of Australian-based Internship programs (Queensland Board of Teacher Registration, 2004, pp. 52–55) and examples of overseas-based Internship programs (Queensland Board of Teacher Registration, 2004, pp. 55–57) are provided. Some of the Australian examples referred to models being explored at the University of Western Sydney (Cameron, 2001), Charles Sturt University (Dobbins & Mitchell, 1995), University of Western Australia (Goody, 2001), University of Sydney (Hatton, 1996), University of Newcastle (McCormack, 1997), and James Cook University (Matters, 2001). Some of the overseas or international examples were drawn from Los Angeles, California (Basinger, 2000), Kansas City, Missouri (Kennedy Manzo, 2002), State University of New York (Kramer Schlosser & Blazano, 2002), Kentucky (McCormick & Brennan, 2001), and Memorial University, Canada (Singh, Doyle, Rose, & Kennedy, 1997).

The Australian and the international examples highlighted a range of reconceptualisations of supervised practicums so that the Internship models would enhance the transition of ITE students to the profession through building their self-efficacy to teach. Common characteristics of the various models were the envisioning of new roles and expectations of the Interns and their Mentor Teachers. For example, there were notions of the ITE student transitioning from a 'Student Teacher' to a 'Co-teacher' (See Carpenter & Franklin, 2010), though research suggested that the developmental phases experienced by ITE students is not a simple, continuous or sequential skill collection process (Cameron, 2001). Moreover, some models (e.g., McCormick & Brennan, 2001) were intended to reduce the number of teachers who leave the profession in their first year.

However, Kennedy and Doyle (1995) appropriately warned of the importance to distinguish between an apprenticeship model with an Internship, which they suggested integrates theory and practice and facilitates ITE students to critically analyse and implement change. More recently, Broadley, Sharplin and Ledger (2013) highlighted the continuing concerns about quality ITE programs, and the challenge of strengthening the theory-practice nexus, and noted that there has been advocacy to "change perceptions that these are competing domains" (p. 96). Furthermore, they highlight the perceptions of practising classroom teachers that view the "credentials of teacher educators with distrust, misunderstanding and scepticism" (p. 96) and that "teacher educators are perceived as removed from the real world of classrooms, behaviour management, parents, marking and the education bureaucracy, in a realm separate to schools" (p. 96). Broadley, Sharplin and Ledger make the valid argument that "Partnerships offer a means for changing these stereotypical views" (2013, p. 96).

Le Cornu (2015) in a paper titled *Key components of effective professional experience in initial teacher education*, highlighted research about teacher quality, teachers' work, and teacher educators' work. In addition, Le Cornu noted that the Australian Government's response to the TEMAG report (TEMAG, 2014a) focused on improvements needed in ITE. While not directly referring to Internships, Le Cornu identified seven key components within three categories for effective professional experiences; viz.

(A) High quality integrated initial teacher education programs

   A.1 Well-structured integrated ITE programs
   A.2 Well managed integrated ITE programs
   A.3 Well supported integrated ITE programs

(B) High quality placements

   B.1 High quality supervising teachers
   B.2 High level commitment from School Leadership

(C) High quality partnerships

   C.1 High quality school-university partnerships
   C.2 High quality systems based partnerships

Elsewhere, Foxall (2014) more directly focused on Internships, in asking principals to provide their perceptions of the work of Intern and Non-Intern graduate teachers. She noted that the Internship model she studied in Western Australia faced several challenges, including the workload faced by Interns and the Mentor Teachers, and the lack of clarity in School-University partnerships. Despite these challenges, Foxall indicated that the supporters of an Internship model "hoped the potential benefits would outweigh the negative aspects, as these perceived benefits revolved around the idea that an extended practicum, with additional mentoring and professional learning, might improve the performance of the mentee and the mentor" (p. 111). Importantly, the study's key findings were very positive as the principals in the study perceived that their Intern graduates performed at a higher level than their Non-Intern graduates, and while there are limitations in generalising beyond this study, Foxall reported that it seemed that employability was enhanced for those students who undertook Internships. Her study showed that "the principals interviewed would seek to employ more Intern graduates if given the choice" (Foxall, 2014, p. 112). In addition, Foxall reported that attrition rates were positively impacted upon. Thus, Foxall's research holds implications in relation to perceived capabilities, employability and attrition.

In developing the conceptual framework, as displayed in Fig. 1, to guide this case study, the *Griffith Career Development and Employability Framework* (Employment Service & Griffith University, 2014) informed this conceptualisation through its use of the stages of the student lifecycle, and associated career development tasks and career development learning curriculum. The conceptual framework foregrounds the *Australian Professional Standards for Teachers – Graduate Teachers* (AITSL, 2014) as quality graduates will be required to demonstrate those standards expected of Graduate Teachers in relation to Professional Knowledge, Professional Practice and Professional Engagement. Le Cornu's three major categories, namely, (1) high quality integrated ITE programs, (2) high quality placements, and (3) high quality partnerships are included as essential components to inform ITE program design and implementation and the professional experience continuum within a high quality ITE program. This conceptual framework provides space for the key Internship considerations discussed in this literature review, as it positions Internships as a culminating, advanced ITE professional experience to enable high quality University-school partnerships to co-construct quality graduates.

4 The Methodology: Qualitative Case Study

A qualitative case study approach (Merriam, 1998) of *The Griffith Education Internship* was adopted, as the intention of this chapter was to present "an intensive, holistic description and analysis of a bounded phenomenon, an institution, a person, a process or a social unit" (p. xiii) and to have the following characteristics:

1. Particularistic – by focusing on *The Griffith Education Internship* to provide insights into its design, implementation and impact;
2. Descriptive – by providing a 'thick, vivid narrative' (Hoaglin, Light, McPeek, Mosteller, & Stoto, 1982) of *The Griffith Education Internship* by drawing upon various sources of evidence;
3. Heuristic – by illuminating meaning and insights into *The Griffith Education Internship*; and
4. Inductive – by developing meaning about *The Griffith Education Internship* from the data.

Data collection was aligned with Yin's guidance (1994) to gather data from a range of sources which fit the purpose of the case study, and included:

- Document analysis – *The Griffith Education Internship* Learning @griffith information and resources, including the Course Profile and assessment design;
- Survey data – Student Experience of Course (SEC) data from 2011 to 2015, and Bachelor of Education (Primary) Course Evaluation Questionnaire data from 2011 to 2014, focusing on Graduate Outcomes and Graduate Success data; and
- Perspectives, especially on the Internship Action Plans (IAPs), of School Coordinators, Mentor Teachers, Interns, and Course Convenors.

The following case study relates to *The Griffith Education Internship* which is conducted with Bachelor of Education (Primary) ITE students at the Mount Gravatt (MG), Logan (LG) and Gold Coast (GC) campuses of Griffith University in Queensland, Australia. In Semester Two 2015, 211 ITE students undertook this Internship as a mandatory capstone experience in their ITE program. In developing this case study, data are drawn upon from the past five years of its implementation.

The authors identify that a limitation of a case study approach is *generalizability*, as this case study is situated in a specific set of contexts and the design and implementation might not be able to be generalised to other contexts. Rather, our position is that we encourage a *transferability* lens, which is appropriate for case studies by encouraging the reader to make the connections and identify the similarities, differences and applicability in relation to their own experiences of ITE professional experience and Internships.

5 Analysis and Discussion: Case Study: *The Griffith Education Internship*

The analysis and discussion is presented through a case study of *The Griffith Education Internship*, with specific attention given to key findings and their implications.

5.1 Historical Development of the Griffith Education Internship

The early development of an Internship throughout the mid-1990s at the Gold Coast campus of Griffith University, and the innovative approaches to Internships at the Mount Gravatt and Logan campuses of Griffith University later became *The Griffith Education Internship* in 2007. The earlier history at the Gold Coast campus, documented elsewhere by Carpenter and Franklin (2010), noted that it commenced with a trial in 1994, with a voluntary Internship at the Gold Coast campus of Griffith University. This trial was used to inform the subsequent design and introduction of a compulsory Internship experience in the fourth and final year of the Bachelor of Education (Primary) program in 1997.

Key features of this Internship model were: ITE students became known as 'Interns' or 'Co-teachers', rather than 'Student Teachers'; Quality Mentor Teachers were identified and matched with Interns; A formal mentoring process was implemented, and; Strong University-school partnerships co-designed the Internship to link theory and practice. The following section of this case study outlines the current design of *The Griffith Education Internship*.

5.2 Design of the Griffith Education Internship

The current design of *The Griffith Education Internship* is discussed in terms of it being a Capstone Semester advanced professional experience, the structure of the Internship, important role expectations of the University-School partnership, the

Internship Action Plan (IAP), and concludes with a succinct identification of key findings, including the outstanding features of *The Griffith Education Internship* model.

5.2.1 Capstone Semester

The Bachelor of Education (Primary) requires students to undertake the Internship as a capstone experience in their final semester of study. As an advanced professional experience, the Internship allows opportunities for them to demonstrate the Professional Knowledge, Professional Practice and Professional Engagement consistent with the expectations of the *Australian Professional Standards for Teachers – Graduate Teachers* (AITSL, 2014).

5.2.2 Internship Approval

The Griffith Education Internship has been 'authorised' by the Queensland College of Teachers (QCT), in meeting QCT expectations that the Internship provides a transition into the teaching profession through a reduced workload, and the support of a mentor. In accordance with QCT requirements, an *Application for Internship Authorisation* form must be completed by the University and submitted to the QCT for approval prior to the commencement of the Internship. As required by the QCT:

> An Internship authorisation must be obtained from the QCT prior to any preservice teacher commencing an Internship. Preservice teachers are unable to commence the roles and responsibilities of an intern until the approval is granted.
>
> The authorisation is valid only for the period of internship. It is not a form of teacher registration and preservice teachers should be advised that they must apply for teacher registration in the usual way following completion of their teacher education program (QCT, 2015).

5.2.3 The Structure of *The Griffith Education Internship*

The structure of the Internship was characterised by three phases; i.e. Orientation; Phase 1; and Phase 2.

The Orientation Phase of the Internship covered the period of preparation on campus. During the Orientation Phase, the Interns undertook activities negotiated with their Mentor Teacher. They were expected to develop their Internship Action Plan (IAP) and attend *The Griffith Education Internship* information evening with their Mentor Teacher. The information evening provided an opportunity to discuss the specific role and responsibilities for everyone involved in the Internship, to discuss the negotiated context of the Internship, and for the Intern and Mentor Teacher to engage in a workshop on the IAP.

Phase 1 of the Internship related to weeks 1–3 (inclusive) in schools, and it required the Intern to enact the IAP steps. At the conclusion to Phase 1, Mentor Teachers and Interns discussed the Interim Appraisal. The key focus was the IAP and the progress which the Intern had made. In finalising the Interim Appraisal, the Mentor Teacher determined whether or not the Intern was meeting the expectations of the *Australian Professional Standards for Teachers – Graduate Teachers* (AITSL, 2014). This phase also provided mentors with the professional development opportunity to attend the Mentor Teacher Cluster meeting, which allowed them to discuss the progress of their Interns as a 'moderating' experience.

Phase 2 of the Internship related to weeks 4–6 (inclusive), and it provided Interns with the opportunity to continue to teach co-operatively, and transition to assume the role of a beginning teacher. At the conclusion of Phase 2, Mentor Teachers completed the "Statement of Completion", which confirmed that the Intern had completed all 30 days, successfully completed the Interim Appraisal assessed at the end of Phase 1, and successfully completed Phase 2.

5.2.4 University-School Partnership: Role Expectations

The effectiveness of the University-school partnership in co-designing and co-constructing the Internship has been pivotal for its success. Considerable, high quality, respectful engagement between schools and the University has been established and maintained. Interns, Mentor Teachers, School Coordinators and University Internship Convenors have clear role expectations and make important partnership contributions. Teacher Education Industry Advisory Groups at the Gold Coast, Logan and Brisbane campuses highly value the Internship and provide ongoing support and advice to ensure that the Internship is relevant and informed by industry needs and demands.

School Coordinators play a key role in matching Mentor Teachers with Interns before Interns begin their Internship. It is important that the Mentor Teachers who are selected work with their Interns in a mentoring role. School Coordinators are well placed to ensure the best match possible. Additionally, Interns are included into wider school routines, and this full immersion approach contributes greatly to the success of the Internship.

Mentor Teachers played critically important roles, and their role moved beyond supervision to a relationship that required them to 'negotiate' a professional partnership with their Intern. To assist in facilitating this discussion, the Interns developed their IAP. In this way, the Internship required more from the Intern than a general professional experience or practicum would, for example, through taking responsibility for their own professional learning. Interns were supported through the IAP which assisted in providing both agency and focus for them.

Interns and Mentor Teachers were expected to collaboratively plan, taking into account their contexts. To illustrate, the amount of teaching done by the Intern depended upon the familiarity and demonstrated competence which the Intern already had with the class and their relationship with their Mentor Teacher.

These considerations informed the negotiations about when and for how long the intern taught, and informed decisions about responsibility for planning, teaching and assessing Learning Areas. Mentor Teachers provided regular feedback to Interns, through informal discussions that enabled the Interns to self-reflect on their teaching performance and other professional aspects. More formal feedback utilising a peer coaching approach is incorporated, focused on a pre-planned aspect of teaching, and was developed through a supportive conferencing arrangement.

5.2.5 Internship Action Plan (IAP)

The IAP was based on the three domains of the *Australian Teachers Professional Standards for Teachers*; i.e. Domain 1: Professional Knowledge; Domain 2: Professional Practice; and Domain 3: Professional Engagement. Under each of the domains, the Intern, in consultation with their Mentor Teacher, identified one objective that the Intern will undertake. Special consideration and emphasis was given to ensuring that the IAP included evidence of impact on student learning. Interns were required to ensure that the chosen activities showed development of:

1. **A strength**. This aimed to assist the Intern in developing a 'point of difference' in preparation for their employment application processes.
2. **An area needing improvement**. This encouraged a proactive approach to self-reflection and professional learning.
3. **A professional role yet to be experienced**.

A critically important aspect of this process was the agency given to Interns as they identified their own performance targets based upon an understanding of their own professional learning needs. The objectives were also negotiated with their Mentor Teachers to develop a shared understanding of how the Internship would progress. In addition, the Interns were required to carefully detail all of their action steps for achievement of each of the domains, including resources needed, who would be involved in each step, explicit links to curriculum documents, school based policies and guidelines. Finally, Interns were also required to provide a timeline that outlined when they anticipated each action step would be completed, and a statement for every step that described what the step would look like when it was successfully completed.

In addition to those three IAP objectives, Interns also engaged with a broad range of activities expected of a teacher and enabled by the QCT Internship Authorisation outlined earlier in this chapter. This process fed into the Interim Appraisal process, with a key design feature being the professional conversations between the Intern and the Mentor Teacher conducted at the end of Phase 1. The Interns shared two key reflections with their mentor teachers; namely, their progress towards each of the objectives to date; and where they saw each objective developing for the remainder of the Internship. Importantly, Interns were required to demonstrate the *Australian Professional Standards for Teachers – Graduate Level*, and include evidence of improvements in student learning. Reflections shaped the ways in which the Intern progressed, with a continual focus on improving student learning.

To further elaborate on the conceptualisation of the model in the final year of the Bachelor of Education (Primary) program, Table 1 outlines the progression from the 'Final Professional Experience/Practicum' with a Supervising Teacher – Student Teacher relationship to *The Griffith Education Internship* with a Mentor Teacher – Intern relationship. It illustrates specific and targeted strategies used by the Mentor Teacher and Intern in the University-school partnership which co-constructs the Internship experience.

5.3 Key Findings and Implications: Intern, Mentor Teacher and School Coordinator Perceptions

The positive impact and outcomes of this Internship model were reflected in a range of data gleaned from Interns, Mentor Teachers and School Coordinators. To illustrate, Student Experience of Course (SEC) data from 2011 to 2015, as displayed in Table 2, show consistently high ratings by Interns. To complement those data, strong Satisfaction with Program, Graduate Success and Post-Graduation Employment data, as shown in Table 3, also aligned with positive perceptions of ITE quality by schools as employers of these ITE graduates. This success is largely due to the way in which Mentor Teachers, Interns and the Course Convenors work collaboratively and effectively. Interns consistently reported that their Internship experience enabled their professional growth to navigate the transition from a student teacher to a Co-teacher, and to becoming a beginning teacher. Many Interns commented that the Internship had been the most valuable course in their entire ITE program. For example, a comment from an Intern in Semester Two 2015 reflected this "…I know I speak for the whole cohort when I say that the Internship experience we all had will be forever valued as a meaningful part of our development as a teacher".

Key themes identified through the qualitative comments by Interns, in relation to "What worked well?" and "What might be improved?" in the Student Evaluation of Course (SEC) surveys, highlighted the importance and value of a well-designed and well-supported Internship. Specifically, Interns strongly affirmed the value of the IAP, assessment design, professional discussions and reflection, and transition to employment as a teacher. To illustrate, Interns made positive comments, such as "The Action Plan is a useful piece of assessment – I am seriously considering using it as part of my 'evidence' for the EQ interview process", "All assessment is geared towards Internship and helping us develop resources and plans to help us be successful", and, "This course really prepared students for their Internship and future employment opportunities".

However, as shown in Table 2, there were some instances, such as Semester Two 2013 at two campuses, and Semester Two 2014 at one of the campuses, where the evaluations were not as strong. While it is difficult to attribute reasons for this, as current Internship convenors, we suggest that this highlights the importance of valuing the significant roles played by all in ensuring successful implementation of the

Table 1 Making the transition to Mentor Teacher – Intern relationship

		Final Professional Experience/Practicum		The Griffith Education Internship	
		Term 1	Term 2	Term 3	Term 4
Assessment		Portfolio: A response to the Australian Professional Standards for Teachers (APST); Curriculum Vitae; Teaching philosophy	Professional experience interim and final reports (based on APST)	The Griffith Education Internship (IAP) (based on the APST)	The Griffith Education Internship interim appraisal (based on the IAP)
		Professional experience reports and University transcript			Statement of Completion
		On campus	Professional experience (in school)	On campus	Internship (in school)
University		Unpack the APST (Graduate Level)	During the professional experience, University Liaison staff work with the students and the supervising teachers to support the professional growth of the ITE student	Development of deeper relationship with the teacher as Mentor, and the ITE student teacher as an Intern	Mentor Teacher cluster meetings as a professional development opportunity
		Provide real life examples of what counts as evidence			Intern cluster meetings where interns hare their stories and resources
		Students create their own observation forms, lesson plans, and reflection strategies to develop their professional judgement			
		Initial teacher education student - Student Teacher identity		Intern - Co-Teacher identity	
ITE students		Using the APST self-audit tool, students map their level of competence	Students continue to use the APST self-audit tool to map their skills development throughout the professional experience	IAP, aligned with APST, requires each Intern to identify 3 objectives which become part of the Interim Appraisal	Interns take on teacher duties as negotiated with their Mentor Teachers, and implement their IAP
					Take part in the Interim Appraisal process
		Supervising Teacher		New relationship as a Mentor Teacher	
Supervising/ mentor teachers		The Supervising Teacher works with the ITE student to induct them into the class over the 5 lead in days, and models a range of effective pedagogy and behaviour management techniques	The Supervising Teacher will continue to model effective teaching, provide feedback, and make suggestions on the way in which they can improve	Mentor Teachers attend an internship information evening	Interim appraisal:
					Mentor Teacher has a professional conversation with their Intern on achievements to date
				Interns and Mentor Teachers work together on the IAP	Mentor Teacher gives advice on projected actions of the Intern

Table 2 The Griffith Education Internship – Student Evaluation of Course 2011–2015

Campus cohort	Sem 2 2011 Mean	Sem 2 2012 Mean	Sem 2 2013 Mean	Sem 2 2014 Mean	Sem 2 2015 Mean
MG	4.4	4.1	3.6	4.6	4.3
	Total cohort N=92	Total cohort N=111	Total cohort N=71	Total cohort N=71	Total cohort N=62
	Responses N=33	Responses N=16	Responses N=14	Responses N=26	Responses N=15
	Resp. rate 35.9%	Resp. rate 14.4%	Resp. rate 19.7%	Resp. rate 36.6%	Resp. rate 24.2%
GC	4.0	4.7	3.9	3.7	4.7
	Total cohort N=145	Total cohort N=151	Total cohort N=136	Total cohort N=110	Total cohort N=125
	Responses N=23	Responses N=36	Responses N=17	Responses N=7	Responses N=56
	Resp. rate 27.9%	Resp. rate 23.8%	Resp. rate 12.5%	Resp. rate 6.4%	Resp. rate 44.8%
LG	4.4	4.3	4.1	4.1	3.9
	Total cohort N=68	Total cohort N=55	Total cohort N=42	Total cohort N=34	Total cohort N=24
	Responses N=19	Responses N=12	Responses N=10	Responses N=16	Responses N=13
	Resp. rate 27.9%	Resp. rate 21.8%	Resp. rate 23.8%	Resp. rate 47.1%	Resp. rate 54.2%

Source: Experience@Griffith Student Evaluation of Course – SEC – data
Scale 1–5; where 1 = strongly disagree: 2 = disagree: 3 = neutral: 4 = agree: 5 = strongly agree
GC Gold Coast campus, *MG* Mt Gravatt campus, *LG* Logan campus

Internship. To elaborate, it is important that the academics and teaching staff have a deep understanding of the principles underpinning the Internship. It is also important that the intensity and complex demands of an excellent Internship experience is realised through positive relationships and University-school partnerships. Schools must be supported by an authentic University presence and connectedness. For example, changes in University and staffing require change management and communication plans. In addition, the institution needs to recognise that an Internship should not be seen as restricted to being an administrative task of assigning the placements of Interns. Rather, an Internship needs to be seen as an advanced professional experience in which the Interns undertake professional growth in transitioning through a high quality, deep process of engagement of becoming a graduate teacher. That is, a well-designed Internship, by itself, does not ensure successful implementation, and the roles played by all involved and the value assigned to it by Universities and schools are crucial to enabling its success.

The following key themes were identified from the perspectives obtained from School Coordinators and Mentor Teachers through substantive conversations and

Table 3 Bachelor of Education (Primary) Graduate Success data – 2011–2014

Program performance indicators		2011	2012	2013	2014
Program profile	Total EFTSL – MG	361.6	349.3	334.9	331.5
	Total EFTSL – GC	639.2	611.6	561.9	549.4
	Total EFTSL – LG	237.1	192.8	157	126
Graduate outcomes	Graduate success – MG (%)	83.33	81.25	92.45	93.33
	Graduate success – GC (%)	69.62	80.52	82.14	68.63
	Graduate success – LG (%)	76.92	89.66	91.67	100
	Post-graduation employment – MG (%)	83.33	80.85	92	92.59
	Post-graduation employment – GC (%)	69.23	79.45	80.39	66.67
	Post-graduation employment – MG (%)	76.32	89.66	91.67	100
Graduate perceptions	Satisfaction with program – MG (%)	82.43	84.75	81.82	85
	Satisfaction with program – GC (%)	82.14	60.87	77.27	85
	Satisfaction with program – LG (%)	87.18	96.88	87.88	88
	Satisfaction with program – national median (%)	79.85	81.23	82.35	80.77

Source: Griffith University Program Performance Indicators Report which summarises data from the Australian Graduate Survey Course Experience Questionnaire for this program
GC Gold Coast campus, *MG* Mt Gravatt campus, *LG* Logan campus

Internship feedback, including reflections obtained at the Mentor Teacher Cluster meetings:

- The Internship is the most important, authentic capstone experience for the purposes of both professional growth and employment of ITE students;
- The University-School partnership is critically important in co-constructing quality teacher graduates;
- The Internship success is dependent upon 'wisdom of practice' and collaborative inquiry, which is characterised by high quality, active engagement, and respectful professional interactions between the University and schools.

In summary, the outstanding features of *The Griffith Education Internship* outlined in this case study might be considered by others in either designing an ITE Internship model, or in comparing these features with the design features of their Internship model. In particular, the Internship model required ITE students to:

- Develop an actual IAP that enabled agency to plan, enact and assess their own performance targets;
- Identify and build upon a strength to the 'next level' as a 'point of difference' for employability;

- Be proactive about any areas in need of development and produce a practical plan to address them;
- Undertake highly individualised Internship experiences that were aligned with the needs of the Interns, the Mentor Teachers, the class contexts, and *Australian Professional Standards for Teachers – Graduate Level*; and
- Be 'work ready' and 'professional' graduates.

6 Conclusion

Following a review of relevant literature on ITE Internships in Australia, an outline of the methodological approach was provided to present a case study of *The Griffith Education Internship* model. This case study included a summary of the historical development and key features of *The Griffith Education Internship* to illustrate the process of co-design through University-school partnerships to then co-construct quality graduate primary school teachers. Insights into the effectiveness of that Internship model were described and outstanding features of the model were summarised to inform further innovation and practice in improving the quality and impact of ITE programs through designing Internships.

In this chapter, we have argued that an effective Internship designed as a capstone, advanced professional experience can assist in the professional growth of ITE students in their process of becoming a teacher. In providing this case study, we have suggested that the transition from being a 'Student Teacher' to a 'Co-teacher' needs to occur in the important culminating semester of an ITE program. The design and implementation of an effective Internship which requires an IAP linked to the professional standards can contribute to achieving this. Importantly, this approach can assist in addressing TEMAG's (2014a) call to lift public confidence in ITE programs and the quality of teacher graduates, to address the evidence of poor practice in a number of programs, to ensure that there is sufficient integration of teacher education providers with schools and systems, and to improve the application of the professional standards.

References

Australian Institute for Teachers and School Leaders (AITSL). (2014). *Australian Professional Standards for Teachers – Graduate Teachers*. Retrieved from: http://www.aitsl.edu.au/australian-professional-standards-for-teachers/standards/list?c=graduate.

Australian Institute for Teaching and School Leadership (AITSL). (2012). *Accreditation of ITE programs in Australia: Guide to the accreditation process April 2012*. Retrieved from: http://www.aitsl.edu.au/verve/_resources/Guide_to_accreditation_process_-_April_2012.pdf.

Basinger, J. (2000, May 18–19). Teacher education extends its reach. *The Chronicle of Higher Education*.

Broadley, T., Sharplin, E., & Ledger, S. (2013). New frontiers or old certainties: The pre-service teacher internship. In D. E. Lynch & T. Yeigh (Eds.), *Teacher education in Australia:*

Investigations into programming, practicum and partnership (pp. 94–108). Tarragindi, Australia: Oxford Global Press.

Cameron, R. B. (2001). *Identifying the developmental phases encountered by beginning teachers during an internship*. Australian Association of Research in Education (AARE) Conference, 2–6 December, 2001, Fremantle, Western Australia.

Campbell-Evans, G. (1995). We did it our way: School based semester (SBS). *Journal of Teaching Practice, 15*(1), 18–23.

Carpenter, L., & Franklin, R. (2010). *The Griffith Education Internship Gold Coast campus*. Gold Coast, Australia: Griffith University.

Careers and Employment Service, Griffith University. (2014). *Griffith career development and employability framework*. Retrieved from: https://www.griffith.edu.au/__data/assets/pdf_file/0010/698959/employability_framework.pdf.

Chadbourne, R. (1995). Student reluctance to take up school-based teacher education: One university's experience. *Journal of Education for Teaching, 21*(2), 219–226.

Department of Education, Training and Employment. (2013). *A fresh start: Improving the preparation and quality of teachers for Queensland schools*. Retrieved from: http://flyingstart.qld.gov.au/SiteCollectionDocuments/A-Fresh-Start-strategy.pdf.

Dobbins, R. & Mitchell, J. (1995). The extended practicum program: A learning journey. *Australian Association of Research in Education (AARE) Conference*, 27–30 November, 1995, Hobart.

Finger, G. (2013). *TPACK and Initial Teacher Education: Implications from the Teaching Teachers for the Future Research* (Australian Teacher Education Association (ATEA) Conference). Brisbane, Australia: Queensland University of Technology.

Foxall, G. (2014). *A primary school internship model: Graduate teacher performance as perceived by employing principals*. Unpublished Master of Education Thesis, Faculty of Education and the Arts, Edith Cowan University, Western Australia, Australia. Retrieved from: http://ro.ecu.edu.au/cgi/viewcontent.cgi?article=2402&context=theses.

Goody, A. (2001). Preparing postgraduate students as future university teachers: The UWA teaching internship scheme. In A. Hermann & M. M. Kulski (Eds.), *Expanding horizons in teaching and learning. Proceedings of the 10th Annual Teaching Learning Forum*. Perth, Australia: Curtin University of Technology.

Government of South Australia. (2013). *Building a stronger South Australia: High quality education*. Retrieved from: http://stronger.sa.gov.au/wp-content/uploads/2013/11/building_a_%20stronger_sa-high_quality_education.pdf.

Hatton, N. (1996). Changing initial teacher education: Limitations to innovation in the United States, Australia and the United Kingdom. *Australian Journal of Teacher Education, 21*(2), 35–42. Retrieved from: http://ro.ecu.edu.au/cgi/viewcontent.cgi?article=1200&context=ajte.

Hoaglin, D. C., Light, R. J., McPeek, B., Mosteller, F., & Stoto, M. A. (1982). *Data for decisions: Information strategies for policymakers*. Cambridge, MA: Abt Associates.

Jones, D., Ball, T., & Smart, M. (1995). *A case study of a pilot internship program*. Paper presented at the Second National Cross-Faculty Practicum Conference, 3–6 February, Surfers Paradise, Australia.

Kennedy, W., & Doyle, C. (1995). *Perceptions of internship evaluation*. St. John's, Canada: Faculty of Education, Memorial University of Newfoundland.

Kennedy Manzo, K. (2002). Kansas City turns classrooms over to interns. *Across the Nation, 5*, 2002.

Kramer Schlosser, L., & Blazano, B. (2002). Making or breaking new teachers. *Principal Leadership, 3*, 36–39.

Le Cornu, R. (2015). *Key components of effective professional experience in initial teacher education in Australia: A paper prepared for the Australian Institute for Teaching and School Leadership*. Melbourne, Australia: Australian Institute for Teaching and School Leadership.

Matters, P. N. (2001). *Beginning teacher partnerships, telementoring and ICT – newfangled or new ways? Journeys of discovery*. Australian Association of Research in Education (AARE) Conference, 2–6 December, 2001, Fremantle, Western Australia.

McCormack, A. (1997). *Impacting on the socialisation of beginning teachers of physical and health education through collaboration*. Brisbane, Australia: Australian Association of Research in Education (AARE) Conference.

McCormick, K. M., & Brennan, S. (2001). Mentoring the new professional in interdisciplinary early childhood education: The Kentucky teacher internship program. *Topics in Early Childhood Special Education, 21*(3), 131–149.

Merriam, S. B. (1998). *Qualitative research and case study applications in education*. San Francisco, CA: Jossey-Bass.

Millwater, J., & Yarrow, A. (1997). Practernship: A theoretical construct for developing professionalism in preservice teachers. *Teacher Education Quarterly, 24*(1), 23–26.

Mishra, P., & Koehler, M. (2006). Technological pedagogical content knowledge: A framework for integrating technology in teachers' knowledge. *Teachers College Record, 108*(6), 1017–1054.

New South Wales Government Education and Communities. (2014). *Great teaching: Inspired learning*. Retrieved from: http://www.dec.nsw.gov.au/our-services/schools/%20great-teaching-inspired-learning.

Queensland Board of Teacher Registration. (2004). *The multiple faces of internships: A report of the Working Party on Internships in Teacher Education*. Toowong, Australia: Queensland Board of Teacher Registration.

Queensland College of Teachers (QCT). (2015). *Internships*. Retrieved from https://www.qct.edu.au/education/internships.html.

Shulman, L. S. (1987). Knowledge and teaching: Foundations of the new reform. *Harvard Educational Review, 57*(1), 1–21.

Singh, A., Doyle, C., Rose, A., & Kennedy, W. (1997). Reflective internship and the phobia of classroom management. *Australian Journal of Education, 41*(2), 105–118.

State of Victoria Department of Education and Early Childhood Development. (2013). *From new directions to action: World class teaching and school leadership*. Retrieved from: http://www.education.vic.gov.au/about/department/pages/teachingprofession.asp.

Teacher Education Ministerial Advisory Group. (2014a). *Action now: Classroom ready teachers*. Retrieved from: https://docs.education.gov.au/system/files/doc/other/action_now_classroom_ready_teachers_accessible.pdf.

Teacher Education Ministerial Advisory Group. (2014b). *Teacher Education Ministerial Advisory Group issues paper*. Retrieved from: http://www.studentsfirst.gov.au/teacher-education-ministerial-advisory-group.

Yin, R. K. (1994). *Case study research: Design and methods* (2nd ed.). Thousand Oaks, CA: Sage Publishing.

Young, W. (1995). Internship: Integrating theory and practice. *South Pacific Journal of Teacher Education, 23*(1), 97–107.

Advancing Partnership Research: A Spatial Analysis of a Jointly-Planned Teacher Education Partnership

Josephine Ryan, Helen Butler, Alex Kostogriz, and Sarah Nailer

1 Introduction

Australian governments, like those in the United States of America (USA) and the United Kingdom (UK), are currently under pressure to improve the performance of their education systems, demanding changes in teacher education. As a result, the governments show a great deal of interest in ways of identifying, standardising and measuring the "quality" of teacher education (Plecki, Effers, & Nakamura, 2012). This has included raising entrance scores for teacher education programs, creating literacy and numeracy tests for graduates as a way of assuring their classroom readiness, identifying ways of bridging theory and practice and improving support for beginning teachers (Teacher Education Ministerial Advisory Group (TEMAG), 2014). In the USA the climate of accountability has led some universities, with the controversial assistance of commercial operator Pearson (Singer, 2013), to address the demand for "evidence" of quality by creating their own assessment process for graduate teachers (Stanford University, 2014). Varied government responses to the teacher "quality" debate in the UK reveal the contested nature of the teacher education issue. Universities in England, Scotland, Wales and Northern Ireland are in a range of situations in terms of power in teaching education (British Education Research Association (BERA), 2014), with the extremes being universities in England that have been marginalised in the teacher education process in favour of school-based teacher education (Beach & Bagley, 2013); whereas in Scotland policy-makers have supported links between universities and schools in initial teacher education (BERA, 2014). In Australia, too, policy-makers have intervened in university teacher education with the teacher education accreditation authority, the Australian Institute of Teaching and School Leadership (AITSL), being charged

J. Ryan (✉) • H. Butler • A. Kostogriz • S. Nailer
Australian Catholic University, Melbourne, Australia
e-mail: jo.ryan@acu.edu.au; helen.butler@acu.edu.au; alex.kostogriz@acu.edu.au; sarah.nailer@acu.edu.au

with identifying ways to measure the quality of teacher education programs and/or their graduates (AITSL, 2015). At this time of heightened scrutiny and accountability, it is important that teacher educators take an active role in setting the teacher education agenda. This chapter reports an investigation of such an initiative.

Australian university teacher educators, while under accountability pressure, are better positioned in comparison to some of their European and American colleagues (Beach & Bagley, 2013; Zeichner, 2010) in that they have not lost their central place as providers of teacher education. Australia's government-mandated review of teacher education from TEMAG (2014) has been in broad agreement with university teacher educators (Australian Council of Deans of Education (ACDE), 2014) in stating that high quality teacher education is based on partnerships between universities and schools. As is an accepted view in much contemporary teacher education, the report argues that high quality teacher education is a shared enterprise between schools and universities, between the academic and the practical aspects of teachers' work (BERA, 2014; Kruger, Davies, Eckersley, Newell & Cherednichenko, 2009; TEMAG, 2014; Zeichner, 2012). In the English context, this is not the belief embodied in the move to make schools the primary sites for the education of teachers (Beach & Bagley, 2013; Department for Education (DfE), 2010). In the USA, views of the best approach to teacher education are highly divergent with programs such as *Teach for America* and other work-based pathways to teaching gaining ground (Zeichner, 2010). In contrast, the TEMAG report recommends school-integrated rather than school-based teacher education (TEMAG, 2014). Although the TEMAG report is clear in its support of school-university partnerships in teacher education, it argues that there is a lack of research on how these partnerships might improve what the report sees as the critical indicator of quality teacher education – school "student outcomes" (p. 41).

The link between teacher education programs and student outcomes is complex (Dinham, 2015). Candidates in teacher education programs are only in schools for relatively brief periods and assembling data on graduates of various programs is a long term proposition that governments might find unpalatable (Dinham, 2015). Yet, the evident complexity does not mean that it is not useful to focus on understanding the impact of schools and universities working together. The TEMAG report's support of partnerships suggests that a renewed approach to researching them is timely. In terms of an appropriate approach to investigating school-university partnerships, a recent meta-analysis of the field of international teacher education research (Cochran-Smith et al., 2015) identifies a significant absence of jointly planned school-university projects to explore the "connections between teacher and student learning" (p. 117). Such projects are important as they "provide alternative ways to think about teacher and student success" (Cochran-Smith et al., 2015, p. 117), thereby bridging the apparent theory-practice divide which has represented universities and schools as different or even oppositional spaces of professional learning.

Australia is currently generating a multiplicity of school-university partnership activities (ACDE, 2014) and, clearly, this work presents opportunities for research about their value for teacher and student learning. It is critical knowledge for governments, not only in Australia but around the world, to understand the ways in which these often expensive university-school initiatives enhance both pre-service teacher (PST) and student outcomes. As a country with a small population and number of jurisdictions, Australia has the capacity to enact national educational reform (Dinham, 2013), and should use this capacity to create a strong research base for its current move to partnerships, thereby contributing to international knowledge about successful teacher education (Cochran-Smith et al., 2015).

This chapter addresses the identified gap of jointly planned school-university research through discussing the research outcomes of a project which was planned to meet both school and university interests. The Catholic Teacher Education Consortium (CTEC), an on-going university-school partnership, began in 2013 between 14 Catholic schools in the north and west of Melbourne, Catholic Education Melbourne (sector leadership) and Australian Catholic University (ACU). The project findings are valuable because they investigate the partnership outcomes and experience from the viewpoints of PSTs and teachers as well as from the vantage point of university and school leadership.

2 Research on School-University Partnerships

School-university partnerships in teacher education have been variously defined (Ryan & Jones, 2014). A relationship of some kind between schools and universities is essential to all but the most "learn on the job" kind of teacher education pathway because schools and universities must cooperate to organise and assess the PSTs' practicum experiences. Commentators have categorised these partnerships in terms of the extent of engagement between partners (Kruger et al., 2009). In some partnerships such as the Professional Development School partnerships in the USA, universities and schools agree to work together on a range of mutually agreed activities (Darling-Hammond, 2005). In others there is a more limited relationship such that schools agree to host the PSTs' practicum and there is little shared activity other than to achieve this goal (Kruger et al., 2009). In much of the research on these relationships between schools and universities there has been an interest in investigating how the theoretical knowledge of the university partner is translated into practice by the PST (Darling-Hammond, 2006).

This view of university and schools as having different concerns has led to studies interested in identifying factors which create and sustain closer relationships, such as the development of shared goals and on-going funding (Darling-Hammond, 2005; Kruger et al., 2009), as well as exploring the varieties of partnerships from cooperative to transformative (Kruger et al., 2009). There has been a body of partnership research that has viewed school-university activity as clinical practice in which the teachers and teacher educators induct PSTs into the professional practices of expert educators (McLean Davies et al., 2013), thereby emphasising the specialised knowledge of teaching. Another element of the literature has defined school-university partnerships as communities of practice into which PSTs are socialised, the most effective ones being those which create maximum interaction between university and school personnel (Le Cornu, 2012). Adding to the study of how the partnerships work and can be improved, those committed to teacher education in partnerships are interested in collecting evidence of their impact on the indicator of school performance outcomes. Effers, Plecki, and McGuigan (2014) have presented evidence that partnerships which require teacher candidates and lecturers to work more intensively in high-needs schools have contributed to improved school achievement.

A critique of international university-school partnership research has been that it has often been small scale, self-study investigations by teacher educators (Cochran-Smith & Fries, 2005; Nuttall, Murray, Seddon, & Mitchell, 2006). University teacher educators' concern with identifying the strengths and weaknesses of their work has meant a proliferation of analyses of partnerships in terms of their own experience and that of PSTs with whom they work. Such perception data, while useful, have often not included that of school leaders, teachers and students (Cochran-Smith & Fries, 2005). As well as the tendency to be self-study, it has been argued that partnership research has failed to show why a school-integrated teacher education approach might be better than a traditional separated academic and practical approach to teacher education (Cochran-Smith & Fries, 2005). In some instances, the opposite appeared to be the case because teacher education candidates in programs that required them to manage university and school activities at the same time were more stressed than those whose preparation did not involve managing these transitions (Cochran-Smith & Fries, 2005; Allen, 2010).

As well as the "small-scale" claim, another critique of teacher education research, including partnership research, has been that the assumptions and theoretical frameworks have been so diverse that it is difficult to connect findings from various studies (Cochran-Smith & Fries, 2005; Nuttall et al., 2006; Sleeter, 2014). The research discussed in this chapter seeks to address this claim by adopting a framework that connects it with other studies of teacher education (Zeichner, Payne, & Brayko, 2015), in particular the most recent large-scale Australian study of the effectiveness of teacher education (Rowan, Mayer, Kline, Kostogriz, & Walker-Gibbs, 2015).

3 Framework for the Current Study

This present study takes the position that the current teacher education context with its concern to make teacher education accountable for school outcomes is based on a binary view of teacher education partnerships. That is, the context of accountability reproduces, in most cases unintentionally, a spatial politics of teacher education that does not transcend the boundaries established by traditional models of partnerships in which school-based professional learning is simply integrated into university-based teacher education courses. Such a partnership model does not challenge the lines of jurisdictional maps and the relations of power associated with them, and hence, sustains the divide between theory and practice, the imagined and the real, preparedness for work and the teachers' work proper. As a result, PSTs find it difficult to bridge the gap between the theoretical knowledge coming from the university and the practical knowledge developed in schools.

More helpful in describing the development of knowledge about teaching is the view of teacher education as taking place in the *boundary zone* where teacher educators, teachers and PSTs can jointly construct professional knowledge. This view of partnerships presupposes dialogical relationships on the boundary between universities and schools. Teacher education partnerships are best seen as activities in which hybridization of theory and practice can occur. In this view of partnerships hierarchies of knowledge are diminished (Zeichner et al., 2015) through dialogical interaction of the theoretical and the practical, the abstract and the particular. This boundary zone has the potential to be the place of production of new professional knowledge for all involved. Teacher education is not a process of making theory into practice but best understood as zones of mixing, blending and hybridization – as a *thirdspace* where both theoretical and practical dimensions of teacher work and power relations between stakeholders come together (Bhabha, 1994; Kostogriz, 2005, 2006; Soja, 1996).

The concept of thirdspace draws our attention to the dialectical and dynamic nature of professional learning through university-school partnerships, if these are open to dialogue and continuous negotiation of meanings and professional identities. As Rowan et al. (2015) argue, it is not useful to see teacher education in a simple or singular way. Drawing on the work of Soja (1996), they suggest that teacher education needs to be seen in terms of the *conceived space* of its visions and goals; the *perceived space* of the teacher education programs that enact the vision; and the *lived space* of day-to-day teaching and learning. Their analysis of teacher education attempts to keep these distinctions in mind in making judgements about what is "effective" in teacher education. Spaces of partnerships in this understanding are outcomes of the interplay of the lived practices of teacher educators, teachers and PSTs in their places (institutions), and representations about how relations between them and their workplaces are made and how they should be made (e.g., ideals negotiated through and imbedded in partnership arrangements). The analysis of the teacher education partnership, CTEC, presented here focuses on the lived space in which the various participants endeavoured to do the day to day work of enacting the project vision. The main objective of the research is to explore the everyday experience of teachers, PSTs, teacher educators and other collaborators as they collectively negotiate the spatial production of meanings related to partnership development.

4 Methodology

The CTEC research project is a 4 year longitudinal case study of a partnership between ACU, Catholic Education Melbourne and initially 14 schools, with an additional school joining in 2014 and another in 2015. The partnership has the aims to:

1. increase the number and quality of graduates coming to teach in CTEC schools;
2. increase numbers of students from CTEC schools undertaking teaching at ACU; and
3. enhance understanding of effective PST education delivered through university-system-school partnerships in urban growth and low SES areas.

Information about increased recruitment of graduates from ACU at CTEC schools is not yet available as the initial cohort of PSTs will not graduate until 2016, monitoring of ACU entrants from CTEC schools is being tracked and compared with the period prior to CTEC to see whether there has been growth in enrolments. The third aim of understanding teacher education delivered through partnerships is a focus in this chapter and will be addressed through investigation of the lived experience of participants as they work in partnership. In pursuing this objective, data sources from the first 2 years of activity in the planned 4 year study will be examined.

Case study is an appropriate methodology to investigate the spaces of a teacher education partnership because a variety of data sources can be included in order to create the case (Harland, 2014). Also analysis of a particular case can be used to consider the value of contemporary theories in the field. In this study, thematic analysis of project documents, such as formal agreements between the parties, shows the vision and goals of participants (conceived space), and evidence about how the participants carried out their vision through planned programs and on-going initiatives are presented (perceived space). Most substantially, attention is given to the lived experience of participants collected through surveys and individual and small group interviews. Examination of these data sources enables the analysis of a case of teacher education on the boundary with a view to assessing the value of the idea that partnerships can be a creative space of dialogical relationships and shared responsibility between universities and schools; as well as the site of disruptions that put the collaboration at risk. The research was planned to investigate both participant perceptions of the project as well as findings about recruitment and eventual employment of CTEC PSTs at CTEC schools.

To address the issue of possible bias in researching a program in which researchers were also designers and teachers, data were collected by research/administration staff who were not working directly with the PSTs. At the start of the program in 2013 researchers collected initial data about the perceptions of the recently-recruited PSTs. Later, in 2013 and in the following year, the following were collected:

- Questionnaires with the 2013 and 2014 cohorts of PST participants;
- Individual and small group interviews conducted with the 2013 and 2014 cohorts of PSTs;

- Small group and individual interviews conducted with school staff, including principals, careers advisors and student teacher co-ordinators, in 2013 and 2014;
- Small group and individual interviews conducted with relevant academics from Australian Catholic University in 2013 and 2014;
- Small group and individual interviews conducted with Catholic Education Melbourne staff in 2013 and 2014.

In the following analysis, project documents have been used to explore findings about the CTEC partnerships as have perception data gathered from all groups of participants. The comments made in interviews and questionnaires have been analysed for recurring themes related to their experience of the partnership. Informed by the work of Miles and Huberman (1994) an inductive approach to coding the responses was used with Nvivo 10 software.

5 Analysis and Discussion

5.1 The Conceived Space: The Catholic Vision of the Partnership

The CTEC – Northern and Western Pilot Project – was the vision of ACU's Victorian Chapter which is a consultative body, led by ACU Executive members and includes University stakeholders, such as the representatives of Catholic Education Melbourne and Catholic school principals. Details of the partnership's origin are significant in that it was a joint venture representing the goals of both the University, sector leadership and some school principals. The Chapter group identified a need for adequate staffing with a commitment to the Catholic ethos to work in Catholic secondary schools in the northern and western suburbs of Melbourne to keep pace with the growing enrolments in these areas. Between 2007 and 2013 there was a 12.2 % growth in enrolments overall in the northern and western suburbs. Growth in the outer north and outer west had been strongest, with an 18.9 % increase between 2007 and 2013 (Catholic Education Melbourne, 2014). Given these numbers and the continuing housing developments on the suburban fringes it was believed that staffing for Catholic schools was an issue in need of a dedicated approach. The partnership, which began with 14 and grew to 16 Catholic secondary schools from the focus areas, planned to address this need by developing a specialised program within the Bachelor of Teaching/Bachelor of Arts (BT/BA) course, a 4 year undergraduate secondary teacher education program. The specialised program was aimed at developing PSTs who were particularly prepared for and interested in working in the Catholic schools in the area.

The partnership vision pursued by the project was to create maximum engagement of PSTs in the CTEC school communities through a dedicated tutorial for them within course units, holding classes in CTEC schools where possible; completion of PST Community and Professional Experience within CTEC schools and other opportunities to immerse themselves in schools with a view to becoming a teacher in the area. These elements were adaptions of elements of similar projects already established between ACU, Catholic Education Melbourne and Catholic primary schools which had shown promising results for partnerships in teacher education (Butler, Larkins, & Cahir, 2013; Summers & Weir, 2012). The project also had the goal of promoting enrolment in teacher education programs of students from CTEC schools to ensure the long term sustainability of staffing for Catholic schools in the north and west of Melbourne. A broader goal of improving access to university of students from the area was also part of the initial vision. The project concept incorporated both the staffing goals of schools and the University's central strategic goal to support the "historic Mission of Catholic educational institutions" (ACU Strategic Plan 2012–2014, p. 4). For the Faculty of Education and Arts, CTEC offered the opportunity to "contribute to the evidence base for effective PST education delivered through university-system-school partnerships in urban growth and low SES areas" (Ryan, Dawson, Nailer, & Podporin, 2015, p. 16). It is clear that, in terms of the vision of CTEC at least, the partnership was a space for collaboration between the diverse groups to create a shared future.

5.2 The Perceived Space: CTEC's Implementation

Planning conversations began in 2011 with a Memorandum of Understanding negotiated by the partners in 2012. A Steering Committee representing all CTEC partners continued to meet regularly to oversee and review implementation of project elements. The first cohort of PSTs entered what was called a "Pilot" program in 2013; the pilot phase being the 2 years for which the program was initially funded, allowing two cohorts of PSTs to enter. The initial commitment of all parties was to complete the pilot with the expectation that if it proved successful further cohorts would enter the project. Based on initial positive findings (Butler, Dawson, Love, Nailer, & Podporin, 2014) the project did take in further cohorts in 2014 and 2015 who will graduate after the end of the pilot phase. Activities were facilitated with in-kind resources from Catholic Education Melbourne and from the schools, 2 years of funding from the University Executive as well as Equity Pathways funding, the latter being a University equity and access program. However, as documented by researchers on partnership sustainability, insecurity of funding is a constant in most teacher education partnerships (Darling-Hammond, 2005; Kruger et al., 2009). Therefore, perhaps predictably, as noted in the 2014 and 2015 CTEC reports (Butler et al., 2014; Ryan et al., 2015), the level of funding was reduced after the program's initial years, putting its continuation at risk. But, despite this threat, further internal support was eventually found for the CTEC work in schools to continue. Unlike government funded school-university partnerships, whose duration can be dependent on the external political context (Jones & Ryan, 2014), it seemed that a program which was close to the strategic direction of the Faculty and University was one which continued to find University support.

An investigation of the activities of the project Steering Committee and its leadership team in the years 2013–2015 suggests the project team undertook a range of activities that were designed to maintain the profile of the partnership with its supporters. Bi-annual reports were made to ACU Chapter; a project newsletter was regularly published which gave details of CTEC achievements; an annual CTEC dinner was held where the University Executive celebrated the CTEC experience with Catholic Education Melbourne representatives, principals and PSTs; CTEC school staff were integrated into University classes creating strong links between the academic and practical aspects of the program. Such activities were opportunities to share experiences and research findings and argue for the continuation of the program.

The 2015 report noted that connections between Catholic institutions were strengthened during the implementation phase through mechanisms such as on-going email and newsletter communication and regular meetings with Catholic Education Melbourne consultants and principal representatives from the northern and western regions. It also recommended that "the Pilot Project be continued as planned, with research findings informing its further development and implementation" (Ryan et al., 2015, p. 27). The project's concern with enhancing educational outcomes in the north and west of Melbourne, where socioeconomic factors contribute to limiting access to higher education, meant that the University's access program Equity Pathways continued to provide funding for CTEC activities (Ryan et al., 2015). The sector partners, Catholic Education Melbourne, and the school principals helped to maintain the shared vision through their attendance at meetings and participation in CTEC's regular evaluation activities. Despite the on-going threat of loss of funding the partnership continued into its third and fourth year.

5.3 The Lived Experience of CTEC

5.3.1 The Catholic Ethos

Thirdspace theory (Bhabha, 1994) suggests that to create successful teacher education in the boundary between university and schools there needs to be a space for discussion and negotiation among the parties to create a shared and/or new understanding of the enterprise. As has been noted, the CTEC project enjoyed high level support from the University as well as from sector leadership and principal representatives during its development and implementation phases. An important issue in terms of the success of the program is whether the vision was shared among those who were engaged in the implementation of the program at the school and university level. There is evidence in data collected from interviews with principals and ACU staff that suggests that the shared sense of "Catholic" identity and community was significant in their commitment to the project. One principal identified the role of CTEC in enhancing the opportunity "to nurture the Catholic ethos of the schools" (Principal, 2014). Another principal talked about the importance of supporting PSTs at ACU as part of a broader commitment to Catholic education: "This is about investing in our Catholicity and our education system" (Principal, 2013).

The interview data also showed that the vision of a Catholic education was shared by those who were involved in the day-to-day operation of CTEC but not as part of the project leadership. A PST Coordinator, charged with organising CTEC school experience, noted that the engagement of the PSTs in the school community meant that teachers could show them "what it means to be a Catholic person, a person working in a Catholic school" (Teacher, 2014). One of the ways in which the CTEC program sought to engage in the northern and western school communities was by situating the mandated BT/BA Community Engagement experience within the social justice programs of the CTEC school communities. PSTs undertook a variety of activities in the communities such as helping in soup kitchens, homework clubs and camps. The PST Coordinator commented, "From a Catholic perspective there's the links to the other organisations outside the school to, you know, the [Catholic social justice project]" (Teacher, 2014). Another teacher in a different school said that, even if the PSTs didn't return to teach at their school, "at least they know the feeling of supported community in a Catholic education setting, and may foster that somewhere else" (Deputy principal, 2014). Some of the CTEC PSTs had themselves attended a Catholic school, sometimes a CTEC school, and a careers advisor interviewed saw the value of the project in promoting access to education for students in the area stating that "something like this may encourage those students to feel like university is a genuine aspiration… And for those interested in going into teaching … they've shown an interest in wanting to revisit the schools that they've been part of" (Teacher, 2013). The PSTs also commented on the significance of the Catholic ethos in both choosing to be part of CTEC in the first place and then as an aspect of the program that they appreciated. Findings from the questionnaire indicate that the proportion of students wanting to work in Catholic secondary schools upon graduation remained fairly consistent across the two rounds of data collection, with the strong majority (83%) continuing to indicate a desire to teach in Catholic secondary schools. Two PSTs who had not attended Catholic schools explained their initial perceptions and the impact of participating in the program on their attitudes.

> I went to a government school and had nothing to do with religion. So that …would have put up a lot of barriers for me applying for a school that had religion involved with it. Now I'm not as afraid of that … it's not a barrier to me. (PST, 2014)
>
> I was really sceptical about Catholic schools. I'd never been to one and I was just like, oh, church school, but seeing how much they really care about their students and how much they really try to engage the families into the school, I really like it. So I was like, oh, Catholic schools are great. (PST, 2014)

5.3.2 The Value of Being Part of a Cohort

Although PSTs in CTEC highlighted the value of being involved in a Catholic school as a positive of the project for them, at the end of the first year and again in the following year the more significant element for them was their enrolment in a CTEC-only tutorial and therefore being part of a cohort of learners. One PST gave the following response:

> I really enjoyed being part of [CTEC project team member's] tutorial group. I think she … really went out of her way for us as well … And it was nice, yeah, knowing that you're part of a group and you know who's going to be in your class and … well we had [CTEC project team member] for … three semesters in a row, so that was pretty good. Like that consistency. (PST, 2014)

The benefits of being with the cohort were seen as both academic and social as in the following comment, "I notice … with the presentations that we've had so far, you know, we're all laughing and being comfortable 'cause [sic] we know each other" (PST, 2014). There was evidence that the creation of a cohort experience also helped to make the theory-practice connection so sought after in teacher education:

> The way our tutorial was staged directly after placement, I thought was great because … it meant that we were able to go straight from being there to talking about it and to rehash what we'd learnt and observed throughout the day. (PST, 2013)

Another participant from the 2014 cohort echoed this idea when asked about her motivation for getting involved in CTEC. "I really like the idea of having like the same cohort of students, like staying with the same class all the way through" (PST, 2104). This group also saw future professional relationships being developed. One PST commented, "And potentially we'll be getting, hopefully, jobs in the same areas anyway so you've got that like connection with all your other peers and staff as well" (PST, 2014).

5.3.3 Long-Term Relationships

While the idea of creating professional relationships was not highlighted in the broad aims of CTEC, as with the primary school projects from which CTEC had been adapted (Butler et al., 2013; Summers & Weir, 2012), the idea that teacher education partnerships created opportunities for close professional relationships was important in a key CTEC approach of intensive PST engagement in schools. This vision was appreciated by those who were involved in the project at the school level, they tended to emphasise the long-term nature of the relationships that were facilitated. A teacher said "the ongoing nature of it I think is fantastic" (Teacher interview, 2014). A Deputy Principal made the comment, "I'm a fan of anything that's long-term" (Principal interview, 2014). A principal noted, "I think having students assigned to us on a long-term basis is good … you know, they're not just here 3 weeks and you never see them again … they become quite connected with the school" (Principal interview, 2013). One principal even saw its impact into the distant future.

> My sense to it would be that if we persevere with it, and this is not something over a year or two, we've got to be committed to this over a five to 10-year … then you can get your measure of it … do they take up leadership roles in our schools? (Principal, 2014).

5.3.4 Disruptions to Relationships

While participants' satisfaction with being involved in a program which developed relationships over time was one element of the project discourse expressed by participants in a range of roles, the concept was interrupted somewhat by experiences of communication breakdowns and organisational frustrations. Such challenges were raised by ACU, Catholic Education Melbourne, school staff and PSTs. Ensuring that information about CTEC reached the different relevant staff at schools was difficult, as was ensuring clear communication between and within ACU and Catholic Education Melbourne. As noted in other partnership research (Darling-Hammond, 2005), face-to-face meetings were very helpful in clarifying project goals and roles but were difficult to schedule, given the different work patterns of schools and universities, as well as the busy workloads of university and school-based staff. The biggest challenge with communication occurred in relation to the Community Engagement experience. As this was something different from a standard teaching placement, both the PSTs and the schools were somewhat unsure of exactly what it entailed. The comments below indicate how a teacher education partnership vision may be created by leadership but it has to be enacted by teachers and PSTs in their day to day work in schools. A PST co-ordinator charged with organising placements at a school said:

> I think there's still a lot of work to be done. I'm not sure whether it's just me, because all the information goes to the principal and then is fed into me. I'm not sure whether I've just been kept out of the loop, but I don't feel like I've had much information from any of the involved partners. But, as I said, maybe that's just because I haven't been given the information from the principal. (Teacher, 2014)

PSTs found themselves in the middle of this absence of communication. One said it would have been good in schools to:

> have someone call us or reply or, you know, we've spoken to one person that wasn't the right person, and then we got pushed to someone else who hadn't spoken to that person and had no idea what we were about. (PST interview, 2014)

Complaints about communication breakdown seem endemic to partnerships between schools and universities (Allen, 2010; Darling-Hammond, 2005). In the case of CTEC, the frustrations have not led to significant numbers of PSTs leaving the program. The 2013 cohort of 18 PSTs lost two due to them choosing to exit or defer the BT/BA course and one because of relocation away from the CTEC area. The 2014 cohort of 23 PSTs lost five because of exiting or deferring the course but gained three new participants (Ryan et al., 2015). Teachers involved in the program had choices whether or not to agree to supervise a CTEC PST but did not have significant power over the project apart from this.

5.3.5 Experience Beyond Catholic Schools

A concern, which goes closer to providing a challenge to the Catholic vision of the project, noted by some PSTs as well as staff from Catholic Education Melbourne and schools, was that PST experience might be limited through only being placed in Catholic schools. One PST said "I would like to see a state school, 'cause [sic] I went in primary and secondary both Catholic. I'd love to see and be involved in a state setting once" (PST, 2014).

This comment reveals a certain tension for some participants in the lived experience of the Catholic vision of the project. In response, the Steering Committee expressed the view that as long as PSTs had the opportunity to be placed at/visit a range of different Catholic schools (7–12, Senior, Single-sex, Co-Educational) within the Consortium this limitation would be addressed (Ryan et al., 2015). As noted, the vast majority of the initially recruited PSTs have remained with the program despite the concern of some that their experience might be limited by only experiencing Catholic schools. Some CTEC participants have been further engaged in CTEC schools by gaining casual paid employment in one of the schools, for example as integration support officers. This was an element of the original project design, planned to enable further immersion of PSTs in school communities when the cohort was in the third year of their BT/BA.

5.3.6 Workload Issues

For the CTEC team at the University and Catholic Education Melbourne there have been on-going comments about the viability of CTEC in terms of the workload it required, an experience which has been shown to be frequently connected to partnership work because of its position outside the teacher education norm, usually dependent on insecure grant funding (Darling-Hammond, 2005; Kruger et al., 2009).

The CTEC reports also document many staff changes which show the program's vulnerability to changes in personnel, likewise identified as a high risk element in teacher education partnerships' success (Kruger et al., 2009). However, as noted earlier, the fact that CTEC has continued to enjoy some financial support because of its coherence with the University's mission has meant that participants' workload issues have not threatened the survival of the project to date.

5.3.7 Policy Disruptions

In 2015 an intrusion from the perceived space of Australian national and University policy had the potential to challenge CTEC more than any of the previously encountered disruption. After submitting to its mandatory periodic review the BT/BA course lost its embedded Community Engagement unit in favour of PSTs having more discipline study and more supervised teaching days in schools, this being in line with AITSL accreditation policy (AITSL, 2014). Community Engagement undertaken in CTEC school communities had been consistently identified by participants as a strength of CTEC, allowing PSTs to know about their school community before undergoing formal teaching experience at the schools:

> I think a benefit [or] highlight is to actually meet the students, not just for teaching purposes. So we have PSTs from other universities but they ... their involvement is just purely classroom oriented. So the two students that we've had from ACU over the year have been able to get to know us as a community ... get to know the students, so then when they go into the classrooms there's even a connection there because they've met the students in a community forum first" (PST Coordinator 2014).

The impact of this change has not been felt by CTEC participants as the revised course is only in its early stages, but that it has occurred demonstrates that the quality of teacher education is affected by factors in the conceived and perceived spaces as much as by what participants experience in the lived space.

Another intrusion on the CTEC experience from the policy space occurred at the beginning of 2015 when some of the original CTEC schools were offered state government funding for a different partnership activity and one school declined some of CTEC's PSTs for placement out of a concern that they would not be able to support both partnership programs. Within the thirdspace framework such disruptions are part of the challenge of working in the hybrid space between the University and schools

6 Conclusion

Examination of CTEC in terms of its conceived, perceived and lived spaces illustrates that engagement in a university-school partnership involved participants in complex activities to establish arrangements which met a vision created at a leadership level. Perceptions of the program revealed that the Catholic ethos underlying the partnership was shared by many of the participants in schools – PSTs and teachers. The partnership investigation suggested that the shared vision gave some strength to the partnership in that participants were able to see where they were going with the work even when it was demanding. While the school participants were more likely to describe the significance of the partnership in terms of valued professional relationships in a shared Catholic context rather than as a vision for the Catholic education system overall, they did not express doubts about this vision. They supported the idea of the partnership despite experiencing communication and other challenges in the boundary zones in which they worked. Participants at the leadership level of university and school were also required to manage changes in policy and resources which threatened the partnership. Ongoing investigation of the program into its third and fourth year will reveal whether it is able to remain resilient.

In terms of what the CTEC project contributes to research on partnerships in teacher education, the research suggests that joint planning and execution of a teacher education initiative prevents universities from becoming narrowly focused on preoccupations like finding placements for PSTs. Instead it means that there is a joint articulation by both the schools and the university participants of what the desirable future teachers might be like. This discussion in the boundary zone is very important for managing the on-going work of constructing the specifics of the program and carrying it out.

The CTEC model presents an alternative notion of partnerships that presupposes dialogical relationships on the boundary between the University and schools. Boundary is presented as an open zone of collaboration and production of professional knowledge and as a space of rich experiences for all involved. In the case of CTEC the partnership has disrupted the status quo of the members and invited participants to join resources, knowledge and experience in and for collaborative teacher education practice. Whether or not the participants accept this invitation becomes a matter of their responsibility evident in an ability to respond to others and their needs, standpoints and understandings. This project therefore redefines partnerships in teacher education as an ethical practice that is open to and includes all the parties involved. By locating teacher education in thirdspace – on the boundary between universities and schools – responsibility of partnership members is less about their own interests, power and control than about exposure to the event of PSTs' professional becoming. This responsibility does not come from either teacher educators or teachers but rather from this event that calls to them and that has been articulated in the original idea of the CTEC project – that is, to increase the number of quality teachers in Catholic schools that are located in socially disadvantaged suburbs. It will be important for the project team to investigate the ways in which the dialogical partnership model continues to be useful in describing the work of participants in the next years of the project. Given the need for teacher education research studies to connect with each other, the project is also an invitation to other researchers to investigate teacher education partnerships based in other contexts in terms of the idea of relationships in the boundary zone.

References

Allen, J. (2010). Stakeholders' perspectives of the nature and role of assessment during practicum. *Teaching and Teacher Education, 27*, 742–750.
Australian Catholic University (ACU). (2011). *ACU strategic plan 2012–2014*. North Sydney, Australia: ACU Office of Planning and Strategic Management.
Australian Council of Deans of Education. (2014). *Teaching for excellence*. Submission to Teacher Education Ministerial Advisory Group. Australian Council of Deans of Education Inc.
Australian Institute of Teaching and School Leadership. (2014). *Australian professional standards for teaching*. http://www.aitsl.edu.au/
Australian Institute of Teaching and School Leadership. (2015). *Research agenda for initial teacher education*. Retrieved from http://www.aitsl.edu.au/docs/default-source/aitsl-research/ITE-researchagenda.pdf?sfvrsn=4.
Beach, D., & Bagley, C. (2013). Changing professional discourses in teacher education policy back towards a training paradigm: a comparative study. *European Journal of Teacher Education, 36*(4), 379–392. Retrieved from http://dx.doi.org/10.1080/02619768.2013.815162.
Bhabha, H. (1994). *The location of culture*. London: Routledge.

British Education Research Association. (2014). *Research and the teaching profession. Building the capacity for a self-improving education system.* Final report of the BERA-RSA inquiry into the role of research in teacher education. Retrieved from https://www.bera.ac.uk/wp-content/uploads/2013/12/BERA-RSA-Research-Teaching-Profession-FULL-REPORT-for-web.pdf?noredirect=1.

Butler, H., Dawson, A., Love, K., Nailer, S., & Podporin, M. (2014). *Catholic Teacher Education Consortium (CTEC) Northern and Western Pilot Project* (2014). CTEC Final report. Unpublished document, Faculty of Education and Arts.

Butler, H., Larkins, G., & Cahir, S. (2013). *Partnerships in learning (PiL): Enhancing quality teaching.* East Melbourne, Australia: Catholic Education Office Melbourne.

Catholic Education Melbourne. (2014). *Enrolment in catholic schools 2007–2013.* Unpublished material.

Cochran-Smith, M., & Fries, K. (2005). Researching teacher education in changing times: Politics and paradigms. In M. Cochran-Smith & K. Zeichner (Eds.), *Studying teacher education: The report of the AERA panel on research and teacher education. AERA.* Mahwah, NJ: Lawrence Erlbaum.

Cochran-Smith, M., Villegas, A., Abrams, L., Chavez-Moreno, L., Mills, T., & Stern, R. (2015). Critiquing teacher preparation research: An overview of the field, Part II. *Journal of Teacher Education, 62*(2), 109–121.

Darling-Hammond, L. (Ed.). (2005). *Professional development schools. Schools for developing a profession.* New York: Teachers College Press.

Darling-Hammond, L. (2006). *Powerful teacher education: Lessons from exemplary programs.* San Francisco: Jossey-Bass.

Department of Education (DfE). (2010). *The case for change.* London: DfE.

Dinham, S. (2013). The quality teaching movement in Australia encounters difficult terrain: A personal perspective. *Australian Journal of Education, 57*(2), 91–106.

Dinham, S (2015). *Issues and perspectives relevant to the development of an approach to the accreditation of initial teacher education in Australia based on evidence of impact.* Australian Institute for Teaching and School Leadership, Melbourne, Australia. Retrieved from http://www.aitsl.edu.au/docs/default-source/initial-teacher-education-resources/ite-reform-stimulus-paper-03-dinham.pdf?sfvrsn=6.

Effers, A., Plecki, M., & McGuigan, C. (2014, May). *Teaching teams in residency-based teacher preparation: when learning to teach is a collaborative endeavour.* Paper presentation at meeting of AERA, Philadelphia. Retrieved from http://www.aera.net/Publications/OnlinePaperRepository/AERAOnlinePaperRepository/tabid/12720/Owner/98111/Default.aspx.

Harland, T. (2014). Learning about case study methodology to research higher education. *Higher Education Research & Development, 33*(6), 1113–1122. doi:10.1080/07294360.2014.91125

Jones, M., & Ryan, J. (2014). Successful and 'transferrable' practice. In M. Jones & J. Ryan (Eds.), *Successful teacher education: Partnerships, reflective practice and the place of technology* (pp. 177–194). Dordrecht, The Netherlands: Sense Publishers.

Kostogriz, A. (2005). Dialogical imagination of (inter)cultural spaces. In J. K. Hall, G. Vitanova, & L. Marchenkova (Eds.), *Dialogue with Bakhtin on second and foreign language learning: New perspectives* (pp. 189–210). Mahwah, NJ: L. Erlbaum.

Kostogriz, A. (2006). Putting "space" on the agenda of sociocultural research in education. *Mind, Culture, and Activity, 13*(3), 176–190.

Kruger, T., Davies, A., Eckersley, B., Newell, F., & Cherednichenko, B. (2009). *Effective and sustainable university-school partnerships. Beyond determined efforts of inspired individuals.* Canberra, Australia: Teaching Australia. Retrieved from http://hdl.voced.edu.au/10707/144200.

Le Cornu, R. (2012). School co-ordinators: Leaders of learning in professional experience. *Australian Journal of Teacher Education, 31*(3), 18–33.

McLean Davies, L., Anderson, M., Deans, J., Dinham, S., Griffin, P., Kameniar, B., et al. (2013). Masterly preparation: Embedding clinical practice in a graduate PST education programme. *Journal of Education for Teaching: International Research and Pedagogy, 39*(1), 93–106.

Miles, M. B., & Huberman, A. M. (1994). *Qualitative data analysis: An expanded sourcebook* (2nd ed.). Thousand Oaks, CA: Sage.

Nuttall, J., Murray, S., Seddon, T., & Mitchell, J. (2006). Teacher Education in Australia: Charting new directions. *Asia-Pacific Journal of Teacher Education, 34*(3), 321–332.

Plecki, M., Effers, A., & Nakamura, Y. (2012). Using evidence for teacher education program improvement and accountability: An illustrative case of value-added measures. *Journal of Teacher Education, 63*, 318–335. doi:10.1177/0022487112447110

Rowan, L., Mayer, D., Kline, J., Kostogriz, A., & Walker-Gibbs, B. (2015). Investigating the effectiveness of teacher education for early career teachers in diverse settings: The longitudinal research we have to have. *Australian Educational Researcher, 42*, 273–298. doi:10.1007/s13384-014-0163-y

Ryan, J., Dawson, A., Nailer, S., & Podporin, M. (2015). *Catholic Teacher Education Consortium (CTEC) Northern and Western Pilot Project (2015)*. CTEC Final Report. Unpublished document, Faculty of Education and Arts, ACU.

Ryan, J., & Jones, M. (2014). Communication in the practicum: Fostering relationships between universities and schools. In M. Jones & J. Ryan (Eds.), *Successful teacher education: Partnerships, reflective practice and the place of technology* (pp. 103–120). Dordrecht, The Netherlands: Sense Publishers.

Singer, A. (2013, January). *Problems with Pearson's student teacher evaluation system – It's like déjà vu all over again* [Web blog post]. Retrieved from http://www.huffingtonpost.com/alan-singer/problems-with-pearsons-te_b_4093772.html.

Sleeter, C. (2014). Towards teacher education research that informs policy. *Education Researcher, 43*(3), 146–153.

Soja, E. (1996). *Thirdspace: Journeys to Los Angeles and other real-and-imagined places*. Oxford, UK: Blackwell.

Stanford University. (2014). EdTPA. Pearson Ed. Retrieved from http://www.edtpa.com/Home.aspx.

Summers, B., & Weir, L. (2012). Partnerships in teacher education: An emerging landscape. *Journal of Catholic School Studies, 84*(2), 54–64.

Teacher Education Ministerial Advisory Group (TEMAG). (2014). *Action now: Classroom ready teachers*. Retrieved from http://www.studentsfirst.gov.au/teacher-education-ministerial-advisory-group.

Zeichner, K. (2010). Competition, economic rationalization, increased surveillance, and attacks on diversity: Neo-liberalism and the transformation of teacher education in the U.S. *Teaching and Teacher Education, 26*, 1544–1552.

Zeichner, K. (2012). The turn once again toward practice-based teacher education. *Journal of Teacher Education, 63*(5), 376–382. doi:10.1177/0022487112445789

Zeichner, K., Payne, K., & Brayko, K. (2015). Democratizing teacher education. *Journal of Teacher Education, 66*(2), 122–135.

Activating Teaching Dispositions in Carefully Constructed Contexts: Examining the Impact of Classroom Intensives

Amanda McGraw, Sharon McDonough, Chris Wines, and Courtney O'Loughlan

1 Introduction

In Australia a focus on 'classroom readiness' in teacher education implies a physical, organisational stance; of new teachers well prepared and complete. A recent Australian review into teacher education conducted by the Teacher Education Ministerial Advisory Group (TEMAG, 2014) argues that pre-service teachers (PSTs) should be consistently and rigorously assessed against national professional standards which outline what beginning teachers should know and be able to do. Interestingly, the current *National Graduate Standards* lack any mention of affective qualities like passion, inspiration and humour. They fail to focus explicitly on important ways of thinking that enable good teaching and professional learning like curiosity, creativity and reflection. Relational elements that are central in teaching are also rationalised and 'flattened' out so that there is little sense of nuance and sensitivity (Gannon, 2012). Reductionism occurs when the system focuses on what is easiest to measure rather than seeking to develop ways to assess what is critical (Diez, 2007). This chapter focuses on the research of a team of teacher educators from a regional Australian university who believe that a focus on dispositions is central to effective teacher education. We have developed a *Dispositions for Teaching Framework* which underpins pedagogical practices, school partnership initiatives, and assessment within a Master of Teaching program for prospective secondary teachers. The framework is not a list of personal characteristics or personality traits, rather it aims to capture ways of thinking that enable teachers to engage deeply in their work and continue to learn. The challenge to avoid a checklist mentality pervades our thinking and so we have focused on constructing contexts where these dispositions can be understood, activated, made visible,

---

A. McGraw (✉) • S. McDonough • C. Wines • C. O'Loughlan
Faculty of Education and Arts, Federation University Australia, Ballarat, Victoria, Australia
e-mail: a.mcgraw@federation.edu.au; s.mcdonough@federation.edu.au; c.wines@federation.edu.au; c.oloughlan@federation.edu.au

documented, and over time, habituated. While issues related to the authentic assessment of dispositions continue to challenge us, we focus in this chapter, on the nature of one of our 'leading practices' (the *Classroom Intensive*) and we examine whether practices like these have the potential to activate dispositions so that they can be recognised.

2 Dispositions for Teaching

The recent national review of teacher education in Australia (TEMAG, 2014) reported that in addition to having academic skills, prospective teachers require "strong interpersonal and communication skills, a willingness to learn and the motivation to teach" (p. 13). While this suggests an important move away from selection processes based solely on performances in high stakes tests, Edwards and Nuttall (2015) argue that the very title of the TEMAG (2014) report *Action Now: Classroom ready teachers* "belies a lack of acknowledgement of the complexity of pre-service teacher preparation" (p. 181). Personal qualities and dispositions required for teaching and for effective, ongoing professional learning enable teachers to deal with what Barnett (2007) would call 'supercomplexity': "a term that we may apply to the open-endedness of ideas, perspectives, values, beliefs and interpretations" (pp. 36–37). In a world of supercomplexity we are subject to "conceptual overload" (Barnett, 2000, p. 415) due to the existence of a multiplicity of changing and contestable frameworks that increase uncertainty and unpredictability. While Cochran-Smith (2003) suggests that teaching is "unforgivably complex" (p. 5), she argues that in the face of simplistic accountability measures and narrow definitions of teacher quality, we must preserve and honour complexity. We would argue that teaching for and within complexity demands high-quality learning and agree with Entwistle (2012) when he suggests that "quality in learning depends on acquiring the attitudes and ways of thinking and practising that are the hallmark of committed professionals" (p. 15). The link between certain dispositions and quality of learning is well established through educational research (Entwistle & McCune, 2009; Perkins, 1995; Ritchhart, 2002; Riveros, Norris, Hayward, & Phillips, 2012). The challenge for teacher educators is to not only articulate which dispositions they aim to link to program goals, but to develop shared understandings of how dispositions are developed in complex teaching and learning contexts.

The National Council for Accreditation of Teacher Education (NCATE) in the United States has mandated the identification and assessment of dispositions. NCATE (2002) contend that dispositions are values, commitments and professional ethics that influence behaviours. They suggest that "dispositions are guided by beliefs and attitudes related to values such as caring, fairness, honesty, responsibility, and social justice" (NCATE, 2002, p. 52). The term 'disposition' is open to multiple interpretations and is sometimes used interchangeably with other concepts like traits, attitudes, competencies and characteristics. Confusingly, the NCATE do not provide any theoretical framework for their definition of dispositions (Freeman,

2007) and while there is agreement in the U.S.A. about the value of dispositions for teaching, there is less agreement about what they constitute and how they can be developed and assessed (Diez, 2007). Some time ago, Arnstine (1967) argued that dispositions are central to effective teaching and defined dispositions as behaviours that are "thoughtful and discriminative of situations" (p. 28), while others equate dispositions to habits of mind and refer to Dewey who suggested that dispositions are habitual and persistent (Dewey, 1922). Costa and Kallick (2000) argue that dispositions are intellectual resources that help activate relevant knowledge and capacities. They contend that they are essential when encountering complex problems and suggest dispositions should "become the subject of curriculum, instruction, student assessment and even teacher evaluation" (Costa & Kallick, p. 3). Other researchers also link dispositions to the quality of learning and thinking suggesting they are abilities like thinking critically, being reflective and having an open mind (Perkins & Ritchhart, 2004; Riveros et al., 2012). Dispositions, however, are more than having an inclination to think and act; they also consist of an "awareness of occasions for appropriate action" (Ritchhart, 2002, p. 51). Entwistle (2012) argues that the disposition to understand for oneself is essential in a climate of complexity and uncertainty. This involves a willingness to learn, a sensitivity to context, the capacity to integrate understandings, and the capacity to use understandings in challenging situations. Central to this notion is the capacity to understand oneself: to hold maps in one's head about how to plan, act and review what we do (Argyris & Schön, 1974); and to create, evaluate and reimagine those personal maps through metacognition and reflection.

Developing a new Master of Teaching program in our university gave us the opportunity to start from scratch and devise a program that is research informed, integrates partnership initiatives and builds upon our educational values, beliefs and experiences. We began the design process not with professional standards but with the question: *What sort of teachers do we want our PSTs to become*? We found that a focus on personal dispositions were just as evident in our responses as desired practices and knowledge and decided that, in the absence of a focus on dispositions in the National Teaching Standards, we needed to formulate our own framework to inform teaching practice and curriculum. Over time, the work of researchers like Gardner (1983), Goleman (1995), Perkins (1995), and Ritchhart (2002) has helped us to rethink intelligence. The notion of 'intellectual character' as dispositional (Ritchhart, 2002; Tishman, 1994) underpins our framework. Ritchhart suggests that thinking dispositions "represent characteristics that animate, motivate, and direct our abilities toward good and productive thinking and are recognised in the patterns of our frequently exhibited, voluntary behaviour" (p. 21). Our framework (see Fig. 1), which is inspired by the work of Perkins (1995) and Ritchhart (2002) and draws upon the research of Entwistle (2009, 2012), attempts to capture key thinking dispositions that are essential in the discipline of education and for learning in higher education contexts. The framework does not intend to provide an exhaustive list of dispositions but instead aims to articulate the dispositions we intend to focus on explicitly in our teaching and through our school partnership activities. The framework provides us with a conceptual map that enables us to build shared vocabulary

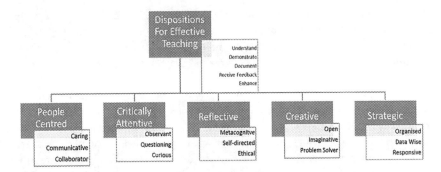

Fig. 1 Dispositions for effective teaching framework

related to thinking dispositions, relevant learning activities, opportunities for making the dispositions visible through documentation, approaches for self-reflection, and strategies for feedback and assessment.

We do not intend to describe the thinking dispositions here, but instead want to focus on a key challenge for teacher educators: how do we construct learning contexts which enable thinking dispositions to be developed and made visible? We see an increasing focus on using classroom observation as a professional learning experience as a significant opportunity to activate and develop key thinking dispositions.

2.1 Classroom Observation as an Opportunity to Activate Dispositions

Observing in classrooms is a central element of initial teacher education programs (Gore, 2015), however, observations are usually focused on PSTs and their teaching in the context of offering them feedback to improve skills. In our Master of Teaching program we place an emphasis on the nature of observation itself and aim to enhance the disposition to critically attend to what is seen in classrooms by providing PSTs with structured opportunities to closely observe what happens there. We use the term 'critically attentive' to describe a disposition involving close observation, curiosity and questioning. We use the work of McCrary Sullivan (2000) to examine the notion of sustained attention and what it means to observe with "keen eyes and fine sensibilities" (p. 212). Danielson (2012) argues that classroom observations provide the ability to "observe the interactive work with students, and this is the heart of teaching" (p. 33). Rather than focus on the work of teachers as a primary focus in classroom observations, we ask PSTs to focus their watching on students' learning and thinking and to then look at the contextual factors that are enabling learning to occur. Worryingly, in both Australia and overseas, classroom observations are increasingly used as a means by which to judge the quality of teachers and teaching

(Danielson, 2012; Gore, 2015; O'Leary, 2014). An intentional focus on learners and learning ensures that PSTs are building curiosity and understanding the complexity of teachers' work.

2.2 Classroom Intensives

A structured, thoughtful approach to classroom observations was required and with the support of teachers and school leaders from our cluster of partnership schools, we developed the practice we call *Classroom Intensives*. Each partnership school hosts a *Classroom Intensive* for one or more days and teachers and school leaders from other partnership schools are also invited to participate. We schedule *Classroom Intensives* across the course of the program the first one being held in March and the final one in October. This enables dispositions to be understood and strengthened over time. The *Classroom Intensive* involves PSTs, experienced teachers, school leaders and teacher educators (up to 60 people are involved in each Intensive) which creates rich opportunities for multiple perspectives to be shared and complexity to be foregrounded. The observation groups consist of six educators who complete observation rounds of 20 min in a variety of classes during the course of a day. Our partnership schools are keen to be actively involved in the process as it enhances the professional learning approaches they are using in their schools. For all of us, the collaborative observation of whole lessons is seen as a way to open up discussions of teaching practice in ways that move "beyond the technical delivery of teaching" (Gore, 2015, p. 9). The power of a collegial approach like this is that it enables the development of "insights that are brought to bear individually and collectively" (Hoyt & Terantino, 2015, p. 211).

The *Classroom Intensive* is structured using a *Visible Thinking* routine that aims to build inquiry habits of mind (Timperley, 2011). O'Leary (2014) argues against using quantitative approaches with pre-conceived categories as a means of documenting and measuring what is observed in classrooms and contends that such approaches need to be questioned for their effectiveness in providing an insight into the "complexity of behaviours, interactions" (p. 54). As a way of purposely building the thinking dispositions in our Framework, we use the *Visible Thinking* routine *See, Think, Wonder* designed by Ritchhart and his colleagues (http://www.visiblethinkingpz.org/VisibleThinking_html_files/03_ThinkingRoutines/03c_Core_routines/SeeThinkWonder/SeeThinkWonder_Routine.html) to focus and frame the thinking and documentation process. While in classrooms, observers focus on the *See/Hear* aspect of the routine and describe without interpretation what they observe and hear in relation to students' thinking and learning. Building the disposition to pay attention and describe complex interactions and behaviours requires access to subject-specific vocabulary which we explicitly build during the course of the program. In doing this, rich theory/practice connections can be made. The whole group comes together during the lunch break to focus on the second part of the routine: to create *thinking* or interpretive statements based on the patterns which emerge from the observations. The intensive focus on observation builds the disposition to be data wise and evidence-based when making interpretations. Thinking statements are shared publicly in the whole group and once everyone has shared at least one statement, we ask participants to again identify emerging patterns. Finally, we focus on the third part of the routine at the end of the day when we ask participants to consider what they have seen and thought during the course of the day and develop statements of *wonder*. During this stage participants wonder about larger ethical, educational, cultural and political issues and demonstrate a disposition to reflect critically. The overall process provides "the foundation for greater insights, grounded interpretations, evidence-based theory building, and broad – reaching curiosity" (Ritchhart, Church, & Morrison, 2011, p. 55).

3 The Research Project

The focus of this research project was to examine the links between the *Classroom Intensive* and the thinking dispositions in our Framework. The questions that most intrigued us were:

1. Did the experience of the *Classroom Intensive* prompt those ways of thinking?
2. Did it activate some dispositions more than others? And,
3. How could we collect evidence of dispositions in action?

The research project is based on one two-day *Classroom Intensive* experience held in one of our partnership schools toward the end of the school year. The school is a P-12 rural school and participants in the *Classroom Intensive* stayed overnight in the rural town to enable them to have an intense two day observation experience in the school. Participants observed in primary as well as secondary classrooms. Participants in the research are PSTs enrolled in the Master of Teaching (Secondary) program together with the teacher educators' (excluding the researchers) who teach in the program and who also participated in the *Classroom Intensive*.

3.1 *Methods*

The research makes use of a mixed method approach in the collection of data. Our decision to adopt such an approach acknowledges and values the unique qualities of information derived from both qualitative and quantitative research methods, and recognizes the uniqueness and complexity of educational research which focuses on human activity and learning (Pring, 2000). Because educational practice is a complex phenomenon, we suggest, like Pring that the "qualitative investigation can clear the ground for the quantitative – and the quantitative be suggestive of differences to be explored in a more interpretive mode" (p. 55). We take a *concurrent approach*, which according to Cresswell (2013) is one "where the researcher converges quantitative and qualitative data in order to provide a comprehensive analysis of the research problem" (p. 16). The concept of the *bricolage*, in the sense that it was initially used by Denzin and Lincoln (2000), is a useful one in conceptualising the method of this research. In essence, when we use the term here we are referring to a research process "dedicated to a form of rigour that is conversant with numerous modes of meaning-making and knowledge production" (Kincheloe & Berry, 2004, p. 16). We, like Kincheloe and Berry, acknowledge that *bricoleurs* operate within a space "where the multiple inputs and forces facing the researcher in the immediacy of her [his] work are acknowledged and embraced" (p. 5). Such an approach "exists out of respect for the complexity of the lived world. Indeed, it is grounded on an epistemology of complexity" (Kincheloe & Berry, 2004, p. 2). With such complexity comes an attendant difficulty in maintaining what Kincheloe and Berry term "theoretical coherence" (p. 3) when engaging in the process of interpreting the data and drawing out generalisations from within its various formats.

3.2 Data Collection

Data collection occurred through the use of four differing techniques, although not all participants completed all four of the data collection activities. Three of the techniques were qualitative in nature; these were the use of participant field notes, a narrative response, and 'on the spot' conversational interviews. Participants completed the field notes (n=36) over the course of the two day *Classroom Intensive*. These notes contain participants' descriptions as they look for visible evidence of thinking and learning at work. They were provided with a template based on the *See, Think, Wonder* routine and were asked to record their non-judgmental observations of what they saw/heard in each of the classrooms they entered. The field notes also include participants' interpretive statements as they search for patterns within, or derived from their observations, and also what they wonder about at the conclusion of the Intensive. The second qualitative method was that of a narrative response (n=13) where participants responded to the following prompt: *Think of a moment or an idea from the Classroom Intensive experience that was significant for you and write about it*. Thirdly, a series of short, on-the-spot conversational interviews were conducted over the course of the Classroom Intensive (n=18). The open questions posed in the interviews centred on the prompts contained within the field notes; that is, 'What are you seeing/thinking/wondering about?' Finally, quantitative data was generated through participants' completion of a survey (n=28) where they identified how frequently thinking dispositions were activated during the *Classroom Intensive*. The 15 items in the survey were derived from the *Thinking Dispositions Framework*, and required participants to indicate how strongly they agreed with statements along a three point Likert-scale. In the design of the survey, we aligned specific statements with the various dispositions from the *Teaching Dispositions Framework*, but students were not made explicitly aware of this alignment.

3.3 Data Analysis

We examined both qualitative and quantitative data as part of our concurrent approach. For the quantitative survey data, we graphed PSTs' survey responses to all statements based on the frequency with which they identified themselves as thinking in the specified ways. We then aggregated the three statements related to each disposition so as to produce a snapshot of the activation of each one separately. In order to activate our own thinking dispositions we used the *See, Think, Wonder* routine as a framework to understand and analyse the data. Using the thinking routine enabled us to give close attention to the data, before we moved to the next stage of interpretation. We each independently formed thinking statements that represented our interpretations of the data and then collaboratively constructed statements emerging from these individual interpretations. The collaboratively created thinking statements are presented for discussion in the following section of this chapter. They represent our findings from the analysis of data but more importantly they represent our learning that will inform the development of our practice as teacher educators in relation to teaching and assessing dispositions.

4 Discussion

4.1 Statement 1: Dispositions Are Activated in Carefully Constructed Professional Learning Contexts

The *Classroom Intensive* is a carefully constructed professional learning experience that provides the context within which all five of the dispositions for effective teaching can be activated. The summary of the survey data in Table 1 shows that PSTs saw themselves thinking in these ways on multiple occasions, although it appears that the tendency to recognise and display some dispositions is more frequent than others. It can be seen in Table 1 that 93 % of PSTs found themselves engaging with the thinking dispositions 'frequently' or 'sometimes'. This clearly shows that the constructed context activates the thinking dispositions. We suggest that key elements of this experience which work to activate the dispositions include: its communal nature; the use of the *See, Think, Wonder* routine as a framework to structure, prompt and notice thinking; the initial focus on students' learning and thinking as opposed to a focus on teaching; and the intensity of the experience. We discuss each of these elements in the following paragraphs.

Table 1 Summary of results for dispositions survey

	Question	Frequent	Sometimes	Never	No answer
Critically attentive disposition	9: I found myself being deeply intrigued by what I was seeing in classrooms	46	50	0	4
	11: I found myself posing critical questions based on what I was seeing	61	39	0	0
	13: I found myself looking closely at particular interactions and incidents	86	11	4	0
	Average	64	33	1	1
People centred disposition	2: I found myself caring deeply about students in particular learning situations	61	39	0	0
	8: I found I had language to communicate what I was seeing, thinking and wondering	57	39	0	4
	12: I found myself being moved by the collaborative and communal nature of the learning experience	75	25	0	0
	Average	64	35	0	1
Reflective disposition	3: I found myself thinking metacognitively about my assumptions and ideas	46	54	0	0
	14: I found myself wondering about the ethical implications of some classroom interactions	29	46	25	0
	15: I found myself prompting my own thinking through questioning	54	43	4	0
	Average	43	48	10	0
Strategic disposition	4: I found myself developing ideas for action that could improve learning for students	86	14	0	0
	6: I found myself organising my field notes into categories	7	43	50	0
	10: I found myself analysing my observations, identifying interesting patterns and reaching conclusions	57	36	7	0
	Average	50	31	19	0
Creative disposition	1: I found myself imagining how I can operate as a teacher in the future	86	11	4	0
	5: I found myself having an open mind about the possibilities related to teaching and learning	75	18	0	7
	7: I found myself identifying and solving problems related to teaching and learning	39	57	0	4
	Average	67	29	1	4

4.1.1 The Communal Nature of the Classroom Intensive

The communal nature of the *Classroom Intensive* assists in the activation of the dispositions within our framework. Opportunities to informally discuss and share the field notes; engage in dialogue between classroom observation sessions; publicly share thinking and wondering statements in structured situations; and be involved in an inclusive learning experience with PSTs, practising teachers, school leaders and teacher educators, all contribute to creating emotional as well as intellectual engagement. This is illustrated in the survey data where 75 % of the participants responded 'frequently' to item number 12: *I found myself moved by the communal and collaborative nature of the learning experience*. This demonstrates the activation of the people-centred disposition and suggests that the PSTs are emotionally connected through a disposition to care, within the learning experience.

4.1.2 The Routine as a Framework to Prompt Thinking Dispositions

The *See, Think, Wonder* routine acts as a powerful framework to structure, prompt and notice thinking dispositions. In analysing the field notes we see that the critically attentive and reflective dispositions are mostly activated through the use of this tool. The survey revealed that 86 % of participants frequently found themselves looking closely at particular interactions and incidents. The field notes show close attention to actions and thinking moves: they watch students using trial and error; they notice students finishing one another's sentences during a problem solving activity; they hear students making connections between content and personal life experiences; they hear students reaching conclusions in conversations; they notice isolated students with wandering minds; they identify facial expressions which show intent concentration; they see students closing their eyes during a story so that they can visualise; they hear the hesitation in voices as students guess and make their ideas public. The routine makes thinking deliberate and conscious and builds the disposition to think metacognitively about one's own thinking. As the survey results show, all participants were aware of their own thinking at least on some occasions during the Intensive.

4.1.3 A Focus on Student Learning

By asking PSTs to focus first on students' thinking and learning, the disposition to care most about student experiences and see learning as people-centred is foregrounded. This also enables PSTs' strategic thinking to stem from a learning-centred basis. A small proportion of the PSTs focus mostly on what teachers do even though they were urged against doing this. Some PSTs focus only on the students and list their movements, comments and interactions. The majority of PSTs begin with a gaze on students; however, their notes capture interactions and show that students' thinking is rarely isolated from what teachers and peers do and say.

The thinking and wondering statements show that PSTs believe a student-centred focus in teaching is important. "I wonder how I can develop my teaching practice so it is less content delivery based and more questioning and student driven as I have seen here", wonders one PST. The *Classroom Intensive* enables PSTs to make theory-practice connections as they see concepts they have explored in the university program being enacted in the classroom. They engage in strategizing, problem solving and thinking creatively as they visualise how they might apply approaches that enable good learning, in their future practice as teachers. This is reflected in the survey data with 86% of PSTs finding that they frequently found themselves 'developing ideas for action'.

4.1.4 The Intensity of the Experience

There is an intensity embedded in the experience as the group works together for up to two full days and this provides multiple opportunities for conversations, questions, narrative connections and reflections to emerge. Rich discussions happen as PSTs move between classrooms and there is scope to continue discussions at the conclusion of the day. PSTs have time to process what they have seen and to think in various ways about the observations that they are making. They also have the opportunity to move backwards and forwards between personal and communal spaces which gives participants silent thinking time as well as time to connect verbally and emotionally with others. The shared nature of the experience and the diverse perspectives that are shared amongst PSTs, experienced teachers and teacher educators in moments when connections occur are like catalysts in a chemical reaction.

4.2 Statement 2: Multiple Forms of Documentation Are Required to Show a Tendency Toward Dispositions

In making visible the way that dispositions are activated through the *Classroom Intensive* we have identified that multiple and diverse forms of documentation are needed to enable their recognition. Our analysis of the data suggests that using only one form of documentation and evidence is inadequate in capturing the complex and holistic nature of the way the dispositions are activated. When we examined the survey data we identified that the strategic and reflective dispositions were the least often self-identified (with 50% and 42% of participants commenting that they found themselves frequently thinking in these ways). Analysis of the field notes and interview data; however, highlights that those dispositions are displayed and discussed in meaningful ways by PSTs. These forms of data indicate the ways PSTs are thinking strategically, as represented by this example: "I think that I need to use an 'oral planning' strategy". Evidence of a reflective disposition is also demonstrated in these data forms, with this example highlighting the way the PST is critically reflecting on their own thinking processes:

> When I am observing ... I'm a very visual person, so first I get distracted and have to get my bearings, so I look around the room see what's on the wall ... but then I sort of, because of the See, Think, Wonder sheet we are filling out, focus in on what the teacher is doing, what the students faces are doing, how are they responding? That's the kind of order I do it [observe] in, I think.

Examples from across multiple data sources which demonstrate the activation of various thinking dispositions reinforce our view that observation schedules that are of a checklist nature are blinkered and fail to allow PSTs to represent their knowledge, skills and dispositions in a range of ways. Capturing the complexity of thinking requires multiple modes and opportunities for expression.

Another example of the need for multiple and diverse documentation forms was evident in the responses of a particular PST who through the field notes revealed very little evidence of the thinking dispositions in action. His field notes contained information related to the physical environment only, for example 'Learning intention on whiteboard', and did not demonstrate a critical attention to the processes of learning and thinking occurring in the classroom. Interestingly, this PST was interviewed during the Intensive with the interview revealing his ability to use a range of thinking dispositions. He shows the disposition of paying critical attention when he comments: "There was a real sense of bringing the focus away from the 'right' answer, that is something I have noticed across the whole school". He also demonstrated his use of a reflective disposition in making connections between personal prior experiences and his observations:

> Even on my placement ... I asked students to sit up the front – they might have moved a row forward, but didn't have that real engaged 'I want to be right here, actively engaged' thing like students do here.

If we only drew from one written source of documentation for displaying dispositions our understanding of this PSTs' dispositions would be limited. This reinforces the need for diverse forms of documentation to enable expression, recognition and articulation of the dispositions.

Our analysis of the multiple forms of documentation also indicated that there are two elements at work in relation to the recognition and display of thinking dispositions. The first of these is that through the *Classroom Intensive* PSTs demonstrate an awareness of how the thinking dispositions are being used by others within classrooms to enhance thinking and learning. The second is related to the fact that in identifying dispositions in practice, they are also displaying their own awareness and use of the dispositions. The data from the collective sharing of statements illustrates the way the experience activates an awareness of the people-centred, creative, critically attentive and strategic thinking dispositions in particular. In verbally sharing the 'I think' statements PSTs demonstrate the tendency to use the people-centred thinking disposition, as illustrated in this example: "I think that the connections with the community are a great teaching and learning resource. I think that the majority of students I have encountered feel as though they are part of the learning community." In making this observation, the PST is both able to identify the collaborative and caring nature of a people-centred disposition at work in the classroom and the school culture, and also demonstrate that this is a priority in their own thinking. Similarly, another PST wrote: "I think that the language and questioning used by teachers encourages the students to think for themselves/encourages independent learning/connects students to the learning as they engage and think more deeply". In this example, the PST both identifies the way the critically attentive disposition has been fostered in the classroom, and engages in using this disposition themselves as they pay critical attention to what is occurring in the learning and teaching situation. In sharing these statements publicly and identifying the commonality of interpretations, PSTs, teachers and teacher educators generate a shared, collegial knowing about the nature of what they are observing and engage actively in using the thinking dispositions.

4.3 Statement 3: Dispositions Interconnect and Rely Upon One Another

The pressure to generate lists of dispositions to inform selection procedures as well as teaching and assessment is mounting. Whilst this is a useful activity to aid explicitness, it can lead to crude classifications which dismiss the contextual, personal nature of dispositions and assumes that dispositions are activated in discrete, isolated ways. In searching for evidence of dispositions at work in the data collected during the *Classroom Intensive*, we found that thinking dispositions were most powerful and evident when they interconnected and were activated in clusters. Thinking dispositions that are central to effective teaching and to understanding complex interactions operate in dynamic ways and seem to rely upon one another for meaning-making. In order to demonstrate the challenges in identifying and assessing dispositions we take one student at random and by examining her responses across the different data collection contexts, show how the dispositions in our framework exist in a web-like formation; interconnected and reliant upon each other for strength.

4.3.1 Hazel

Hazel's field notes are a collection of close observations which highlight her ability to notice and name what students do to learn. She observes close interactions between students and between students and teachers and shows that critical attention is the cornerstone of understanding student learning and effective teaching practice. Her eyes dart around the room identifying students' ways of thinking. Notes in the See/Hear column of the *See, Think, Wonder* chart, show that she notices students getting ready to learn, making predictions, posing clarifying questions, referring to learning intentions, persisting with problems, thinking aloud, developing their understandings through talk in small groups, and responding excitedly to established routines. She also notes the features of the classroom and in some moments, what teachers do and say. She includes snippets of conversation from teachers: "What's worse than failure? The failure to try"; "I'm interested in what you already know and understand"; "If you put it out there you've got to justify it." Her descriptive notes show that student learning and teachers' practice are entwined and that what students largely do is in response to what teachers do or to routines that teachers have established. Her thinking statements show a strategic disposition which enables her to organise her thinking and make broad interpretations from the data she has collected. Her thinking statements include the following:

> I think expectations of teachers to teach thinking is explicit and constantly reinforced through classroom displays, discussions with peers and the pedagogy.
> I think that students are encouraged to make predictions and not afraid to search for answers.
> I think that a lot of activities are centred around real life situations in order to make learning relevant.

Hazel's narrative writing after the *Classroom Intensive* reveals her disposition to reflect and be creative. She reflects on a particular classroom experience drawing out important approaches that the teacher uses to build positive relationships with students. In repeating the line "This teacher knows how to build positive relationships with students" she emphasises her people-centred disposition and how important relationships are for her own teaching and learning, along with how keen she is to identify approaches that can be used in a practical sense to know students and help them to enjoy the experience of learning at school. She begins the narrative with a focus on the environment: "It's hot today. The flies attach themselves to the backs of the students on the way through the door and now buzz overhead." Creatively, she paints a picture of the classroom built upon vivid imagery and the critical attention she has given to watching students and teachers at work. Suddenly she focuses her attention on an interaction that captures her curiosity:

> I see something that catches my interest. There are three students in this class with disabilities. They seem pretty excitable and the teacher calmly and quickly gets them on task. There is absolutely no disruption. I watch the teacher more closely. She smiles. A lot. She looks fresh and cool in this muggy room. She moves from table to table checking students' work. Students offer insights into their personal lives and she puts aside the work for a moment to focus on the student. And then the moment comes, she asks a student: "How can you incorporate that into your story today?" Instantly the student is on task … This teacher knows how to build positive relationships with her students.

Hazel's disposition to be people-centred is strong in this writing. She shows the ability to care and to value relationships and emotions in the context of teaching.

In the focus group interview where Hazel engaged in dialogue with her peers the critical attention she gave to classroom learning saw her move into reflection and thinking ethically about dilemmas as well as creative problem solving. In a discussion about teachers' use of questioning she says:

> I often worry that that's becoming patronising ... because they are quite short closed questions. It might be like herding sheep, very, very tightly herding sheep. I know they are asking questions all the time, but they are asking very pointed questions all the time, so it can sort of narrow thinking. I feel like it's 'guess what's in my head', having a specific answer in mind.

She fears that this sort of questioning creates "drones" and that set curriculum can drive teachers in directions away from students engaging in more exploratory and critical thinking.

Through the use of the *See, Think, Wonder* routine, the narrative writing task and the opportunity for dialogue with her peers Hazel shows that she has important dispositions for teaching and that those dispositions interconnect and rely upon one another to fuel good thinking about her profession. What exists is a complex web of thinking interactions which can only be identified and appreciated by examining the thinking that occurs in rich, purposefully constructed professional learning contexts. The challenges for teacher educators working to value dispositions are multi-layered. Not only is there the challenge to pinpoint key dispositions and to construct meaningful contextual experiences that activate them, but even more challenging in relation to assessment, is the task of identifying and documenting dispositions as they interact in web-like formations.

5 Conclusion: What Are We Learning and Where to Next?

Through our research we understand the power carefully constructed professional learning experiences can have in providing PSTs with opportunities to build and demonstrate the dispositions identified in our framework. We believe that school/university partnerships provide the basis for the construction of such experiences and contend that partnerships which only focus on enhancing professional placements are limited. We appreciate the complexity of engaging in work related to dispositions in teaching and feel that this complexity is something to be cherished rather than dismissed. We understand that we must draw upon multiple forms that are written and verbal, expository and narrative in order to make dispositions visible. Rich, contextualised experiences enable dispositions to work collectively and they cannot easily be captured in single snapshots or in checklists that decontextualise and separate them into discrete parts. This challenges us to continually develop our processes for recording, demonstrating and evaluating the way the learning experiences in our program contribute to the activation of dispositions. We find that the process of researching our practice is generative and sparks new possibilities for the ways we can strengthen the constructed professional learning experiences in our program. The incorporation of the narrative writing task as part of the research process highlighted to us its potential in enabling PSTs to make visible their use of the thinking dispositions and this is an aspect we will formally build into future experiences.

In order to deepen our understandings we need to collect data in ongoing ways that will enable us to identify what PSTs say about the *Classroom Intensive* and how it fosters their understanding and activation of dispositions. We need to consider how the activation of dispositions might become habituated for PSTs and whether the dispositions are activated in similar ways during professional placements. In building a knowledge base of research that demonstrates how dispositions intersect and are activated through carefully constructed professional learning experiences we can begin to speak back to reforms and approaches that are limited and superficially framed. This will also enable us to strategically embed these approaches within our programs so that PSTs have multiple opportunities to develop dispositions for effective teaching and learning. Developing PSTs' understandings of thinking dispositions and how they foster quality learning is also essential – because then they will be able to infuse a focus on dispositions into their own teaching.

Acknowledgements This research was supported by funds from the Faculty of Education and Arts Small Grants Scheme, Federation University Australia. The authors are grateful for this support and for the feedback from the reviewers.

References

Argyris, C., & Schön, D. (1974). *Theory in practice: Increasing professional effectiveness*. San Francisco: Jossey-Bass.
Arnstine, D. (1967). *Philosophy of education: Learning and schooling*. New York: Harper & Row.
Barnett, R. (2000). University knowledge in an age of supercomplexity. *Higher Education, 40*, 409–422.
Barnett, R. (2007). *A will to learn: Being a student in an age of uncertainty*. Berkshire, UK: Open University Press and Society for Research into Higher Education.
Cochran-Smith, M. (2003). The unforgiving complexity of teaching: Avoiding simplicity in the age of accountability. *Journal of Teacher Education, 54*(1), 3–5.
Costa, A., & Kallick, B. (2000). *Habits of mind: A developmental series*. Alexandria, VA: Association for Supervision and Curriculum Development.
Creswell, J. W. (2013). *Research design: Qualitative, quantitative, and mixed methods approaches*. Thousand Oaks, CA: Sage.
Danielson, C. (2012). Observing classroom practice. *Educational Leadership, 70*(3), 32–37.
Denzin, N., & Lincoln, Y. (2000). *Handbook of qualitative research* (2nd ed.). Thousand Oaks, CA: Sage Publications.
Dewey, J. (1922). *Human nature and conduct: An introduction to social psychology*. New York: Modern Library.
Diez, M. (2007). Assessing dispositions: Context and questions. In M. E. Diez & J. Raths (Eds.), *Dispositions in teacher education* (pp. 183–201). Charlotte, NC: Information Age Publishing.
Edwards, S., & Nuttall, J. (2015). Professional learning in pre-service and in-service teacher education: Contexts and issues. *Asia-Pacific Journal of Teacher Education, 43*(3), 181–182.
Entwistle, N. (2009). *Teaching for understanding at university: Deep approaches and distinctive ways of thinking*. Basingstoke, UK: Palgrave Macmillan.

Entwistle, N. (2012). The quality of learning at university: Integrative understanding and distinctive ways of thinking. In J. R. Kirby & M. J. Lawson (Eds.), *Enhancing the quality of learning* (pp. 15–31). New York: Cambridge University Press.

Entwistle, N. J., & McCune, V. (2009). The disposition to understand for oneself at university and beyond: Learning processes, the will to learn and sensitivity to context. In L. F. Zhang & R. J. Sternberg (Eds.), *Perspectives on the nature of intellectual styles* (pp. 29–62). New York: Springer.

Freeman, L. (2007). An overview of dispositions in teacher education. In M. E. Diez & J. Raths (Eds.), *Dispositions in teacher education* (pp. 117–138). Charlotte, NC: Information Age Publishing.

Gannon, S. (2012). Changing lives and standardising teachers: The possibilities and limits of professional standards. *English Teaching: Practice and Critique, 11*(3), 59–77.

Gardner, H. (1983). *Frames of mind*. New York: Basic Books.

Goleman, D. (1995). *Emotional intelligence*. New York: Bantam Books.

Gore, J. (2015). *Evidence of impact of teacher education programs: A focus on classroom observation*. Melbourne, Australia: Australian Institute for Teaching and School Leadership.

Hoyt, K., & Terantino, J. (2015). Rethinking field observations: Strengthening teacher education through INFORM. *Action in Teacher Education, 37*(3), 209–222.

Kincheloe, J., & Berry, K. (2004). *Rigour and complexity in educational research: Conceptualizing the bricolage*. Berkshire, UK: Open University Press.

McCrary Sullivan, A. S. (2000). Notes from a marine biologist's daughter: On the art and science of attention. *Harvard Educational Review, 70*(2), 211–227.

National Council for Accreditation of Teacher Education (NCATE). (2002). *Professional standards for the accreditation of schools, colleges and departments of education*. Washington, DC: NCATE.

O'Leary, M. (2014). *Classroom observation: A guide to the effective observation of teaching and learning*. Oxon, UK: Routledge.

Perkins, D. N. (1995). *Outsmarting IQ*. New York: Free Press.

Perkins, D. N., & Ritchhart, R. (2004). When is good thinking? In D. Y. Dai & R. J. Sternberg (Eds.), *Motivation, emotion and cognition: Integrative perspectives on intellectual functioning and development* (pp. 351–384). Mahwah, NJ: Erlbaum.

Pring, R. (2000). The 'false dualism' of educational research. *Journal of Philosophy of Education, 34*(2), 247–260.

Ritchhart, R. (2002). *Intellectual character: What it is, why it matters, and how to get it*. San Francisco: Jossey-Bass.

Ritchhart, R., Church, M., & Morrison, K. (2011). *Making thinking visible: How to promote engagement, understanding, and independence for all learners*. San Francisco: Jossey-Bass.

Riveros, A., Norris, S. P., Hayward, D. V., & Phillips, L. M. (2012). Dispositions and the quality of learning. In J. R. Kirby & M. J. Lawson (Eds.), *Enhancing the quality of learning* (pp. 32–50). New York: Cambridge University Press.

Teacher Education Ministerial Advisory Group. (2014). *Action now: Classroom ready teachers*. Canberra, Australia. http://www.studentsfirst.gov.au/teacher-education-ministerial-advisory-group. Accessed 15 Oct 2015.

Timperley, H. (2011). *Realizing the power of professional learning*. Berkshire, UK: McGraw-Hill Education.

Tishman, S. (1994). *Thinking dispositions and intellectual character*. Paper presented at the 1994 Annual Meeting of the American Educational Research Association, Apr 4–8. New Orleans, LA.

Classroom Ready? Building Resilience in Teacher Education

Caroline Mansfield, Susan Beltman, Noelene Weatherby-Fell, and Tania Broadley

1 Introduction

An ongoing concern for teacher educators, teacher employers and more recently policy makers, is the extent to which graduating teachers are "classroom ready". National and international research has shown that teachers face numerous challenges, especially in the early career years, and difficulties managing challenges may lead to distress, burnout and a decision to leave the profession. Early career teachers often experience "reality shock" (Friedman, 2004) and report feeling under prepared as they transition from university to the profession, despite having had extended periods of professional experience during their degree. In Australia, teacher education providers are now charged with the challenge to prepare "classroom-ready" teachers (Teacher Education Ministerial Advisory Group, 2014) and a raft of recommendations has been made regarding particular teacher education experiences and assessment to ensure classroom readiness. For example, one recommendation is that suitable candidates for teacher education should be selected

C. Mansfield (✉)
School of Education, Murdoch University, Perth, Australia
e-mail: caroline.mansfield@murdoch.edu.au

S. Beltman
School of Education, Curtin University, Perth, Australia
e-mail: s.beltman@curtin.edu.au

N. Weatherby-Fell
School of Education, University of Wollongong, Wollongong, Australia
e-mail: noelene@uow.edu.au

T. Broadley
School of Education, Curtin University, Perth, Australia

Faculty of Education, Queensland University of Technology, Brisbane, Australia
e-mail: tania.broadley@qut.edu.au

according to the balance of "academic skills and personal characteristics" (p. vii) that are required for the profession. The non-academic key capabilities that are deemed important for teacher education students include motivation, strong interpersonal and communication skills, and resilience (Australian Institute for Teaching and School Leadership, 2015).

In the context of preparing "classroom-ready" teachers who will manage the everyday challenges of the profession, grow and thrive throughout their career, we argue that a resilience-focused approach to developing such non-academic key capabilities, or personal resources is beneficial. Personal resources such as motivation, efficacy and social and emotional competence are important both for success and enabling resilience (Beltman, Mansfield, & Price, 2011). Furthermore, research evidence shows that teacher resilience is associated with positive outcomes such as professional commitment, engagement, enthusiasm and job fulfillment (Day & Gu, 2014). Teacher resilience has been positively associated with student achievement and teacher quality (Gu & Li, 2015), which also feature strongly in current conversations about the profession.

If resilience is an important capability for pre-service and in-service teachers, how might this be developed? Researchers in the field of resilience posit that resilience may only be demonstrated in times of adversity (Doney, 2013), yet recently teacher resilience researchers have argued that teachers require "everyday resilience" (Gu & Day, 2013; Gu & Li, 2013) to manage uncertainty as well as the ongoing intellectual and emotional challenges of their work. Everyday resilience involves more than bouncing back from particular difficulties, rather it is the capacity to manage ongoing and multiple challenges over time, while continuing to grow and thrive professionally. Particular skills and coping strategies are commonly associated with resilience and empirical research has shown professional, motivational, social and emotional dimensions of teacher resilience (Mansfield, Beltman, Price, & McConney, 2012). Capacity building in these areas during teacher education is one way of developing teacher resilience.

As teacher education curriculum becomes increasingly prescribed and crowded, innovative approaches to developing resilience skills and strategies are needed. In recent years, online learning experiences have been developed in relation to wellbeing and mental health issues. For example, resources such as *thedesk* (www.thedesk.org.au) focus on assisting university students with mental and physical health and wellbeing (Ryan, Shochet, & Stallman, 2010). Online resources have the advantage of being instantly accessible and enabling self-paced learning and engagement (Bonk & Graham, 2006).

This chapter describes the development and evaluation of an innovative online learning resource designed to support pre-service teachers in building capacity for professional resilience. The online modules were developed as part of the Building Resilience in Teacher Education (BRiTE – www.brite.edu.au) project (Mansfield, Beltman, Broadley, & Weatherby-Fell, 2013), which aimed to help pre-service teachers build awareness of the skills and practices that will help facilitate resilience in their future teaching career.

2 Literature Review

As a starting point for developing the online modules and to ensure that the modules were underpinned by empirical and conceptual work in the field, we undertook an extensive review of the teacher resilience literature (environmental scan) over the past 15 years to identify the personal and contextual resources, as well as strategies that contribute to positive resilience outcomes for teachers (Mansfield, Beltman, Broadley, & Weatherby-Fell, 2016). The review identified a range of personal and contextual resources that influence teacher resilience, as well as particular strategies that promote resilience, and offered recommendations as to how these could be implemented in teacher education courses. The following paragraphs provide an overview of these.

Personal resources that enhance teacher resilience included intrinsic motivation (Kitching, Morgan, & O'Leary, 2009), and self-efficacy for both pre-service (Le Cornu, 2009) and in-service teachers (Howard & Johnson, 2004). Having a sense of moral purpose (Day, 2014), a sense of vocation (Hong, 2012), optimism (Tait, 2008), and social and emotional competence (Ee & Chang, 2010) were also seen as important. Contextual resources could be drawn upon to support teacher resilience and in the literature the key resource was relationships within and outside of the workplace. For example, relationships between teachers and school leaders (Peters & Pearce, 2012), with trusted colleagues (O'Sullivan, 2006), with whole school communities (Ebersöhn, 2012), with supporters outside of school or online (Papatraianou & Le Cornu, 2014) and between teachers and their students (Morgan, Ludlow, Kitching, O'Leary, & Clarke, 2010) were all found to support teacher resilience. The literature also indicated that teachers use a variety of strategies to harness the available personal and contextual resources. Problem-solving (Johnson et al., 2014), help-seeking (Sharplin, O'Neill, & Chapman, 2011) and goal-setting were important, as were strategies to achieve a work-life balance (Le Cornu, 2013). Engaging in professional learning had a number of positive outcomes (Patterson, Collins, & Abbott, 2004) as did other activities involving reflection (Leroux & Théorêt, 2014). Using good communication skills was also an important strategy (Schelvis, Zwetsloot, Bos, & Wiezer, 2014) as was the ability to regulate emotions (Morgan, 2011).

The literature reviewed also provided suggestions with regard to the types of learning experiences that could occur within teacher education that may help build resilience. There were ideas regarding how to develop personal resources and strategies such as developing reflective skills (Leroux & Théorêt, 2014), enhancing emotional competence (Hong, 2012), managing stress (Curry & O'Brien, 2012) and developing coping strategies (Mansfield, Beltman, & Price, 2014). Other suggestions were connected to the importance of building relationships and included assertiveness training (Ee & Chang, 2010), managing relationships (Keogh, 2010) and dealing with parents (Fantilli & McDougall, 2009). Still other strategies were recommended that focused on the broader context such as increasing sociocultural awareness (Ebersöhn, 2014). It was seen as crucial that any strategies used were connected to the profession through being situated around authentic classroom situations using case-studies and realisitic problem-solving (e.g. Huisman, Singer, & Catapano, 2010).

Although the review identified a range of existing resilience programs, those involving teachers typically were about supporting student resilience (see for example, KidsMatter, www.kidsmatter.edu.au and ResponseAbility, www.responseability.org). Programs were delivered via a series of workshops or as part of a whole school approach. There was a notable absence of programs for teachers and pre-service teachers, as well as programs that were freely available.

The review enabled us to identify the range of factors associated with teacher resilience and the types of learning experiences recommended for pre-service teachers. As a result of the review, we identified developed a BRiTE framework, which determined the content our five modules:

- **B**uilding resilience – what is resilience and why it matters for teachers;
- **R**elationships – maintaining support networks, building new relationships in schools;
- Wellbeing – personal wellbeing, work-life balance, maintaining motivation;
- **T**aking initiative – problem solving, ongoing professional learning, communicating effectively; and
- **E**motions – developing optimism, enhancing emotional awareness, managing emotions.

3 Conceptual Framework

Based on the review and our previous empirical research in the field (Beltman et al., 2011; Mansfield et al., 2012, 2014) we conceptualise resilience as a *capacity*, a *process* and also as an *outcome*. Figure 1 (based on Biggs & Moore, 1993) shows the process of resilience whereby personal resources related to resilience (e.g. motivation; social and emotional competence), and contextual resources (e.g. relationships, school culture, support networks) interact as individuals harness resources and use particular strategies (e.g. problem solving, time management, maintaining work-life balance) to enable resilience outcomes (e.g. commitment, job satisfaction, wellbeing, engagement). Furthermore, resilience outcomes influence future resources and strategies and so resilience develops with experience and over time. Bi-directional arrows in Fig. 1 also illustrate that the resilience process may not necessarily be strictly linear, but that resources and strategies interact with each other in cycles over time, before resulting in adaptive outcomes.

In relation to teacher education, the focus of the modules is on building capacity through development of personal resources and learning ways to harness contextual resources, as well as developing resilience focused strategies for managing challenges. Because the school contexts pre-service teachers work in are varied, in using

Classroom Ready? Building Resilience in Teacher Education

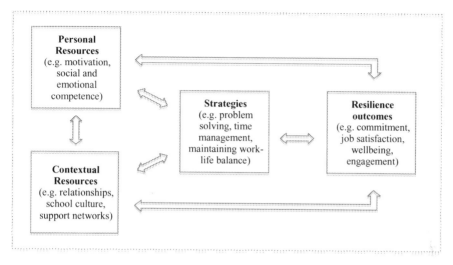

Fig. 1 The teacher resilience process

this conceptual framework, our aim in developing modules was to assist pre-service teachers to build on existing personal resources and strategies and understand how to mobilise contextual resources to manage challenges.

4 Methodology

4.1 Module Development

The module development process was informed by design-based research methodology, "a methodology designed by and for educators that seeks to increase the impact, transfer, and translation of education research into improved practice" (Anderson & Shattuck, 2012, p. 16). Applying this systematic but flexible methodology enabled the researchers to employ a cyclical, iterative process of analysis, design, development and implementation, as illustrated in Fig. 2. Within this process, the project team gathered integral feedback from a broad range of trial participants, including users and experts in the field of teacher education and resilience research. An important aspect of the process was to be cognisant of the constructive alignment of the modules, both vertically and horizontally. Learning outcomes, learning activities and feedback mechanisms were considered and planned through a methodical approach that ensured users of the resilience modules were scaffolded in appropriate ways.

The modules were developed in a staged approach, and the process involved trials with stakeholder groups (project reference and advisory groups and pre-service teachers) providing feedback to inform module content and design, resulting in the final version. Figure 2 shows the module design process where initially the

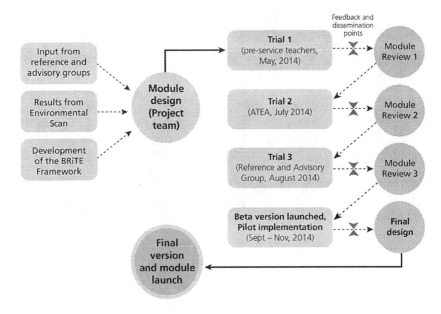

Fig. 2 The BRiTE module design process

environmental scan (in this case undertaken through an extensive literature review), input from stakeholder groups and the BRiTE framework provided a basis for the module development. With input from online learning experts and highly qualified, educational web designers, one module was completed to trial with three stakeholder groups. These trial groups included pre-service teachers, reference and advisory groups and teacher educators from around Australia. The first module trialed was focused on Relationships (R) and included the design principles established by the project team (i.e. personalised, interactive, grounded in the literature and connected to the profession) that were considered the foundation of future module design. The release of a single module allowed the stakeholders at each trial to focus on one module specifically within the timeframe available. Further module development was based on the refinement of the previous module trial, and included further refinement based on feedback.

Trial One in May 2014 included 48 second year pre-service teachers (22 primary; 26 secondary) from an Australian university, who had completed one school placement. Participants were invited to work through the Relationships module in a computer laboratory, at their own pace. A paper-based evaluation process to provide feedback regarding content and online design was employed. The evaluation included 18 questions with a five-point Likert scale (strongly agree to strongly disagree) asking users to evaluate aspects of the module including knowledge and skills, overall design and aesthetic appeal. Two open-ended questions asked for users to identify the time they had taken to participate and any additional comments. In line with design-based research methodology, further module review and refinement were undertaken to incorporate the feedback from this trial.

Trial Two in July 2014 comprised 13 participants who attended the Australian Teacher Education Association (ATEA) conference. These teacher educators were asked to access the Relationships module and provide feedback on a paper-based survey about usability, technical aspects, layout and content-specific input from relevant disciplines. Refinements were made to the module prior to the third trial.

The project reference and advisory group members included consultant psychologists, exercise physiologists, teacher educators (national and international), international experts in the field of teacher resilience, and online learning/instructional design experts who provided feedback on all key design features of the modules prior to release. Local group members were invited to engage with the Relationship module, in the third and final trial in August 2014 and 11 of the group participated in this trial.

4.2 Final Design and Online Design Features

Following the iterative design process described above, results from the trials were used to develop a Beta version of all five modules. The module design was informed by four key principles: personalised learning, interactive engagement, activities and content grounded in the literature and connected to the teaching profession.

Personalised learning is defined as the provision to each user "of content or an experience which has been tailored to suit their specific needs based on implicit or explicit information about that user" (O'Donnell, Lawless, Sharp, & Wade, 2015, p. 23). In order to provide a personalised experience, the modules began with a self-reflection quiz that provided information about the user and then automatically prioritised their learning path through the topics in the module. The requirement for users to input their own thoughts on key themes, added to the personalised learning experience, as did the opportunity to build a personal toolkit (which could be downloaded) throughout the modules.

The personal toolkit also aligned with the focus on *interactivity*. The toolkit is developed throughout the learning journey and allows users to "pin" and save information (including inspirational quotes, tips, strategies) to their toolkit to support their journey toward resilience. Learning activities such as responding to questions (multiple choice, true/false responses) with feedback specifically designed for each response were developed to enhance engagement. The interactivity of modules was further exemplified through authentic teaching scenarios designed to allow users to apply their resilience related skills, have opportunities for reflection, and contribute ideas regarding useful additional strategies.

The comprehensive review of the literature enabled writing of "what do the experts say?" sections to highlight that topics addressed were *grounded in the literature*. These sections summarised key research related to aspects of resilience and offered further references for users to follow if interested.

The modules were *connected to the teaching profession* with teacher voices frequently "heard" through videos, direct quotes from research featuring pre-service and early career teachers (Mansfield et al., 2012, 2014) and explicit connection to teaching standards (Australian Institute for Teaching and School Leadership, 2011), the Australian Curriculum (http://www.australiancurriculum.edu.au/), Early Years Learning Framework (2013) and further resources from related professional organisations.

4.3 Beta Version Evaluation

4.3.1 Participants

Once the Beta version of the modules was developed and live, users were invited to evaluate modules to inform the final design. Two cohorts of participants evaluated the modules with Cohort A comprising pre-service teachers (n = 144) and Cohort B non-pre-service teachers (n = 37). Participants accessed and completed some, or all, modules during an 8-week period and provided feedback regarding content and online design. All participants were volunteers and university ethics approval was obtained for the study.

As shown in Table 1, the majority of the 144 Cohort A pre-service teacher participants were studying a Graduate Diploma of Education (85%). In addition, 79% of the overall cohort was female with most of these aged between 20 and 30 years.

Table 1 Demographics of Cohort A: pre-service teacher (PST) participants

Course	Number	% of cohort	Gender (n)	Age range (n)
Bachelor of Education	20	14%	Female (19)	20–30 (8)
				31–40 (8)
				41–50 (3)
			Male (1)	51+ (1)
Graduate Diploma of Education	122	85%	Female (94)	20–30 (53)
				31–40 (23)
				41–50 (17)
				51+ (1)
			Male (28)	20–30 (14)
				31–40 (7)
				41–50 (5)
				50+ (2)
Master of Teaching	2	1%	Female (1)	20–30 (1)
			Male (1)	20–30 (1)
Totals	144	100%	F = 114	20–30 = 77
			M = 30	31–40 = 38
				41–50 = 25
				51+ = 4

The average age of all participants in Cohort A was 32 years, with 31.5 for females and 33.6 for males. The spread of age ranges is also shown in Table 1.

Cohort B participants (n=37) were also mainly female (76%), and included consultants from educational organisations (n=5), psychologists (n=3), researchers (n=2), teachers (n=9) and teacher educators (n=18). The average age of these participants was 46.7 years (range 25–66).

4.3.2 Instruments

The evaluation for both cohorts was conducted online with a combination of Likert scale response items and open-ended questions. At the completion of each module, users were asked to complete a short evaluation (1 = strongly disagree; 5 = strongly agree) comprised of a rating scale for 18 items related to module content (e.g. *I found the content of this module relevant*), to module online design (e.g. *The information in the module is well organised*) and to possible future use (e.g. *I will refer to this module again in the future*). Users were asked to indicate the time it took to complete the module and an open-ended question was included if they had any further comments. The non pre-service teachers, Cohort B, completed similar questions but they focused on perceived relevance for pre-service teachers and use as a teacher educator (e.g. *The content of this module will be relevant for pre-service teachers*; *I will refer to the content in this module in my teaching*).

5 Results

5.1 Quantitative Results

Tables 2 and 3 present the quantitative results from the evaluation rating items for each cohort and show highly positive evaluations for both cohorts trialing the Beta version of the modules with all ratings above 3.5. Not all participants completed all module evaluations and module evaluations declined over modules 1–5. Even so, it is worth noting that the mean scores for those who completed all evaluations were fairly consistent, indicating that users engaging with later modules rated these equally useful and engaging. As Cohort B participants were asked to provide feedback about use of the modules in teacher education and for pre-service teachers, this may have contributed to the decline in evaluations across the modules. Cohort B participants may also have been more familiar with the content and may also have been more "time poor", juggling other end of year work demands. The findings also showed alignment of feedback on the relevance and the usefulness of the BRiTE modules for teacher education from both cohorts.

Table 2 BRiTE module evaluation: Mean scores for Cohort A participants

Module question	1	2	3	4	5	Overall mean
Content						
Useful	4.2	4.0	4.2	4.2	4.3	4.2
Interesting	4.1	3.9	4.2	4.1	4.3	4.1
Relevant	4.4	4.1	4.3	4.3	4.4	4.3
Appropriate level	4.4	4.2	4.3	4.4	4.3	4.3
Enjoyable	3.9	3.8	4.0	3.9	4.1	3.9
Enabled reflection	4.1	3.9	4.2	4.3	4.3	4.2
Raised awareness	4.1	4.1	4.2	4.2	4.2	4.2
Enabled development of knowledge and skills	4.0	3.8	4.0	4.1	4.2	4.0
Consider new ideas	3.8	3.8	3.7	3.8	4.0	3.8
Will use content in Professional Experience	4.0	3.9	3.9	4.0	4.0	4.0
Will use content in teaching career	4.2	4.1	4.1	4.2	4.3	4.2
Will refer to in future	4.0	3.7	3.9	4.0	4.0	3.9
Will recommend to friends	3.9	3.8	3.8	3.9	3.9	3.9
Content mean	*4.1*	*3.9*	*4.1*	*4.1*	*4.2*	*4.1*
Online design						
Appealing	4.3	4.2	4.3	4.3	4.4	4.3
Graphics appropriate	4.3	4.3	4.3	4.3	4.3	4.3
Navigable	4.5	4.2	4.2	4.3	4.4	4.3
Organised	4.5	4.3	4.4	4.4	4.4	4.4
Links work	4.6	3.8	3.7	4.3	4.2	4.1
Online design mean	*4.4*	*4.2*	*4.2*	*4.3*	*4.3*	*4.3*
Overall mean	**4.2**	**4.0**	**4.1**	**4.2**	**4.2**	**4.2**
No. (%) participants completed evaluation	117 (81%)	81 (56%)	73 (51%)	71 (49%)	67 (47%)	

5.2 Qualitative Results

Qualitative data were also gathered via open-ended questions at the end of each module evaluation. Cohort A participants were asked: "Are there any comments you'd like to make about this module?" In response, participants identified strengths of the modules and made suggestions for improvement.

5.2.1 General Comments

General comments about the content and design were given: "Interesting information, interactive design and visually appealing" (P78). Organisation and usefulness of the module content was a strength: "The module was well organised and the

Table 3 BRiTE module evaluation: Mean scores for Cohort B participants

Module question	1	2	3	4	5	Overall mean
Content						
Useful for PSTs	4.3	4.3	4.1	4.4	4.3	4.3
Interesting for PSTs	4.0	4.3	3.9	4.3	4.6	4.2
Relevant for PSTs	4.3	4.3	4.2	4.6	4.4	4.4
Appropriate level for PSTs	3.9	4.4	4.0	4.4	4.3	4.2
Enable reflection for PSTs	3.9	4.3	3.9	4.0	4.0	4.0
Enable development of knowledge and skills	3.7	4.3	3.9	4.0	4.0	4.0
Will refer PSTs to module	4.1	4.2	4.0	4.3	4.0	4.1
Will refer to content of module in teaching	3.8	4.1	4.0	4.1	4.1	4.0
Content mean	*4.0*	*4.3*	*4.0*	*4.3*	*4.2*	*4.2*
Online design						
Appealing	4.1	4.5	4.0	4.1	4.3	4.2
Graphics appropriate	4.2	4.5	4.2	4.1	4.1	4.2
Navigable	4.2	4.6	4.1	4.4	4.2	4.3
Organised	4.1	4.6	4.1	4.3	4.4	4.3
Online design mean	*4.2*	*4.6*	*4.1*	*4.2*	*4.3*	*4.3*
Overall mean	**4.1**	**4.4**	**4.0**	**4.3**	**4.2**	**4.2**
No. (%) participants completed evaluation	26 (70%)	10 (27%)	9 (24%)	8 (22%)	9 (24%)	

content useful, in particular the provision of practical examples" (P14). Comment was also made about use of different media and activities maintained engagement: "Breaking up the reading with questions was an effective way to maintain engagement. The use of different media, including the YouTube video was also good for providing different ways to access the content" (P26). True-false response questions were used in a number of modules and participants liked these "because it gave me the opportunity to revise knowledge I had learnt previously" (P33) and "interactive activities made it easier to understand" (P34).

Additional resources were appreciated: "I also appreciated the links to the resources if I would like to follow up on any points" (P38), and the strategies and tips were noted as "simple but very practical and useful" (P33). One participant wrote "I have saved some of the links to look over again a later date. Thank You" (P96). The capacity for users to "pin" items to their personal toolbox was also praised: "I really enjoyed [sic] that the tips and pages were able to pinned to my personal toolbox" (P38).

5.2.2 Comments About Specific Modules

Specific comments were made about each module. For example, referring to the Relationships module, a participant noted: "This module gave me some great suggestions on how to build and maintain relationships in a new school environment" (P95). Participants also noted how the information aligned with their previous experiences.

> The content in this module is of great value and from my personal experience, the value of relationships and mentors cannot be understated. Students perform at their best when they respect/have a connection with the person who is passing on knowledge. This may also be said for working relationships – a positive team oriented mindset promotes a positive environment for others. (P62)

Some users, perhaps with more life experiences made comments such as: "I was already aware of most of the content in this module. Good to refresh" (P67) and "it was common sense but good to read and review" (P79).

Referring to the Wellbeing module, a participant said: "I thought this module was extremely helpful in making me think of ways of how to deal with stress. I would definitely use the strategies" (P24). Particular activities in the module were seen as beneficial: "I think the section about reflecting on a situation, whether it's permanent or pervasive etc. really useful, it's a really positive strategy to employ" (P11). This participant also "appreciated the factual content" of the Emotions module. One user noted that "we need more around this at uni" (P35).

5.2.3 Reflection and New Ideas

Participants described the benefits of reflection stimulated throughout the modules. One noted: "I enjoyed the process of reflecting on what I knew about resilience before and after accessing information" (P38). Another said: "It allowed me to reflect on my own teaching practice. I will definitely be using this during my next PEX [Professional Experience] and also in my future teaching career" (P15). Comments were also made about new ideas in the module content that "made me think of things I wouldn't have usually. Provided me with some excellent suggestions!" (P56), and was "very helpful for professional development!" (P59). Another pre-service teacher said: "This module was very well thought out and provided me with some new ways to approach teaching but also it was able to reinforce some of my own personal and professional goals and qualities" (P64).

Participants also noted how their understanding of resilience had developed, as illustrated by the following two quotes:

> I had a fairly good understanding about resilience (or so I thought) I can see now how well developed my current protective factors are and how some of these will assist in my future wellbeing- BUT – I also have some work to do in building another set of protective factors in each school that I will casual teach in. (P43)

> The information on this website has been interesting and extremely useful and helpful. Resilience is definitely much clearer to me now, and I now know a few helpful strategies and ideas to help build the resilience/confidence with my students. I would definitely recommend this website to others. (P15)

5.2.4 Ideas for Future Teaching

Some participants noted the applicability of their learning for future teaching, remarking, for example, that "I will be teaching at a challenging high school … and will incorporate a lesson on resilience for all of my classes – thank you!" (P55). Participants also engaged with modules, based on how they viewed their immediate employment prospects and their prior experiences. For example, with regard to the Relationships module a participant noted:

> I struggled to stay attentive in this module- probably because I felt that it was more useful for pre-service teachers that expect to get a permanent position – during my life I have had to move a lot and change work a fair bit so many of the bits of advice were practical in nature and something I do almost automatically- I will think more about my personal learning network and support network though. (P16)

5.2.5 Suggestions for Improvement

Even though the majority of comments noted positive aspects of the modules, users also noted technical glitches that needed attention and made suggestions for how the modules may be improved. These included having more case studies, a better balance between secondary and primary schooling examples, downloadable tips, motivating quotes from famous people, strategies for dealing with negative colleagues and conflict resolution. Suggestions were also given by the non-pre-service teachers for how the modules may be improved through adding in-depth scenarios, connections to research and challenging some of the assumptions made. All comments were used to refine specific aspects of the modules and to inform decisions about the final version of the modules.

5.2.6 Value for Teacher Education

Cohort B participants were asked: "How do you think this module could be used in teacher education programs?" These participants noted the importance of the resource for pre-service teachers, the engaging and well-presented learning design, effective use of the Australian Professional Standards for Teachers (Australian Institute for Teaching and School Leadership, 2011) and said it had "A good balance of theory, videos of personal experiences and practical advice. It is easy to navigate and the tips and advice is given in a supportive non-judgemental way" (P22). Others commented on how they could use the resource: "This is an excellent resource for teachers and teacher educators to help stimulate discussion, reflection and training on all areas related to resilience" (P8).

More specific suggestions were also made regarding how the modules could be valuable in initial teacher education programs, as illustrated by the following three comments.

> This module provides some great strategies for pre-service teachers to learn to cope with the stressors of the profession, and hopefully these strategies will be carried forward well into their careers. The importance of this cannot be underestimated, as burnout is not necessarily sudden; it can be a very drawn-out and painful process. (P2)
>
> Students could complete the module right before a practicum placement as they will likely see much of the examples given in schools as well go through their own challenges as they cope with the pressure of these learning experiences. Perhaps it could be used in a professional practice unit, where students all complete the module as a group with opportunity to ask questions, discuss and complete the activities together. (P20)
>
> This module could be incorporated into the Professional Practice unit to equip pre-service teachers with mental strengths before being placed in a school for their practicum. The knowledge in the module will be necessary for pre-service teachers to deal with various levels of stress and adversity in the classroom. (P10)

6 Discussion

The BRiTE project provided an opportunity to explore how resilience related skills for teachers may be promoted through the development of an online learning resource that is personalised, interactive, connected to the profession and grounded in the literature. In summary, the findings of the evaluation were highly positive in terms of content and online design for the pre-service teachers and education experts trialling the modules. The findings also showed that both cohorts of participants were closely aligned in their evaluative feedback on the relevance and the usefulness of the BRiTE modules for teacher education. This unique resource is shows how innovative online resources may be used to complement teacher education experiences.

On a conceptual level, one strength of the modules was the comprehensive literature review on which the BRiTE framework was developed (Mansfield et al., 2016). Conceptualising resilience as a *capacity*, *process* and *outcome* that is multidimensional, dynamic and developing over time allows for a more nuanced understanding of resilience processes and a positive view of the concept. Often pre-service teachers describe resilience as the capacity to "bounce back", however equally, if not more important, is the capacity to "bounce forward" (Walsh, 2002), which not only has a restorative function, but promotes ongoing growth, development and learning through the lifespan. Data showing that users developed their understanding of "resilience" by engaging with the modules reinforces the importance of conceptually (rather than popularly) driven understandings of the construct. It is important that trait views of resilience are challenged and teachers understand the broader social ecologies (Ungar, 2012) in the teaching profession that enable resilience.

The development of this resource raises the issue of the extent to which an online self-paced accessible resource focused on non-academic key capabilities (Australian Institute for Teaching and School Leadership, 2015) may be a valuable addition to pre-service teacher education for both pre-service teachers and teacher educators. As higher education programs continue to embrace online and blended learning and look towards MOOCS (Massive Open Online Courses) as a source of future students and revenue (Burd, Smith & Reisman, 2015; EDUCAUSE, 2012), these modules show how an engaging online resource can be developed to raise awareness of resilience strategies in a particular professional context (see also, Wosnitza et al., 2013). In recent years, online resources for mental health and wellbeing have become more prevalent with research suggesting that individuals are more likely to seek online help than traditional or face to face help (Crisp & Griffith, 2014; Ryan et al., 2010) even with increasing levels of distress. Online resources have the advantage of being instantly accessible and can be visited and revisited when needed. How BRiTE users engage with the resource and their site visiting (and revisiting) behavior is an important avenue for future research. Likewise, the extent to which engagement with such a resource may influence teacher resilience in the short term and long term requires future longitudinal research.

Although both groups in the reported evaluation were positive about the value of the modules, there remains the challenge of developing content that meets the needs of the diverse group of pre-service teachers in Australia (Australian Institute for Teaching and School Leadership, 2013). Teacher education courses at the undergraduate, graduate and postgraduate level attract students with a range of life experiences, motivations and aspirations. Some participants described some of the content within the modules (knowledge and skills) as "common sense" even though there was an acknowledgement that a review and reinforcement of the learnings and wisdoms was both timely and valuable. Similarly, user engagement was influenced by the view they had of their future teaching, which included working in a casual capacity. Consideration of the range of work profiles beginning teachers may have and including targeted support for the unique challenges of casual teaching would be a valuable avenue for future module development. Another further development may involve the option to engage with content at different levels, further personalising the learning experience. It may also be appropriate to consider that at times pre-service and practicing teachers require a reminder to be aware of the knowledge each bring to the teaching profession, to classrooms, schools and the broader community.

How the modules may be used in teacher education programs was also considered as part of this project. Guidelines have been developed to assist teacher educators to use the modules in various ways. For example, in a flipped learning environment (Bergman & Sams, 2012) students could engage with a module scenario and bring their responses and further ideas to class for a discussion. Modules may also be embedded into Learning Management Systems via a Widget and connected to particular unit content. For individuals, engagement with the modules provides opportunity for professional growth, with opportunity to revisit responses, thereby providing evidence of reflective practice which may be used in a portfolio.

As the modules are aligned with the Australian National Professional Standards for Teachers (Australian Institute for Teaching and School Leadership, 2011) they may be also used to provide part of the body of evidence illustrating achievement of standards. As the modules have been designed to support development of resilience skills and strategies, we wish to caution against use of the resource in a remedial manner, as a "go to" package for students in crisis.

On a broader level, a resource such as BRiTE may have application beyond the teacher education experience. The modules may complement teacher induction programs, provide resources for mentor teachers and be adapted for use in professional learning settings for more experienced teachers. The opportunity to engage with current resources regarding resilience may also be beneficial for teachers and their students particularly in the face of ongoing professional challenges. Although the modules are specifically developed for the Australian context (which may also be a limitation) the content and online design of modules is readily adaptable for other countries and other "caring" professions.

7 Conclusion and Future Directions

In Australia, teacher education providers are under pressure to "identify and admit only those candidates who can demonstrate they have the necessary academic as well as non-academic capabilities that will enable them to successfully graduate as classroom ready teachers from a rigorous initial teacher education program" (Australian Institute for Teaching and School Leadership, 2015, p. 1). Such non-academic capabilities include "motivation to teach, strong interpersonal and communication skills, willingness to learn, resilience, self-efficacy, conscientiousness, organisational and planning skills" (p. 8). Although nearly all these capabilities are addressed in the BRiTE modules, what the literature shows, as illustrated in the introduction to this chapter and in Fig. 1, is that resilience is a complex, multidimensional construct which incorporates factors such as motivation and relationship skills. We also know that these are developed in an ongoing way over time, not only through individual capacities, but also with support from various contexts and as a result of personal experiences. Responsibility for the development of an effective, committed teacher therefore is a shared one. Individuals, workplaces, employers and professional development providers all have a role to play. Pre-service programs clearly have a key role to play in the very early stages of a career and the BRiTE modules, as indicated by their evidence-informed nature and positive evaluations of their role in teacher education, indicate that skills and capacities related to resilience can be developed during a pre-service program. Rather than being a fixed quality that can be measured at one point, resilience is "the culmination of collective and collaborative endeavours" (Gu & Li, 2013, p. 300) and should be viewed as an ongoing process occurring as a result of interactions in particular contexts.

Acknowledgements Support for this research has been provided by the Australian Government Office for Learning and Teaching, grant number ID13-2924. The views expressed in the publication do not necessarily reflect the views of the Australian Government Office for Learning and Teaching.

References

Anderson, T., & Shattuck, J. (2012). Design-based research: A decade of progress in education research? *Educational Researcher, 41*(1), 16–25. doi:10.3102/0013189x11428813

Australian Institute for Teaching and School Leadership. (2011). *Australian National Professional Standards for Teachers*. Victoria, Australia: Education Services Australia.

Australian Institute for Teaching and School Leadership. (2013). *Initial teacher education: Data report*. Retrieved from http://www.aitsl.edu.au/docs/default-source/initial-teacher-education-resources/2013_aitsl_ite_data_report.pdf.

Australian Institute for Teaching and School Leadership. (2015). *Action now: Selection of entrants into initial teacher education*. Melbourne, Australia: AITSL. Retrieved from http://www.aitsl.edu.au/initial-teacher-education/ite-reform/selection.

Beltman, S., Mansfield, C. F., & Price, A. (2011). Thriving not just surviving: A review of research on teacher resilience. *Educational Research Review, 6*(3), 185–207. doi:10.1016/j.edurev.2011.09.001

Bergman, J., & Sams, A. (2012). *Flip your classroom: Reach every student in every class every day*. Washington, DC: International Society for Technology in Education.

Biggs, J., & Moore, P. J. (1993). *The process of learning* (3rd ed.). Sydney, Australia: Prentice Hall.

Bonk, C. J., & Graham, C. R. (2006). *The handbook of blended learning: Global perspectives, local designs* (1st ed.). San Francisco: Pfeiffer.

Burd, E., Smith, S., & Reisman, S. (2015). Exploring business models for MOOCS in higher education. *Innovative Higher Education, 40*(1), 37–49. doi:10.1007/s10755-014-9297-0

Crisp, D. A., & Griffiths, K. M. (2014). Participating in online mental health interventions: Who is most likely to sign up and why? *Depression Research and Treatment, 2014*, 11. doi:10.1155/2014/790457

Curry, J. R., & O'Brien, E. R. (2012). Shifting to a wellness paradigm in teacher education: A promising practice for fostering teacher stress reduction, burnout resilience, and promoting retention. *Ethical Human Psychology and Psychiatry, 14*(3), 178–191. doi:10.1891/1559-4343.14.3.178

Day, C. (2014). Resilient principals in challenging schools: The courage and costs of conviction. *Teachers and Teaching: Theory and Practice, 20*(5), 638–654. doi:10.1080/13540602.2014.937959

Day, C., & Gu, Q. (2014). *Resilient teachers, resilient schools: Building and sustaining quality in testing times*. Oxon, UK: Routledge.

Doney, P. A. (2013). Fostering resilience: A necessary skill for teacher retention. *Journal of Science Teacher Education, 24*(4), 645–664. doi:10.1007/s10972-012-9324-x

Early Years Learning Framework for Australia. (2013). Retrieved from https://education.gov.au/early-years-learning-framework

Ebersöhn, L. (2012). Adding 'flock' to 'fight and flight': A honeycomb of resilience where supply of relationships meets demand for support. *Journal of Psychology in Africa, 27*(1), 29–42. doi:10.1080/14330237.2012.10874518

Ebersöhn, L. (2014). Teacher resilience: Theorizing resilience and poverty. *Teachers and Teaching, 20*(5), 568–594. doi:10.1080/13540602.2014.937960

EDUCAUSE. (2012). *What campus leaders need to know about MOOCs: An EDUCAUSE executive briefing*. Louisville, CO: EDUCAUSE Publications. Retrieved from http://www.educause.edu

Ee, J., & Chang, A. (2010). How resilient are our graduate trainee teachers in Singapore? *The Asia-Pacific Education Researcher, 19*(2), 321–331.

Fantilli, R. D., & McDougall, D. E. (2009). A study of novice teachers: Challenges and supports in the first years. *Teaching & Teacher Education, 25*(6), 814–825. doi:10.1016/j.tate.2009.02.021

Friedman, I. A. (2004). Directions in teacher training for low-burnout teaching. In E. Frydenberg (Ed.), *Thriving, surviving, or going under: Coping with everyday lives* (pp. 305–326). Greenwich, CT: Information Age Publishing.

Gu, Q., & Day, C. (2013). Challenges to teacher resilience: Conditions count. *British Educational Research Journal, 39*(1), 22–44. doi:10.1080/01411926.2011.623152

Gu, Q., & Li, Q. (2013). Sustaining resilience in times of change: Stories from Chinese teachers. *Asia-Pacific Journal of Teacher Education, 41*(3), 288–303. doi:10.1080/1359866X.2013.809056

Gu, Q., & Li, Q. (2015). *Resilience of Chinese teachers: Confirming a new construct*. Paper presented at the 16th biennial conference of the European Association for Research on Learning and Instruction (EARLI), Limassol, Cyprus, August.

Hong, J. Y. (2012). Why do some beginning teachers leave the school, and others stay? Understanding teacher resilience through psychological lenses. *Teachers and Teaching: Theory and Practice, 18*(4), 417–440. doi:10.1080/13540602.2012.696044

Howard, S., & Johnson, B. (2004). Resilient teachers: Resisting stress and burnout. *Social Psychology of Education, 7*(4), 399–420.

Huisman, S., Singer, N. R., & Catapano, S. (2010). Resiliency to success: Supporting novice urban teachers. *Teacher Development: An International Journal of Teachers' Professional Development, 14*(4), 483–499. doi:10.1080/13664530.2010.533490

Johnson, B., Down, B., Le Cornu, R., Peters, J., Sullivan, A., Pearce, J., et al. (2014). Promoting early career teacher resilience: A framework for understanding and acting. *Teachers and Teaching: Theory and Practice, 20*(5), 530–546. doi:10.1080/13540602.2014.937957

Keogh, J. (2010). Plugging the leaky bucket: The need to develop resilience in novice middle years teachers. *Primary & Middle Years Educator, 8*(2), 17–23.

Kitching, K., Morgan, M., & O'Leary, M. (2009). It's the little things: Exploring the importance of commonplace events for early-career teachers' motivation. *Teachers and Teaching: Theory and Practice, 15*(1), 43–58. doi:10.1080/13540600802661311

Le Cornu, R. (2009). Building resilience in pre-service teachers. *Teaching and Teacher Education, 25*(5), 717–723. doi:10.1016/j.tate.2008.11.016

Le Cornu, R. (2013). Building early career teacher resilience: The role of relationships. *Australian Journal of Teacher Education, 38*(4), 1–16. doi:10.14221/ajte.2013v38n4.4

Leroux, M., & Théorêt, M. (2014). Intriguing empirical relations between teachers' resilience and reflection on practice. *Reflective Practice: International and Multidisciplinary Perspectives, 15*(3), 289–303. doi:10.1080/14623943.2014.900009

Mansfield, C. F., Beltman, S., Broadley, T., & Weatherby-Fell, N. (2013). *BRiTE: Keeping cool by building resilience in teacher education*. Retrieved from http://www.olt.gov.au/project-brite-keeping-cool-building-resilience-teacher-education-2013

Mansfield, C. F., Beltman, S., Broadley, T., & Weatherby-Fell, N. (2016). Building resilience in teacher education: An evidenced informed framework. *Teaching and Teacher Education, 54*, 77–87. doi:10.1016/j.tate.2015.11.016

Mansfield, C. F., Beltman, S., Price, A., & McConney, A. (2012). "Don't sweat the small stuff:" Understanding teacher resilience at the chalkface. *Teaching and Teacher Education, 28*, 357–367. doi:10.1016/j.tate.2011.11.001

Mansfield, C. F., Beltman, S., & Price, A. (2014). 'I'm coming back again!' The resilience process of early career teachers. *Teachers and Teaching, 20*(5), 547–567. doi:10.1080/13540602.2014.937958

Morgan, M. (2011). Resilience and recurring adverse events: Testing an assets-based model of beginning teachers' experiences. *The Irish Journal of Psychology, 32*(3–4), 92–104. doi:10.1080/03033910.2011.613189

Morgan, M., Ludlow, L., Kitching, K., O'Leary, M., & Clarke, A. (2010). What makes teachers tick? Sustaining events in new teachers' lives. *British Educational Research Journal, 36*(2), 191–208. doi:10.1080/01411920902780972

O'Donnell, E., Lawless, S., Sharp, M., & Wade, V. (2015). A review of personalised e-learning: Towards supporting learner diversity. *International Journal of Distance Education Technologies,* 22–47. doi:10.4018/ijdet.2015010102

O'Sullivan, M. (2006). Professional lives of Irish physical education teachers: Stories of resilience, respect and resignation. *Physical Education and Sport Pedagogy, 11*(3), 265–284. doi:10.1080/17408980600986314

Papatraianou, L. H., & Le Cornu, R. (2014). Problematising the role of personal and professional relationships in early career teacher resilience. *Australian Journal of Teacher Education, 39*(1), 100–116. doi:10.14221/ajte.2014v39n1.7

Patterson, J. H., Collins, L., & Abbott, G. (2004). A study of teacher resilience in urban schools. *Journal of Instructional Psychology, 31*(1), 3–11. Retrieved from http://www.projectinnovation.biz/jip_2006.html.

Peters, J., & Pearce, J. (2012). Relationships and early career teacher resilience: A role for school principals. *Teachers and Teaching: Theory and Practice, 18*(2), 249–262. doi:10.1080/13540602.2012.632266

Ryan, M. L., Shochet, I. M., & Stallman, H. M. (2010). Universal online resilience interventions might engage psychologically distressed university students who are unlikely to seek formal help. *Advances in Mental Health, 9*(1), 73–83.

Schelvis, R. M. C., Zwetsloot, G. I. J. M., Bos, E. H., & Wiezer, N. M. (2014). Exploring teacher and school resilience as a new perspective to solve persistent problems in the educational sector. *Teachers and Teaching, 20*(5), 622–637. doi:10.1080/13540602.2014.937962

Sharplin, E., O'Neill, M., & Chapman, A. (2011). Coping strategies for adaptation to new teacher appointments: Intervention for retention. *Teaching and Teacher Education, 27,* 136–146. doi:10.1016/j.tate.2010.07.010

Tait, M. (2008). Resilience as a contributor to novice teacher success, commitment, and retention. *Teacher Education Quarterly, 35*(4), 57–76.

Teacher Education Ministerial Advisory Group. (2014). *Action now: Classroom ready teachers – Australian Government response*. Canberra, Australia: Australian Government, Department of Education and Training. Retrieved from https://docs.education.gov.au/system/files/doc/other/150212_ag_response_-_final.pdf

Ungar, M. (Ed.). (2012). *The social ecology of resilience: A handbook of theory and practice.* New York: Springer.

Walsh, F. (2002). Bouncing forward: Resilience in the aftermath of September 11. *Family Process, 41,* 34–36.

Wosnitza, M., Morgan, M., Nevralova, K., Cefai, C., Henkel, M., Peixoto, F., Beltman, S., & Mansfield, C. (2013). *Keeping cool Europe – Enhancing teacher resilience in Europe.* Application Lifelong Learning Programme. Submission number 539590-LLP-1-2013-1-DE-COMENIUS-CMP.

Building Professional Learning Identities: Beginning Teachers' Perceptions of Causality for Professional Highs and Lows

Ellen Larsen and Jeanne M. Allen

1 Background Context

It has been well documented that beginning teachers can experience "reality shock" upon entering the teaching profession (Keogh, Garvis, Pendergast, & Diamond, 2012). According to Devos, Dupriez, and Paquay (2012, p. 206), "beginning teachers enter a new world, experience an accelerated pace of life, and encounter unexpected situations and challenges." Participation in professional learning and induction programs has been cited as a necessary support for novitiate teachers as they deal with the transition into the profession (Darling-Hammond, Wei, Andree, Richardson, & Orphanos, 2009; Huisman, Singer, & Catapano, 2010), impacting positively on levels of beginning teacher retention (Buchanan et al., 2013; Ingersoll, 2001) and, additionally, assisting teachers to develop the capacity to impact student outcomes and contribute to the collective expertise of their schools (Lovett & Cameron, 2011). As stated in the recent report from the Australian Teacher Education Ministerial Advisory Group (TEMAG) (2014, p. 38), "high-performing and improving education systems demonstrate a commitment to structured support for beginning teachers in their transition to full professional performance and, in doing so, build and sustain a culture of professional responsibility."

The provision of support in this context requires an understanding of both the professional learning needs of the beginning teacher (Lovett & Cameron, 2011), and also of the ways in which the beginning teacher develops an identity with a propensity to engage as a professional learner (Walkington, 2005). Self-efficacy (Devos et al., 2012), motivation, resilience (Doney, 2013) and a positive attribution style (Fineburg, 2010) have all been linked to beginning teachers' ability to cope with the early challenges of teaching. A study of novice coaches by Larsen and

E. Larsen (✉) • J.M. Allen
School of Education and Professional Studies, Griffith University,
Nathan, Queensland, Australia
e-mail: ellen.larsen@griffithuni.edu.au; jeanne.allen@griffith.edu.au

© Springer Science+Business Media Singapore 2016
R. Brandenburg et al. (eds.), *Teacher Education*,
DOI 10.1007/978-981-10-0785-9_14

Allen (2014) also found that those coaches who displayed evidence of strong professional learning identities were able to remain positive in the face of significant challenges. Little is known, however, about what motivates beginning teachers to prioritise professional learning in the development of their teacher identities.

In response to research acknowledging that professional learning is key to teacher retention and success, the "teacher as professional learner" has emerged as significant in educational policy (Australian Institute of Teaching and School Leadership (AITSL), 2011, 2012). The implementation of *The Australian Professional Standards for Teachers* (AITSL, 2011) has established professional learning as an expectation for all teachers through, for example, structured induction programs. According to Phillips (2008), effective engagement in professional learning also requires a sense of responsibility for that learning. There is a need, therefore, for us to understand how teachers entering the profession develop positive professional learning identities. The work reported on in this chapter goes some way to addressing this need.

2 Research Aim

The aim of the research reported on below was to develop an understanding of the ways in which beginning teachers interact within their working contexts to develop their identity as professional learners during their first year of professional practice. For the purposes of this chapter, data analysis and interpretation from the first phase of the study, conducted through an online survey in 2015, will be presented and discussed. In doing so, we respond to the following research question:

> How do beginning teachers attribute causality for the successful and unsuccessful[1] events that they experience in their first year of teaching?

The findings from this study raise important considerations in relation to how such attributions impact the development of beginning teachers' beliefs, values and identities as professional learners. This chapter will acknowledge these considerations as study findings are discussed.

3 Literature

We begin this review by discussing current national and international literature about the development of teacher identity which provides an overarching conceptual framework to this research. We then provide a brief overview of how the literature portrays the professional identity development of the beginning teacher, and the

---

[1] We are not suggesting a polarity between "successful" and "unsuccessful" here. Rather, participants reported a range of experiences across this spectrum. The terms "successful" and "unsuccessful" were used by participants during data collection to identify those events in which successful or unsuccessful outcomes were perceived.

ways in which teacher identity has been shown to be impacted by professional learning. The final part of the review focuses on the process of reflection on and for action—and its relevance to professional learning identity development.

Teacher identity has been an area of increasing focus for some time (Beauchamp & Thomas, 2011; Day, Kington, Stobart, & Sammons, 2006; Gee, 1999). Teacher identity stems from an individual's sense of personal identity, which has been described as the set of beliefs and values that one holds about oneself that exist behind one's "situated identities" (Bullough, 2005) that are specific to the particular roles or contexts in which an individual participates. Referred to as both teacher identity (Flores & Day, 2006) and professional identity (Cohen, 2010), both terminologies refer to the teacher's understanding of what an effective teacher is, and their own beliefs and values about the teacher they want to become (Thomas & Beauchamp, 2007).

Identity research has demonstrated that teachers not only perform a functional role, but also develop an identity reflecting their understandings and inclinations as a teacher practitioner (Beauchamp & Thomas, 2011; Beijaard, Meijer, & Verloop, 2004; Flores & Day, 2006). The seminal work of Lortie (1975) demonstrated that beginning teachers come to teaching with a set of values and beliefs that impact the ways in which they understand their multiple professional responsibilities informed by their experiences as school students, through a process of anticipatory socialisation. The process of occupational socialisation is then further influenced during pre-service professional experience activities (see, e.g., Allen, 2006), and, as the pre-service teacher transitions to practising teacher, through immersion in the institutional environment (Allen, 2006) and through interaction with colleagues (Cook, 2009). Beginning teachers modify their early understandings and beliefs about teaching as they experience the realities and demands of their new role. According to Day et al. (2006), this is an intense time of identity work when new teachers often question current beliefs and values, and reshape their identities as they reflect on the highs and lows of their experiences in the workplace.

According to Hammerness, Darling-Hammond, and Bransford (2005, p. 383), "developing a professional identity is an important part of securing teachers' commitment to their work and adherence to values and norms of practice." The impact of beginning teachers aligning their practice and beliefs to "adjust to the requirements of the conditions of the workplace" (Hargreaves, 1995, p. 80) has been debated within the research. However, teachers are expected as a norm of practice, in Australia and elsewhere, to engage in ongoing professional learning (AITSL, 2011; United Kingdom Department of Education, 2011). It is therefore essential that beginning teachers value and prioritise professional learning as a responsibility of their work.

Researchers agree that such professional learning comprises of more than participation in professional learning events. Mockler (2013, p. 42) argues that "teacher professional learning at its best is not merely about acquisition of knowledge and skills, but the formation and mediation of teacher professional identity." This view represents a shift in attention away from teacher behaviour and towards teacher thinking and reflection (Zuljan, Zuljan, & Pavlin, 2011). From this perspective, engagement in professional learning "promotes the teacher as a flexible, lifelong learner, able to participate in ongoing change" (Walkington, 2005, p. 54). The emphasis is on both the development of knowledge for improved practice, as well as the growth of a professional learning mindset.

Key to the development of such a mindset is a focus on reflective practice. Teachers who engage reflectively can develop the capacity to identify areas for improved practice (Liu & Zhang, 2014). Researchers agree that reflective practice has transformative potential through the "thoughtful, systematic, critical exploration of the complexity of one's own learning and teaching practice" (Samaras & Freese, 2006). Therefore, within the context of this study, reflection can be seen as thinking about, and moving forward from, the highs and lows of teaching.

However, while reflective practice has been clearly identified as a critical factor in teacher professional learning, it continues to be represented in myriad ways (Liu & Zhang, 2014; Toom, Husu, & Patrikainen, 2015). Seminal works by Dewey (1933) and Schön (1983) occupy a prominent position in the literature on reflective practice, albeit from different theoretical perspectives. While Dewey (1933) supports a retrospective approach to reflection through a sequenced and logical practice known as *reflection on action*, Schön (1983) is critical of such a technicist approach, and places value on the tacit and experiential knowledge of the teacher to respond flexibly and spontaneously to experiences as they happen through *reflection in action*.

Reflection on action provides the beginning teacher with the opportunity to make sense of their professional experiences that can be "complex, unpredictable and often challenging" (Jones & Jones, 2013, p. 74). For the beginning teacher, tacit understandings of teaching (Herbert, 2015) and past teaching experiences, upon which to draw while reflecting in action, are obviously more limited (McIntyre, 1993). Reflection on action provides a retrospective opportunity for beginning teachers to make meaning about "themselves as persons and as teachers, events they encounter and the contexts in which their experiences occur" (Toom et al., 2015, p. 322).

While reflective practice of the type proposed by Dewey (1933) is important to understanding past events, Eraut (1995) argues the need for a model of reflection for action that requires beginning teachers to consider future actions and development (Urzua & Vasquez, 2008). Reflection for action focuses on prospective planning for action "that allows novice teachers to interpret their early experiences with a view towards the future" (Urzua & Vasquez, 2008, p. 1944). This future oriented process enables interpretations of experience to generate professional learning intentions. There is a significant gap in the research examining thinking behaviours that facilitate this reflection for future action. Through framing the work presented in this chapter in attribution theory, we go some way towards addressing this gap.

4 Theoretical Framework

Our adoption of Weiner's theory of attribution (1972, 1985, 1986) provides an effective frame within which to examine thinking that facilitates professional learning. Attribution theory explains the process and consequences of seeking a determination of causality following a particular event perceived by an individual as having either a successful or unsuccessful outcome. According to Weiner (1985, 1986), individuals have an innate tendency to seek causality to explain the causes for events that occur in their lives, particularly when such events are novel, unexpected or negative (Perry, Daniels, & Haynes, 2008). The attribution process is therefore highly pertinent to the beginning teacher undergoing a significant transition into an unfamiliar context (Boyer, 2006). Furthermore, attributional processing subsequently influences the behaviour of the individual within that social context (Weiner, 1995).

4.1 Dimensions of Causality

Weiner (1972, 1985, 1986) proposes that individuals allocate causality across three dimensions of locus, stability and controllability. The properties for each dimension (see Fig. 1) are considered as individuals reflect, and determine causality.

Locus of causality: In allocating the locus of causality, an individual seeks to ascertain the source of responsibility for an event outcome as either internal or external to their own self. A locus of causality that is internal includes personal ability and effort. External loci of causality include (a) the abilities or decisions of others, and (b) the context in which the event took place.

Stability: Stability refers to the individual's perception of the changeability of the attributed cause in the future. On one hand, a highly stable cause would be deemed to be fixed, and unlikely to change in the future. On the other hand, an unstable cause would indicate a possibility for change across time.

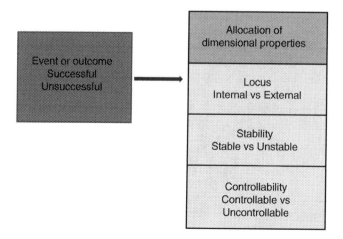

Fig. 1 Dimensions of causality

Controllability: Weiner (2010) defines controllability as the perception of influence over the cause of an event. High controllability refers to a high degree of perceived influence over either an internal or external cause. McAuley, Duncan, and Russell (1992) found that greater reliability of attributional measurement occurs when both personal and external perceptions of control are included.

4.2 Attributional Responses

Significantly, dimensional attributions for the cause of an event outcome impact an individual's subsequent actions, motivations, and emotional responses (Weiner, 1986), as we explain below. These actions and responses have been linked by Weiner to self-efficacy, expectations for the future and the motivation of the attributing individual (see Fig. 2).

Attributions for locus of causality have been closely linked to self-efficacy (Weiner, 2010). When attributing a successful outcome internally, the individual is likely to experience a sense of pride and self-efficacy. Conversely, external attributions for successful outcomes may lower the individual's sense of self-efficacy due to feelings of failure (Bandura, 1989). Where causality for an unsuccessful outcome is determined to be external, self-efficacy can be preserved (Coleman, 2013). In contrast, self-attribution for an unsuccessful outcome can lead to feelings of guilt and lowered self-efficacy.

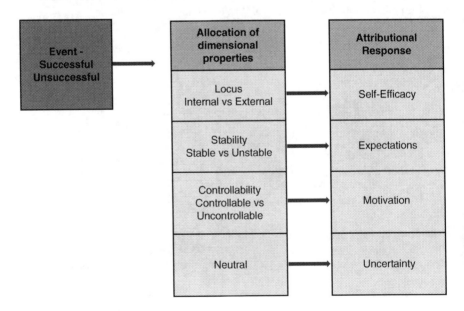

Fig. 2 Attributional responses

Stability gives rise to expectancy shifts for future achievements and is a powerful determinant of perceived hope for success, while controllability creates a perception of influence over the cause. There is a strong link between controllability and Bandura's (1989, 2001, 2006) work on human agency. A high sense of agency leads the individual to perceive that they have the ability to influence factors impacting their success. In contrast, a low sense of agency elicits the perception that circumstances are controlled by others, which can impact negatively on the motivation to act.

Martinez, Martinko, and Ferris (2012, p. 17) introduced the concept of "fuzzy attribution style." Whereas the attributions above indicate a "crisp set" of attributional decisions by the individual, a fuzzy attribution results from an uncertainty, or an unwillingness to commit, to a particular causal decision. These attributions are characterised by neutral responses when reflecting about causality.

As alluded to above, this chapter focuses on the attributions of causality across these dimensions, reported by a sample of beginning teachers in response to their perceived successful and unsuccessful experiences during their first year of teaching.

5 Methodology

This is the first phase of a larger sequential mixed methods study (Creswell & Clark, 2011), involving the online collection of survey data in 2015 following ethics clearance from the University's Human Research Ethics Committee. Fifty-seven first-year teachers working in independent schools in Queensland completed the online survey consisting of an adaptation of the Causal Dimension Scale II (CDSII) (McAuley et al., 1992), designed to measure participants' attributions of causality for events in which they were involved in their first year of teaching. This sector provides a richly diverse and previously under-researched context for investigation. With a return rate of 30.6% from a possible sample of 186 beginning teachers, demographic data indicated that there was representation of independent school contexts across geographic location, school size and year level (Prep to Year 12).

6 Data Analysis

To remain within the scope of this chapter, two of the four sections of the survey data have been selected for presentation here. These include open responses providing participants' reported experiences and associated perceptions of causality, and quantitative data from a bi-polar scale providing detailed attributions across the dimensions pertaining to each cause.

Analysis firstly involved the coding of attributed causes for the event outcomes. Each cause was coded using key words, and iterative coding led to the development

Table 1 Total scores for the causal dimension scale II

Dimension of attribution	Bi-polar survey statements		
Total scores	27–16	15	14–3
Locus of causality	That reflects an aspect of yourself	Neutral	Reflects an aspect of your context
	Within you		Outside of you
	About you		About others
Controllability (personal)	Manageable by you	Neutral	Not manageable by you
	You can control		You cannot control
	Over which you have power		Over which you have no power
Controllability (external)	Over which others have control	Neutral	Over which others have no control
	Within the power of other people		Not within the power of other people
	Other people can control		Other people cannot control
Stability	Permanent	Neutral	Temporary
	That is stable across time		That varies across time
	Unchangeable		Changeable

Adapted from McAuley et al. (1992)

of categories (Miles, Huberman, & Saldana, 2014). Frequency counts and percentages were calculated for each category to ascertain the prevalence of causes identified by this first-year teacher sample.

Total scores were then calculated for each causal dimension (locus, controllability and stability) attributed to each cause (see Table 1). The higher the total score, the higher the personal responsibility (internal), perception of both personal and external control, and perceived stability of the cause; the lower the score, the lower the sense of personal responsibility (external), personal and external control and stability of the cause. A score of 15 was considered neutral.

7 Findings

We present our findings in four parts: (1) Causes[2] of successful outcomes; (2) Causes of unsuccessful outcomes; (3) Dimensional attributions for successful causes; and (4) Dimensional attributions for unsuccessful causes.

---

[2] As previously noted, this is a perceptual study and, therefore, these are participants' reported perceptions of the causes of "successful" and "unsuccessful" event and experience outcomes.

Table 2 Successful cause categories

Attributed causes	Survey response exemplar	Frequency count	%
Own practice	Providing an interesting activity	54	38.57
Colleagues	I asked other teachers what they used for behaviour management	35	25
Own relational/ communication work	I developed a positive relationship with the student at the beginning	16	11.43
Collaboration	Everyone was on the same page doing the same things	10	7.14
Own professional learning	Personal study/research and preparation	8	5.71
Students	The student's willingness and motivation to take on extra learning	8	5.71
Context	I work with these girls in a small class environment	3	2.15
Own life experience	My previous work and life experience has assisted me	2	1.43
Professional learning	I attended Professional Development that was inspiring and practical	2	1.43
Pre-service experience	My teaching internship has allowed me to accumulate lots of ideas and resources	2	1.43

7.1 Causes of Successful Outcomes

Ten cause categories for success were established (see Table 2). Of these categories, participants were most likely to attribute success internally to their own practice. In total, participants attributed causality internally in 57.14% of survey responses. While there was a propensity for these beginning teachers to attribute internally, external causes were also represented, with support from colleagues accounting for the majority of external attributions. Table 2 includes the attributed causes, an exemplar survey response and the frequency count. Other external causes were also acknowledged, such as collaboration, students, contextual conditions, professional learning and pre-service experiences to lesser extents (see Fig. 3).

7.2 Causes of Unsuccessful Outcomes

Similarly, participants were most likely to attribute causality for unsuccessful outcomes to their own practice (see Fig. 4).

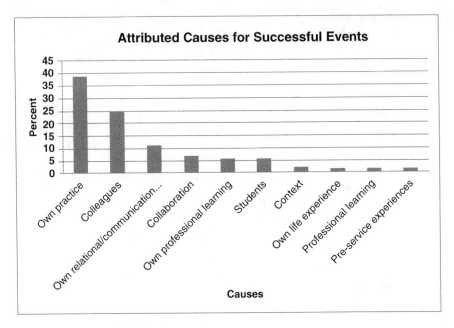

Fig. 3 Successful cause distributions

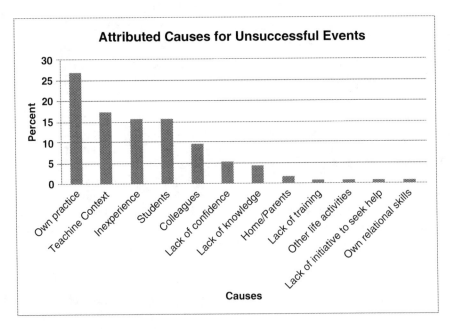

Fig. 4 Unsuccessful cause distributions

Table 3 Unsuccessful cause categories

Attributed causes	Survey response exemplar	Frequency count	%
Own practice	I did not prepare my materials enough	31	26.97
Teaching context	Not enough time, lack of teacher aide support, small sized classroom	20	17.39
Inexperience	If I was more experienced I may have been able to try something different	18	15.65
Students	This was due to the student's attitude towards his work	18	15.65
Colleagues	My mentor does not seem keen to impart her knowledge	11	9.58
Lack of confidence	I felt I was not confident about talking to parents about learning difficulties	6	5.21
Lack of knowledge	I didn't have enough knowledge about the topics I was teaching	5	4.35
Home/parents	There was no support from home	2	1.73
Lack of training	Inadequate training and preparation to manage behaviour	1	0.87
Other life activities	My sporting career influenced this	1	0.87
Lack of initiative to seek help	I did not speak with my mentor about it	1	0.87
Own relational skills	I am extremely driven and find it hard to forgive the laziness of others	1	0.87

Internal categories, which included inexperience, a lack of confidence, a lack of knowledge, a lack of professional learning initiative and relational skills, totalled 53.92% of responses (see Table 3). Notably, causes pertaining to external causes such as teaching context, students, colleagues, parents and the home, lack of training and other life activities combined to yield 46.09% of responses.

7.3 Dimensional Attributions for Successful Causes

Attribution sets for each cause were developed combining dimensions of locus of causality and stability. Our data analysis generated five types of personal and external attributions for successful experiences (see Table 4). Two types of personal or internal attributions featured, with the first illustrating a perception of high stability and the second attributing low stability. These two attribution types were categorised as "Personal 1" and "Personal 2" consecutively. Similarly, two external attribution types were developed with the first featuring attributions of high stability, and the second, low stability. We labelled these types "External 1" and "External 2." The last attribution type included attribution sets where locus of causality was perceived as neutral, and was thus categorised as "Neutral."

Table 4 Attribution sets (locus of causality and stability) for successful events

Attribution set (L Locus, S Stability)	Attribution type and description	Frequency count	Percent
L internal S high	Personal 1	46	44.66
	I can always achieve success		
L Internal S Low	Personal 2	22	21.34
	This success was mine, but may not continue		
L External S High	External 1	10	9.71
	They can always achieve success		
L External S Low	External 2	10	9.71
	This success was not mine and may not continue		
L Neutral S Neutral	Neutral	15	14.56
	I am not sure who is responsible for this success		

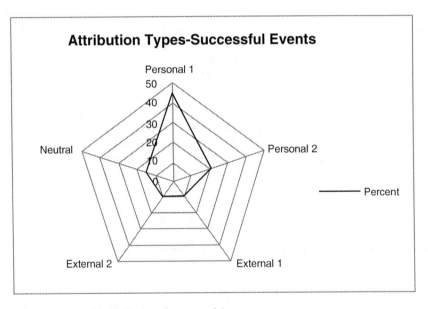

Fig. 5 Attribution type distributions for successful events

These findings indicate that the majority of participants attributed success to internal causes that they perceived as constant (see Fig. 5). The second most common attribution type demonstrated a propensity to attribute internally, but to perceive the cause for success as unstable. A total of 19.42 response sets attributed causality externally, with 50% of these perceiving this cause to be stable into the

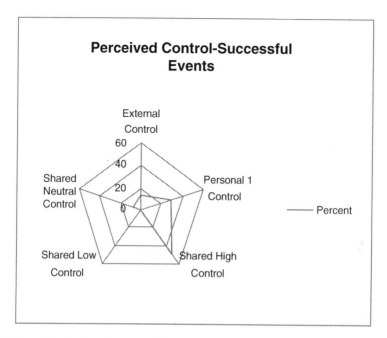

Fig. 6 Control distributions for successful events

future. Significantly, 14.56% of responses were recorded as neutral, which suggests that, for a portion of these beginning teachers, decision making with regard to locus, stability and/or controllability remained undetermined.

Through the analysis of personal and external control data, we found that participants reported a significant level of shared high control for successful experiences (see Fig. 6). This was particularly significant where the locus of causality was perceived to be internal, calculated at 40% of responses (see Fig. 6), compared to shared high control for externally attributed successes at 8.57%. Aside from shared control, participants were also more likely to express higher levels of personal control for successful causes than external control. It is noteworthy that there were also a number of participants who perceived success to be the responsibility of, and within the control of, others in their context.

7.4 Dimensional Attributions for Unsuccessful Causes

Analysis of attributional sets combining locus and stability dimensions for unsuccessful causes generated two dominant types. Significantly, participants were most likely to perceive high levels of personal responsibility for unsuccessful events, but

Table 5 Attribution sets (locus of causality and stability) for unsuccessful events

Attribution set (L Locus, S Stability)	Attribution type and description	Frequency count	Percent
L Internal S High	Personal 1	9	9.47
	I am responsible and it probably will not change		
L Internal S Low	Personal 2	36	37.9
	I am responsible but the cause may change		
L Internal S Neutral	Personal 3	3	3.16
	I am responsible but the cause may or may not change		
L External S High	External 1	8	8.42
	Others are responsible and it probably won't change		
L External S Low	External 2	26	27.37
	Others are responsible but it could change		
L External S Neutral	External 3	2	2.11
	Others are responsible and it may or may not change		
L Neutral S High	Neutral 1	1	1.05
	It is nobody's responsibility in particular and it probably won't change		
L Neutral S Low	Neutral 2	5	5.26
	It is nobody's responsibility in particular but it could change		
L External S Neutral	Neutral 3	5	5.26
	It is nobody's responsibility in particular and it may or may not change		

to also see these causes as unstable (see Table 5). External causes, although less significantly represented, were also perceived to be likely to alter across time see (Fig. 7). Attribution sets consisting of neutral attributions accounted for 16.84% of responses. Additionally, a total of 17.89% of responses indicated a perception that causes would be unlikely to change across time.

Analysis revealed that control over causes for unsuccessful experiences was mostly perceived as personal (see Fig. 8), with highest perceptions of personal control where participants also held themselves to be responsible for the cause. Similarly, external causes were linked to external control. However, in 17.02% of the responses, despite an attribution of internal responsibility, participants also reported perceiving that others shared high levels of control with them over this cause (see Fig. 8). For some participants, a neutral attribution of responsibility for unsuccessful experiences was compounded by a lack of definitive attribution for who had any control over the cause.

Building Professional Learning Identities: Beginning Teachers' Perceptions...

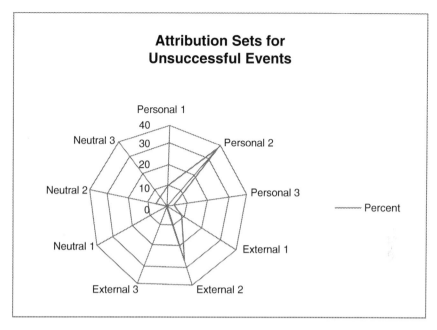

Fig. 7 Attribution set distributions for unsuccessful events

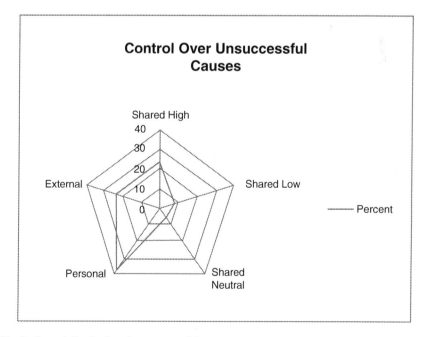

Fig. 8 Control distributions for unsuccessful causes

8 Discussion

We now turn to a discussion of the findings and, in doing so, respond to the research question underpinning this study: *How do beginning teachers attribute causality for the successful and unsuccessful events that they experience in their first year of teaching?*

8.1 Successful Causes

The findings indicate that, when reflecting on a particular successful experience, these beginning teachers are likely to attribute responsibility for that success to their own practice. These findings could be indicative of self-serving bias, described by Harvey, Martinko, and Gardner (2006) as the tendency for individuals to attribute success internally, and to attribute failure to external causes. Research has shown that such attributions assist individuals to maintain self-efficacy. In a study of attribution styles and teacher burnout, Fineburg (2010) found teachers perceiving an internal locus of causality for successes avoided burnout and loss of efficacy in the profession. We can thus deem such attributions to be positive in the lives of teachers as they face ongoing challenges.

Participants also display a tendency to associate internally attributed causes with high stability, or persistence, of the successful cause into the future. According to Fineburg (2010), such attributions also fall into a positive attribution style whereby there is an optimistic expectation for the future. While facilitating a positive outlook for future practice, this tendency raises the question as to how such a reflection on action would lead to reflection for action. Where professional improvement is not deemed necessary, a view of continuous professional learning may be compromised.

Furthermore, participants' reported perceptions of dual high control over causes for success presents as an interesting trend. Controllability creates for the individual a perception of influence over the cause. For these first-year teachers, shared high control indicates a perceived duality of power. An attribution of shared control could, according to Turner and Stets (2006), be a consequence of the individuals' acknowledgement of power, or fair treatment, by others in the context. Where a less powerful individual feels that they have been treated fairly by a more powerful other, that individual may choose to attribute success to a disposition of their own, but also acknowledge the disposition of another (Turner & Stets, 2006). The question then arises over the impact of shared controllability on proactive reflection and planning for action by the first-year teacher.

8.2 Unsuccessful Causes

Participants also made internal attributions to both their own practice and inexperience in response to unsuccessful events. These are important findings in light of the fact that internal attributions for failure are categorised as negative, with a tendency to lower self-efficacy (Weiner, 1985). According to Schlenker, Weigold, and Hallam (1990), concern over criticism may activate a more cautious approach when attributing responsibility for unsuccessful outcomes. This may indicate that first-year teachers are less comfortable attributing responsibility to others in their context for unsuccessful outcomes, such as colleagues, leaders or mentors. The influence of power and positioning on the reflections of first-year teachers may in turn influence their attributions, despite the negative impact that this thinking may have on perceptions of self-efficacy.

It is important to note that this sample of first-year teachers, regardless of attributions of responsibility, perceived the cause for their unsuccessful experiences to be temporary and changeable. It could thus be reasonably anticipated that such an attribution style would facilitate these teachers' positive reflection for action. However, such action planning for transformation (Toom et al., 2015) requires a perception of controllability. While the majority of participants reported a perception of high personal control, there was also a significant group that considered causes to be controlled either in part, or completely, by others in the context. Given that controllability influences agency to make change, it would be reasonable to expect that some first-year teachers may anticipate dependency upon others, either completely or in part, to action change.

8.3 Neutrality

Martinez et al. (2012) suggest that the more fuzzy, or neutral, an attributional style, the more incapable the individual is to make a definite decision as to how to move forward. Such individuals would avoid making decisions as to appropriate action. Across all attributions, participants demonstrated a tendency to include in part, or completely, neutral attributions for successful and, even more commonly, unsuccessful causes. In light of these concerns, these first-year teachers may be at risk of focusing solely on reflection on action, without "looking forward" (Toom et al., 2015) to engage in refection for action. Limited experience (McIntyre, 1993) and concerns over the response of colleagues to attributions made by the beginning teacher (Schlenker et al., 1990; Turner & Stets, 2006) could play an influential role in attributional neutrality.

9 Limitations

We acknowledge several limitations pertaining to our presentation and discussion of this research study. First, for the purposes of this chapter, we report only on the first phase of our larger mixed methods study; a more comprehensive report, drawing from the full study, is forthcoming. Second, there are a number of areas that we point to in this chapter that require further exploration. These areas, which include neutral responses and the role of power and authority on attributional styles, will be further explored in Phase Two of the study, as well as in ensuing research projects. Third, given the space limitations of this chapter, we were unable to engage with additional literature, such as that of Daniels (2011) that could potentially add to and enrich our attributional framework. Again, this will be incorporated into our future work.

10 Conclusion

The findings from this study provide important insights into the ways in which first-year teachers reflect on their practice and make meaning from the experiences they encounter during their work. In this chapter, we reported on the first phase of a larger research study aiming to develop an understanding of the ways in which beginning teachers interact within their working contexts to develop their identity as professional learners during their first year of professional practice. The findings from an online survey used to elicit responses from a sample of first-year teachers working in independent school contexts across Queensland shed light on the ways in which participants reflected upon particular experiences and attributed causality for the associated outcomes.

In sum, this study found that the sample of first-year teachers displayed common patterns of attribution in response to perceived successful and unsuccessful events. Particular patterns representative of positive attribution styles included self-attribution for success and a perception of the instability of causes for unsuccessful experiences. The propensity for first- year teachers to self-attribute causality for unsuccessful events, and the neutrality of some attributional thinking, was evident within our findings. Notably, the extent to which causes for successful outcomes were perceived as constant and the perception of shared control over causes of both successful and unsuccessful events has raised questions as to the influence of such attributional thinking on the development of dispositions valuing ongoing professional growth and learning.

We will focus on these questions in Phase Two of the study where semi-structured interviews will be conducted. In light of the findings from this study, understanding how beginning teachers attribute causality for the highs and lows experienced during their first year of teaching could provide an important key to supporting beginning teachers' development as professional learners.

References

Allen, J. (2006). Beginning teacher socialization in the workplace: Some perspectives from the literature. In B. Walker-Gibbs & B. A. Knight (Eds.), *Re-visioning research and knowledge for the 21st century* (pp. 101–115). Teneriffe, Australia: Post Pressed.
Australian Institute of Teaching and School Leadership (AITSL). (2011). *Australian professional standards for teachers*. Melbourne, Australia: Australian Institute for Teaching and School Leadership.
Australian Institute of Teaching and School Leadership (AITSL). (2012). *Australian charter for the professional learning of teachers and school leaders*. Melbourne, Australia: AITSL.
Bandura, A. (1989). Human agency in social cognitive theory. *American Psychologist, 44*(9), 1175–1184.
Bandura, A. (2001). Social cognitive theory: An agentic perspective. *Annual Review of Psychology, 52*, 1–26.
Bandura, A. (2006). Toward a psychology of human agency. *Perspectives on Psychological Science, 1*(2), 164–180.
Beauchamp, C., & Thomas, L. (2011). New teachers' identity shifts at the boundary of teacher education and initial practice. *International Journal of Educational Research, 50*, 6–13.
Beijaard, D., Meijer, P., & Verloop, N. (2004). Reconsidering research on teachers' professional identity. *Teaching and Teacher Education, 20*, 107–128.
Boyer, W. (2006). Accentuate the positive: The relationship between positive explanatory style and academic achievement of prospective elementary teachers. *Journal of Research in Childhood Education, 21*, 53–63.
Buchanan, J., Prescott, A., Schuck, S., Aubusson, P., Burke, P., & Louviere, J. (2013). Teacher retention and attrition: Views of early career teachers. *Australian Journal of Teacher Education, 38*(3), 112–129.
Bullough, R. J. (2005). The quest for identity in teaching and teacher education. In G. Hoban (Ed.), *The missing links in teacher education design* (pp. 237–258). Dordrecht, The Netherlands: Springer.
Cohen, J. (2010). Getting recognised: Teachers negotiating professional identities as learners through talk. *Teaching and Teacher Education, 26*, 473–481.
Coleman, M. (2013). Emotion and the ultimate attribution error. *Current Psychology, 32*, 71–81.
Cook, J. (2009). "Coming into my own as a teacher": Identity, disequilibrium, and the first year of teaching. *The New Educator, 5*, 274–292.
Creswell, J. W., & Clark, V. (2011). *Designing and conducting mixed methods research* (2nd ed.). Thousand Oaks, CA: SAGE Publications.
Daniels, H. (2011). Analysing trajectories of professional learning in changing workplaces. *Culture Psychology, 17*(3), 359–377.
Darling-Hammond, L., Wei, R., Andree, A., Richardson, N., & Orphanos, S. (2009). *Professional learning in the learning profession: A status report on teacher development in the United States and abroad*. Stanford, CA: National Staff Development Council.
Day, C., Kington, A., Stobart, G., & Sammons, P. (2006). The personal and professional selves of teachers: Stable and unstable identities. *British Educational Research Journal, 32*(4), 601–616.
Devos, C., Dupriez, V., & Paquay, L. (2012). Does the social working environment predict beginning teachers' self-efficacy and feelings of depression? *Teaching and Teacher Education, 28*, 206–217.
Dewey, J. (1933). *How we think: A restatement of the relation of reflective thinking to the educative process*. Chicago: Henry Regnery.
Doney, P. (2013). Fostering resilience: A necessary skill for teacher retention. *Journal of Science Teacher Education, 24*, 645–664.
Eraut, M. (1995). Schön shock: A case for reframing reflection-in-action. *Teachers and Teaching: Theory and Practice, 1*(1), 9–22.

Fineburg, A. (2010). *Examining explanatory style's relationships to efficacy and burnout in teachers*. Doctor of Philosophy Dissertation, The University of Alabama, Alabama.

Flores, M. A., & Day, C. (2006). Contexts which shape and reshape new teachers' identities: A multi-perspective study. *Teaching and Teacher Education, 22*(2), 219–232.

Gee, J. P. (1999). Identity as an analytic lens for research in education. *Review of Research in Education, 25*, 99–125.

Hammerness, K., Darling-Hammond, L., & Bransford, J. (2005). How teachers learn and develop. In L. Darling-Hammond & J. Bransford (Eds.), *Preparing teachers for a changing world: What teachers should learn and be able to do* (pp. 358–389). San Francisco: Wiley.

Hargreaves, A. (1995). Realities of teaching. In L. W. Anderson (Ed.), *International encyclopedia of teaching and teacher education* (2nd ed., pp. 80–87). Oxford, UK: Elsevier Science Ltd.

Harvey, P., Martinko, M., & Gardner, W. (2006). Promoting authentic behaviour in organisations: An attributional perspective. *Journal of Leadership and Organisational Studies, 12*(3), 3–11.

Herbert, C. (2015). Knowing and/or experiencing: A critical examination of the reflective models of John Dewey and Donald Schon. *Reflective Practice, 16*(3), 361–371.

Huisman, S., Singer, N., & Catapano, S. (2010). Resiliency to success: Supporting novice urban teachers. *Teacher Development, 14*(4), 483–499.

Ingersoll, R. M. (2001). Teacher turnover and shortages: An organisational analysis. *American Educational Research Journal, 38*(3), 499–534.

Jones, J. L., & Jones, K. A. (2013). Teaching reflective practice: Implementation in the teacher education setting. *The Teacher Educator, 48*, 73–85.

Keogh, J., Garvis, S., Pendergast, D., & Diamond, P. (2012). Self-determination: Using agency, efficacy and resilience (AER) to counter novice teachers' experiences of intensification. *Australian Journal of Teacher Education, 37*(8), 46–65.

Larsen, E., & Allen, J. M. (2014). *The novice literacy coach: Exploring motivation and persistence in the face of challenge*. Paper presented at the AARE, Brisbane.

Liu, L., & Zhang, Y. (2014). Enhancing teachers' professional development through reflective teaching. *Theory and Practice in Language Studies, 4*(11), 2396–2401.

Lortie, D. C. (1975). *Schoolteacher: A sociological study*. Chicago: University of Chicago Press.

Lovett, S., & Cameron, M. (2011). Schools as professional learning communities for early career teachers: How do early career teachers rate them? *Teacher Development, 15*(1), 87–104.

Martinez, A., Martinko, M., & Ferris, G. R. (2012). Fuzzy attribution styles. *Journal of Leadership and Organisational Studies, 19*(1), 17–24.

McAuley, E., Duncan, T., & Russell, D. (1992). Measuring causal attributions: The revised causal dimension scale (CDSII). *Personality and Social Psychology Bulletin, 18*, 566–573.

McIntyre, D. (1993). Conceptualising reflection in teacher development. In J. Calderhead & P. Gates (Eds.), *Theory, theorising and reflection in initial teacher education* (pp. 39–52). London: Falmer Press.

Miles, M. B., Huberman, A. M., & Saldana, J. (2014). *Qualitative data analysis: A methods sourcebook* (3rd ed.). Thousand Oaks, CA: SAGE Publications.

Mockler, N. (2013). Teacher professional learning in a neoliberal age: Audit, professionalism and identity. *Australian Journal of Teacher Education, 38*(10), 35–47.

Perry, R., Daniels, L., & Haynes, T. (2008). Attributional (explanatory) thinking about failure in new achievement settings. *European Journal of Psychology of Education, 23*(4), 459–475.

Phillips, P. (2008). Professional development as a critical component of continuing teacher quality. *Australian Journal of Teacher Education, 33*(1), 1–9.

Samaras, A. P., & Freese, A. R. (2006). *Self-study of teaching practices primer*. New York: Peter Lang Publishing.

Schlenker, B. R., Weigold, M. F., & Hallam, J. R. (1990). Self-serving attributions in social context: Effects of self-esteem and social pressure. *Journal of Personality and Social Psychology, 58*, 855–863.

Schön, D. (1983). *The reflective practitioner*. New York: Basic Books.

Teacher Education Ministerial Advisory Group (TEMAG). (2014). *Action now: Classroom ready teachers*. Canberra, Australia: Department of Education.

Thomas, L., & Beauchamp, C. (2007). Learning to live well as teachers in a changing world: Insights into the development of a professional identity in teacher education. *The Journal of Educational Thought, 41*(3), 229–243.

Toom, A., Husu, J., & Patrikainen, S. (2015). Student teachers' patterns of reflection in the context of teaching practice. *European Journal of Teacher Education, 38*(3), 320–340.

Turner, J. H., & Stets, J. E. (2006). Sociological theories of human emotions. *Annual Review of Sociology, 32*, 25–52.

United Kingdom Department of Education. (2011). *Teachers' standards: Guidance for school leaders, school staff and governing bodies*. London: United Kingdom Department of Education.

Urzua, A., & Vasquez, C. (2008). Reflection and professional identity in teachers' future- oriented discourse. *Teaching and Teacher Education, 24*, 1935–1946.

Walkington, J. (2005). Becoming a teacher: Encouraging development of teacher identity through reflective practice. *Asia-Pacific Journal of Teacher Education, 33*(1), 53–64.

Weiner, B. (1972). *Theories of motivation: From mechanism to cognition*. Chicago: Rand McNally.

Weiner, B. (1985). An attributional theory of achievement motivation and emotion. *Psychological Review, 92*, 548–573.

Weiner, B. (1986). *An attributional theory of motivation and emotion*. New York: Springer.

Weiner, B. (1995). *Judgments of responsibility: A foundation for a theory of social conduct*. New York: Guilford.

Weiner, B. (2010). The development of an attribution based theory of motivation: A history of ideas. *Educational Psychologist, 45*(1), 28–36.

Zuljan, V., Zuljan, D., & Pavlin, S. (2011). Towards improvements in teachers' professional development through the reflective learning paradigm. *H.U. Journal of Education, 41*, 485–497.

Teaching and Teacher Education: The Need to Go Beyond Rhetoric

John Loughran

1 Introduction

> There have been debates about how, where, by whom, and for what purposes teachers should be educated ever since teacher education emerged ... For just as long, there have also been debates about what kind of an activity teaching is and what knowledge and skills teachers need to have in order to teach well. (Cochran-Smith & Demers, 2008, p. 1009)

As has been demonstrated time and time again, when questions about the quality of teaching and teacher education arise, responses are often based on individuals' personal experiences and opinions, education systems' expectations, demands and/or politicians' desires for higher rankings through various international educational testing schemes. It is not surprising then that views about teaching and teacher education end up being influenced by sweeping generalisations that masquerade as evidence and that the type of data used to shape policy is based on bold statements such as, 'Parents are concerned about teacher quality ...'; or 'Principals see a decline in standards of beginning teachers ...'; or 'Teacher education does not make student teachers classroom ready'.

Cochran-Smith and Demers (above), like many before them, highlighted the recurrent nature of debates about teaching and teacher education. As has been argued elsewhere, teaching and teacher education are complex and sophisticated enterprises (Bullock, 2011; Labaree, 2000; Loughran, 2015; Richardson, 1997) although they are not necessarily recognized as such by the casual observer. So why is it that the same debates continue and that public expectations of teaching and teacher education do not appear to be realized? Darling-Hammond (2006) offered one way of interpreting the situation:

J. Loughran (✉)
Faculty of Education, Monash University, Melbourne, Australia
e-mail: John.loughran@monash.edu

> One of the most damaging myths … is the notion that good teachers are born not made. This superstition has given rise to a set of policies that rely far too much on some kind of prenatal alchemy to produce a cadre of teachers … and far too little on systematic, sustained initiatives to ensure that all teachers have the opportunity to become well prepared.
>
> A companion myth is that good teacher education programs are virtually non-existent and perhaps even impossible to construct. As a consequence of the first myth or their own experience, a startling number of policy makers and practitioners appear to believe one or more of these notions: that teaching is mostly telling others what you know and therefore requires little more than subject matter knowledge, that people learn[ing] to teach learn primarily from (more or less unguided) experience, or that education schools can offer little more than half-baked "theories" that are unnecessary and perhaps even an impediment in learning the practical requirements of teaching. Thus there is little reason to require much in the way of teacher preparation or to invest in the institutions that are expected to prepare teachers to teach. (p. ix)

If teaching is not understood as complex and sophisticated business then there is little wonder that teacher education is also dismissed as simplistic and superficial leading to front loading views of, and sadly, approaches to, what teaching teaching should entail. Hence, Darling-Hammond's conclusion (above) that such thinking leads to a view that there is little need to invest in teacher preparation, unfortunate though it may be, poses major challenges for mounting claims to the contrary. But, just stating that teacher education is complex and sophisticated business does not resolve the situation.

This chapter examines four issues (the notion of a prescribed curriculum for teacher education; a vision for teaching; professional knowledge of practice; and, evidence of impact) that offer a starting point for a more informed debate about teaching and teacher education – something that is crucial if Darling-Hammond's myths are to be addressed and the situation is to substantially change. In so doing, the challenge is to go beyond the common rhetoric associated with existing practice and make clear that teaching and teacher education is complicated, sophisticated and important business.

2 Prescribed Curriculum

Criticism and ridicule of teaching and teacher education is not new, Labaree (2004) encapsulated the ever persistent complaints well when he stated that:

> Education in general is a source of chronic concern and an object of continuous criticism … [yet] citizens give good grades to their local schools at the same time that they express strong fears about quality of public education in general … [Such] threats include everything from multicultural curricula to the decline in the family, the influence of television, and the consequences of chronic poverty. One such threat is the hapless and baleful education school, whose incompetence and misguided ideas are seen as both producing poorly prepared teachers and promoting wrong-headed curricula. For the public at large, this institution is remote enough to be suspect (unlike the local school) and accessible enough to be scorned … [making] it the ideal scapegoat, which allows blame for problems with schools to fall upon teacher education … for critics of public education, the ed school's low status

and its addiction to progressive educational rhetoric make it a convenient target for blame. (p. 3)

To some, the idea of a prescribed teacher education curriculum is enticing; the argument often being that 'if teacher education taught the right things, the right way, then students of teaching would be properly prepared for the demands of teaching'. But as studies of curriculum consistently illustrate, just setting a mandated curriculum does not necessarily lead to the desired learning outcomes; not least because of the range of issues associated with curriculum alignment, i.e., the hidden curriculum, excluded curriculum, recommended curriculum, written curriculum, supported curriculum, tested curriculum, taught curriculum and learned curriculum (Glatthorn, 1999). Clearly, the interactions between these curricula challenge the perceived cause and effect expectations that tend to flow from a misguided belief that mandating the curriculum will resolve the situation.

With all that we know about teaching and learning, although the notion of a linear relationship might be comforting, it does not apply in education in the ways so often expected – in contrast to some areas of science where the experimental and control approach is steadfast. In fact, as the literature on educational change continues to illustrate, when a linear cause and effect problem solving approach is applied to teaching and learning, an ever-growing set of issues that influence the perceived problem tend to emerge as opposed to leading to a generalizable solution. As a consequence, the suggested solutions begin to create their own new sets of problems, all of which tend to distract from the original problem initially set to be 'solved'. Much of the 'can be solved with a single solution' approach is as a consequence of assuming that teachers can (should) be told what to do, ignoring the fact that teachers are professionals who in the normal course of their work are constantly making judgements about what to do, how and why, in response to not just the curriculum but more importantly, their learners and their pedagogical context.

There is furious agreement that quality in teaching matters, "even among those who argue for diametrically opposed approaches to teacher preparation, there is an apparent consensus that teaching quality is a critical influence on how and what students learn. The frequency of citations by researchers and policy makers of all stripes ... [is] that individual teachers are the single largest factor that adds value to student learning" (Cochran-Smith, 2003, p. 95). The same clearly applies in teacher education. Teacher educators matter; they critically influence how students of teaching learn about, and come to understand, teaching.

It seems reasonable to suggest then that, rather than attempting to mandate the correct 'what and how' of teacher education, it is more judicious to consider the vision it projects for teaching; a vision that should be strong and clear. It is hard to argue against the notion that teacher education should be able to create a vision of what teaching is (or should be) and purposefully build ways of making that tangible in the work of students of teaching. If that is the case, then support of that vision requires at least two foundational components: the ability to develop teachers' professional knowledge of practice that is articulable, useable and therefore highly valued; and, the expectation that that knowledge will impact teachers' practice and, as a consequence, lead to enhanced student learning. If that were the case, then teacher education would be in a position to offer the evidence necessary to push back against Darling-Hammond's myths and superstitions that continue to confound and trivialise the serious work of teaching and teacher education. That is a challenge that must be addressed and is the imperative for going beyond rhetoric.

3 A Vision for Teaching

The notion of a vision for teaching offers an opportunity to create a meaningful way to argue against views of practice that are primarily based on a transmissive or banking model of teaching (Freire, 1972). In a study of priorities for teacher education, Kosnik and Beck (2009) found that their participating teachers "gave a high priority to having a general teaching approach or philosophy … a "vision" for teaching. Being helped to develop such a vision was one of the things they appreciated most in their pre-service program" (p. 147). However, they also cautioned that there were problems with creating a vision for teaching in teacher education programs. Three issues in particular that they noted were that visions were often: too abstract; too narrow; and/or, unrealistic. They proposed nine principles that they considered vital to creating a sound vision for teaching:

1. Pursue a broad range of goals
2. Select and prioritize objectives, topics and activities
3. Connect to students' lives
4. Engage students
5. Teach for depth
6. Integrate learning
7. Build community in the classroom
8. Teach inclusively
9. Build close teacher-student relationships. (p. 157)

Kosnik and Beck's principles are certainly laudable, but it is not difficult to see how they could unwittingly be interpreted by a teacher as being realized in practice without necessarily questioning the nature of one's existing practice. Such a perspective was not uncommon when teachers were initially introduced to PEEL (Project for Enhancing Effective Learning; Baird & Mitchell, 1986; Baird & Northfield, 1992), a teacher-led project that aimed to develop students as active learners by explicitly developing their metacognitive skills by teaching for understanding as opposed to teaching through transmission. Despite the major shift to teaching and learning inherent in the aims and practices of PEEL, many teachers introduced to the project were often of the view that they were already teaching in a manner congruent with a PEEL approach.

Teachers involved in PEEL were typically attracted to the project because they recognized the poor learning tendencies (see, Mitchell, 1992, p. 179 for full details)[1] that fostered passive learning in their classrooms. Interestingly, many teachers not involved in the project also acknowledged these features as typical in their students. But the difference between involvement and non-involvement in PEEL often hinged on whether, as a teacher, there was some acceptance of responsibility for their students' learning behaviours. For example, when first introduced to PEEL Hynes (1997) stated:

> I listened carefully to what Ian [Mitchell] and John [Baird] were saying and how they saw what the program meant. I spent a great deal of time thinking over a couple of basic issues which left me with an insecure feeling – my reaction to the meetings and what everyone was saying was 'but I do this anyway! – I can't quite grasp onto how their ideas are different to what has been said and tried before'. (pp. 28–29)

Many teachers were of this view. They recognized that their students were passive learners however they tended to consider passive learning to be a part of 'normal schooling', rather than being linked to the nature of their teaching. Hence the 'we already do this' view of teaching masked the reality of their existing classroom practice. It is not hard to see then how important it is to create a vision for teaching through which the rhetoric and reality match!

As this brief PEEL example suggests, the challenge for teacher education is to consistently create meaningful pedagogical experiences through which purposeful teaching transforms subject matter through learning, and in so doing, to make the links between teaching and learning explicit. Because the long recognized *apprenticeship of observation* (Lortie, 1975) dramatically influences how many students of teaching have experienced, and therefore conceptualize teaching, the ability to create a realistic vision that challenges their experiences of teaching and learning is no simple task.

Many aspects of teacher education can rightly be criticized for reinforcing transmission as the dominant mode of practice rather than challenging it. If students of teaching are to understand teaching as more than transmission then telling them it is not so can never suffice. Teacher educators need to embrace what it means to genuinely model teaching for understanding in order to consistently reinforce the development of pedagogical relationships that result in quality learning. Creating opportunities for students of teaching to see into their teacher educators' pedagogical reasoning is crucial in order to illustrate that good practice is not innate, but thoughtfully structured and conducted.

To challenge the 'we already do this' view of teaching, teacher education must primarily be a site in which practice is opened up for scrutiny, exploration and research. Teacher educators must be able to illustrate that teaching is more than telling and learning is more than listening. They must consistently model not just good

---

[1] Briefly, the list of Poor Learning Tendencies (PLTs) is: (1) superficial attention; (2) impulsive attention; (3) premature closure; (4) inappropriate application; (5) staying stuck; (6) non-retrieval; (7) ineffective eradication; (8) lack of internal reflective thinking; and, (9) lack of external reflective thinking.

teaching, but illustrate how that teaching is conceptualized, structured, implemented and reviewed. In that way, the complex and sophisticated nature of teaching can be made clear to students of teaching as they experience it.

Going beyond an 'activities that work' (Appleton, 2002) approach to the teaching *and* learning of teaching matters. Teacher educators' practice needs to be responsive to, whilst also challenging, the needs and expectations of their students of teaching. There is a constant need to extend learning about teaching so that students of teaching seriously engage with the complexity of practice.

> The remarkable feature of the evidence is that the greatest effects on student learning occur when teachers become learners of their own teaching, and when students become their own teachers. When students become their own teachers, they exhibit the self-regulatory attributes that seem most desirable for learners (self-monitoring, self-evaluation, self-assessment, self-teaching[2]). Thus it is visible teaching and learning by teachers and students that makes the difference. (Hattie, 2012, p. 18)

In essence, a vision of teaching should be sufficiently concrete and useable to genuinely shape one's practice. Teaching for quality learning requires sophisticated knowledge *of* and *in* practice. Teacher education should therefore support students of teaching to make that vision robust, articulable and realizable in their practice. In that way, teachers' professional knowledge of practice might be catalysed.

4 Professional Knowledge of Practice

A strong example of how an important aspect of a vision for teaching might unwittingly be undercut is encapsulated in academic arguments about teachers' professional knowledge of practice. There has long been debate about knowledge in relation to teaching and the ways in which definitions of such knowledge shape what does, and does not, count and the perceived status flowing from such decisions and allocations. Fenstermacher (1994) drew attention to the distinction between the knowledge that "teachers generate as a result of their experience as teachers, in contrast to the knowledge of teaching that is generated by those who specialize in researching teaching" (p. 3). In so doing, he posed an important question about the nature of teachers' knowledge of practice – whose knowledge is it and what purpose does it serve?

Schön (1983, 1987) captured some of the salient features of differences in understandings about, and perceived value of, knowledge. He examined the nature of theoretical knowledge emanating from the 'ivory towers' and the practical knowledge imbued in the 'swampy lowlands'. His exploration of these forms of knowledge focused in on how a technical rational approach to practice contrasted with a practitioner's knowing in action. Schön began to articulate the tacit knowledge

---

[2] These points resonate well with PEEL and the importance it places on fostering students' metacognitive skills through teaching aimed at supporting such an active approach to knowledge development and understanding.

deeply embedded in a practitioner's doing and initiated a new wave of interest in reflection that had its crescendo in teaching and teacher education - thus complementing and extending Dewey's (1904, 1933) earlier work in the field.

By refocusing attention on the role of reflection, Schön heightened interest in knowledge of practice. Importantly, in teaching and teacher education, it also triggered new ways of exploring practice, specifically from the privileged position of the teacher. Teacher research (Clarke & Erickson, 2003; Cochran-Smith & Lytle, 1990, 1993; Mitchell, 2002), practitioner research (Cochran-Smith & Lytle, 2004; Zeichner & Noffke, 2001) and self-study (Bullough, 1994; Hamilton et al., 1998; Loughran, Hamilton, LaBoskey, & Russell, 2004) led to the development of knowledge of practice, *for* practice, *by* practitioners. As these practice-based research approaches gained momentum, they initially sat 'uncomfortably in the hallowed halls' as their products were not necessarily considered commensurate with the more highly valued public/codified knowledge from more traditional research approaches. As teacher education has long jockeyed for position in the hallowed halls of academia, it too has struggled to come to grips with how to portray, enact and value knowledge of teaching. Unfortunately that struggle has heightened tensions around the theory-practice gap (Nuthall, 2004), most notably exacerbating tensions for students of teaching through their professional experience.

Students of teaching need to be able to see, and experience, knowledge of teaching as making a difference in their practice and, as a consequence, enhance their students' learning. Therefore, teacher educators need to be able to make informed choices not only about what knowledge is important in teaching about teaching, but also how it might be used by their students of teaching and support their learning about teaching.

> Research is often seen by teachers as too theoretical, too idealistic, or too general to relate directly to the practical realities of classroom life ... they consider [research reports] primarily as a source of useful ideas about things they might try when circumstances permit. They evaluate research by finding out if its recommendations can be effectively adapted to their own classrooms. (Nuthall, 2004, p. 274)

Nuthall (above) accurately describes a major issue in relation to research and teaching; and by extension, teacher education. If teachers apply recommendations from research in their classrooms and they are found to be wonting, it tends to reinforce the view that theory is less than helpful in practice.

There is a great need for research findings to resonate with teachers' experience of their understanding of student learning in their classrooms. From a teacher's perspective, it does not matter how generalizable research findings might be, nor how robust or rigorous the method that led to those findings might be, if when applied they do not make a difference in an individual's classroom, they do not matter. As a consequence, a teacher's knowledge (however that might be defined) derived of personal experience tends to be more highly regarded by that individual than research knowledge that can too easily be seen as abstract and removed from the reality of classroom practice.

If teacher education cannot illustrate the value of research and portray the resultant knowledge in meaningful ways for students of teaching, then it more than likely reinforces the oft' bemoaned theory-practice gap (Korthagen & Kessels, 1999). Munby and Russell (1994) described how students of teaching are confronted by the tension between the *authority of position* and the *authority of experience*. Authority of position can be seen as carrying similar intentions to that of 'telling as teaching', therefore how teacher educators navigate the teaching of theory is clearly important as the *how* perhaps matters more than the *what*. Teacher educators need to ensure that students of teaching do not experience a situation in which 'knowledge from on high is transmitted to them'; teaching IS the message (Russell, 1997) and in teacher education there is little doubt that actions speak louder than words.

Teachers typically share their knowledge of practice through stories of classroom experiences, activities and teaching procedures. Being able to unpack those experiences, to explore why activities and procedures work facilitates a shift in focus from doing to thinking. It is in the underlying pedagogical reasoning that the ability to create knowledge of practice begins to come to the surface, and it is in teacher education that such reasoning should be nurtured and enhanced.

Understanding the nature of knowledge in teaching is crucial to understanding how it might impact practice so who determines that knowledge, why and how matters. Teacher education must be at the forefront of making that knowledge clear, useable and meaningful in the developing practice of students of teaching. In so doing, teachers' professional knowledge of practice is able to be articulated, portrayed and applied - despite the problematic nature of teaching which is, "an interactive process in which teachers must always be creating or adapting methods to meet the requirements of the curriculum as it relates to the specific needs and abilities of their pupils at particular moments in time" (Nuthall, 2004, p. 276).

If students of teaching are to see beyond teaching as doing, they need to have such practice modelled by their teacher educators, they need to see that teachers' professional knowledge of practice is informative, useful and valued. Teacher education must be at the forefront of so doing.

5 Evidence of Impact

> ... research about teacher education needs now to be undertaken using methods that will increase our knowledge about important features of teacher education and its connections to the outcomes that are important in a democratic society ... however ... although empirical research can inform important decisions about research and policy, it cannot tell us what to do. Simply because something has been researched does not tell us much about what people actually do or should do in preparation programs. Indeed, we see many instances where the same research is interpreted to justify dramatically different practices and policy decisions. (Cochran-Smith & Zeichner, 2005, p. 31)

One of the enduring issues around the perceived effectiveness of teacher education is the difficulty associated with offering acceptable evidence of impact. This issue is one that disturbs education more generally. Those things that can be measured to show impact tend to assume a short term, perhaps superficial, linear cause and effect relationship; something that troubles efforts to support and better value deeper learning in contrast to the simple accumulation of information. And, herein lies the recursive nature of the educational paradox. When telling as teaching and listening as learning dominates, measurement appears as a relatively straightforward process. Thus, assessment seeks to answer two major questions: If the information was delivered (read taught) can it be recounted? If so, how accurately is it recounted and how proficiently can it be used (read learnt)?

In seeking quality in teaching and learning there is a need to go beyond recall of propositional knowledge in order to pursue deeper levels of understanding. However, in so doing, assessment becomes increasingly complex and resource heavy. Evidence of impact therefore requires research that purposefully goes below the surface. In education that has typically taken the focus away from large-scale studies with generalizable outcomes, to small scale, context specific cases of particular instances or situations. Despite what might be uncovered through specific small scale studies, they tend to be less influential in the public domain than studies that offer generalizable findings – especially so in the political world where proof of improvement in numeric terms inevitably dominates.

That does not mean that small scale, context specific cases are not important. Rather, it is about being clear about purpose and intent. Purposefully investigating a situation, seeking to better understand how teaching shapes learning, or being able to describe quality of outcomes, may well precede quantification. Understanding the relative value of the nature of evidence matters - it goes hand in hand with the nature of the research. For example, Hattie's (2012) visible learning has attracted a great deal of attention in recent times because it speaks to issues around teaching and learning in ways that can be seen to offer evidence of solutions. His extensive meta-analyses underpinning effect-size across a large range of specific outcomes is both informative and impressive. Having such knowledge is helpful; how to do something as a consequence requires pedagogical expertise.

Expert teachers are skilled and knowledgeable professionals (Loughran, 2010) who must constantly manage competing pedagogical needs, issues, concerns and expectations.

> The act of teaching requires deliberate interventions to ensure that there is cognitive change in the student; thus the key ingredients are being aware of the learning intentions, knowing when a student is successful in attaining those intentions, having sufficient understanding of the student's prior understanding as he or she comes to the task, and knowing enough about the content to provide meaningful and challenging experiences so that there is some sort of progressive development. It involves a teacher who knows a range of learning strategies with which to supply the student when they seem not to understand, who can provide direction and redirection in terms of the content being understood and thus maximize the power of feedback, and who has the skill to 'get out the way' when learning is progressing towards the success criteria. (Hattie, 2012, p. 19)

Evidence of the ability of a teacher to perform in the way described by Hattie (above), must surely be powerful. Clearly, the same applies to teacher education where the knowledge, skills and ability necessary to teach teaching abounds. The ability to demonstrate expertise carries with it an invitation for teacher educators to develop research programs that actively address issues about quality, impact and value in teaching *and* learning about teaching.

Now is the time to decide how to respond to the recurring questions placed before teaching and teacher education and to do so in ways that have impact. There have been countless studies that offer insights into aspects of quality in teaching and teacher education. It is time to develop coherent, well-linked research programs that build on these findings and offer opportunities to demonstrate (qualitatively and quantitatively) that which makes a difference. That which has been learnt from small scale, context specific descriptive studies needs to be built upon. For example, if teachers' professional knowledge of practice is able to be captured, articulated and portrayed, how is it used and to what extent? In a similar vein, what aspects of a pedagogy of teacher education influence teacher educators' practice? To what extent do the results of standardized tests influence teachers' practice? There is a pressing need to be able to 'scale up' research and seek convincing evidence of impact beyond the particular in order to embrace the general. Challenging as it may be, there is a need to be able to offer measures of improvement that speak to the demands to be able to show that expertise in teaching and teacher education makes a discernible difference. Without such evidence, the technical-rational approach will always be seen as a simple solution.

6 Conclusion

If teaching really is complex and sophisticated business, then teachers themselves need to be able to illustrate why that is so. The same applies in teacher education. There needs to be a concerted, coherent and thoughtful approach to illustrating what teacher education has to offer and how it makes a real difference in the development of the next generation of skilled professionals. If teacher education is to be a valued starting point for a career as a teaching professional, then teacher educators need to lead the way in responding to questions that have, for so long, been answered in less than convincing ways to the sceptical observer.

> As every seasoned teacher educator can attest, the work is all-encompassing, sometimes exhaustively so. The press of time, of building programs, of dealing with bureaucracies, of endless meetings with collaborators, of countless hours with candidates, of getting from one school to another, of applying for grants, and more can make philosophical reflection seem like a remote luxury ... the politicized environment surrounding teacher education generates anxiety, anger, distraction, and confusion. The environment places relentless pressure on teacher educators to showcase and defend their work ... all of these factors militate against calm, tenacious, and honest reflection on purpose. (Hansen, 2008, p. 5)

If we as teacher educators do not take the time for 'calm, tenacious and honest reflection on purpose' as Hansen (above) suggests, and make decisions about what to do, how can we expect the situation to change? Although the issues in teaching and teacher education lie heavily on the profession, the response inevitably begins with the individual. The challenges are clear; at a personal level, how will you respond?

References

Appleton, K. (2002). Science activities that work: Perceptions of primary school teachers. *Research in Science Education, 32*(3), 393–410.
Baird, J. R., & Mitchell, I. J. (Eds.). (1986). *Improving the quality of teaching and learning: An Australian case study - the PEEL project*. Melbourne, Australia: Monash University Printing Service.
Baird, J. R., & Northfield, J. R. (Eds.). (1992). *Learning from the PEEL experience*. Melbourne, Australia: Monash University Printing Service.
Bullock, S. M. (2011). *Inside teacher education: Challenging prior views of teaching and learning*. Rotterdam, The Netherlands: Sense Publishers.
Bullough, R. V. J. (1994). Personal history and teaching metaphors: A self-study of teaching as conversation. *Teacher Education Quarterly, 21*(1), 107–120.
Clarke, A., & Erickson, G. (Eds.). (2003). *Teacher research*. London: RoutledgeFalmer.
Cochran-Smith, M. (2003). Teaching quality matters. *Journal of Teacher Education, 54*(2), 95–98.
Cochran-Smith, M., & Demers, K. E. (2008). How do we know what we know? Research and teacher education. In M. Cochran-Smith, S. Feiman-Nemser, D. McIntyre, & K. E. Demers (Eds.), *Handbook of research on teacher education: Enduring issues in changing contexts* (3rd ed., pp. 1009–1016). London: Routledge press.
Cochran-Smith, M., & Lytle, S. L. (1990). Research on teaching and teacher research: The issues that divide. *Educational Researcher, 19*(2), 2–11.
Cochran-Smith, M., & Lytle, S. L. (Eds.). (1993). *Inside/outside: Teacher research and knowledge*. New York: Teachers College Press.
Cochran-Smith, M., & Lytle, S. L. (2004). Practitioner inquiry, knowledge, and university culture. In J. J. Loughran, M. L. Hamilton, V. K. LaBoskey, & T. Russell (Eds.), *International handbook of self-study of teaching and teacher education practices* (Vol. 1, pp. 601–649). Dordrecht, The Netherlands: Kluwer Academic Press.
Cochran-Smith, M., & Zeichner, K. (Eds.). (2005). *Studying teacher education: The report of the AERA panel on research and teacher education*. Mahway, NJ: Lawrence Erlbaum Associates.
Darling-Hammond, L. (Ed.). (2006). *Powerful teacher education*. San Francisco: Jossey-Bass.
Dewey, J. (1904). The relation of theory to practice in education. In C. A. McMurry (Ed.), *The relation of theory to practice in the education of teachers (Third Yearbook of the National Society for the Scientific Study of Education, Part 1)* (pp. 9–30). Bloomington, IL: Public School Publishing.
Dewey, J. (1933). *How we think*. Lexington, MA: D.C. Heath and Company.
Fenstermacher, G. D. (1994). The knower and the known: The nature of knowledge in research on teaching. In L. Darling-Hammond (Ed.), *Review of research in education* (pp. 3–56). Washington, DC: American Educational Research Association.
Freire, P. (1972). *Pedagogy of the oppressed*. New York: Herder & Herder.
Glatthorn, A. (1999). Curriculum alignment revisited. *Journal of Curriculum and Supervision, 15*(1), 26–34.
Hamilton, M. L., with, Pinnegar, S., Russell, T., Loughran, J., & LaBoskey, V. (Eds.). (1998). *Reconceptualizing teaching practice: Self-study in teacher education*. London: Falmer Press.
Hansen, D. T. (2008). Why educate teachers? In M. Cochran-Smith, S. Feiman-Nemser, D. J. McIntyre, & K. E. Demers (Eds.), *Handbook of research on teacher education: Enduring questions in changing contexts* (pp. 5–9). London: Routledge.

Hattie, J. (2012). *Visible learning for teachers: Maximizing impact on learning*. London: Routledge.

Hynes, D. (1997). Theory into practice. In J. R. Baird & I. J. Mitchell (Eds.), *Improving the quality of teaching and learning: An Australian case study - the PEEL project* (3rd ed., pp. 28–44). Melbourne, Australia: Monash University.

Korthagen, F. A. J., & Kessels, J. (1999). Linking theory and practice: Changing the pedagogy of teacher education. *Educational Researcher, 28*(4), 4–17.

Kosnick, C., & Beck, C. (Eds.). (2009). *Priorities in teacher education: The 7 key elements of pre-service education*. London: Routledge.

Labaree, D. F. (2000). On the nature of teaching and teacher education: Difficult practices that look easy. *Journal of Teacher Education, 51*, 228–233.

Labaree, D. (2004). *The trouble with ed schools*. New Haven, CT: Yale University Press.

Lortie, D. C. (1975). *Schoolteacher*. Chicago: Chicago University Press.

Loughran, J. J. (2010). *What expert teachers do: Teachers' professional knowledge of classroom practice*. Sydney, Australia: Allen & Unwin, Routledge.

Loughran, J. J. (2015). Thinking about teaching as sophisticated business. In D. Garbett & A. Ovens (Eds.), *Teaching for tomorrow today* (pp. 5–8). Auckland, New Zealand: Edify.

Loughran, J. J., Hamilton, M. L., LaBoskey, V. K., & Russell, T. (Eds.). (2004). *International handbook of self-study of teaching and teacher education practices*. Dordrecht, The Netherlands: Kluwer Academic Publishers.

Mitchell, I. J. (1992). A perspective on teaching and learning. In J. Baird & J. Northfield (Eds.), *Learning from the PEEL experience* (pp. 178–193). Melbourne, Australia: Monash University Printing Service.

Mitchell, I. J. (2002). Learning from teacher research for teacher research. In J. J. Loughran, I. Mitchell, & J. Mitchell (Eds.), *Learning from teacher research* (pp. 249–266). New York: Teachers College Press.

Munby, H., & Russell, T. (1994). The authority of experience in learning to teach: Messages from a physics method class. *Journal of Teacher Education, 4*(2), 86–95.

Nuthall, G. (2004). Relating classroom teaching to student learning: A critical analysis of why research has failed to bridge the theory-practice gap. *Harvard Educational Review, 74*(3), 273–306.

Richardson, V. (1997). Constuctivist teaching and teacher education: Theory and practice. In V. Richardson (Ed.), *Constructivist teacher education: Building a world of new understandings* (pp. 3–14). London: Falmer Press.

Russell, T. (1997). Teaching teachers: How I teach IS the message. In J. Loughran & T. Russell (Eds.), *Teaching about teaching: Purpose, passion and pedagogy in teacher education* (pp. 32–47). London: Falmer Press.

Schön, D. A. (1983). *The reflective practitioner: How professionals think in action*. New York: Basic Books.

Schön, D. A. (1987). *Educating the reflective practitioner*. San Francisco: Jossey-Bass.

Zeichner, K. M., & Noffke, S. (2001). Practitioner research. In V. Richardson (Ed.), *Handbook of research on teaching* (4th ed., pp. 298–330). Washington, DC: American Educational Research Association.

Index

A
Access, 39, 44, 119, 133, 135, 148, 182–184, 197, 217, 221
Accreditation, 15, 17, 18, 20, 24, 39, 50, 63, 140, 160, 175, 187
Agency, 58, 83, 87, 118, 119, 166, 167, 171, 237, 247
AITSL, 11, 40, 158, 160, 163, 165, 166, 176, 187, 232, 233
Analysis
 content, 120–125
 discourse, 118, 120, 124, 126, 131
 discourse analysis, 11
Apprenticeship of observation, 257
Articulable, 255, 258
Assessment, 26, 51–56, 58–60, 67, 134, 140, 142, 147, 153, 163, 168, 175, 193–196, 205, 207, 211, 258, 261
Assessments, 18, 75
Attribution theory, 234
Attributional thinking, 248
Australian Government and the Minister for Education and Training, 16–18, 20, 24, 29
Australian Institute for Teaching and School Leadership (AITSL), 64, 140
Australian Institute for Teaching and School Leadership, 218, 223, 225, 226
Australian Institute of Teaching and School Leadership, 40
Australian Institute of Teaching and School Leadership (AITSL, 175
Australian Institute of Teaching and School Leadership (AITSL), 39, 232
Australian Institute of Teaching and School Leadership [AITSL], 16
Australian Professional Standards for Teachers, 19, 53, 158, 160, 163, 165–167, 169, 172, 223, 232
Australian Professional Standards for Teachers (APSTs)., 103
Australian Teacher Education Association (ATEA), 217
Authoritative discourse, 144, 147, 148
Authoritative discourses, 144
Authority of experience, 260
Authority of position, 260

B
Bachelor of Education, 38, 39, 67, 81, 99, 100, 102, 118, 120, 124, 134, 135, 158, 160, 163–165, 168, 218
Beginning teachers, 19, 20
BRiTE, 212, 214, 216, 219–221, 224–226
Building Resilience in Teacher Education (BRiTE), 211–226

C
Capabilities
 key capabilities, 55, 59
 non-academic key capabilities, 212, 225
Causality, 232, 235–239, 241–244, 246, 248
 perceptions of causality, 231–248

Challenge, 7–9, 16, 27, 29, 35, 45, 76, 99, 109, 129, 132, 134, 135, 144, 147, 149, 161, 179, 186–188, 193, 194, 196, 207, 211, 225, 254–257
Challenges, 3, 5, 9, 12–13, 16, 18, 22, 23, 36, 45, 51, 59–60, 66, 74, 76, 92, 95, 101, 105, 109, 117, 132, 140–144, 146, 150, 162, 186, 188, 205, 207, 211, 212, 214, 215, 224–226, 231, 232, 246, 254, 257, 263
Classroom
    classroom intensives, 6, 193–208
    classroom observations, 88, 93, 113, 196, 197, 202
    classroom readiness, 17, 19, 52–55, 59, 60, 175, 193, 211
Classroom Observation, 196–197
Clinical practice, 25–27, 177
Collaborative learning, 60
Collaborative teaching, 151
Conceived space, 181–182
Conceptual framework, 26, 158, 160–163, 214–215, 232
Content Knowledge (CK), 39, 40
Contextual resources, 213–215
Coping, 45, 212, 213
Curriculum, 8, 10, 21, 28, 36, 37, 41, 43–44, 46, 53, 55, 57, 58, 64, 66, 67, 80, 82, 93, 99–105, 108, 111–115, 125, 126, 131, 133–137, 162, 167, 195, 207, 212, 218, 255, 260
    curriculum studies, 255

D
Design-based research, 11, 215, 216
Dialogical relationships, 179, 180, 189
Digital credentialing, 8, 49–52, 54–60
    design systems for digital credentialing, 52, 54, 55, 60
Discourse
    analysis, 120, 124, 126, 131
    discourse analysis, 11
    dominant, 124, 127, 134, 135, 137
    marginalized, 124, 131–133, 135, 137
    marginalized discourse, 10
Discourses
    dominant, 135
Disposition, 246
Dispositions, 6, 10, 21, 51, 56, 58, 193–208, 248
Disruptive innovation, 59–60
Diversity, 10, 124, 131, 132

E
Education system, 12, 18, 37, 184, 188
Education systems, 36, 38, 175, 231, 253
Emotions, 7, 117, 118, 206, 213, 214, 222
Evidence, 1–3, 8, 12, 17–23, 29, 40, 50–55, 58–60, 74, 81, 85, 86, 91, 126, 140, 141, 158, 163, 167–169, 172, 175, 178, 180, 182, 184, 185, 198, 199, 203–205, 212, 225, 226, 232, 253, 254, 256, 258, 260–262
Exceptional Teachers for Disadvantaged Schools, 20–24
Exceptional Teachers for Disadvantaged Schools (ETDS), 20–24

H
Hardy, 87
History of teacher education, 40
Hybridization, 144, 179

I
Identities, 7, 133, 149
Identity, 7, 117–120, 129, 137, 142–143, 149, 184, 231–248
    teacher, 117, 119, 128, 136
    teacher identity, 110, 142, 143, 232, 233
Ideological becoming, 143
Images of teaching, 117–137
Impact, 1, 4–13, 17, 20–22, 26, 27, 29, 49–51, 53–55, 89, 94, 119, 133, 136, 140, 142, 163, 167, 168, 172, 176, 178, 184, 186, 188, 193–208, 231–233, 236, 237, 246, 247, 254, 255, 260–262
    teacher impact, 255
Impacts, 17, 25, 57, 80
Inclusion, 105, 152
Inclusive teaching, 256
Initial teacher education, 3, 5, 6, 8, 11, 16, 18, 19, 21, 25, 26, 35–46, 63, 65, 66, 76, 99, 100, 112, 114, 153, 175, 196, 224, 226
Initial Teacher Education, 17
Initial teacher education (ITE), 3, 49, 157–172
Initial Teacher Education (ITE)
    Initial Teacher Education policy reform, 49
Innovation, 8–10, 12, 13, 20, 35–46, 49, 50, 54, 55, 59, 60, 63, 64, 66–68, 73, 74, 79–82, 93, 101, 172
    disruptive innovation, 49, 51, 54–55
Intern, 102, 158, 161, 162, 165–172
Interns, 161–170, 172

Index 267

Internship
   Internship Action Plan, 158, 163, 165–169, 171, 172
   Internship authorisation, 165, 167
Intervention, 8–10, 12, 13, 28, 81
Interventions, 7–8, 118, 261

K
Knowing in action, 258
Knowledge
   hierarchies of knowledge, 179
   Technological Content Knowledge (TCK), 169
   Technological Pedagogical and Content Knowledge (TPACK), 160
   Technology Knowledge (TK), 160

L
Learning
   learning strategies, 261

M
Mandate, 255
Master of Teaching, 15, 20, 24–28, 38–39, 140, 193, 195, 196, 198, 218
Master of Teaching (MTeach), 20, 24–29
Mentor teacher, 9, 68, 74, 108, 149, 150, 161
   mentor professional learning, 100, 101, 103, 112, 115
Mentor Teacher, 158, 165–172
Mentor teachers, 9, 89, 161–164, 166–168, 170, 172, 226
Mentor Teachers, 166, 167
Mentoring
   Massive Open Online Course (MOOC), 225
   whole school mentoring, 106
Methodologies, 120
Methodology, 136, 137, 158, 163–164, 180–181, 215–224, 237
Motivation, 56, 57, 60, 69, 185, 194, 212–214, 226, 231, 236, 237, 239
Motivations, 57, 225, 236
Myths, 254, 256

N
National Exceptional Teachers for Disadvantaged Schools (NETDS), 20
National' Exceptional Teachers for Disadvantaged Schools (NETDS), 21
Non-academic key capabilities, 212, 225

O
Online learning, 212, 216, 217, 224

P
Partnership, 5, 10, 52, 64, 66, 87, 99–102, 114, 134, 158, 164, 166–168, 171, 175–189, 193, 195, 197, 198
   school-university partnership, 99, 153, 162, 176, 178, 182
Partnerships, 16, 19, 64–67, 99, 115, 124, 139, 140, 152–153, 162–164, 170, 172, 207
Pedagogical relationships, 257
Pedagogy
   PCK, 117
   Pedagogical Content Knowledge (PCK), 5, 6, 12, 160
   Pedagogical Knowledge (PK), 29
   Pedagogy of teacher education, 262
Perceived space, 182–183
Placement
   benefits of paired placements, 141–142
   challenges of paired placements, 141–142
   confidence in paired placements, 149–150
   conflict in paired placements, 142, 145
   paired placement, 7, 9, 64, 74, 76, 139–153
   tension in paired placements, 142–143
Policy
   impact of policy, 49
   policy reform, 1–13
Policy makers, 1, 2, 6, 29, 53, 65, 211, 254, 255
Policy-makers, 175
Politicians, 1, 2, 253
Portfolio, 52–54, 59, 225
Portfolio of evidence, 53, 54
Portfolios, 52–54
Pre service teachers, 63–76, 117–137
Prescribed curriculum, 254–256
Preservice teacher, 17, 165
Pre-service teacher, 50, 51, 55, 63–76, 100, 102–104, 106, 107, 109–115, 194, 233
Pre-service teacher (PST), 218
Preservice teachers, 21, 165
Pre-service teachers, 3, 6, 9, 18, 21, 50, 51, 53, 54, 56, 59, 79, 94, 99–103, 106, 107, 109–115, 117–137, 139–153, 212, 214–216, 218, 219, 223–225
Pre-service teachers, 27
Pre-service teachers (PSTs), 79, 193
Primary teacher education, 40
Principal, 4, 183–186
Principals, 1, 36, 41, 43, 45, 88, 142, 162, 181, 183, 184, 253

Professional
  identity, 117–137
  knowledge, 126
  practice, 128
  professional becoming, 139, 143–153, 189
  professional engagement, 76, 163, 165, 167
  professional identity, 7, 9, 54, 63, 140, 179, 232, 233
  professional knowledge, 50, 51, 112, 113, 143, 163, 165, 167, 179, 189, 254, 255, 258, 260, 262
  Professional Learning Communities (PLCs), 27, 28
  professional learning identity, 231–248
  professional practice, 26, 28, 163, 165, 167, 177, 224, 232, 248
Professional commitment, 212
Professional experience
  professional experience curriculum, 3
  professional experience models, 63–65, 67, 76
  quality professional experience, 27
Professional Knowledge, 258–260
Professional practice
  professional experience, 50, 112, 113, 143, 254, 258–260, 262
  professional standards, 53, 151, 172, 193, 195
Professional StandardsProfessional practice
  professional standards, 18, 19
Project for Enhancing Effective Learning (PEEL), 256–258
PST's, 79, 89, 90
PSTs, 63–76, 79–82, 85–95, 139–142, 144–147, 149–153, 177–189, 193, 195–198, 200, 202–204, 207, 208

Q
qualitative research, 104
Qualitative research, 10, 87
Quality
  quality teaching, 8, 23–29, 80, 83, 95, 101
  teaching quality, 255
Queensland College of Teachers (QCT), 165, 167

R
Reflection
  reflection for action, 234, 246, 247
  reflection on action, 234, 246, 247
Reflective practice, 68, 74, 75, 124, 225, 234

Research
  mixed methods, 11, 198
  qualitative, 10, 87, 104
  research methodology, 10–12, 215, 216
Resilience, 6, 10, 211–226, 231
Rhetoric, 20, 29, 65, 253–263

S
School Based Semester (SBS), 160
School-university partnerships, 177–178
School-University partnerships, 162
Self-efficacy, 161, 213, 226, 231, 236, 246, 247
Small scale studies, 2, 11, 261
social competence, 213, 214
Social competence, 212
Sophisticated, 5, 9, 13, 53, 253, 254, 258, 262
Space
  conceived space, 10, 179, 180
  lived space, 10, 179, 188
  perceived space, 179, 180, 187, 188
  third space, 101, 102, 110, 114, 115
Spatial analysis, 11, 175–189
Standard, 186
Standards, 17, 18, 20, 36, 49, 50, 64, 118, 140, 151, 158, 160, 163, 172, 218, 226, 253
Stereotypical images, 118, 128, 134
Student
  Student Experience of Course (SEC), 163, 168
Supervising teacher, 139–142, 145, 147–151, 161, 169
Supervising Teacher, 168, 169
Supervising teachers, 43, 79, 139–147, 150–153, 162, 169
Support network, 223
Support networks, 214

T
Teacher
  as knowledgeable, 124, 135
  as professional, 124, 130–131
  as the charismatic and caring subject, 124, 127
  beginning, 137
  beginning teacher, 10, 24, 166, 168, 175, 193, 225, 231–248, 253
  characteristics, 161
  graduate, 117, 118, 136
  graduate teacher, 6, 10, 18, 40, 41, 43–46, 54, 158, 160, 162, 163, 165, 166, 170, 175
  highly accomplished teacher, 83

identity, 117, 119, 128, 136
lead/leading teacher, 9, 148
primary teacher, 37, 39, 43
quality, 162
secondary teacher, 36, 37, 39, 40, 152, 181, 193
teacher as professional, 232
teacher characteristics, 212
teacher identity, 110, 142, 232
teacher preparation, 3, 16, 19, 22, 35–40, 45, 254, 255
teacher quality, 27, 95, 194, 212, 253
Teacher education
  history of teacher education, 37
  primary teacher education, 40
  secondary teacher education, 36, 37, 39, 40, 181, 193
  Teacher Education Ministerial Advisory Group (TEMAG), 1, 3, 4, 6, 9, 11, 12, 15, 19, 20, 22, 50, 52–54, 59, 65, 99, 100, 115, 139, 140, 152, 153, 157, 158, 160, 162, 172, 175, 193, 194, 211, 231
  teacher education reform, 29
  TEMAG, 117
Teacher Education Ministerial Advisory Group (TEMAG), 140, 175, 176, 193, 211
Teaching
  as complex, 124, 127, 129–131
  as transmission, 124, 126–128
  effective teaching, 3, 39, 195, 196, 200, 205, 208
  quality teaching, 8, 23–27, 29, 80, 83, 95, 100
Teaching rounds, 43
  quality teaching rounds, 25, 27, 28

Technological pedagogical and content knowledge (TPACK, 160
Technological Pedagogical and Content Knowledge (TPACK), 160
Technology Knowledge (TK), 160
TEMAG, 193, 194
Theory-practice connections, 203
Theory-practice gap, 50, 53, 99, 114, 259, 260
Thinking routine, 200
Third space, 101, 102, 110, 114
Triadic relationship, 144, 147, 148, 153
Triadic relationships, 143

U
UK, 175
United Kingdom, 23, 233
United Kingdom (UK), 175
United States of America (USA), 175
USA, 60, 175–177

V
Visible Thinking, 197
Vision for teaching, 254, 256–258
Visual representation, 120, 121, 123–126, 134–136
Visual representations, 10, 11, 120, 121
  methodology, 136, 137

W
Wellbeing, 212, 214, 222, 225
Wilkinson, 87
Wittgenstein, 84

Printed in the United States
By Bookmasters